Praise for *Sufi Encounters*

"The 21st century must be a century dominated by messages of universal peace and understanding, as delivered by the great sages of our shared history. I am grateful to Shaykh Fadhlalla, a sage of our times, for dedicating his life as a spiritual beacon, and working to promote peace across continents through his universal message of love and understanding."

Ambassador Akbar Ahmed,
Ibn Khaldun Chair of Islamic Studies,
American University, Washington, DC

"*Sufi Encounters* offers us a compelling view of Sufi history together with vivid personal remembrances of living mystics. By taking up topics like Sufi women as well as jihad, the book also challenges us with an honest assessment of the place of Sufism and the Muhammadi mystical path in today's world. This is an inspiring and at the same time beautifully subtle book, with light-filled insights on every page."

Saadi Shakur Chishti, author of The Sufi Book of Life

"*Sufi Encounters*' combination of autobiography and generous quotes, many of which the reader would not normally encounter, makes for a rich offering."

Kabir Helminski, Sufi master, music director, poet and
author of Love's Ripening: Rumi on the Heart's Journey

"Sufism is a path, a path to the Great Unknown, the Cosmic Force beckoning humankind to its highest destiny. That path has a celestial goal but a terrestrial map. In *Sufi Encounters* the discerning reader will find the map marked by stations, from tombs in South Asia, both Pakistan and India, to sites in the Maghrib (North Africa) and also South Africa as well as Iran. The authors are well-travelled guides, familiar with the multiple twists and turns of the path. Here they provide a lyrical light, clarifying both the path and its way stations with their own transformative vision of 'a new life beyond change, where the mulberry tree is ever in fruit, and Divine Love is never in dispute'. The method and the message of this book are wondrous, making the path broader, its passage more accessible and assured for all travellers."

Bruce B Lawrence, Professor Emeritus, Duke University,
Adjunct Professor, Fatih Sultan Mehmet Vakif University,
co-author of Sufi Martyrs of Love

"Here is a living tapestry of Sufism woven by a life following the path of love. Shaykh Fadhlalla Haeri gives us a penetrating glimpse into the inner and outer landscape of this mystical path, its history and living saints. In our present time of so much divisiveness, it is a blessing to know of these luminaries who have lived a light of oneness beyond any division."

Llewellyn Vaughan-Lee, PhD, Sufi teacher and author

Shaykh Fadhlalla Haeri is a revered spiritual master and teacher who for over 40 years has guided students from all over the world on the path of Sufism. His approach emphasizes practical, actionable knowledge that leads to self-transformation, and provides a natural bridge between seemingly different Eastern and Western approaches to spirituality. He is the author of more than 50 books on Islam, the Quran and Sufism.

Muneera Haeri is the author of *The Chishtis: A Living Light* and has a special interest in the history of Sufism.

Sufi
ENCOUNTERS

SHARING THE WISDOM OF THE ENLIGHTENED SUFIS

Shaykh Fadhlalla Haeri
& Muneera Haeri

Preface by Seyyed Hossein Nasr

WATKINS
Sharing Wisdom Since 1893

This edition published in the UK and USA 2018 by
Watkins, an imprint of Watkins Media Limited
Unit 11, Shepperton House
89-93 Shepperton Road
London
N1 3DF

enquiries@watkinspublishing.com

1 2 3 4 5 6 7 8 9 10

ISBN: 978-1-786781-85-7

Typeset in South Africa by Mizpah Marketing Concepts
Printed and bound in the United Kingdom

British Library Cataloguing-in-Publication data available
Library of Congress Cataloguing-in-Publication data available

www.watkinspublishing.com

TABLE OF CONTENTS

PUBLISHER'S NOTE

The invocation of "peace be upon him" is implied every time the Prophet Muhammad's name is mentioned.

Throughout the book, wherever two sets of dates are mentioned, the first will be Hijri (usually marked AH) and the second Common Era (CE).

Any reference to "men" in text with the connotation of "mankind" equally refers to "women" and should be regarded as non-gender specific.

ACKNOWLEDGEMENTS

My gratitude to all who have accompanied me on this journey and supported my work in the preparation of this book, in particular Shaykh Hosam Raouf, Muna and Abbas Bilgrami, Omar Essa and Abu Bakr Karolia. My thanks to Ayesha Powell, Anjum Jaleel, Ahmed Bàasid Sheriff and Max Lohnert, who assisted with editing and photos.

Many thanks are also given to others, as well as the above, who helped make my travels in India, Iran and Pakistan enjoyable and safe. These include Tahmina Bawany, the late Meher Bashiruddin, Ali Bilgrami, Aziza Bilgrami, Irfan Butt, Zaheer Cassim, Ambassador Asghar Ebrahimi Asl, Nayyar Ali Gauhar, Ali H Gokal, Dr Khalid Iqbal, Fatima Iqbal, Syed Salim Abbas Jilani, Aziza Pir Mahfooz Jilani, Mumtaz and Shamim Khan, Mustafa Khokhar, the late Makhdoom Mazhar Hussain, Mumtaz Mazhar Batool, Syed Mostafa Mossavi-Azad, Pir Muhammad Harun Riedinger, Mr and Mrs Sahibzada Sultan Hameed and Dr Hamid uz Zaman Xaigham. There were many others whose hospitality I enjoyed and to whom I also give my thanks.

ACKNOWLEDGEMENTS

PREFACE

I have known Shaykh Fadhlalla Haeri for three decades, during which I have met him on different continents, but I feel as if I have known him for my whole lifetime. Although his mother tongue is Arabic and mine Persian, we both hail from a Persian background. The famous Shaykh 'Abd Allah Ha'iri, one of the distinguished members of his family, was a close friend of my father and I have known many other members of the Haeri family. Like Shaykh Fadhlalla, I hail from a Shiite background and at the same time belong to the Shadhili Sufi lineage, which is primarily a Sunni *tariqa*. And, like Shaykh Fadhlalla, I was first educated in the sciences before turning to philosophy and Sufism. I have also, again, like him, been exiled in the West (and in his case later in South Africa) for the past few decades. When in his presence, I feel to be not only in the company of a spiritual brother, but in the presence of a family member. When I read in the present book his chapter on Iran, I felt sad that I was not able to be present there in his company. I wished so much that I could have been his tour guide in Nayshapur, Isfahan and so many other historical sites of my homeland.

The son of a distinguished family of religious scholars, Shaykh Fadhlalla was born and brought up in Karbala near the tomb of my ancestor, the third Shiite imam, Husayn ibn 'Ali – upon whom be peace – on whose birthday I was born and after whom I was named. A brilliant child, Shaykh Fadhlalla studied in Iraq in the field of engineering and science and then turned to the field of business, in which he became very successful. In this matter there is a contrast between us for I have never had a gift for business administration and so went immediately into the field of scholarship and teaching upon finishing my doctoral studies at Harvard. But even then we were both seeking the same goal, which is the world of the Spirit, and so both ended up in the embrace of Sufism. Shaykh Fadhlalla also began to study the Islamic philosophical and Sufi traditions and, like myself, became a great admirer of Mulla Sadra.

The tumultuous events in Iraq and then Iran caused him to move to the West, as was also to be in my case. He became the master of his own Sufi order and established centres for the dissemination of knowledge of Islam and Sufism in several places in the Occident from Texas to London. He also began to spread spiritual teachings through writing while he devoted much energy and resources to the education of the young. After many years, he left the West – but not for back home. He settled in South Africa with a large group of his followers, continuing in this new setting his activities as a spiritual teacher, educator and philanthropist. May he continue to be a source of light and charity for many years to come.

A very important point that needs to be mentioned about Shaykh Fadhlalla, in this age of rampant modernism on the one hand and so-called fundamentalism on the other, is that he is completely orthodox and traditional on both the *shari'a* and *tariqa* levels and at the same time a universalist who respects other authentic religions, a perspective that I share with him completely. At the present moment one sees in the Islamic world on one side modernists who are usually relativizers and want to change religion according to the tenets of modernism, and on the other side fundamentalists, who believe that only they possess the truth, being exclusivist and at the same time limited in their understanding of their own religion. And then there are some Sufis with a kind of Salafi tendency that prevents them from having the universalist perspective on revelation that is stated so majestically and so often in the Noble Quran. These days in the Islamic world, rare indeed are those who share the universality of an Ibn al-'Arabi, a Rumi or a Djan-i-Djanan. Shaykh Fadhlalla is one of those rare Muslim contemporary masters who is both orthodox and universalist, possessing a trait that has drawn me so much to him over the years.

Sufi Encounters is a work that reflects these qualities. It is at once an autobiography, a didactic treatise and a literary opus full of wonderful translations of the words of earlier Sufis as well as his own poetry, which reveals his art as a poet. The book is not only about Sufism; it is also a Sufi book. The autobiographical parts reveal an exceptional life imbued by the Grace of God Who has provided the author the opportunity to see so much, to experience so many different aspects and parts of the contemporary world, to meet so many remarkable human beings, to visit so many holy places and to familiarize himself with so many works of a spiritual nature from both East and West. In reading the autobiographical section, one feels as if one is experiencing the life of the author and somehow sharing it with him.

The didactic teachings are interspersed within the text of the book. The author turns again and again from the account of his life experiences to the exposition of Sufi doctrines concerning the nature of God, the Universal Man, the cosmos and other important doctrinal teachings. Shaykh Fadhlalla provides expositions of even difficult doctrinal issues in a clear and simple language as only a master who has digested fully such knowledge could do.

The quotations from various Sufis from the width and breadth of the Islamic world are like an anthology of Sufi writings, especially poetry, interspersed throughout the book. They reveal the author's deep knowledge of the Sufi tradition and of Sufi literature, especially in Arabic and Persian. His own poetry reveals how much he is part of this tradition himself.

Sufi Encounters is an important work for several reasons. It casts light upon the life of a man originally from Iraq and brought up in a traditional Muslim family but confronted by the modern world within which he searches for the Truth, giving up worldly life in order to find the Beloved. The book also reveals much about the present-day Islamic world, where, despite the tragedies that are to be seen everywhere, tradition and spirituality survive. The work is also a metaphysical and spiritual guide as well as a compendium of Sufi sayings and poems.

I pray that God grant Shaykh Fadhlalla a long life to continue his exceptional services to God and His creatures. May the effusion of his spiritual presence continue, *damat barakatuhu.*

Seyyed Hossein Nasr
Washington, DC
Muharram 1438 AH/September 2016 CE

INTRODUCTION

Some have said that the seed of Sufism was sown
in the time of Adam,
It germinated in the time of Noah,
sprouted in the time of Abraham,
developed in the time of Moses,
reached maturity in the time of Jesus
And produced pure wine in the time of Muhammad.
Those who drank this wine lost themselves,
Their soul then declared its victory
Allahu Akbar.
This is where truth lies.

Shams-i-Tabriz

The Prophet Muhammad (peace be upon him)[1] had taught, "Die before you die." The Sufi sage retold this teaching to his disciples as, "Lose your (lower) self and there will remain only the (higher) soul – Allah's light within your heart." This is the purpose of human life.

Authentic religious teachings and spiritual practices lead the seeker past ordinary states of consciousness and experiences toward a new state of infinitude that is the source of the universe. In this state there is no duality or otherness – an indescribable Oneness: perfect, sacred and constant. When personal and conditioned consciousness yields to its root and essence – supreme consciousness – spiritual evolution is complete. This book is essentially about people who have disciplined their minds and conduct and have attained a high degree of awareness of inner light and pure consciousness.

The Prophet Muhammad taught that while you would never get to know the Truth through men, you would understand men through the light of Truth. After many encounters with acknowledged spiritual masters and sages, I realized the wisdom of this teaching. No one could give me the Truth or take it away. However, I knew that others may help me overcome my self-acquired barriers, false values and other mental veils. The fact is that there is nothing that is durable or eternal other than Truth itself. To experience this state, you need to switch off all thoughts and emotions and touch higher consciousness. Pure and boundless consciousness begins at the borderline between self and soul, or falsehood and truth. This ocean of Reality is beyond all notions of space and time.

The enlightened ones link the seen with the unseen; living in full awareness and self-accountability, while illumined by the presence of the perfect light of the One Reality – perfect integration.

> *Were it not for the ability of souls to wander in different arenas, progress for the seekers would not be realized. There is no distance between you and Him to be traversed, nor is there any severance between you and Him that you need to overcome in order to arrive.[2]*
>
> *Ibn 'Ata' Allah*

> Human souls wander in the world of activities like horses being trained. Allah, Who is closer to us than closeness itself, has decreed that His Mercy and Light permeate all existences. We cannot improve on His Constant Presence and Mercy. The journey you imagine you are taking is simply to do with exploring the self and transcending it toward its source and origin – the soul. We are stimulated to increase in consciousness of Him by His Grace.

Sufism is the Islamic spiritual package which enables the serious seeker to understand the interconnectedness of all realities and their unity at both source and termination. Beams of energies and energetic entities, such as angels, radiate from that source and bring about multi-universes and countless levels of consciousness in creation.

Soul consciousness is the ultimate quest of intelligent human beings, who need a constant reference that sheds light upon ever-changing worldly dualities. A fulfilled personal life means the realization of eternal life –

before and after the cycles of birth and death. It is the transformative declaration that there is no god but God (Reality) and all of creation depends upon this truth and realizes it to the degree of its potential.

The way of the enlightened Sufis is the practical application and outcome of original Islam, whose teachings were modified due to political reasons, cultural distractions and lower human tendencies. The transformative path of Islam was recast as a structured religion imbued with more fear than hope. Religions, like viruses, mutate, and whenever they focus excessively on the outer rules and regulations, mystic movements, like Sufism, rise from within them to redress imbalance. Judaism has the Kabbalists; Christianity the Gnostics and Rosicrucians, for example.

The Sufis I met over the years were all trying to live according to the Prophetic model of the universal being with consciousness spanning the whole range of the limited, discernible and what is concealed. There was a sense of presence in all of them and those who had a sense of humour directed it mostly at the uncertainties and constant changes in the world. Their outer courtesy was exemplary. The animal self had been contained due to reference to higher consciousness. This is what made them attractive, so people desired to be in their presence. They represented role models for those of us who want to live in a world that prepares us for what is after death.

I was fortunate that during my travels I had the opportunity to study and discuss Islam, the history of Muslims and Sufism with scholars and illumined beings in numerous locations and circumstances. I often questioned why the perfect, original teachings of Islam had not become the foundation for the life of Muslims over the centuries, despite adherence to the *shari'a* (Islamic law or code of conduct, outward path) and *sunna* (customary practice and conduct of the Prophet Muhammad). It was upsetting to witness how the Muslims' culture and way of life had lost its vitality and was going through a serious crisis. The challenge for me, as it is for other concerned Muslims today, is how to reconcile the perfection of the message of the Quran and the Muhammadi Way with the confused lives of Muslims, individually and collectively. Is this dichotomy due to their failure to live this message with sincerity? What had gone so wrong or why did it not go right?

> There is loud talk that Muslims have disappeared from the earth's face.
> We ask you; did true Muslims exist anywhere in any place?
> Your style of living is Christian, your culture that of the Hindus;
> A Jew would be ashamed if he saw Muslims such as you.
> You are Seyyeds as well as Mirzas, and you are Afghans –
> You are all these, but tell us are you also Mussalmans?[3]
>
> *Muhammad Iqbal*

There have been numerous reflections and comments, like those of the poet, philosopher and politician Allama Iqbal (1877–1938 CE), addressing the Muslims of India, on what scholars or committed Muslims see as the discrepancy between the ideal of Islam and the practice of the Muslims. A similar situation is observed also with other religions. There is a difference between looking at a map and following it correctly; hence the gap between the teachings of original Islam and Muslims' life and conduct. To live a fulfilled life on earth we need to address the obvious needs of body, mind, self and heart – all within our conditioned consciousness. Constant effort and hope is needed to connect heart and soul with mind and self. The ultimate human purpose is to live and interact in the world of dualities, where everything that exists and everything we experience is in twos, with constant reference to the light of our soul's unity. Humanity is not separate from divinity and we all yearn to experience this truth. Islam's purpose is seen clearly within Sufism.

> The way of the Sufi is to experience life and yet to remain above it; to live in the world and not let the world own him.[4]
>
> *Hazrat Inayat Khan*

The Quran and the Prophetic traditions describe the link between the seen and unseen, human life on earth and the hereafter, and the inseparability between limited consciousness and full consciousness. The Sufis strive on this path to be transformed and awakened to a lasting illumined state. The purpose of life is to awaken to this truth and avoid fears and sorrows.

> *If I had known any science greater than Sufism, I would have gone to it, even on my hands or knees.*
>
> *Imam Junayd*

The following memoirs are a personal interpretation of aspects of Sufi teachings, the role Sufism has played historically and its relationship to the *deen* (religion, life-transaction between Allah and man). Family and friends had also encouraged me to write about my encounters with individual Sufis and people of light. Muneera as my co-author has worked on this manuscript from its beginning. Her considerable background research has enriched and framed my writings.

Initially, I was reluctant to recall the past and write retrospectively about these experiences. I had not kept diaries, as I always enjoyed living these experiences without interruptions of writing.

Few people today have had the time and opportunity to travel as I did in search of Reality. My passionate desire along the spiritual path led me to journey all over the world, meet people of knowledge, visit the shrines of great masters, and study the inspired works of bygone years. On some occasions I traversed a continent in order to spend an hour with an enlightened being. May these musings celebrate the lives of those beings I had the privilege to meet over the years and shed some light on questions that commonly perplex seekers on the path.

Today's global upheavals and ignorant misinterpretations of religion, which have produced barbaric behaviour and injustice, encouraged me to weave this tapestry of my inner quest. Born into a family of traditional Shiite *'ulama*, a Hindu master guided my first steps toward a spiritual path and sent me to find the Sufis. A Sunni shaykh of Scottish origin then became my teacher. The North African Shadhilis became my first point of reference on the Sufi path, permission from masters of the Chishti and Rifa'i orders followed. I was a reluctant teacher, as I could feel the onslaughts of outer discords and religious differences will overshadow the real quest for awakening to the divine light within the heart.

These are subjective recollections of past events, encounters and teachings that touched my heart and explained various key issues of concern, as we progress to our destiny in life. These writings do not claim to be either an academic or inclusive work on the history or practices of Sufism. Translations from Arabic or Farsi, unless otherwise stated, are mainly my own. A chapter on Sufis and Mahdis in *jihad* was written in response to current interest in this issue. The chapter on female Sufis celebrates the important role women, starting with my mother, Bibi Fadhila, have played in my life, as family members and pupils. It also expresses my belief that, had the teachings of Islam been truly honoured, the position of women in the Muslim world would have been very different.

Sufi Encounters is a companion work to *Son of Karbala*, my earlier autobiography. Some of the illumined beings mentioned in *Sufi Encounters* are also referred to in *Son of Karbala*; in *Sufi Encounters* there is more emphasis on the history and teachings of Sufism, with particular reference to a few well-known *tariqas* (Sufi paths or orders) which I have been associated with or exposed to.

The human make-up contains personal subjective conditioned consciousness, as well as a higher dimension, so the foundation of spiritual growth can be seen as having less concern about personal and material needs and more focus on durable values and the purpose of life. The Sufi objective throughout the ages has been to move from self-concern to soul awareness. This shift can only occur as a result of numerous incremental changes. The Sufis in this book all made deliberate and wilful changes in perceptions, viewpoints and attitudes in their quest for enlightenment. The way they expressed themselves or conveyed their message was subject to their own station and the overriding culture and language of their day. All awakened beings have realized the same Truth – the sacred Oneness – that envelops and regulates the entire universe. Enlightened beings see every aspect of duality as a natural veil of cover upon absolute unity. Our relative life on earth is an introduction to experiencing perpetual life free from space and time limitations. However, if taken out of context, their sayings can be misinterpreted and the clarity of their revelations clouded. It is important to remember as you peruse these pages that their outer differences belie their inner sameness.

The Sufis were the guardians of transformative Islam but many of the traditional practices, in particular the teacher/pupil relationship, will have to adapt to accommodate the massive societal changes of the past 100 or so years. We must live according to our times and pursue our desired destiny in the clear understanding of our cultural limitations and potential. The primal maps that govern existence show clearly our drive toward higher consciousness and the discovery of our sacred origin. The ultimate desirable state is to live our humanity with cheerful acceptance, while in constant unison with the light of divinity which is the ever-living force which energizes all existence.

Chapter 1
EARLY STEPS

Nothing comes to you from anyone;
nothing comes from you to anyone;
everything comes from you to you.
                    Khwaja Abdullah Ansari

I was born in Karbala, Iraq, in 1937, on the day of the birth of Imam Hussein, to a family of distinguished Shiite *ulama* (those trained in the religious sciences). Karbala had its own special blend of Iraqi/Iranian culture plus a nomadic Arab element with its particular concept of honour. I grew up speaking Arabic and Farsi, respected and felt equally at ease with either culture, coming as I did from both.

My father's grandfather, Shaykh Zayn al-'Abideen, had moved to Najaf and Karbala from Mazanderan, a province of Iran. Khursheed, his wife's family, was also from that area. Shaykh Zayn al-'Abideen's family had originated from Shirvan in present-day Azerbaijan but had moved to Mazanderan in the early 1800s following a Russian invasion, which brought much change and upheaval.

My mother was Arab, from a Seyyed (denotes males accepted as descendants of the Prophet through his grandsons, Hasan and Hussein) family with Turkoman blood on my grandmother's side. She came from the Bani Asad (Sons of the Lion), a prominent Arab tribe. It was tribesmen from the Bani Asad who buried the martyred body of Imam Hussein.

My religious education followed the traditional pattern of an elite, scholarly Shiite Muslim household. Islam was simply a way of life and conduct, and its heritage and beliefs the foundation upon which society was built. As a child I loved reciting the Quran, enjoying the reverberations of the sounds within my head and breast. I recall my anguished crying when I wanted to offer *salat* (ritual prayer) aged three and was unable to do it properly.

The city of Karbala was a favoured destination for numerous *dervishes* (followers of Sufism). They came from different regions in the Islamic world such as Turkey, Central Asia, Iran, the Arab world, North Africa and elsewhere. They belonged to different Sufi orders, each with distinct cultures and practices. The majority of them were practicing Muslims and *shari'a* adherents. There was noticeable respect and courtesy amongst them.

There were always amongst them a few colourful *dervishes*, ascetics and other types of mystics. It was quite natural for me to connect traditional Islam with *dhikr* (invocation, remembrance of Allah), chanting and other esoteric practices. I was sometimes drawn to the more eccentric Sufis, who preferred isolation and a reflective life to public acclaim or leadership. For me, at that young age, an acceptance of fate and the unseen was a natural, everyday norm.

The only close family member with a connection to Sufism was my great-uncle, Shaykh Abdullah Haeri Mazanderani. He became a Sufi as a result of his encounter with Mullah Sultan, a great Sufi master, from Gonabad in northeastern Iran.

Some of the Sufi brotherhoods were considered by both the Sunni and the Shiite orthodoxy to have diverged from aspects of traditional Islamic teaching, often provoking opposition to them. Sufism had been regarded with suspicion by the Shiite *'ulama* since the Safavid period, when Twelve Imam Shiism was adopted as the state religion of Persia. Ironically, the first Safavid ruler, Shah Ismail, was himself the head of a Sufi sect, but the Shiite Arab *'ulama* he brought into Persia from the Levant to educate a largely Sunni population were generally opposed to Sufism. Over the years the Persian people developed a negative connotation with Sufism, considering it to be outside mainstream Islam and full of superstitious practices. In Persia, the study of *tasawwuf* (Sufism) became known as *'irfan* (gnosis, enlightenment) to distinguish it from the Sufism practiced in the Sunni world. Persian *tariqas* existed but were not in the public eye, and when any of the *'ulama* took an interest in *'irfan*, they did so discreetly.

Initially, Shaykh Abdullah had avoided meeting Mullah Sultan for these reasons. Their first encounter came when Shaykh Abdullah was returning from the public baths and saw Mullah Sultan in the street but continued walking on and did not greet the Sufi master. Mullah Sultan called after him, "I know that you will finally come to me."

This eventually came to pass, for Shaykh Abdullah left Karbala, gave up his formal religious status and devoted the rest of his life to the Sufi path. In time, he became an acknowledged Sufi shaykh of one of the Gonabadi orders with pupils of his own. For many years he was estranged from most of his family, particularly his elder brother, Shaykh Muhammad Hussein, who was my grandfather.

My father, Shaykh Ahmad, had a deep affection for his uncle and was eventually able to reconcile his own father, Shaykh Muhammad Hussein, with Shaykh Abdullah. When the two brothers finally met, Shaykh Muhammad Hussein realized that a man who upholds the *shari'a* or outer boundaries, like himself, was ultimately at the same altar of worship as the man who upholds *haqiqa* (Truth, inner reality) or inner boundlessness. I could well imagine Shaykh Abdullah saying that *tasawwuf* or *'irfan* is the original Muhammadi Way but, due to cultural diversity and the emergence of dubious sects, the real Sufis remained a minority. They can be described as those who combine the notion of living well in this world in preparation for the hereafter. Whenever my father told this story he would give a joyful sigh of relief, acknowledging the unity of the outer and inner or seen and unseen – *tawhid* (oneness)!

My childhood exposure to Sufism, or what I call now "transformative Islam", and to numerous enlightened people from different cultural backgrounds, prepared me in later years to explore past and contemporary Sufi life. But it was not until I was 40 years of age that I was to follow in the footsteps of my great-uncle, Shaykh Abdullah.

As a 16-year-old, I had won a government scholarship to study science (physics, chemistry and mathematics) in the United Kingdom. The years that followed exposed me to a very different world from the traditional milieu in which I had been raised. My emphasis was on personal excellence, first as a student, then as an engineer for the Iraqi Petroleum Company, and later as a businessman in the Middle East. During those years I was plunged into a Western business arena whose priorities and values were dramatically different to the world of my childhood.

This period was largely dedicated to the development of life skills, but there was a meeting of hearts and minds with the Irish writer Anthony C West, which enabled me to reflect on the contrasts between the God-centric world I had come from and the Western materialism that now confronted me. He was the author of a much-acclaimed novel called *River's End* and had devoted his life to literary pursuits. He was also something of a philosopher and during the long walks we enjoyed together on the Welsh beaches he would talk about the unifying field that permeates this world and its play as it manifests. Anthony was able to reassure me of the correctness of my basic childhood upbringing, which was the fruit of a living faith, not mere ritual or superstition.

> *Allah was, and there was nothing beside Him, and He is now as He was.*[5]
>
> *Ibn 'Ata' Allah*

Allah is the Unique, Absolute Truth and the Essence of all creations, known and unknown. He is totally independent of all existential creations and realities, and yet everything in existence is dependent upon Him, connected to Him and acts according to His Decrees. He was the Unique, Independent, Absolute and Self-reliant and continues to be the same. Allah is the creator of time

and space and is thus the First, and the Last. He is both
Evident and Unseen.

During these walks we would talk about ethics, morality, the purpose
of life and different religions. Anthony regarded them all as having the
same essence and purpose, although he believed that contemporary
Christianity had lost its original spiritual impetus. I, too, had felt
the spiritual barrenness of Western society but had to admit that the
traditional way of life in the East was also no longer sustainable. A
culture that had existed for hundreds of years with minimal change and
protected from outside influences was now facing the rapid onslaught of
the modern world. The people of the East would be forced to adapt to a
new lifestyle with global consciousness.

My father was to pass away while I was still studying in the UK. I was
barely 20 years old. He was a remarkable, enlightened being whose
knowledge and wisdom was respected by all. Shaykh Ahmad was an
'alim (one trained in the religious sciences), as well as an accomplished
alchemist, as were his father and grandfather before him. He once
explained to me that the alchemical process is to turn a base metal into
a higher one, from lead to gold, from an unstable and confused state
to noble, beautiful gold. Its pursuit enables the seeker to experience
how time and the timeless are related; how thousands of years can be
shrunk by accelerating the natural process. It is, thus, a spiritual exercise,
reflecting the quality of the practitioner's state and the people who want
to turn metals into gold for material gains will not succeed. My mother
told me that just before Shaykh Ahmad stopped his alchemy, she had
seen some of his rings, which had originally been silver, turn gold in
colour. He had then stopped wearing them.

Shaykh Ahmad died on New Year's Eve, 1957, having shown no sign of
illness during the day. After the sunset prayers he retired to his bedroom,
saying he was feeling a little weak. At midnight he collapsed on the

veranda just outside his room. Bibi Fadhila, my mother, stayed with him as my brother, Fadhil, rushed to call the doctor. When he returned my father was still lying on the veranda. It was a cold winter night and the doctor recommended they take him inside. As my brother tried to move him, Shaykh Ahmad turned to him with a serene smile on his face and calmly said, "There is no point, it is complete."

> *You ask me the marks of a man of faith?*
> *When death comes to him, he has a smile on his lips.*
> *Muhammad Iqbal*

There were a number of indications that Shaykh Ahmad foresaw his own death. The day before he had given Baba Mahmood, his manservant, a list of shops where accounts were to be settled. In all the years Baba worked for him, he had never settled all his accounts at the same time. Some time before his death, he had been tending to his favourite orange tree, which adorned the courtyard, standing at the centre of a ring of trees. Try as he might to revive it, the old orange tree had become weak and barren. As he pruned and watered it, he turned to his daughter, Fodhla, who was standing by his side and said, "It is a sign."

A few weeks before, he had taken my brother Fadhil on a trip by horse-drawn carriage half an hour into the desert. When the carriage was well beyond the sprawling public cemetery, he pointed out a place and said this was where he wanted to be buried. He told Fadhil that he had already shown the undertaker the exact spot. It was considered a strange place for Shaykh Ahmad to want to be laid to rest as the family had a handsome mausoleum at the entrance to the shrine of Imam Hussein, which was own to the local population. It was a matter of great prestige to be buried close to the tomb of Imam Hussein. There were two other private mausoleums next to the shrine but with the shrine's expansion they had already been incorporated into the public areas.

On the day of his funeral, Karbala closed down. Thousands came from all over – religious leaders, tribal chiefs, government officials and the king's representative, as well as merchants, shop owners and street vendors.

He was deeply loved and respected by all. For 40 days, the traditional mourning period, relatives came to the family's house dressed in black and Quranic recitation reverberated through the rooms.

I returned to Iraq a year after he died and wanted to go alone and visit his grave, but when I got there I found a new cemetery had sprung up around where he was buried. There were so many graves that I could not find his. I had to go back to town to get Baba Mahmood to guide me. At the time of his burial not a single grave in that area had been dug. The people obviously felt something special about the place that such a man wished to be buried there. In fact, next to his grave, a water spring had come up. Until recently it was known as "the fountain of Ahmad" in his honour.

My father left this world with complete ease and readiness. He had settled his accounts outwardly and inwardly. He had acted appropriately in whatever he did, always faithful and cheerful to the needs of the moment with reference to the divine. His memory has always remained with me as a source of inspiration. I would recall how I used to walk behind Shaykh Ahmad in the late afternoon, as he did some maintenance work around the house. As a boy I would help him plaster walls, mix the gypsum and knock in nails. It always gave me a great sense of pride to be my father's apprentice.

Shaykh Ahmad had encouraged me to take the government scholarship and study modern science abroad. In retrospect, I always felt that he realized the changes that would take place with the passing of a way of life that had gone on for centuries. He knew that for me to flourish both in the inner and outer I had to go out into a wider world.

INEVITABLE EXIT

Time has come to bid farewell
To the mulberry tree,
For time has come to embark
On the journey to meet destiny.
Back again, riding the sea,
Lost in the ocean,
Following the chart of devotion
With constantly changing undercurrents
Uncertain about the direction
Except at sunrise,
Then at sunset
And in between a practice
Of being diligent and acting wise
From morning to evening
From evening to dawn
Leaving behind
The orchard
And the birds
And the secret whisper of
The mountain breeze
And all other comforts
That make life smooth and bring ease.

Life is indifferent
To human experience
For its only concern
Is the disposal of time
In confined space
With an exit called death
To a new life beyond change,
Where the mulberry tree is ever in fruit
And Divine Love is never in dispute.[6]

Shaykh Fadhlalla Haeri

In the years that followed my father's passing, Seyyed Hussein Dallal, a family friend, was a great support to us all. He came from a prominent tribal family from Hillah in central Iraq, where ancient Babylon was. Hillah is also not far from Karbala. Hussein moved amongst the scholarly *'ulama*, as well as in senior government circles, due to his own credentials. He was a respected lawyer who only took on cases where he felt there was injustice and wouldn't charge for his services. Seyyed Hussein had a bedroom in a modest, old-fashioned hotel in Baghdad near the River Tigris, in the area where all the bookshops and libraries were located. It was a small room with a steel bed, underneath which lay a small suitcase containing all of his belongings. There was no closet or any other furniture.

On one of the two occasions that I visited him there, he opened the suitcase and gave me a turquoise ring. I wore it for many years, until it was lost. Seyyed Hussein had considerable political influence and commanded respect amongst people who mattered. The despotic government of Saddam Hussein in its early years tired of his crusades against injustice. He was charged with treason for trying to negotiate with the Kurds and his bullet-ridden body, sloped on a chair, was shown on television as a warning to those who would dissent. Before his death, he had written me a letter asking me to concentrate on my studies in England and other aspects of culture and education but to avoid at all costs local politics, warning that no good would come out of it the way it was going. Afterwards I learned that Hussein had been subjected to several days of torture before he was ruthlessly shot by a machine gun. Often when individuals stand up to a tyrant they will be cut down, unless a movement springs up to overwhelm the old regime.

> *The Messenger was asked what kind of striving in Allah's way was the best. He replied, "Speaking the truth in front of a tyrannical ruler."[7]*
>
> Prophet Muhammad

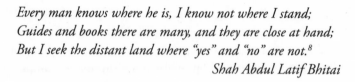

Every man knows where he is, I know not where I stand;
Guides and books there are many, and they are close at hand;
But I seek the distant land where "yes" and "no" are not.[8]
Shah Abdul Latif Bhitai

When I was living in Beirut during my early 30s, a chance encounter with an Indian Swami on a flight from Kuwait marked the true beginning of my spiritual journey. Having lost my father of form at a young age, I was now to find my father of meaning.

Swami Chinmayananda, an Indian Brahmin, Vedantic scholar and Guru, radiated love and serenity. I was intrigued by this exotic stranger with his flowing robes and friendly, yet regal, manner and instigated a conversation. I asked the Swami about the coloured dot on his forehead. Swami Chinmayananda replied that I was not really asking about the dot. My curiosity concealed a deeper question about the purpose of life and the pursuit of deep joy and sustainable contentment. This meeting marked the beginning of a pupil–master relationship between a Muslim and a Hindu sage.

Test religion before condemning it! Try the spiritual life for two
years, then, you decide for yourself its benefits.[9]
Swami Chinmayananda

I recognized in Swami Chinmaya an enlightened being and knew that I could never rest until I, too, had achieved an inner state of contentment and peace. Over the next few years there were frequent travels in India and other countries with the Swami. My Islamic heritage was part of my persona, but I found much spiritual nourishment in the universal teachings of the Hindu master. Swami Chinmaya's teachings enabled me to access my own inner reality. He taught me that there is only one Truth, which permeates all cultures and religions – it is not exclusive to a specific language, place or time. Swami Chinmaya himself exemplified *haqiqa* and in his wisdom he knew the importance for me of combining it with *shari'a*. Swamiji regularly reminded me of my link with my Islamic heritage, often greeting me with *assalamu alaykum* (peace be upon you) and even suggested that I visit Makka. He also warned me against the deviations and distortions from the original Prophetic message.

The Swami knew that I lived by the Islamic Prophetic path and so a full return to it would be a natural completion for my spiritual journey. A day came when Swamiji told me the time had arrived for me to find the Sufis and return to the Islam of my youth. The Guru advised that I take the first clear path that presented itself, and not to be distracted by anything I might see that did not directly concern me. These two guidelines became beacons in my approach throughout life. At first there was a sense of desolation at losing proximity to the master, who had been my spiritual father for several years. As events unfolded, I came to realize the deep wisdom of Swamiji's guidance.

> *World perfection through individual perfection! The world can only be changed by the spiritual unfoldment of each individual – not by political revolution, but by spiritual evolution.*[10]
> *Swami Chinmayananda*

Chapter 2
PATHS AND QUESTS

*For all lovers their passion can never be satisfied except
by prayers upon the beloved Muhammad for light is
only in contemplating his beauty. Follow his path and
you will be well guided for there is no other guidance
and keep admiring Muhammad with love and repeat
his qualities and you will realize that honour. It will only
increase you in love and understanding. Be sincere to the Ahl
al-Bayt with love and his companions constantly.*

Ibn al-'Arabi

When Swamiji told me to leave and find the Sufis, my first thought was
to journey around Iran. Perhaps, like my great-uncle, Shaykh Abdullah,
I too would discover men of light in the mountains of Khurasan. I nearly
bought a motor caravan with this intention in mind. Before this trip
could take place, I returned to England where my family was living.
Shortly after my arrival, I went into a London bookshop and picked
up a book entitled *The Way of Muhammad*. This book marked another
turning point in my life.

When I read of the Prophet's conduct and constant reference to the
Higher, it struck a deep cord in my heart that this is the only way to a
good life. During my years with Swami Chinmaya I had been inspired
by the advice given by Krishna to Arjuna in the Bhagavad Gita, that he
is most beloved, who is the same in praise and censure. The Prophet
Muhammad had lived his life with transformative virtues or divine
attributes, which are nearest to living Truth. When I discovered the dual
nature of man, an evolved animal, alive due to the divine soul within
him, then the meaning of perfect man became clear. The complete
being lives according to the perfect light within, not some fancy idea of

perfection. Our material life, as body and mind, is temporary but it is the driving force to discover the permanent truth of our soul within the heart, a reflector of the cosmic soul – Allah.

Later, reading about the so-called "complete man" referred to in Abd al-Karim Jili's (d. c1410 CE) book, *Al-Insan al-Kamil* (*The Perfect Man*), I realized that Muhammad was that being. He, other Prophets and a few enlightened beings are considered to have completed their journey in consciousness.

The Way of Muhammad had kindled in me a great love of the Prophet and a desire to emulate his qualities. Whoever had written this book I thought was worth meeting; so I contacted the publishers at their address in Berkeley, California.

Some time passed, then one day the answer came to my London home. Standing outside was a European man with a touch of the *dervish* in his clothes and demeanour. The author of *The Way of Muhammad*, Shaykh Abdalqadir as-Sufi, had sent his pupil, Abdul Rahman Wolf, with an invitation to meet him. A chance visit to a bookshop, a book that attracted me – seemingly unimportant incidents, but they changed my life.

This meeting took place in an apartment owned by Ibrahim, a pupil of Shaykh Abdalqadir. The shaykh was a Scottish convert to Islam, whose birth name was Ian Dallas. I was immediately struck by his charisma and intelligence. The shaykh had taken as his guide Shaykh Muhammad ibn al-Habib, a Moroccan Darqawi shaykh. He was a cultivated man, writer and actor, who had even starred in a Fellini movie before he embraced Islam. He and his pupils maintained a strong link with the cultural trappings of Moroccan Islam, including their attire and food. It is quite natural for new converts to a faith to adopt the trappings of that culture and live the new identity.

Shaykh Muhammad ibn al-Habib was a master of the Shadhili-Darqawi Sufi order, a prominent North African *silsila* (chain, spiritual lineage). He was an old man when Shaykh Abdalqadir met him, and was acknowledged as one of the greatest North African Sufi masters of his time.

Another important influence on Shaykh Abdalqadir had been the Raja of Mahmudabad (1914–73 CE). Shaykh Abdalqadir told me how much he had benefitted from the Raja's counsel, after he had first embraced Islam. The Raja was the first director of the Islamic Cultural Centre in London and devoted the last years of his life to supervising the building of the Regent's Park Mosque, which he had donated the land for. The governments of Egypt, Iran and Pakistan contributed to this project. He was most helpful to Shaykh Abdalqadir and other British converts to Islam, especially with regard to the universality of the *deen*.

Shaykh Abdalqadir respected not only the Raja's knowledge of Islam but also his asceticism, inner light and willingness to sacrifice everything for his beliefs. Born to a high position of power and wealth, he was a prominent member of the All-India Muslim League. Initially he had not been in favour of a separate Muslim state, but eventually was persuaded by Mohammad Ali Jinnah, an old family friend, to support Partition. Jinnah's early death so soon after Partition and the politics at that time made it impossible for the Raja to stay in Pakistan. He moved to Iraq in 1959 and later went to London.

My father had been on friendly terms with the Raja and his family during their stay in Iraq. There had been a long connection between our two families. When I visited Mahmudabad in the early 1980s, I discovered more about this old link. The strong Jafari heritage of that area is attributed to the influence and work of Shaykh Zayn al-'Abideen, my great-grandfather. In the Raja's main palace there was a beautiful *firman* (edict) declaring the Raja of Mahmudabad of that time was authorized to represent Shaykh Zayn al-'Abideen, who had sent him a prayer mat, *tasbih* (prayer beads) and an agate ring as tokens of this bond.

Farid ad-Din Attar, in his *Tadhkiratu'l-Awliya* (*Memoirs of Saints*), tells the story of another illumined ruler, Hazrat Ibrahim bin Adham (730–

777/78 ce), the King of Balkh, who gave up his kingdom and family to live as a *dervish*.

One day the Sultan had gone hunting. During the pursuit of a beautiful deer, his fast horse outstripped all his companions. Ibrahim bin Adham then found he was alone in the wilderness. He heard the Divine Voice repeatedly say to him, "Wake up, before death overtakes you." The Sultan fainted from shock. When he came to, he saw the deer was standing close by him. He aimed at the animal but before his arrow could leave the bow, the deer addressed him in a human voice. He told the Sultan that he would not be able to kill him as he had come to hunt the Sultan, not to be hunted by him. The deer asked whether he had ever wondered if the Lord had not created him for more important pastimes than the hunt. Once Ibrahim had heard these words, he felt a great sense of desolation and fear of the next world. He realized how meaningless his life was.

The Sultan said goodbye to his companions, who had by this time joined him. He went alone into the interior of the jungle, where he exchanged his costly robes for a shepherd's deerskin. He found a cave in the wilderness, where he lived alone for nine years. Ibrahim spent his time in prayer, lamenting his past sins. He only left his cave on Fridays, when he would collect some fuel from the forest to sell in the market. He spent the proceeds on his keep and for the ascetics, who dwelt close by him. Once his devotions attracted too much attention, he left the cave and went to Makka.

Ibrahim bin Adham became the prototype of the Sufi renunciate and a source of inspiration for later mystics.

Shaykh Abdalqadir initially encouraged me to live the Muhammadi model fully and adopt all the ritual practices of Islam. I found great joy returning to the practices of my youth, experiencing inner meanings and benefits in all aspects of the path. I was able to resonate with the *deen* in a fresh way that would not have been possible for a traditional Muslim. The Prophetic saying, *"Haqiqa* is my inner state, *tariqa* is my path and the *shari'a* is my actions"* resonated fully. I knew then that the lights of *haqiqa* that I had experienced with Swamiji would be fully reinforced and strengthened by adopting *tariqa* and *shari'a*. To follow the Muhammadi Way was to align oneself with desirable destiny, to act with discrimination and discernment and be steadfast with outer humility and inner dignity.

> *Salat is purification for hearts and a means of opening*
> *up the doors to the unseen.*[11]
>
> *Ibn 'Ata' Allah*

Effective *salat* is disengagement from the visible worlds
and a re-confirmation of total connection with the Lord
of creation, for the heart gets tarnished due to attachments
and desires in this world. This "rust" can only be removed
through *dhikr* and *salat*. It is only then that the windows
of inspiration open and the lights of the Unseen shine
through to reflect upon the mirror of the heart.

I had already tasted with Swamiji moments of oblivion and disappearance from self-awareness. The Sufi concept of *fana'* (annihilation of self) was thus familiar. Swami Chinmaya had taught me to stop the mind chatter and to enter into timeless Presence. Shaykh Abdalqadir showed me that everything emanates from the self and if the self is purified the soul will illumine things as they are. The purpose of life is to groom and purify the self and live as a sacred soul.

Shortly after our first meeting, Shaykh Abdalqadir came to stay with me at my home in Sharjah in the United Arab Emirates. He had recently been in a car accident and came both to recover his health and write in the pleasant sea air. The day he arrived he wanted to go to the beach. I drove him there and said I would collect him later. I returned later than anticipated, and he was nowhere to be found on the long and empty beach. When I finally got back home, he was already safely installed being served tea by the manservant, Narayan. When I asked him how he had managed to get back, he just said, "Allah did it," with a wave of his hand. His trust in divine guidance was impressive.

During the following days I was transfixed with the freshness of the Sufi teachings and the path of inner awakening. He introduced me to the poems of Shabistari and other Persian classical Sufis, especially Yahya al-Suhrawardi.

> *The stakes are high for real prayer.*
> *You must gamble your self*
> *And be willing to lose.*
> *When you have done this,*
> *And your self shakes off*
> *What you believed yourself to be,*
> *Then no prayer remains,*
> *Only a sparkle of the eyes.*
> *Knower and known are one.*
>
> *Mahmud Shabistari*

Later I read the *Hikmat al Ishraq* (*Wisdom of Illumination*) of Shaykh Shihab ad-Din Yahya al-Suhrawardi (1155–1191 CE), which was another description of the prevailing presence of the sacred light at all times. Suhrawardi came from northwestern Iran but spent much of his life in Iraq and Syria. He blended pre-Islamic Iranian gnosis, including Zoroastrian symbolism, with Ancient Greek and contemporary Islamic philosophy. Suhrawardi's illumination is therefore an important link between the pre-Islamic and post-Islamic wisdom of Iran. He was executed in Aleppo in 1191 CE on the order of al-Malik al-Zahir, a son of Saladin, on grounds of heresy.

Shaykh al-Ishraq, as he is commonly known, taught that all things in this universe are different reflections of the original Light, while some are direct reflections, others are accidental and some more refracted. This is a good model to show that all material existence and creation are modified and transformed aspects of a mysterious energy or life force, which we designate as God and His lights. This teaching seemed familiar to my heart and had a reassuring impact on me.

Another gift from Shaykh Abdalqadir at this time was the *diwan* (collection of odes) of the Shadhili-Darqawi masters. These gnostic revelations contained the songs of Shaykh Muhammad ibn al-Habib, as well as those of Shaykh Ahmad al-'Alawi, Shaykh al-Fayturi and Bu Madyan. These songs gave me the keys to blissful oblivion. The impact of these poetic couplets was so intense that whenever I remembered them in the years to come it felt like visiting a pavilion in paradise.

One of the odes that came from the *diwan* of Shaykh Muhammad ibn al-Habib, entitled "Withdrawal from all that is other-than-Allah", was particularly compelling.

> *My soul informs me that its reality is the Divine light, thus do not see other than that.*
> *If I wasn't a light, I would be something else and everything else is not real. Thus do not accept it.*
> *When you look with your inner eye you will not see other-than-Allah in His earth or in His heavens.*
> *But the illusion of other-than-Him hides Him. So leave your whims and desires behind, if you want to see Him.*
> *Board the ship of the path and you will be rescued by it, and accept the authority of its captain in his ways.*
> *Unite the wine with the goblet and be extinguished, and thus you will obtain sublime enlightenment.*
> *Witness with your insight His oneness but differentiation is His law on earth, so do not forget that.*
> *Make your concern one only. Thus all other needs will vanish and you will enter into His protection.*
> *Hand over all your affairs to He who knows best, for He is the expert of what goes on in hearts and desires.*
> *Oh Lord, bless the Prophet Muhammad, who carried the secrets of existence and its splendid source.*

Another favourite ode from Shaykh Muhammad ibn al-Habib was "Annihilation in Allah":

> *Oh he, who seeks oblivion in the reality of Allah, call always Allah, Allah,*
> *And vanish in Him from all else and then witness with your heart the presence of Allah.*
> *And gather your concerns in Him. It will suffice for you from all otherness.*
> *Be a pure slave to Him and you will be free from everything other-than-Allah.*
> *Submit yourself to Him with humbleness and you will be granted the secret of Allah's essence.*
> *Invoke Him with seriousness and truthfulness in the presence of the dedicated slaves.*
> *Conceal what lights come to you indicating His universal essence.*
> *With us, other-than-this is not possible for real existence, for life belongs and emanates from Allah.*
> *As for your illusions, sever them all the time by reference of the oneness of Allah.*

Shaykh Abdalqadir wanted to go to Pakistan in 1977 and visit one of his pupils, an American Indian healer, who was then studying in Karachi. At that time I had never been to Pakistan and had no interest in visiting it. I travelled there reluctantly, and was not happy in Karachi. The next day I visited the ancient cemetery of Thatta in Sind with its early Muslim graves. There I found an old Arab-style village with wooden shutters overlooking alleyways. It reminded me of Karbala. There was more life coming from the graves than from all the bustle and noise of Karachi! An old man emerged from a domed grave in the cemetery and began telling his long story of how he had walked to Makka for the *Hajj* (pilgrimage to Makka) with only a silver coin in his pocket for provision on this six-month journey there and back. He then produced this Maria Theresa silver crown, presenting it to me with a beaming smile. It remained with me for years until one day it disappeared from its usual pocket, never to return.

Shaykh Abdalqadir had fanned the flame that Swamiji had ignited in my heart. I grew increasingly restless, longing for some inner certainty and stillness, and would pace up and down the beach outside my Sharjah house, calling out for some opening. Then there came an invitation from Shaykh Abdalqadir for me to spend time with him in America and also to make an exploratory trip to Bolivia and South America.

I followed Shaykh Abdalqadir's directions diligently in the hope that they would lead me to more permanent and reliable states of inner awakening. He suggested a visit to Bolivia to explore possibilities of setting up a Sufi centre there and I went readily. To travel to an alien culture in order to serve others would help my own evolvement. To know one's self, one must go beyond its limits – go beyond the familiar to come to the most intimate innermost. On this trip I became the project, going to the other side of the "Mountain of Qaf". In Sufi terminology, "Qaf" refers to a state not a place; there are two zones of reality, one measurable, mental and human, yet behind it is the metaphysical and sacred. As human beings we live within space and time but we can allude to higher consciousness or eternal life on the other side. If you go beyond the "Mountain of Qaf", you leave conditioned consciousness for higher illumination and openings.

The outer journey yielded no result, but in the inner it confirmed my willingness to follow my teacher's instructions unquestioningly and with total trust in a good outcome that could not be expected beforehand. A sample of the traditional courtesies a pupil was expected to follow:

TEN RULES OF BEHAVIOUR OF THE YASSAVIYA SUFI ORDER

Nobody should be more respected than the murid's [seeker on Sufi path] master.

*The murid should be clever enough to understand the hints
and symbols of his master.*
*The murid should accept whatever his master says or does
without challenge.*
The murid should seek riza [acceptance] of the master.
Be honest and faithful, do not give way to doubt.
Be ultimately loyal to the master.
Be ready to give up everything for the sake of the master.
Keep the secrets of the master and don't reveal them.
Follow what is advised by the master.
*The murid should be ready to give his life for the sake of the
master and for union with Allah.[12]*

*What has never been disappears, and what has never ceased
to be remains.*

Ibn al-'Arabi

When Shaykh Abdalqadir visited me in the Gulf he mentioned his wish
to establish a centre in Tucson, Arizona. A sizeable building, which he
named the Ribat, was later purchased there. I rented an apartment in
town close by. The shaykh was actively engaged in writing, teaching and
holding circles of *dhikr*. There was a small but dedicated community
around him, mainly of Western converts to Islam. I respected their
sincerity and commitment to Islam.

Since meeting the shaykh, my drive to experience truth and be content
with that inner certainty had intensified. I was on a path of stripping off
past habits and identities. The blueprint clearly existed in the Quran and
Sufi teachings, but would this awakening ever come to me? When would
I be truly enlightened?

My state of high expectation soon reached a point of almost indifference.
I decided to leave Tucson in two days' time. When I told Shaykh

Abdalqadir about my plans, he asked me to extend my stay. He was going to put me in *khalwa* (spiritual retreat, seclusion). The literal meaning of *khalwa* is "emptying out", and signifies a time of retreat in which the pupil neither sees nor talks to anyone for a period of several days in invocation and silence. Shaykh Abdalqadir said that this exercise was well overdue for me.

> *Nothing benefits the heart more than a spiritual seclusion, whereby it enters the domain of true reflections.*[13]
>
> Ibn ʿAtaʾ Allah

> For spiritual health we need to turn away from desires and struggles, confusions and dualities. The heart needs to experience its stillness and be replenished by contemplation and increased awareness of the One. We need to balance outer experience with inner space and light until such time as we see all manifestations and experiences emanating from the One Divine Essence.

Any fantasy I had ever had of a spiritual take-off from a hidden cave or mountain ledge with a magnificent view was rudely shattered. Instead, there was a dreary third-floor apartment overlooking a noisy highway, with the constant swish of rain and traffic coming from the streets below.

I was alone for three days, the same time Shaykh Abdalqadir had spent in *khalwa* under the direction of his second spiritual master, Shaykh al-Fayturi. I wept so much that my clothes were drenched with my tears. One of my many visions during this period was that of my own funeral. I saw young men carrying my body. They were men in their late 30s or 40s. There were about 100 people close by, sombre but not grieving. To witness the end of one's biographical existence is most liberating, for it is witnessed by one's own perfect, eternal soul.

It is a futile attempt to specify how an epiphany, great insight or spiritual opening occurs. Even the desire for it, except at an earlier stage of one's spiritual journey, can be a blockage. A point comes in any meditative practice that the attempt to concentrate or focus the mind is in itself a hindrance. The no-man's land between mindfulness and heartfulness is difficult to traverse, as the mind always tries to take over. The teacher prepares the earth, plants the seed and cares for the young tree, but the way and time of its flowering and bearing fruit is a magical outcome that holds us all in awe.

Words from the *diwan* of Shaykh Muhammad ibn al-Habib transmit something of the experience of my *khalwa*:

REMEMBRANCE OF MY LORD

I am in ecstatic bewilderment by remembering my Lord.
And that remembrance is the healing.
I have loved a Lord upon whom I fully depend. Whatever
he decrees I adopt.
Any love for other-than-He in it is agony and grief.
What a victory for he who has gone past the idea of death,
for him eternal life and on-goingness.
Oh Lord, bless Muhammad, from whose essence the lights
are radiating.
His family and noble companions. They make the trusts.
They keep them too.

From then on, I often wondered how people could read any of these couplets without stepping out of themselves and being shattered. "Remembrance of my Lord" became my signature tune and I sang it whenever I attended *dhikrs* or alone by myself.

After my retreat I wrote to Swamiji Chinmaya thanking him for everything he had done for me and telling him that now, for me, "the obvious had become obvious". During the times we had spent together, I always noticed how, despite the purposefulness with which he approached all his actions, nothing in the outer world seemed to disturb him. I now came fully to understand that he possessed that stable emotional core sustained by his knowing the Truth that is timeless and ever constant. This had enabled him to deal with all kinds of apparent conflicts and difficulties. The spirit always triumphs. God is the victor. The human soul is the agent of knowing and experiencing truth.

> *At the start of the journey, the relationship is the same as that of a mother and her child but at the end of the journey there may come a time when separation and weaning are necessary, especially in the outer relationship. The inner relationship between the serious murid and his shaykh continues, since the everlasting connection is through the light of the ever-present connector, Allah, and true love continues.*
>
> *Sidi Ali al-Jamal*

Focused awareness or freedom from thought – a clear mind – is the doorway to that vastness for which we yearn. *Fana'* means loss of personal control and will. You are no longer the doer and able to act from the self or ego. *Baqa'* is ongoingness in the perfection of the now; thus this state follows *fana'*. The so-called "you" continues its journey through life but with a different lightness at heart – an illumined being.

After the experience of the *khalwa*, it was difficult to adjust to the world around, particularly to drive a car, which seemed most unnatural. Everything I saw, for the next six months, appeared hazy, illumined or translucent. The simplest of objects, like a bird or some fruit, possessed a special radiance. My eyes were moist with tears much of the time.

Shaykh Abdalqadir gave me the *idhn* (permission) to teach as a Shadhili Sufi shaykh. In later years, a shaykh of the Chishti Sufi order and another one of the Rifa'i order also gave me their *idhn*. It is a part of Sufi tradition that when a person reaches a stable stage in their higher understanding and spiritual awakening, acknowledged masters will honour him by bestowing their lineage.

After my *khalwa*, Shaykh Abdalqadir asked me to teach Quran to a group of ladies at his Ribat in Tucson. It was my first teaching experience and the Quran came to life for me, accompanied by the desire to transmit its deeper meaning. I came also to understand that what I had seen on the horizons of the Vedanta was also embedded in the Quran.

My new state inspired me with the desire to create a community that was going to live an effulgent Islam, inspired by the message of the Quran. America seemed fresher and contained a greater sense of hope and possibility than Europe. It was also the land where my eyes opened in the spiritual sense. The question was where to set up the community centre.

One evening, while studying the map of the USA, I was seeking guidance and inspiration. The name Medina in Texas caught my attention. It seemed an auspicious omen, as *madina* means "city" in Arabic and was the name given to the first place where the Prophet Muhammad established a Muslim community. The Texas Medina was near a small town in the hill country called Boerne; the nearest city being San Antonio.

Following my intuition, I was soon in San Antonio to explore the possibilities of a centre there. The waiter who answered my request for room service in the hotel spoke with an Iranian accent. Hussein and I struck up a friendship and a pot of his mother's home-cooked rice soon arrived in my room. An introduction to the Iranian community in San Antonio followed. Shortly afterwards I purchased a property between San Antonio and Boerne and the next phase of my life began. A few Muslims gathered around me and joined in sessions of Quranic interpretations.

Shaykh Abdalqadir visited San Antonio later on and we remained in contact. Years later, when I decided to move to South Africa, he suggested looking at the Lowveld area, which became my base. He particularly pointed out the abundant nuts and fruit of the area, knowing my fondness for them. Our paths in life diverged and on some topics our views differed, but I shall always remember with gratitude his gift of the legacy of the great Shadhili-Darqawis. Shaykh Abdalqadir said to me on several occasions, "It is like we are on two ranges of mountains, every now and then we pop up and greet each other." We met recently in Cape Town and shared some pleasant recollections of those early years.

Destinies meet and destinies depart.

*This day have I perfected for you your religion and completed
My favour on you and chosen for you Islam as a religion.*
Quran 5:3

The Sufi teachings had guided me toward my own inner unfoldment and rediscovery of the Way of Muhammad. I was inspired not only to share the openings I had with other seekers, but also to explore the origins and development of Sufism within the Islamic cosmology – why it had come about in all its different flavours and how the traditional teachings could be adapted to suit the world of today. It has proved to be a lifetime's search!

The following thoughts on the origin and development of Sufism have been in part expressed in my earlier book, *Elements of Sufism*. They are the culmination of exposure and studies in the USA and the years that followed, so they are retrospective, but I thought it might be of interest to the reader to see this broadbrush picture of some key figures in early Sufism, before embarking on travels with the Sufis.

Early Islam united the warring Arab tribes and produced a multiracial, polyethnic community united in the belief in one ever-present God, the Originator of all creation, to Whom everything returns.

The Arabs were fervent tribalists and the Quraysh was a leading elitist tribe in Makka with considerable monopoly on trade, backed by the prestige of their guardianship of the Kaaba, the Arabian ancient sacred place of worship. The ways of those ancient times were called the Era of *Jahiliyya* (ignorance), which was to be superseded by Islam – the path of enlightenment and readiness for the hereafter – here and now.

The first generation of Muslims lived, practiced and preached their religion without there being a special class of priesthood or need for a monastic way of life. Religious teachers were not paid as it was everybody's duty to learn and live their chosen path of life. Islam was regarded as a *deen*, a complete way to interact in life, rather than a new religion. The other Abrahamic paths had fallen into the natural pitfalls of excessive structure and a priestly class.

Within a few decades after the death of the Prophet Muhammad, however, a more organized tribalism with dynastic rule emerged. Religion was used to reinforce the rulers' policies. The early great religious and social revolution of Islam with its spiritual vitality, faith and exemplary conduct was modified, structured and made to support an elitist political system with a strong Arabist cultural bias. Individual men of piety and groups began to revolt against this betrayal and call for the return of the original, transformative Islam.

With Mu'awiya's dynastic rule in Damascus, religion became a major tool in the hands of the Umayyads and its emphasis shifted to ensure blind obedience to the rulers and their earthly-wise religious employees. The spiritual and liberating aspects of Islam were side-tracked by the authorities; individual men of piety and groups of dissenters, who revolted openly against this derailment, were often brutally obliterated. In some cases revolt took the part of political activism.

Others took to the path of piety and self transformation – the seeds of early Sufism. They were quietist in their approach and concentrated on personal efforts to perfect devotion and worship. They lived as ascetics and sought direct communion with God, rather than having their religious life directed and controlled by the *'ulama* of an authoritarian state. These early seekers explored ways of renouncing the *dunya* (this world) to attain the *akhira* (ultimate realm). They reflected on the inner meaning of the Quran and *hadiths* (tradition or saying of the Prophet Muhammad relating to his deeds and utterances), alongside developing techniques through which they could access the soul within. They tended to exist at the margins of society, rejecting materialism and the wealth that conquests had brought to establishment Muslims. Many lived in remote sanctuaries on the borders of Muslim lands. In urban areas, pious scholars began to congregate in groups to discuss gnostic interpretations of the Quran, following teachers such as the famed Hasan al-Basri (d. 110 AH/728 CE).

> *Not he who dies and is at rest is dead,*
> *He only is dead who is dead while yet alive.*
>
> *Hasan al-Basri*

The name "Sufi" became popular at a later period. During the time of the Prophet, a group of pure-hearted, simple folk in Madina were called the people of *suffa*. This name came from the small raised platforms they sat on, which are preserved near the Prophet's tomb. The word may be the origin of the English "sofa". They were poor materially but rich at heart due to their deep trust in God and reliance upon His Grace and perfect decrees. Their closeness to the Prophet and their focus on Quran, meditation and prayers distinguished their life and conduct.

It is also suggested that the origin of the word came from *suf* (wool) because these renunciates wore woollen garments, rather than the linens and cottons preferred by the wealthier Muslims at this time. Whatever the origin of the word, early writers on Sufism tried to show that its teachings were followed by those seriously aspiring to walk in the Prophetic footsteps. Abu Bakr al-Kalabadhi (d. 334 AH/994 CE) from Bukhara in his *Kitab al-Ta'arruf* (*The Doctrine of the Sufis*) claimed that Sufis existed at the time of the Prophet. He wrote that "These Sufis were deposited by God amongst His creation, and chosen out of those whom God made: they were the people of his bench (*ahl al-suffa*), and after his death they were the best of his community."

Ali ibn Abi Talib, the Prophet's son-in-law and the fourth caliph, became the most important genealogical reference for future Sufis. He is considered to have lived the gnostic path due to his attachment and love of the Prophet Muhammad. Imam Ali exemplified a being living fully in the world of dualities and challenges but drawing his reference from divine light and perfections. He is considered as the starting point of all the Sufi chains except the Naqshabandis, who take from Abu Bakr, the first caliph. The Sufis believe Ali is the ultimate transmitter of the esoteric knowledges. Hence, the authenticity of a spiritual master was based on his ability to trace his line of transmission back to Imam Ali.

> *Your remedy is within you – but you do not sense it.*
> *Your sickness is within you – but you do not perceive it.*
> *You presume that you are a small entity –*
> *Whereas within you is concealed the vast world.*
> *You are indeed that magnificent book –*
> *By whose alphabet the hidden becomes evident.*
> *Therefore you have no needs beyond yourself*
> *Your essence and secrets are in you – if only you can reflect.*
>
> *Imam Ali*

Sufis have been generally tolerated by other Muslims, but at times they were regarded with suspicion or persecuted. Although most Sufis adhered strictly to the rituals and prescriptions of Islam, some of their practices – especially shunning the world – caused controversy amongst the establishment. Also, their particular practices of *dhikr*, litanies, and in some cases use of music and dance, were disapproved of by many of the orthodox. This became more significant with the passing of time, when personal piety developed into a group dynamic and challenged the established religious authorities with their interpretation of living Islam.

Sufi ideas and practices continued to emerge in the early centuries of Islam to counter the increasing structure, theology and unqualified leadership. There were, however, many different approaches. In some cases one school of thought will have impacted on another and a new hybrid emerged, but regional and ethnic differences also played their part. The schools of Khurasan and Transoxiana, for example, did not have the renunciate flavour of the dominant Sufism of Baghdad and Basra, which has tended to colour the historical perception of the first Sufis. These early Sufis tended to come from the urban middle classes and often had a strong grounding in the religious sciences.

As time went by, the teaching and personal example of Sufis living a spiritual path began to attract growing numbers of people. Between the

9th and 11th centuries CE, the various Sufi orders began to emerge. Once these Sufi orders, or brotherhoods, came into existence, the centre of Sufi activity was no longer the private house, school or residence of the spiritual master. A more institutionalized structure became the norm. *Dhikr* and other gatherings were held in specially designated mosques or centres. A Sufi centre was called a *khanqah* (Iran and Asia) or *zawiya* (North Africa) or *tekke* (or *tekye*, Turkey). In North and West Africa such a centre was called a *ribat*, the name which was also used to describe the fortresses of the Sufi soldiers who fought in defence of Islam.

Once there were centres with a circle of followers living in close proximity, there had to be rules for the adepts' behaviour. Abu Said ibn Abul-Khayr (967–1049 CE) was a Khurasani master who set down a code of conduct for such establishments:

1. *Let them keep their garments clean and themselves always pure.*
2. *Let them not sit in the mosque or in any holy place for the sake of gossiping*
3. *In the first instance let them perform their prayers in common.*
4. *Let them pray much at night.*
5. *At dawn let them ask forgiveness of God and call unto Him.*
6. *In the morning let them read as much of the Quran as they can and let them not talk until the sun has risen.*
7. *Between evening prayers and bedtime prayers let them occupy themselves with repeating some litany.*
8. *Let them welcome the poor and needy and all who join their company, and let them bear patiently the trouble of (waiting upon) them.*
9. *Let them not eat anything save in participation with one another.*
10. *Let them not absent themselves without receiving permission from one another.*

Furthermore, let them spend their hours of leisure in one of three things: either in the study of theology or in some devotional exercise or in bringing comfort to some one. Whosoever loves this

*community and helps them as much as he is a sharer in their merit
and future recompense.*[14]

These rules were written at a period when groups of like-minded seekers
were coming together in quasi-monastic communities to focus on their
inner unfoldment.

> *It is the custom amongst shaykhs that when they are informed
> about someone's condition, they ask, "With whom does he keep
> company?" From that it also becomes evident to what class of
> people he belongs.*[15]
>
> *Abu Said ibn Abul-Khayr*

Abu Said ibn Abul-Khayr himself was a controversial character, with a
fondness for lavish Sufi gatherings where music, dance and recitals of his
ecstatic poetry featured. He was also regarded by many as an inspired guide
on the mystic path; although many amongst the *'ulama* were critical of
his behaviour. Two hagiographies were written by his descendants, which
contributed to the respect given to him by future generations of Sufis. The
Chishtis often referred to him in their teaching stories.

> *Shaykh Farid ad-Din Ganj-i-Shakur related that Shaykh Abu
> Said Abu-l-Khayr, while on horseback, was approached by a
> disciple who was on foot. The disciple first kissed the shaykh's
> knee. "Lower," ordered the shaykh. The disciple kissed the
> master's foot, then the knee of the horse, then the horse's hoof
> and finally he kissed the ground. The shaykh remarked, "In
> commanding you to go lower and lower my purpose was not
> to have you kiss the ground, but rather [to indicate to you that
> the] lower you go the higher will be your spiritual rank!"*[16]

The various schools of Islamic Law that emerged during the early two
centuries after the Prophet Muhammad's death were the legalistic

attempts to define practices and set boundaries for the application of Islamic law. Many of the early schools of Islamic Law ceased to be propagated and were superseded by those the rulers endorsed. Thus by about 1000 CE there remained about a dozen schools of law in Muslim lands. Later on, this number was reduced to seven or eight. Similarly, there were countless Sufi masters and orders through the centuries, many of which died out with the teacher's death.

The Sufi orders which emerged a few centuries later also intended to define a path for practice of inner purification and individual awakening to God consciousness. Most spiritual masters and teachers of the Sufi orders, like the founders of schools of law, did not expect their teaching to be structured or given rigid interpretation, let alone that these orders or schools of law would be named after them. The backing of a ruler, sultan or other forces, such as wars or disasters, played a big role in wider establishment and longevity of the religious school or path.

A noticeable trend within these mystic orders is that many of them intermingled, often strengthening each other and at times emerging as a new hybrid. Most of them kept a record of their lineage or chain of transmission of knowledge from the old master to the new.

Madrasas (schools for religious studies) were often connected with Sufi activities, and most taught Sufism as part of their curriculum. Religious law and Sufism became entwined. Around the 11th century CE, rules and regulations governing Sufi practices emerged. The importance of the master–pupil relationship was emphasized. Abu Qasim al-Qushayri (d. 1074 CE) from Nishapur, the writer of one of the earliest treatises on Sufism, for example, stated that it was impossible to achieve spiritual enlightenment without a teacher. Initially the master had mainly been a *shaykh al-ta'lim* (shaykh of instruction), whose role was largely to transmit sacred knowledges. He was not intimately involved with his pupil's private life, pupils would often move between teachers and there were no initiation rites or oaths of obedience. Sufis later entered into the era of *shaykh al-tarbiya* (shaykh of upbringing), where the master controlled every aspect of his pupil's life, even monitoring his dreams.

Complete obedience and fidelity to one master was obligatory. The pupil had to replace self-will with divine-will, as obeying the shaykh was part of the process of surrendering to God's will.

The firm contract between master and pupil was sealed by the latter's oath of allegiance, by transmission of a *dhikr* and bestowal of a patched or wool cloak from the former to the pupil. The rituals of a sober, respectable Sufism were now firmly established. Such masters as al-Qushayri associated themselves with the Sufism of Junayd Baghdadi. They rejected the intoxicated Sufism of Mansur al-Hallaj, which was closer to that professed by ecstatics like Abu Yazeed (also known as Bayazid) Bistami. Two different paths emerged: "sober Sufism" and "drunken Sufism". The "sober Sufis" were *shari'a* adherents, while the "drunken Sufis" sometimes, but not always, disregarded the outer courtesies and brought Sufism into disrepute.

Books were written about the Sufi path, outlining the spiritual hierarchy and the road to enlightenment. There were also many hagiographies composed about popular masters, generally extolling their miraculous powers, and often written by their descendants. Shrine culture began to develop. Pilgrimages were made to shrines, as the supplicants believed the dead saints were able to answer their prayers.

As the Sufi brotherhoods spread out geographically and increased numerically, their activities became of interest to those in power. From being associated with a professional urban class, Sufism began to attract the masses and influenced the rise of conversions to Islam, particularly in rural areas. Rulers realized the advantages of friendly association with the more orthodox groups, whose masters were called upon for both practical and spiritual counsel.

The legendary Saladin, for example, gave Sufi visitors to Cairo a beautiful, spacious *khanqah* (Sufi centre) to stay in. This both created goodwill toward the Ayyubid dynasty and ensured government authorities knew what their itinerant mystic population were up to. It also meant that institutionalized Sufism had arrived, and instead of it being a path to inner awakening, it began to resemble a structured religion, hierarchy and all. Theological hair-splitting and rivalry developed between the different orders and distracted from the real purpose of the quest.

> When Ibn al-ʿArabi came to Cairo he went to visit the famous khanqah. He had hoped "to find there the breath of the Supreme Companion". Instead, he observed a group whose "primary preoccupation was cleaning their frocks – or should I say their uniforms? – and combing their beards..."[17]

The following five key figures in the history of Sufism were chosen to show some different outer orientations in spiritual seekers. Abu'l Qasim al-Junayd (d. 298 AH/910 CE) is one of the architects of early Sufi philosophy. He gave his name to the most prominent Baghdadi school of Sufism and many *tariqas* trace their chains of transmission from him. Imam Junayd advocated balancing inner intoxication with outer sobriety. In contrast, Mansur al-Hallaj (244–309 CE) is the most famous example of the ecstatic martyr. Abu Hamid al-Ghazali (1056–1111 CE) popularized Sufism as a necessary addition to the traditional religious sciences, having realized the limitations of only focusing on *fiqh* (Islamic Law). His brother, Ahmad al-Ghazali (d. c1123 CE) was a Sufi from the beginning, devoting himself to his writings and inner experiencing. Muhammad ibn Abdul Jabbar al-Niffari's (d. 354 AH/965 CE) writings represent for me the height of Arab spiritual poetry in their transmission of *Haqq* (Truth, inner reality).

> We did not take Sufism from talk or words, but from hunger and detachment from the world, and by leaving the things to which we were habituated and which were agreeable to us.
> *Imam Junayd*

Imam Junayd was the Chief Judge of Baghdad at one time, as well as being its foremost Sufi master. He wrote on concepts such as *fana'* and *baqa'* for the spiritual elite, believing that Sufism was only for the select few and not for the ordinary Muslim. He maintained seven doors between himself and the public when he was talking to avoid the ignorant from being exposed to teachings they might misinterpret. Junayd carried this spirit of caution into his texts and letters to his pupils, probably in part to protect against any charges of heresy, which were sometimes laid against Sufis in the Baghdad of his times. This quietist approach toward the outer world meant that the mystics around him were largely ignored by the authorities and left to focus on their inner unfoldment undisturbed.

> *I have realized that which is within me*
> *And my tongue has conversed with Thee in secret*
> *And we are united in one respect,*
> *But we are separate in another.*[18]

Imam Junayd

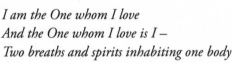

> *I am the One whom I love*
> *And the One whom I love is I –*
> *Two breaths and spirits inhabiting one body*
> *When you see me, you see the One*
> *And when you see the One you see us both.*[19]

Mansur al-Hallaj

Mansur al-Hallaj (244–309 CE) was a very different Sufi. The story of his martyrdom has been popularized in the West due to Louis Massignon's *The Passion of al-Hallaj: Mystic and Martyr of Islam* and other works. He was supposedly executed on grounds of heresy for exclaiming in ecstasy, *"Ana'l-Haqq"* (I am the Truth). The story has been that he represented the intoxicated Sufi, who revealed mystic truths in the marketplace and was condemned as much by the orthodox Sufis, as represented by the School of Junayd, as the political and religious authorities. This has been strongly questioned by contemporary historians, although the generations of Sufis that followed al-Hallaj often referred to him in a manner in keeping with the legend of an ecstatic martyr. Rumi's explanation was:

> When Hallaj's love for God reached its utmost limit, he became his own enemy and he naughted himself. He said, "I am the Real," that is, "I have been annihilated; the Real remains, nothing else." This is extreme humility and the utmost limit of servanthood. It means, "He alone is." To make a false claim and be proud is to say, "You are God and I am the servant." In this way you are affirming your own existence, and duality is the necessary result. If you say, "He is the Real," that too is duality, for there cannot be a "He" without an "I". Hence the Real said, "I am the Real." Other than He, nothing else existed. Hallaj had been annihilated, so those were the words of the Real.[20]

While Shams-i-Tabriz questions his spiritual station:

> The beauty of the spirit had not yet completely shown itself to Hallaj. Otherwise, how could he have said, "I am the Real"? What does "I" have to do with God? What is this I? What are words? Even if he had been immersed only in the world of the spirit, how could letters fit there? How could "I" fit in? How could "am" fit in?[21]

I always took it that the barrier between the voice of truth and the human voice was removed, and the tongue reflected its essence declaring itself to be the truth.

Al-Hallaj was of Iranian origin and his first exposure to Sufism was in Tustar with Sahl al-Tustari, then later with Amr al-Makki, a pupil of Junayd's, in Basra. About ten years after his immersion in Sufism, al-Hallaj became a political activist. It is not known what movement he espoused but it may have been related to some form of extreme

Shiism. He travelled widely as a popular preacher in India, Khurasan and Transoxiana but was no longer accepted in conventional Sufi circles. The last nine years of his life were spent under house arrest in Baghdad for his political views. He maintained some connection with prominent Sufis and was initially protected by powerful establishment supporters. It has been said that al-Hallaj was eventually executed on the trumped-up charge of advocating people performing *Hajj* around a replica of the Kaaba he had erected, rather than going to Makka.

Al-Hallaj was an original thinker; his *Tawasin* presents dramatic dialogues between Allah and Iblis, the Prophet Musa (Moses) and Iblis, in which various issues like predetermination, free will and spiritual intoxication are debated. Al-Hallaj presents Iblis as the lover of Allah, who would not bow down to anything other than Allah, even if commanded to by Allah. There are also other sayings and poetry which have been attributed to al-Hallaj.

> *Oh those of you who love me please kill me, for in death lies my*
> *life, and my death will only lead to real life.*
>
> *Mansur al-Hallaj*

Connection, which is at the foundation of everything in existence, takes place at numerous levels and dimensions. In nature, countless communications take place as stimulation and response. Human language makes bridges between different aspects of experience and consciousness. Al-Hallaj was mostly absorbed with higher consciousness and the subtle lights and delights that relate to the world of spirits. The wide gap in understanding between the common folk and what al-Hallaj's heart felt is such that his utterances are more misunderstood and confusing than connecting. The majority of people, who were obsessed with physical and earthly realities, were often disturbed by al-Hallaj's readings into higher realities. The few that understood his utterances were strongly attracted to him and resonated with his elevated light. Wise enlightened beings often put a barrier between themselves and the common folk, so as not to cause confusion for those who are unfamiliar with the language of hearts and soul.

⸎

Much has been made of the friction between the *'ulama* as the upholders of religious law and the Sufis, particularly the more ecstatic or *qalandari* (wandering *dervishes* who shaved their heads, faces, eyebrows, were known for their outrageous behaviour and often accused of disregarding *shari'a*). The *Ihya al-Ulum al-Din* (*Revival of the Religious Sciences*) of Abu-Hamid al-Ghazali (1056–1111 CE) is often credited with reconciling Sufism with the mainstream. This process had already started some years earlier with the Sufi masters of Nishapur. There the Sufi shaykh tended to be, as was the case with Abu Qasim al-Qushayri, a Shafi'i *'alim*.

Abu-Hamid al-Ghazali was also a distinguished Shafi'i theologian, philosopher and prolific writer on the religious sciences. He came from Tus, studied in Nishapur, and lectured at the prestigious Nizamiyyah Madrasa in Baghdad under the patronage of the Seljuq Vizier, Nizam ul-Mulk. At the peak of his outer success he had a spiritual crisis because he was not experiencing existence through the lens of Oneness. He then became sick and lost his voice so he could no longer teach. The political upheavals of the Seljuq era and the murder of Nizam ul-Mulk may also have influenced his decision to leave Baghdad. The warring factions of his times certainly impacted on him as he wrote on the necessity of firm leadership and the importance of the masses obeying their ruler, regardless of his spiritual credentials, on the grounds that strong governance is always preferable to chaos.

Abu-Hamid gave up his position and left Baghdad with only some manuscripts. These were later stolen; an indication that real knowledge does not come from books. He travelled for a few years looking for answers to his life's questions until he realized that the cure for his sickness was to adopt the Sufi path. He afterwards retired to Tus and spent the last part of his life writing about Sufism and ethics. He had woken up to the fact that while it was essential to follow the *shari'a*, man's ultimate objective is the opening of the heart, and the Sufis have that technology. His later teachings incorporated Sufism into orthodoxy and he became one of the most important reference points for Sunni Islam and sober Sufism.

> *Declare your jihad on thirteen enemies you cannot see – Egoism, Arrogance, Conceit, Selfishness, Greed, Lust, Intolerance, Anger, Lying, Cheating, Gossiping and Slandering. If you can master and destroy them, then you will be ready to fight the enemy you can [see].*
>
> *Abu Hamid al-Ghazali*

His younger brother, Ahmad al-Ghazali (d. c1123 CE), was a Sufi master. He taught famous figures in Sufi history, such as 'Ayn al-Quzat al-Hamadani and Abu al-Najib al-Suhrawardi, the founder of the Suhrawardi order. He is considered by Sufis to be the more illumined of the two brothers.

Shams ad-Din Aflaki, the author of *Menaqibu al-Arifin* (*The Acts of the Adepts*) and a pupil of Rumi's grandson, Chelebi Emis Erif, quotes Rumi as saying that "it would have been better for Abu Hamid if like Ahmad he had had an atom of mystical love, for there is nothing greater than the love of a spiritual master as an introduction to divine knowledges."

Shaykh Ahmad is remembered for his poetry on divine love and His *Risalat al-Tayr* (*Epistle of the Birds*), which uses the metaphor of the journey of a bird to explore man's path to spiritual unfoldment. It is a precursor of the later, more famous, *Conference of the Birds* by Farid ad-Din Attar. The relationship between the two brothers appears close, as Abu Hamid asked Ahmad to take over his post at the Nizamiyya Seminary when he left for his journey of spiritual exploration.

> *It has been said that the final impetus for Abu Hamid to break his ties with the outer world came when Ahmad came into one of his lectures and said, "You lent a hand to them when they hung back, and you yourself have been kept behind, while they went ahead of you. You have taken the role of guide, yet you will not be guided; you preach but you do not listen.*

O whetstone, how long will you whet iron, but will not let yourself be whetted?"[22]

In this case the older brother was guided by the younger on the road to awakening!

I am closer to the tongue from its utterance and whoever witnesses Me will not mention and whoever mentions has not witnessed. Distance is that you never find me and distance is when you give attributes and distance is that signs come to your heart and they are from Me and distance is that you see yourself and I am closer to you than your sight.

Niffari

Muhammad ibn Abd al-Jabbar ibn al-Hasan an-Niffari's (d. 354 AH/965 CE) writings represent for me the pinnacle of mystic outpourings. Niffari is said to be of Iraqi origin, coming from an area not far from Karbala, and according to the commentator Afif al-Din al-Tilimsani (d. 690 CE), he never wrote a book but recorded his revelations on scraps of paper, which were later organized by either his son or grandson. "He was a wanderer in deserts, and dwelt in no land, neither made himself known to any man. It is mentioned that he died in one of the villages of Egypt: but God knows best the truth of his case." There is no mention of him by any of the early Sufi writers, but Ibn al-'Arabi cites him four times.

Some of Niffari's renderings are called *mawaqif* ("when all stops" or "at the stop"). They come from a point where the writer has transcended conditioned consciousness, where self has morphed to soul's presence, like a voice that is no voice, a hearing that does not come from the ear. While most spiritually acknowledged people point out in adoration to the pervasiveness of Reality, Niffari sends beams of transformative light. The voice comes from inside the inner sanctum, from Truth Itself.

When I review my love and affection for the Sufi masters of the past, it becomes obvious to me that an aspect of these beings has had a prominent quality in my mind. Obviously these features resonate within me, so I am drawn to them. Niffari represents the need to migrate to where culture, comfort and ease are not dominant. His insights and unveilings in the desert were written by him and left behind for others to collect. He represents to me the best example of the stripping of identity and dipping into the ocean of unity.

> *In death I witnessed all actions to be vices and fear overtook hope and wealth was fire and when I called for help no answer came and even my past actions and friends ran away from me. And then mercy asked me where is now all your good deeds and I saw fire and then it said, "I am your friend and I am calling you" and I stepped out [of myself].*
>
> *Niffari*

Chapter 3

BAYT AD-DEEN

When the number of my friends and students in San Antonio increased, a farm was purchased half an hour's drive away from the first property on the road to Austin. A community centre was designed and built on the 140-acre plot with the capacity to house 100 people. The area was rocky but had attractive streams and a lake. Muslims from many different racial backgrounds, including converts to Islam, black and white, came to study or work at the centre. There was also a printing press, some farming activities and rearing of domestic animals. My emphasis was on teaching the Quran and the basic practices of Islam; but there was much *dhikr* and singing of *diwan*. A Pakistani ex-army Brigadier General, Razi Bilgrami, left retirement to run Bayt ad-Deen ("House of Religion"), as the centre was named.

Razi Bilgrami had been introduced to me by Wing Commander Qasim Husain, who was a retired Pakistani Air Force officer from a cultured Delhi family. On a visit to Bayt ad-Deen in its early days, Commander Qasim observed that there was a need for co-ordination and supervision of the numerous activities taking place. He suggested that I needed someone like his friend Brigadier Bilgrami to get the place organized. Soon after a phone call to Canada and a brief visit, the Brigadier and his wonderful wife, Aziza, were installed at Bayt ad-Deen. Later on, their youngest son, Abbas, was to marry my eldest daughter, Muna.

Commander Qasim was one of a group of people I had come to know in London during the late 1970s who were playing a role in maintaining Islamic culture, mainly for the people of the Subcontinent. He had been in the circle of the Raja of Mahmudabad, which also included other retired government officers who were mostly based in England. I was to enjoy years of association and friendship with him, and during this time we collaborated on ideas and ways to bring to life the *Ahl al-Bayt* (Household of the Prophet) spiritual model. He visited me a few times in America and was of great help in shaping my own outer activities and orientation. His clarity of thought, asceticism and dedication to his work was appreciated by many. Toward the end of his life, Commander Qasim asked Muneera to make sure that the memoirs of my Sufi journey were written and made available. So this work is in part keeping a promise to an old friend!

An Institute for Quranic Studies was set up; its main focus teaching the Quran and in particular the inner meaning and roots of key words and terms. My first *tafsirs* or interpretations of the Quran come from the insights of this period. My thirst for a deeper understanding of the Quran led me to a more comprehensive study of the Quranic Sciences and the classical commentaries. I knew that any serious revival or awakening would be due to the power of the Quran and its immense effect upon those who approach it with humility and trust. The enthusiasm of the new Muslims who gathered around me was also a big encouragement.

Yet, from the beginning of this project, I thought of it as a temporary phase in my life. The community was completely dependent on my personal resources and it lacked quality teachers and instructors. The only teacher I knew who had a mature and universal perspective was Seyyed Mehdi al-Hakim, a prominent Iraqi *'alim*. From a London base, he was also actively engaged in the opposition to Saddam Hussein.

Seyyed Mehdi came to teach at the centre for several weeks, but existing commitments did not allow him to devote more time to teaching. We had a close friendship and during the many hours we spent together discussing spiritual issues, I came to understand the importance of *shari'a* as giving the outer limits which point toward boundlessness, like the launching pad of a rocket. Adherence to *shari'a* boundaries is the necessary first step for inward access of the infinite. It becomes sweet when it is the foundation of *haqiqa*. When religious people compete with each other regarding the minutiae of religious law, they display their

ignorance as to the real purpose of the *deen*. Our human side of existence
has its constraints and limits, while our soul depicts the infinite and
timeless – and the path is to reconcile and unify these complementary
sides of our nature.

A few years after his visits to Texas, Seyyed Mehdi was gunned down in a
Khartoum hotel by one of Saddam Hussein's assassins. Many of the male
members of his beleaguered family had been executed on the orders of
Saddam and I recall Seyyed Mehdi asking me to pray that he should not
be deprived of the ultimate sacrifice and join the rank of his martyred
brothers.

Seyyed Mehdi worked closely in the UK with Seyyed Bahr al-Uloom, a
man of deep wisdom and understanding of diverse issues in life. Seyyed
Bahr al-Uloom was an accomplished *'alim* with a strong inclination to
research, who also helped me in my studies of *shari'a*. He had arrived in
England because of the heavy persecution his family was being subjected
to in Saddam's Iraq. His friendship and in-depth understanding helped
me considerably in my exposure and comprehension of the history of
Islam and Muslims. He guided me along several important projects,
one of which was a handbook of *fiqh* in Arabic, for which he wrote a
comprehensive introduction, and also for *Prophetic Traditions in Islam*.
He had deep knowledge and respect for those historical figures known
to be Gnostics and had incorporated the light of transformation within
his own cosmology of the *deen*. He established a centre in London with
Seyyed Mehdi, which became a haven for the Iraqi diaspora. Seyyed
Bahr al-Uloom was to play an important role in the governance of Iraq
after the fall of Saddam.

> *You must enjoin what is good and forbid what is evil –*
> *otherwise the worst of men will be placed over you, and the*
> *best of you will call out but no one will answer them.*[23]
>
> *Imam Ali*

*They said, "Would you ever forget whom you love?" and I
answered, "Oh, people, how can I ever forget my soul? Although
it does not appear evident, I have no doubt it is none other
than the nur [light] of Allah."*

Shaykh Ahmad al-Rifaʻi

Amongst the interesting visitors to Bayt ad-Deen was Shaykh Jamali,
a Yugoslavian master of the Rifaʻi Sufi order. The Rifaʻis had a centre
in upstate New York, where the resident shaykh was Asaf Durakovic, a
Bosnian Sufi poet, bio-medical physician and expert in nuclear medicine,
who became a close friend.

Shaykh Asaf's ancestors were feudal landowners in Bosnia. With the
advent of communism they were forced to flee for Croatia and leave the
family estate to be confiscated. He did his master's and doctoral degrees
at Zaghreb University and in 1968 he emigrated to Canada. There he
founded the World Life Institute, an international non-profit humanitarian
organization, based in New York State. Shaykh Asaf has visited me on
several occasions in South Africa and was present to conduct my mother's
funeral. He encouraged friends and students in Gauteng to establish
the Rasooli Centre near Pretoria and was helpful to many of them. His
followers tell stories about him which verge on the miraculous. The shaykh
is a dedicated teacher, who follows uncompromisingly the path of *tajrid*
(literally "stripping off", transcendence from form to meaning).

*If you want to move your soul
Along to Union,
Take the sharp and swift sword
And cut the nafs to pieces.*

Popular Rifaʻi dervish song[24]

On an earlier visit to Shaykh Asaf's centre in upstate New York, I
personally witnessed the sword ritual for which the Rifaʻis are famous.
During the gathering, Shaykh Jamali performed the Rifaʻis' "Miracle of
the Sword". After a period of invocation and Sufi chanting, he called
out several times, "*Allahu Akbar*" (God is Greater) and then inserted a

metre-long sword through his abdomen, right in front of me and of my companions, which included a sceptical Razi Bilgrami. Shaykh Jamali then pulled out the sword smoothly and with ease, without evidence of pain or blood. At the end of the proceedings, he hugged Razi Bilgrami warmly and then left. When we got home, a trace of blood was found on Razi's shirt, a reminder that the event was materially true, although seemed logically inexplicable. Most men of light have a specific flavour or talent. It requires a strong inner not to feel any pain when a sword pierces your abdomen. Most people take notice of events that are out of the ordinary and it encourages them to ask about higher realities and God's ways. The Prophet Isa's (Jesus) miraculous healing powers attracted people to his teachings.

In a moment of intimate conversation with Shaykh Jamali, he lamented the dilution of and deviation from Islam amongst many of his followers. He said that their teachings and practices need to be re-anchored in the original Prophetic Way. Then he asked me if I could produce a compilation of the original Prophetic teachings, especially regarding conduct and behaviour, so that they could translate this work into their local languages. My promise to him to produce this work led to the compilation of the book *Prophetic Teachings on the Authority of His Household*, which was a comprehensive collection of sayings and teachings from the Prophet and the imams on all matters of faith and practice.

Some time later, through Shaykh Jamali and Shaykh Asaf, I was invited to join the Rifa'i order; an honour I accepted with gratitude.

The Rifa'is historically had often been forced to adhere to the official version of Islam, as sanctioned by Muslim rulers, but their aspirations never ceased to be for the original message. They are a Sunni *tariqa* but always express a deep love for the family of the Prophet and maintain a strong inner sense of connectedness and trust in the unseen.

Shaykh Asaf told me a popular Rifa'i story about the death of Imam Hussein. They say that the imam asked his murderer, Shimr, for water before the latter slew him. When Shimr refused, the imam explained that he did not need the water. He was just giving Shimr the opportunity to do one good action so that Allah might forgive him. Imam Hussein then pointed to the water seeping out near his feet.

Shayh Asaf has written eloquently about Imam Hussein and the martyrs of Karbala. When people hear him recite his verses or tell the story, they feel the passion of his delivery as if he had personally witnessed the events.

> *O glory of this world, how brief is your flight*
> *O hand of the tyrant, how weak is your might*
> *O power of the kings and mighty potentates*
> *The sands of time await your demise*
> *Your gold and your sword, how briefly it shines*
> *Your army's no greater than the swarm of ants*
>
> *Almighty Creator, please guide my hand*
> *To open the record covered with desert sand*
> *Where the blood of the martyrs reaches beyond time*
> *Where the truth and honour will forever stand*
> *Grant me Your mercy to recall the times*
> *Of what is written in blood at the Furat banks*
>
> *Over thorns to the stars, our journey contains*
> *The faith of this world, travelled in ten days*
> *From Makka to Kufa, over the burning sands*
> *Over the burning hearts, where human will defends*
> *The truth against the power which always pretends*
> *That destiny is made by the human hands*
>
> *The wicked may triumph but for a short while*
> *The righteous may suffer, the innocent fall*
> *With no apparent justice, while the world still spins*
> *And rewards those who indulge in sins*
> *I ask no further question of honour or treason*
> *For in all matters, You have Your supreme reason*
> *Yet, our hearts are human, so easily broken*

Please forgive my tears and my wrath awoken
At still flowing blood of the victims so pure
That even the stone can't silently endure
For the rocks and sands, and even the skies
Still echo of their sobs and laments and cries

Your last Messenger's house, scattered in the sand
In a glorious light, will forever stand
Above the sinful world, still reaching for the stars
Above the power and gold, healing burning scars
Of hearts so deeply wounded with unending pain
For Ehlel Bayt of your Prophet, for blood of Hussein

All praise is to You! Creator of both worlds
All peace and blessing upon their pure souls
For each Ashura day, we offer salutation
In ten Days, thirty parts of Your final revelation
O reader, for every day of the kudret caravan
Honour the martyrs with three juz of Quran.[25]
                                        Shaykh Asaf Durakovic

Shaykh Ahmad ibn Ali al-Rifa'i was born in 512 AH/1118 CE near Basra, in southern Iraq. His mother was a descendant of Imam Hussein. Shaykh Ahmad lived in the marshlands between Basra and Wasit, leaving the area only once to go on *Hajj*. He inherited a family *silsila* through his maternal uncle, Mansur al-Bataihi (d. 540 AH/1145 CE). Shaykh Ahmad was known for his great knowledge of *fiqh*, his compassion for the poor, sick, elderly and all animals. Despite his great wealth he lived as an ascetic.

Ibn Khalikan, in his famous 13th-century biographical dictionary, wrote of this order:

> *Abu'l-Abbas Ahmad ibn Abi 'l-Hasan 'Ali, commonly known as Ibn ar-Rifa'i, was a holy man and a faqih of the Shafi'i school. By origin he was an Arab and lived in Bata'ih, in a village called Umm 'Abida. A large concourse of fuqara*

attached themselves to him as their guide. The dervish order related to him is known as Rifa'iyya or Bata'ihiyya. His followers experience extraordinary states during which they eat live snakes and enter ovens blazing with fires which then become extinguished. It is said that in their country (the marshlands) they ride on lions and perform similar feats. They hold festival gatherings [mawasim] at which uncountable numbers of fuqara congregate and celebrate.[26]

When Shaykh Ahmad went for his *Hajj*, he walked barefoot with a large number of *Hajjis* (pilgrims) and when he reached the Prophet's tomb he greeted him as if he were his grandfather. An answer was heard from the shrine saying, "O my son!" Thousands of people heard it. Then he recited, "Here I bring you a shadow of a being who begs you to allow him to kiss your hand."

The Rifa'i order became known for the remarkable feats performed by their *dervishes* when in states of ecstasy. Their *dhikr* sounded like howling, so centuries later, when European visitors to Turkey encountered Rifa'is, they called them the howling *dervishes*.

Ibn Battuta, the famous traveller, refers to the distinct characteristics of Rifa'i *zawiyas*, as well as to the practices for which they were famous. When his caravan stayed at Wasit in 728 AH/1327 CE for three days, he writes,

This gave me the opportunity of visiting the grave of the saint Abu'l-Abbas Ahmad ar-Rifa'i, which is at the village of Umm 'Ubaida, one day's journey from the Wasit ... It is a vast convent in which there are thousands of poor brethren ... When the afternoon prayers have been said drums and kettle-drums were beaten and the poor brethren began to dance. After this they prayed the sunset prayer and brought in the repast, consisting of rice-bread, fish, milk and dates. When all had eaten and prayed their first night prayer, they began to recite their dhikr, with Sheikh Ahmad sitting on the prayer-carpet of his ancestor, then they began the musical recital. They had

*prepared loads of fire-wood which they kindled into a flame,
and went into the midst of it dancing; some of them rolled in
the fire, and others ate it in their mouths, until finally they
extinguished it entirely. This is their regular custom and it is
the peculiar characteristic of this brotherhood. Some of them
will take a large snake and bite its head with their teeth until
they eat it clean through.*[27]

The Rifa'i order spread rapidly throughout Egypt and Syria. Originally
it was established in Egypt by Abu-l-Fath al-Wasiti (d. 632 AH/1234 CE),
who is buried in Alexandria. His successor was Ahmad al-Badawi (d. 675
AH/1276 CE), who founded his own *tariqa* called Badawiyya. His shrine at
Tanta remains a popular place of pilgrimage to this day. Abu Muhammad
Ali al-Hariri (d. 645 AH/1248 CE) took the Rifa'i teachings to Syria; his
branch of the order became known as the Haririyya. Under the Ottomans
the Rifa'is were widespread in Turkey; later they expanded into Macedonia,
Kosovo, Bulgaria and Bosnia, and more recently to the USA.

*Come, brother, if it's the Truth you seek,
There's only one way – through a perfect guide.
If it's the Messenger's beauty you seek,
There's only one way – through a perfect guide.*

*Many have come with the guide as their quest;
When they found him, he soon put their troubles to rest.
A millennium of reading you may try to digest;
There's only one way – through a perfect guide.*

*Come now, brothers, come, let's go,
Lovers' hearts will overflow;
Gabriel did Muhammad show,
There's one way only – through a perfect guide.*[28]
                              Shaykh Muzaffer Ozak al-Jerrahi

Shaykh Muzaffer Ozak al-Jerrahi (1916–85) was a remarkable man of light and delight, whom I met during my time in America. He owned a bookshop in Istanbul but travelled extensively in the West, particularly in America, where he had dedicated followers. When he spoke it was in a gruff, slightly brassy tone because of his chain smoking. The transmission of the sound seemed to come from a much higher zone in him – his soul. He had been practicing from his young days as a popular *mu'adhdhin* (the one who calls to prayer). Shaykh Muzaffer enveloped people within his illumined aura, so they basked in his powerful presence. He did not dwell much on intellectual issues. There was no need, for the people coming to him it was enough to be in his presence and touched by spiritual love.

Shaykh Muzaffer had a strong spiritual sense of humour and radiated joy. He knew my dislike of smoking and would joke that it was his only vice. He would then continue that he balanced this vice with a virtue, as he only lit one match first thing in the morning and from that first cigarette all the others he smoked during the day would be lit. No wastage!

On one occasion when I was sitting with him he received a gift. He then put the little parcel on his head and almost vanished into an ecstatic state, travelling in consciousness to acknowledge the one Source behind all. The way he expressed his gratitude to the One was as though there was a direct connection between him and Allah. The gift could have been the answer to an unexpressed desire.

I told Shaykh Muzaffer that the Turkish marquee during Ashura in Karbala had always been my childhood favourite because of all the delicious sweets and perfumes available there. He mentioned that he had been to Karbala 17 times and proudly declared he knew Karbala better than me; he came there for light, while for me familiarity veiled some of the subtler lights of presence that permeated the shrine of Imam Hussein.

When visiting his centre in upstate New York, I asked permission to sing some of the odes from the Jerrahi *diwan*. There were a couple I found particularly potent. Shaykh Muzaffer immediately called one of the men and asked him to give me all the available tapes, as I was now authorized to sing anything from their *diwan*. He also said that any pupils of mine were to be welcomed at his centres. His generosity clearly surprised some of those around him, as I was an outsider to their inner circle.

Shaykh Muzaffer's gatherings in America were open to all and being a Muslim was not a pre-condition. Some of his Muslim devotees wondered why he tolerated the more casual behaviour of the Westerners and other people around him. On his last visit before his passing, he invited everybody who was present at a large meeting to join him for the sunset prayers. Those people who did not wish to pray were asked to leave. Many stayed and prayed with him. By that act he filtered out people who were not serious or committed.

Shaykh Muzaffer gave me a totally fresh perspective on Kemal Ataturk. I had always held a rather negative opinion of Ataturk, as he had banned Sufism in Turkey while he tried to establish a secular regime. Shaykh Muzaffer explained firmly that in fact the old vine of Islam had atrophied and it was necessary to cut it down to ground for new shoots to spring. Thus Ataturk had inadvertently played a role in reviving Islam. He was confident that Islam in Turkey would rise again in a manner appropriate to our time. This is happening in Turkey today with its vibrant, confident youth expressing their interest in the study of Quran and the *deen* without too much concern for past cultural trappings. I have no doubt that the revival of understanding and living the *deen* will emerge from Turkey and Turkic-speaking people.

Thousands followed Shaykh Muzaffer's funeral procession in Istanbul, with no disturbance from the authorities despite the official ban on Sufism. His work in America is carried on by his *khalifa* (deputy appointed by the shaykh), Shaykh Tosun Bayrak.

He was not an acknowledged scholar or *'alim*, but his ability to touch hearts was immense and many were deeply affected and transformed by his presence. Ease and grace always surrounded him. His teachings were primarily based on spiritual love and the relationship between the lover and the Beloved, which he celebrated in beautiful verse and with a booming voice.

> *Pass the rest by and follow love, O heart;*
> *Reality's folk obey love, for their part;*
> *love is more ancient than all that's known to exist:*
> *They sought love's beginning, but found it had no start.*[29]
>
> *Shaykh Muzaffer Ozak al-Jerrahi*

In America, I discovered Ayatollah Moussavi Khelkhali, who was regarded most highly within the Shiite theological establishment but had in the last ten years of his life withdrawn from active life, mainly due to health reasons. I discovered in him a man of immense spiritual wisdom and insights. His exposure to the unseen, past, present and future was as awesome as it was delightful. During the last years of his life he wrote poetry and enjoyed all human contact with ease and peace.

On one occasion I was invited by a group of Middle Eastern Americans in Orange County to give a talk on living Islam in the West. I was quite openly critical about the complacency of Muslims and the assumption that if one was born into this religion and spoke Arabic all was well. I highlighted the fact that knowledge of Arabic is not the same as the in-depth understanding of the language of the Quran. The assumption that one knows is the biggest barrier for inner knowledge. Toward the end of my stay I felt my talk had had a negative outcome and wished in retrospect I could have modified or even avoided the views I expressed. The next day I was visiting Ayatollah Khelkhali in San Francisco, still feeling downcast from this unhappy visit. As I entered his room, where he was sitting on a futon surrounded by his notes and books, he smiled and said, "Here comes a horseman who was accompanying sluggish pedestrians." After my greeting, he continued, "Either you should ride with other horsemen or you should get down and walk with the pedestrians." He knew exactly what I had been exposed to with complacent and cosy professional Muslims in America. My mistake was that I spoke from the heart without regard to the listeners' states and stations of ignorance. Most of my listeners had strong minds and weak hearts – much rationality with little transcendence from body or mind.

> *The perfect wali is he who behaves like the weak amongst the strong and lowers himself from the highest stage to the lowest for the benefit of his companions. He helps the strong in their highest stages, and helps the weak in their lowest stages. The Prophet said, "Talk to the people according to what they understand."*
>
> *Sidi Ali al-Jamal*

> *I do not reside on the earth, nor in the heavens, but I reside in the heart of the true believer.*
>
> *Hadith Qudsi*

The inner state of an enlightened being is the presence and experience of the Supreme light; the Source and Essence of all of existence. Such a person is aware at all times of the cosmic Oneness upon which every existence depends. It is that Divine energy that sustains the heavens and earth and gives rise to perceptions and differentiations of dualities and diverse entities. Outer differences relate to the environment and the circumstances that these beings live in. You may find a shaykh in North Africa who had been in *jihad* (literally "intense striving", often used in context of "holy war" as well as spiritual striving) most of his life, another one in northern Iran who had spent his days in a remote village teaching youngsters, yet another enlightened one who travelled for many years, then remained stationary in one spot for the rest of his life. It is said that there are more hidden saints, both men and women, than those who are known and famous. Ibn al-'Arabi, one of the most celebrated of all Sufi masters, was the student of two ladies who were hardly known to other people of his times.

I met a few amazing beings who lived as ordinary people and were hardly noticed by others. In Karbala there were at least five or six that I remember, who were much respected by the senior religious personages but whose spiritual station was not acknowledged by others. There was a Seyyed Muhammad Pashwari, who was most loved and respected by my father. There were some other *dervishes* with no possessions who would come regularly to the city two or three times a year and would be given hospitality by a few of the more evolved households.

I came across one such being in Kuala Lumpur, on a visit there during my years in America. Toward the end of a talk at the university, I noticed a most unusual person, accompanied by his young wife. After I greeted him I was drawn to have some quiet time with him. He must have picked up my thoughts, as he invited me to his house. After a long drive, we ended up in one of the poorer suburbs and I discovered that his house was a shack on a traffic island, surrounded by larger brick houses. He then told me that he had been living in this area, which was until recently farmland, but as new expensive houses sprung around him he just moved about from one plot to another. His shack comprised of one living area of about three by metres in length and a small room off it, which I guessed was the bedroom. We sat on the floor and were given some tea and water. When I commented on the quality of the water, he said he must show me his constant spring. Just the other side of the corrugated iron wall there was a pipe stuck in the ground from which a stream of water jetted out constantly. My surprise at this sight was met with a mild response, and he said whatever he had needed in his life was provided at the appropriate time.

When he had moved to this new location, the neighbours to begin with were very accommodating and gave him water whenever he asked for it. As time went by, they became less helpful; eventually one day he decided he would not ask anybody anymore. Soon after that difficult time he was inspired to look for a steel pipe from the leftover construction piles around him and stick it into one particular spot. After many prayers one day, he knew that God would provide him with water that morning. He collected whatever containers and bottles in readiness for the flowing well. About midday, water just gushed out.

*My shaykh has instructed me regarding iman [faith] saying,
"Part of iman in the unseen is that your provision comes from
where you do not expect, because the Prophet said, 'Allah refuses
to provide for His servant, the mumin, except from whence he
will not reckon.'"*

Sidi Ali al-Jamal

Like many seekers of truth, I wanted to be with like-minded, like-hearted
people and dreamt of an ideal community. I had grown up in a family
and society which had evolved over a few centuries to be self-reliant
and whose members were openly accountable to each other, referencing
all the time the Prophetic path with its guiding lights and boundaries.
Reflecting back on those years at Bayt ad-Deen, I realize I had tried
to reproduce a similar environment but it could not function properly
without numerous other life-connecting activities which would make it
self-sustaining. There was a need for health care, agriculture, education
projects and workshops, alongside more serious seekers, whose focus was
on meditation and exploring higher consciousness. There were attempts
at some activities but they were not sufficient to make it self-sustaining.

You cannot recreate a monastic ambiance in the middle of the market
place; maybe a few centuries earlier my childhood Karbala's society and
culture could have been transplanted, but not toward the end of the
20th century. Yet, despite its limited lifetime, Bayt ad-Deen was a sincere
attempt. There were gatherings of such sweetness – of Quran, *diwan*
and spiritual outpourings – that although the participants were later to
scatter throughout the world to follow their various destinies, a deep
impression was left on the hearts of most that lived there or visited.

I had designed and built a teardrop-shaped grassy island at the entrance of
the main building of the Institute of Quranic Studies. It symbolized the
tear I would shed before I left this temporary haven. After several years,
this extensive religious centre became the Greek Orthodox Church's

American Headquarters. The public cemetery is still open to all religions.

> *Why, tell me, if what you seek*
> *Does not exist in any place,*
> *Do you propose to travel there on foot?*
> *The road your self must journey on*
> *Lies in polishing the mirror of your heart.*
> *It is not by rebellion and discord*
> *That the heart's mirror is polished free*
> *Of the rust of hypocrisy and unbelief:*
> *Your mirror is polished by your certitude*
> *By the unalloyed purity of your faith.*[30]
>
> *Hakim Sanai*

Chapter 4

PAKISTAN

Some regard knowledge as superior to action,
While others put action first; both are wrong.
Unless action is combined with knowledge,
It is not deserving of recompense.[31]

Ali al-Hujwiri

During the first years of the community at Bayt ad-Deen in the early 1980s, several dozen of the students were sponsored to visit North Africa, Pakistan, India, Sri Lanka and to go on *Hajj*. The Western students in particular were keen to know more about the Sufis and the potential transformation through living faith and belief in the unseen. They wanted to live amongst the Muslims and experience a simpler way of life in the poorer countries of the East. A number of countries were surveyed with a view to set up a base for this exposure and eventually it was decided that the middle of the Pakistani side of the Punjab was the most suitable. Before embarking on this project, I decided to visit Lahore and the shrine of Ali al-Hujwiri for confirmation.

Ali al-Hujwiri of Ghazna had studied under Sufi masters in Transoxiana, Khurasan and Syria. He probably reached Lahore for the first time around 426 AH/1035 CE in the reign of Sultan Masud (422–432 AH /1031–41 CE). The earlier annexation of the Punjab by Mahmud of Ghazna had encouraged a migration of Sufis to that area. Al-Hujwiri's master, Shaykh Abu'l-Fazl Khattali, ordered him to go to Lahore but al-Hujwiri protested as there was already an eminent Sufi there. However, the morning after he reached the city, he saw the coffin of Shaykh Hussein Zinjani, the master in question, being carried out for burial.

The writing on his tomb says al-Hujwiri died in 465 AH/1072–77

CE, although his death may have been a few years after that date. Posthumously, Ali al-Hujwiri was given the title of "*Data Ganj Bakhsh*" (Distributor of Unlimited Treasure).

His book, *Kashf al-Mahjub* (*Uncovering the Veiled*), is considered to be the first significant Sufi manual to be written in Persian. It has been translated into many languages and it is still in print in Arabic, Persian, Urdu and other tongues. In Pakistan, he is often referred to as the father of the Sufi paths. There is a tradition that whenever a new spiritual master arrives in the Subcontinent, he must first visit Data Saheb and take permission for his work. Many of the great masters that followed him, such as the Chishti Shaykhs Muin ad-Din Chishti and Baba Farid ad-Din Ganj-i-Shakar, observed this courtesy. The celebrated poet Allama Iqbal had a vision of a separate country for the Muslims of India while meditating at Data Saheb's tomb. I wondered if the vision meant a separate earthly land or merely an inner state.

The shrine in Lahore has undergone regular refurbishments and expansions, especially during the past few decades. As is usual with saintly shrines, there are numerous bazaars and commercial activities nearby. Old manuscripts are sold next door to local soup kitchens for the poor, while close by are sellers of rosaries and garlands of flowers.

On my first visit to Lahore, I was hosted by a former senior politician, who was also a big land owner. He brought a number of people with him to the airport whom I did not know and had to greet politely. My host assured me that I would be seeing many of these people again at dinner that night. While I was being introduced to these dignitaries, many of whom were dressed up in Western suits and ties, with some in the local *shalwar qameez* (baggy pants and long tunic), I repeatedly recalled my remembrance of Ali al-Hujwiri during the flight to Pakistan. His soul was now admonishing me, "How dare you come to Lahore and not visit me first!" During the last hour of the flight, the remembrance of the great *wali* (friend of God) was so vivid that I became determined to visit his shrine immediately upon my arrival in Lahore.

A member of the welcoming committee was a personal friend, so I confided to him discreetly my dilemma. He suggested that if I excused myself by saying it was Ali al-Hujwiri's wish, everybody would understand or at least acquiesce. The main host was duly approached and he announced to everybody that Shaykh Fadhlalla wished to visit the shrine before dinner, although he must remind him that it was a Thursday night and the place would be exceptionally crowded.

Three people drove me up to the shrine through the throngs of determined visitors. As it was an official car we were driven right up to the entrance, where everyone took off their shoes. I was approached there by a beautiful old lady who appeared not entirely of this world. Her face looked seasoned with both joy and sorrow. She announced to me that she had been expecting my visit. As I was reluctant to have any conversations with anyone before paying my respects to the saint, I promised to speak to her afterwards.

Inside the shrine there was no space to move and I soon lost sight of my three companions. I stood next to the place that marked where the saint had spent his long period of seclusion, or *chilla* as it is called. The root of the word comes from "forty", implying that you stay for 40 days and nights in isolation with no outer connections. The idea is to sever all relationship with body and mind. Even though a large crowd surrounded the tomb, I was taken by an inner state of emptiness and felt a strong link with the soul of the buried saint. After a while I felt at great ease in circumnavigating around the tomb. When I had finished, a good-looking man emerged from the midst of the crowd and embraced me with a beautiful smile on his face and thanked me profusely for the visit.

When I recovered my thoughts and tried to thank him in return, he had vanished, leaving an empty space behind. After a while I was able to retreat with ease. Making my way toward the entrance, I found my three companions, who apologized for having lost me.

At the entrance, the Afghani refugee lady I had met earlier was eager to tell me her story of how she had walked all the way from Kabul with her daughter-in-law and grandson in answer to a call from Ali al-Hujwiri. She then described the miraculous ways her life had been saved several times, although both her husband and son had been killed by the Russians in Afghanistan. She cheerfully handed me my shoes and assured me that the best of Pakistan would open to me with ease. I came to know from other friends and family, who later visited the shrine, that this lady could identify the foreign Sufis and even knew which masters they followed.

My host's house was a gracious, old-fashioned stately home with an enormous garden. It was very jarring after the visit to the shrine to make small talk with the hospitable host and his special guests. My host's father was an ex-prime minister and there were many photographs with other commonwealth prime ministers and dignitaries. In particular, there was a large signed photo of Winston Churchill, which I found especially incongruous. I turned the photo away from the room to create a more neutral atmosphere suitable for prayers and *dhikr*.

One of my companions from Europe was fascinated that the long walkway from the carport to the inside of the house was lined with hundreds of flowerpots. It was explained that this was a legacy of the British Raj, when the *memsahebs* (wives of colonial officers) would often have to move on to another location at short notice. As a result, their favourite flowers were planted in pots that were transportable. In time it became a measure of status: the more flowerpots you had, the more senior you were in the colonial service. That night I had some wonderful dreams of being in vast deserts with limitless horizons – but surrounded by oceans of flowerpots. The seen and unseen worlds are ever connected!

When I visited the shrine of Ali al-Hujwiri again in April 2010, a friend in the government insisted that we be accompanied by special security. Once at the shrine, our group was escorted to the interior of the inner chamber. The guards had to cordon off the area for half an hour. This enabled me to enjoy a very private visit and experience the light that engulfed the tomb. Less delightful was the official interview by a TV news correspondent that I had to be subjected to at the end of the visit. The need for intensive security was subsequently justified when a few months later the shrine was bombed by extremists. Many innocents died or were injured.

In October 2012, there was another visit to Ali al-Hujwiri, with less personal security protection this time because the shrine itself was now more vigilantly guarded against extremist attacks. The atmosphere was as compelling as ever around the tomb but somehow the outer environs had lost the charm of earlier years.

The area of Ahmedpur and Bahawalpur was rich in agriculture and had a stable farming community with a strong Sufi inclination. While in the States I had instigated a programme of educating Muslim prisoners in and around Texas. On one of my visits to a prison, I met Dr Khalid Iqbal, who was doing post-doctoral work in a nearby university, and was also helping the prisoners. I was struck by the man's quality of character and good intentions and advised him that he should return to Pakistan as soon as possible. His presence there encouraged me to set up a base in his home town of Ahmedpur. Dr Iqbal's family recommended the setting up of cotton ginning mills and a few other economically uplifting activities, alongside a hostel and a mosque to be developed for the Americans and Europeans visitors. A homeopathic clinic was headed by a young Pakistani doctor and a few practitioners from the West. The venture lasted a few years and was of great benefit to all.

Soon after my arrival in Ahmedpur, I heard about Seyyed Ikram Husayn Shah Saikir, a Chishti shaykh who was also a Hakim and a healer. He had some followers in the area, although he was based in Hyderabad, Sind.

The Chishtis are amongst the earliest Sufi brotherhoods to have spread in the Subcontinent. The order originated in the 10th century CE in Afghanistan but was brought to India by Shaykh Muin ad-Din Chishti (536–633 AH/1141–1236 CE), commonly known as "*Khwaja Gharib Nawaz*" (Helper of the Poor). Gharib Nawaz originated from Sijistan in eastern Iran and came to India after travelling through the Middle East in search of spiritual knowledge. He first went to Lahore to pray by the tomb of Ali al-Hujwiri, as was the custom with newcomers to the region, and then settled in Ajmer in Rajasthan. His years in Ajmer coincided with the capture of the town by the Muslim Ghurid forces. Even after this event, the Muslims would have been in a minority and Gharib Nawaz lived and taught amidst the Hindu poor. He set an example for his spiritual heirs of adaptation to the environment and culture of the surrounding population. The Chishtis laid great emphasis on service and charitable acts, as a means for their own self-purification. They fed Muslim and non-Muslim alike. Their masters always held open dialogues with Hindu and Buddhist men of knowledge. They lived ascetic lives and avoided contact with sultans and their courts. Above all their *qawwalis* or devotional songs attracted people to them.

I was even more encouraged to meet Seyyed Ikram when I heard the following unusual story. Hakim Badr, the father of a local hakim called Iftikhar, had made a vow that his son would be trained in the art of traditional Islamic healing but in time he had forgotten his vow and the son was attending a local school. One day the boy was on his way to sit an exam and could not make it to the school due to severe abdominal pain. While crouching under a canal bridge, a *qalandari* type of a man appeared and told him that his sickness would only increase unless his father fulfilled his vow. He must be taken to a man called Seyyed Ikram from Hyderabad, who would cure him and be his teacher. This was the beginning of Seyyed Ikram's connection with Ahmedpur. The strange man had already appeared a few times in the locale, saying that he was a Sufi who had been buried some 500 years previously in Damascus. Once he fulfils the task that is the reason for his visitation, he disappears again.

Later I heard another version of this story, which was just as intriguing. After Iktikhar had matriculated he had refused to study more and taken to wandering around shrines and graveyards. One day when he was by a grave in Dera Nawab Saheb, he heard a voice telling him to go to Hyderabad in Sind, where he would find a hakim called Seyyed Ikram. He travelled there by train and asked people to direct him to Seyyed

Ikram's dispensary. When he reached that address, Seyyed Ikram had already left for the day. He found his home address and when he arrived there, Seyyed Ikram himself opened the door. His first words to Iftikhar were, "What took you so long to reach here!" Seyyed Ikram had had a dream telling him that a new pupil was coming to him.

Seyyed Ikram was a modest, self-effacing being. He lived quietly in Hyderabad, Sind with a rural centre at Mirpur Khas for *dhikr* and gatherings, where they celebrated the usual Chishti festivals. In his quiet way he lived a remarkable life by practicing outer medicine with inner healing in a most disciplined and inspired way. He had migrated from Rajasthan and was a descendant of Imam Ali al-Reza. He represented the tapestry of connection between the Sufi *tariqas* and those related to the Prophet, with a strong emphasis on the teachings from the Prophet's family. It is for this reason that until the time of Partition many parts of India maintained aspects of the old Shiite cultural and religious traditions, such as the commemorations of Muharram, the month in which Imam Hussein, the grandson of the Prophet, was martyred at Karbala. Seyyed Ikram's love for Sufi poetry and his delight in hearing and reciting it was a joy to behold.

From the first time Seyyed Ikram met with me he was enthusiastic about Muslims from the States and Europe coming to Pakistan and contributing to a revival of Sufism and Islam. He felt that a connection between the Sufi practices of North Africa and that of the Subcontinent would be an excellent mix. He had read about the Shadhilis and had wanted to meet a teacher from that order. Seyyed Ikram realized that the sweetness and beauty of the Chishtis needed to be balanced by the majesty of the Shadhilis. He would have been pleased to have read these memoirs, which makes reference to the great masters of both these *tariqas*.

Our first meeting in the early 1980s was the beginning of a long friendship. When he came to South Africa toward the end of his life, he mentioned to a gathering that my work on self-knowledge would only be fully acknowledged and used years after my passing.

One day someone asked Seyyed Ikram about curses and blessings from saints. He answered this in a matter-of-fact manner that curses are from us and blessings are from Allah. He then told the questioner, if you hear a really enlightened person condemning someone, it is not from him, he is simply describing the situation as it is. We curse ourselves through our wrong actions and the saint is merely a mirror that shows the results. As for blessings, they are in the original design of the Creator so that we will come back to His mercy. Potentially we are all blessed but we need to take responsibility for the distractions that impede us from moving toward the light that is leading us both outside and within the heart.

Seyyed Ikram became a close friend to my daughter Muna and her husband Abbas Bilgrami. Once she asked Seyyed Ikram about other spiritual masters. His immediate reply was, "You don't look for streams of water when you have the Ganges flowing in your house." When Muna repeated this, I was touched by his confidence in my destiny.

Seyyed Ikram also had a strong link with my youngest son, Ahmad, who he believed had the potential to be a great teacher. When Seyyed Ikram first saw a photo of Ahmad as a small child, he laughed heartily with joy and said he should be called Ahmad Jamal Farid. They spent some time together when Ahmad was in his teens and early twenties and a strong rapport developed between them.

On one visit to Bahawalpur, Seyyed Ikram and I met with Captain Wahid Baksh Sial Rabbani, one of the *khalifas* of Maulana Syed Muhammad Zauqi Shah (1878–1951 CE). Captain Wahid had a most extensive Sufi library and had devoted his time to teaching and promoting the Sufi way of life. On this visit he gifted me with a copy of a handwritten Sufi commentary of the Quran by Ruzbihan Baqli (d. 1209 CE) of Shiraz. Ruzbihan's commentary has always been one of my favourites. He is also known for his spiritual diary, *The Unveiling of Secrets*, his work on divine love, *The Jasmine of the Lovers* and other mystical treatises.

Although my wife, Muneera, never met Captain Wahid, she feels a strong connection with him. Some years after Captain Wahid's death, she was attending a *dhikr* in Islamabad when a lady in the *dhikr* circle called Tehzeeb-un-Nisa Begum learnt Muneera was completing a work on the great Chishti masters. Tehzeeb Begum said that she had been a pupil of Captain Wahid's and that he had told her that one day she would meet a lady from Shaykh Fadhlalla's family who would write a book on the Chishtis. She was to give this lady a copy of Captain Wahid's manuscript, which she had translated into English, on the last *Hajj* of his master Hazrat Zauqi Shah. These writings beautifully record the final days of Hazrat Zauqi Shah, who passed away in Makka while on *Hajj*.

Muneera eventually met Zahra, the granddaughter of Captain Wahid, and recounted to her this extraordinary story. Zahra is married to Bilal, a French convert to Islam. One of her grandfather's last acts before he passed on was to perform her *nikah* (marriage) to Bilal. Bilal had gone to the shrine of Baba Farid, one of the greatest of the medieval Chishtis, in Pakpattan and prayed for a pure and pious Muslim wife. Zahra was the answer.

Dead saints' reputations for answering prayers vary. Some of them are known to respond to specific requests. Baba Farid is considered to be particularly accommodating in this regard. He is generous to all. Shaykh Farid ad-Din Ganj-i-Shakar (575–664 AH/1179–1265 CE), commonly known as Baba Farid, was renowned for his asceticism and the arduous nature of his spiritual disciplines. He is the only one of the Chishti masters who is said to have performed the *Chilla-o-Makus*, in which the *dervish* suspends himself downwards in a well meditating for 40 days and nights. Every day the *mu'adhdhin* of the local mosque, near Uchch, would hoist Baba Farid up by the rope he was tied to and later lower him down again. This extreme practice is said to come from the Hindu tradition.

Baba Farid is considered the originator of the growth of the Chishti order in the Punjab. Today 11 Punjabi tribes claim that their ancestors accepted Islam at his hand. He settled in Ajodhan (modern-day Pakpattan) in the Punjab. The town was surrounded by harsh and desolate areas. His initial journey there was so perilous that his mother was lost in the jungle and eaten by wild animals. Despite the remoteness of the area, rich and poor from far away locales flocked to Baba Farid's *khanqah*, such was his reputation as a teacher. He refused the gift of four villages from Sultan Balban, always advising his pupils that

> *If you desire to attain the position of great saints,*
> *do not pay any attention to the princes.*[32]

On one occasion a man came to him in great distress and asked him to write a letter to Sultan Balban on his behalf. Baba Farid's letter reflected his attitude toward worldly power:

> *I referred this matter first to Allah but you will get the*
> *credit for it. If you do not give him anything, the real*
> *preventer is Allah and you are helpless in this matter.*[33]

Baba Farid always tried to bring contentment to people's hearts. He once refused a gift of a knife, saying, "Bring me instead a needle. The knife is an instrument for cutting, the needle for sewing together."[34]

He is commonly known as Ganj-i-Shakar throughout Pakistan today. This name is said to have come from his encounter with some greedy sugar traders, who were travelling by camel. The master asked them what they were carrying. They did not want to say it was sugar in case he asked for some, so they said it was salt. Baba Farid replied, "Then it will be salt." When they arrived at their destination they found their goods were salt. When they returned to apologize to Baba Farid for their deceit, he turned the salt back to sugar.

Another story says that as a young man he fasted continuously for three days until he was so hungry that he put pebbles into his mouth. The pebbles turned into sugar. At first he was reluctant to eat them in case they were a temptation, sent to distract him from his prayers. He eventually decided to eat them to give him sufficient strength to continue praying. His spiritual master had previously told him to break his fast with something from the unseen, so he decided this was such a gift.[35]

Baba Farid's spiritual heir was Hazrat Nizam ad-Din Awliya of Delhi. In later years he described Baba Farid to his pupils as follows:

> *Despite his longing for solitude, there was no limit to the number of people who were forever visiting him. The door to his hospice was never closed except for half of the night. Yet no one came to the shaykh for material assistance since he himself possessed nothing... If someone came unto his presence for the first time and someone else who had been an acquaintance for some years also came, he would pay equal attention to each, and of kindness and concern he would give them equal measure.[36]*
>
> *Amir Hasan Sijzi*

Baba Farid's shrine is perhaps one of the most frequently visited places on Pakistani Sufi trails. It is possible to make a day trip there from Lahore and it has a very welcoming and cheerful atmosphere. Much *dhikr*, devotional singing and ascetic practices go on there. Legends and facts blend to give a picture of a most ascetic and devout person. When people talk about the Chishtis, Baba Farid is considered amongst the five great Chishti masters of their Golden Age.

On my first visit along the bazaar that leads to the shrine, I was curious about the photographs of a European shaykh that hung in many of the small stalls. The photos were of a British Muslim named Shah Shahidullah Faridi, who became a recognized shaykh and had many followers from abroad as well as Pakistan.[37]

Shah Shahidullah Faridi was born John Gilbert Lennard in 1915 to a wealthy Roman Catholic family of German origin. He was educated at Shrewsbury but left school young, as he found the materialism of his contemporaries and the culture bereft of any purpose and meaning. He refused from a young age to attend church services and was never confirmed in the Catholic Church. His brother, John William, shared his spiritual orientation. A class fellow of John William's at Oxford University had a library of books on Buddhism, which proved of interest to the young men. They progressed to Islamic mysticism through the works of the French philosopher René Guénon. After years of spiritual search, Guénon had become a Muslim, taken the name Abd al-Wahid Yahya and lived in Cairo, following the Shadhili *tariqa*.

Two books greatly influenced the brothers at this time, *An Early Mystic of Baghdad*, on the life and teachings of Shaykh Harith al-Muhasibi, and the *Kashf al-Mahjub* of Ali al-Hujwiri. Inspired in particular by the teachings of Ali al-Hujwiri, the brothers embraced Islam. They took their *shahadah* (declaration of embracing Islam) at the Woking Mosque in 1936. This mosque had been built by Shah Jahan, Begum of Bhopal (1868–1901). John William, who was then 26 years old, became Faruq Ahmad, and John Gilbert, at 21, became Shahidullah. They now set off to find a Sufi master.

Faruq Ahmad had some connection with Frithjof Schuon, a German-Swiss scholar of metaphysics, who was associated with René Guénon. Schuon was also a member of the Shadhili *tariqa* and was known as Shaykh Isa in this context. The brothers could not have found what they were seeking with him in Europe as they travelled to India in 1937.

The Nawab of Bahawalpur, a state in the Punjab, had met the brothers in the UK as he owned property near their family estate. He invited them to stay in Bahawalpur. They were the guests of Brigadier Seyyed Nazir Ali Shah in Dera Nawab, whose home was open to Muslim converts and scholars. Years later and unbeknownst to me, I was to send Western converts to Islam to that very area to experience living in a Muslim community. Traces of seekers were clearly already there!

They travelled widely in the Subcontinent but did not find the master they were seeking. Finally, in Bombay, intending to take a ship back to England, they were recommended to go to a Chishti master, Hazrat Zauqi Shah in Hyderabad Deccan, who spoke excellent English. When the brothers met him they realized they had found their teacher. Shahidullah recognized him from a dream he had had in which the master, accompanied by a small girl, had told him, "Your share is with

me – your portion of the *deen*, as well as your portion of the *dunya*."
Shahidullah immediately became his *murid* (pupil), entering the Chishti
Sabriya order.

When Hazrat Zauqi Shah learnt of Faruq Ahmad's allegiance to Frithjof
Schuon, he told him that he had to ask the latter's permission before he
could become the pupil of another master. If a pupil has given his *bay'a*
(spiritual allegiance) to one master, he must take permission before he
can transfer his commitment to the new teacher. Aside from the question
of courtesy and understanding of the seriousness of such a commitment,
a pupil in the early days of his quest might be confused by a connection
with more than one teacher. Faruq Ahmad took permission from Frithjof
Schuon through correspondence and was later given *bay'a* by Hazrat
Zauqi Shah.

Faruq Ahmad was to die from pneumonia in Lahore, eight years after
he embraced Islam. He had said at an earlier time that he wanted to
be buried near the grave of Ali al-Hujwiri. Nobody had been buried
there for a long time but at the last moment his funeral procession was
diverted to Data Saheb, as al-Hujwiri's shrine is commonly known, and
his wish was fulfilled.

Shah Shahidullah Faridi became a Chishti shaykh and a prolific writer
on Sufism. Hazrat Zauqi Shah gave him his daughter Rashida, the little
girl in the dream, in marriage. He established a centre in Karachi, where
he was buried in 1978, and maintained close links with the shrine of
Baba Farid in Pakpattan, hence his name "Faridi".

When he was recovering from his first heart attack, his doctor advised
him to take better care of his health. Shah Shahidullah replied that no
man has the right to live longer than 63, this being the age the Prophet
Muhammad left this world. His wish was granted as he died at 63.

The main impression I had at the entrance to the courtyard of Baba Farid's shrine was that of ease and welcome. There were several groups engaging in different activities with confidence and contentment. There was singing in one corner, a group reciting the Quran together in another, there were a few ladies a bit further on reciting some prayers quietly and then there was an old man reading Urdu poetry aloud. There was also the usual traffic of circumambulating visitors placing offerings of flower garlands on the shrine.

I followed a friend who was my guide right into the mausoleum where we sat for a few minutes reciting the *Surat Fatiha* ("The Opening", first chapter of the Quran) and greeted the saint. Although there was much activity going on, I eventually found a corner where we could sit quietly in relative seclusion.

At one point in my meditation I felt I was sitting right next to Baba Farid in a cave-like enclosure, engulfed by utter silence and peace. At that exact moment I could feel the presence of someone next to me placing a cloth on my head, which I tried to ignore. After a few minutes I realized that my head was covered with a smooth green cloth with a lot of Quranic inscriptions on it. I later discovered that this was one of the covers from the tomb, which are given to special visitors and often replaced by new donations. The cloth was 3 metres by 2 metres long with *Ayat al-Kursi* (The Throne Verse; Quran 2:255) on it. I thought to myself that it would be wonderful to be under this cover on my deathbed.

After sunset, large cauldrons of food arrived to feed the multitudes, who by then were sitting in anticipation. As I watched this peaceful, philanthropic celebration, a scholarly-looking man approached me. He sat for a moment next to me and greeted me in perfect English, clearly wanting to share with me his disapproval of the *Wahhabi* (puritanical offshoot of Sunni Islam, opposed to Sufism, that originated in the 18th century CE) prohibitions against shrines. He gestured toward the people and said, "Do you think any of these people are worshipping Baba Farid?" He continued: "They are mostly poor peasants and this is both a social event and a spiritually uplifting outlet." I nodded in agreement.

Then he apologized for disturbing me and as he was leaving he gave me his card. He was a lecturer at a university in Lahore.

On another visit I was told that there were several European and American Muslims staying near the shrine. I happened to know one of the couples, an American and his wife with their son. Hajj Uthman was a kindly American Sufi who had generously given away what he had inherited and had been living off charity and grace. I caught a glimpse of their youngster enjoying a frolic in the alleyway, chasing a few chickens.

> *Baba Farid often would say to his visitors, "May Almighty God give you pain!" People would be surprised. "What sort of supplication is this?" they would ask themselves. "Now it is evident," concluded the master [Shaykh Nizam ad-Din Awliya], "what he meant by that supplication [for unless you experience the pain of separation from God, you cannot experience an intense love for Him]."*[38]
>
> Amir Hasan Sijzi

Over the years I came to know more about Baba Farid's states and station through Seyyed Ikram and others and developed a great affinity for his sincerity and light. It was clear to me that this being lived the last few years of his life in almost total detachment from what was going on around him. Maulana Badr ad-Din Ishaq, one of his closest followers, once said that one of Baba Farid's most important qualities was that he was exactly the same under all circumstances.

Many years later when I wrote a book, *Witnessing Perfection*, I often recalled Baba Farid's state of looking at outer events with an inner focus on their meaning and essence – ever constant and ever perfect, the original truth pervades the whole universe. Utter perfection is at the essence of all.

> *The sun, air, water, space and fertile soil are necessary for the rose to bloom; intelligence, inspiration, love, a wide outlook, and guidance are required for the heart to unfold.*[39]
>
> Hazrat Inayat Khan

The original writing of this quote says "soul" rather than "heart", but in my terminology all "souls" are the same, it is the state of the "hearts" that differ.

On a visit to Baba Farid in April 2010, we were hosted by the Deputy Commissioner of Pakpattan. He had a private passion for roses and was producing essential oil and rose water from local rose orchards. As he wanted to uplift the value of locally produced agriculture, he had introduced the favoured cultivar of rose damascena to the area. He had also built large fountains surrounded by large quantities of planted roses in parks and playgrounds for the nearby population to enjoy. We were gifted with litres of his locally produced rose water. The coach was filled with wonderful rose perfume for the next seven days of our tour in the Punjab. This visit to Baba Farid proved an uplifting experience for my grandson, who was then 12 and wrote this about the experience:

> Yesterday we went to a shrine that belonged to Baba Farid. It was pretty amazing because I had this experience. In the room where there are two graves, we put that cloth on and I immediately felt like a type of sweetness in my mouth and in my throat, like maple syrup. And when we left I kept putting my tongue on the roof of my mouth, to get the sweetness again and again. Then, I discovered that the end of his name "Ganji Shakar" meant something about sugar. So I was amazed by that.

> I felt a spark in my heart although normally I don't like going to shrines. I normally fuss and stuff but in that place I felt very different. I was very happy and I couldn't stop smiling. This spark that I felt it was like my ribs were opening up, my heart was growing bigger and bigger by the second. Everything was like opening up. The sweetness in my mouth lasted until we came back to the bus and I had a drink. I wanted to stay there longer. I could feel he was there right next to me and I felt very warm at the time.

During my 2010 travels around Pakistan, I revisited the shrine of Shaykh Baha ad-Din Zakariyya (1171–1267 CE) in Multan. This celebrated Suhrawardi shaykh was a contemporary of Baba Farid and his shrine is amongst the oldest in Multan. Shaykh Baha ad-Din had been a pupil of Shaykh Shihab ad-Din Suhrawardi in Baghdad, whose *Awarif al-Maʿarif* (*The Knowledge of the Spiritually Learned*)was one of the earliest Sufi manuals, and brought his teachings back to India. The Suhrawardis were establishment Sufis and though Shaykh Baha ad-Din lived in great style, his material affluence did not detract from his stature as a teacher. It is said that even the servants in his household were in constant *dhikr*. Despite their different approaches, there was mutual courtesy and good will between Shaykh Baha ad-Din and Baba Farid.

Multan is known as *Madinat-ul-Awliya* (The City of Saints) because of the large number of Sufis that are buried there. Muslims have been in Multan since the 8th century CE. Culturally and spiritually the area has played a key role in the history of Islam in the Indo-Pak Subcontinent. It was a delight to be in Multan again after many years. From my first stay in the early 1980s it had reminded me strongly of Karbala; two cities where life and death walked hand in hand.

This visit to the shrine was memorable because of a special encounter. We found an elderly gentleman sitting doing *dhikr* in the space between two tombs. Abbas asked him why he was there and learned that he had been a successful businessman, but when he was 70 he told his children that he was giving up this world and preparing for the next. He came from a family who had looked after Baha ad-Din Zakariyya's shrine for generations and he had been allocated an area for his own tomb at the spot where he spent his days in prayer and meditation. Every morning his son dropped him off at the tomb on his way to work and picked him up in the afternoon. The old man told us that he was looking after his future abode, just in case anyone else took his tomb space!

Devotion to Muhammad is my faith, his love my way of life,
and obedience to him my goal.
   Hazrat Abu Anees Muhammad Barkat Ali al-Ludhianwi

My desire to meet the interesting Sufis of Pakistan took me further into
the Punjab to meet Sufi Barkat Ali, a well-known and respected Sufi, one
of the greatest of the 20th century. I adored Sufi Barkat Ali. His friends
had all thought he would have a bright future in the Indian Army but
soon his British superiors were disappointed at his lack of ambition and
drive. His love for prayers and litany ended his career with a dismissal
report that he was too God-intoxicated to make a successful officer.
Telling this story, Sufi Barkat Ali would grin joyfully, showing the gap
left by his missing front tooth. "God-intoxication, to be mad about God
– that is the only true sanity!" he said.

He moved to Pakistan after Partition and decided to stay in a poor part
of the Punjab, a distance from Faisalabad. In the early days it would have
been half a day's trek on a cart but when I first visited him it was on
rough roads which took nearly two hours.

Soon after Sufi Barkat Ali settled in this area, landowners and villagers
from neighbouring areas came to recognize this non-worldly lover of
truth and Islam. A centre called Dar al-Ehsan (Abode of Selfless Action)
was established. He gave dictation to the scholarly devotees and asked
others to do research projects regarding the Prophet's life and teachings.
As the number of visitors grew around him he embarked on other
community projects. One was to harbour orphans or children whose
parents could not afford their upkeep, another project was to restore
and house manuscripts of the Quran. Eventually the buildings grew to
shelter a few hundred children, who were taught and fed and in between
chanting songs of praise and Quranic verses.

Over the years many of the grown-up students became involved with the
ongoing project to repair Qurans. Torn pages or parts of the Quran would

be sent to be lovingly patched up and matched to produce a complete Quran. Within a few years, several large halls were filled up with every imaginable script, size and age of Quran manuscripts. I was shown a Quran the size of a thumb and one which was about 3 metres long and over a metre wide, requiring three people to turn the page, otherwise it would be torn. There must have been thousands of Qurans. It was said that every few days a small lorry full of jumbled manuscripts arrived from a depot outside Lahore, which one of his followers had donated as a collecting point. The centre ended up feeding many of the poorer people around it, besides the resident students. A few doctors offered to establish a clinic in the vicinity, which soon expanded to become a popular surgery for glaucoma and cataracts. Well-known surgeons would often visit this clinic for the more specialized operations.

In one of the Quran halls he had lined up on the floor the sets of tunics he had worn over the years. They were made from rough handmade cotton cloth of earth colour. He wore one set a year until it was fully worn out and patched in different locations. The one he was wearing was much stained with red and black ink, a casualty of his writing.

In the centre of another hall, there were piles of rose petals at different stages of preparation. Sufi Barkat Ali used them as remedies for diverse ailments. Rose petals of every colour and size lay in plates and baskets. Only he knew what each was for.

The area was surrounded by orchards of mangoes and other sub-tropical fruits. On late afternoons he would take a stroll under these vast trees with his long *tasbih* of 10,000 beads, which was carried behind him by a couple of young followers who often competed for this task.

On one visit I was so touched by the resident students' sincerity and love for their teacher that I sent from Faisalabad seven gifts of different consumables. I had given the list to a friend and it included a sack of sugar, a tea chest, a sack of flour and a few other things – seven items in all. The gifts had arrived at the centre at sunset and the bearer was told that no food or gifts would be accepted at that time. It had been a tradition that whatever was left over had to leave the centre at dusk and be distributed to all the farms and peasants nearby. When the person protested that there was a whole sack of flowers that would fade by morning, Sufi Barkat Ali held him at the prayer niche and asked everybody to help pelt him with the flowers he had brought. My order had been for edible flour, not the decorative variety. Sufi Barkat Ali had of course understood the error and turned it into a cause for humour.

Perched in the middle of one of the teaching halls, he had an ancient mechanical typewriter that needed constant maintenance, often on a daily basis. With this typewriter he wrote numerous books and articles, as well as regular letters to heads of states, reminding them of divine grace and their responsibility to uphold justice for all. One day someone had asked him whether he had had any response to any of his reminders. He smiled and threw his hands in the air, implying that what mattered was to act appropriately; the results were not in our hands.

When I first visited Sufi Barkat Ali, I was warned that he had been on a vow of silence for the past 30 years. However, when we met he jubilantly expressed his pleasure that he no longer had to wait for our meeting. He then reiterated that he had waited so long for this event. There were always dozens of people around, poor peasants, well-dressed young people, ladies with special requests and a large contingent of serious-looking, long-bearded Sufi types. The latter considered themselves to be the real followers of Sufi Barkat Ali.

On another occasion when I visited him, I was with some of my friends from Sweden. Sufi Barkat Ali turned around and declared that he himself was really a shaykh for the buffalo because of the regular requests from local peasants to pray for their cows and buffalos to give safe birth to several offspring. Laughingly, he pointed at me and declared, "He is a shaykh for people!" He then told the visitors that some of them were men and a few were ladies, but in his case he had unified the mother and the father in his heart and now they were residing as one being, one gender. "I am both," he declared with a wide grin.

Before my last visit to Sufi Barkat Ali I heard that he had left Dar al-Ehsan, which had been continuously expanding for decades. Apparently one day he simply walked away because the trustees had some differences between them regarding management of land or assets. After his morning prayer he walked straight out until he reached a river bank in the afternoon and just stopped there. A new centre grew around him though and when I visited him several halls and buildings were already taking shape. His simple *charpoy*, where he had first slept when he had reached this place, was still left intact on the bank of the river.

When I asked Sufi Barkat Ali why I could not stay in a rural place like him, he laughed and stretched one hand to the east and the other to the west, turned around and said, "This is where you belong." I thought to myself that this must mean to nowhere.

On a previous visit, one of the keepers on the Quran depots told me that no Quran had ever left the centre, although every day dozens were received for rehabilitation. On the day before I left, Sufi Barkat Ali gave me eight beautifully bound handwritten Qurans and told me that these were for the eight centres I would establish.

One day, Sufi Barkat Ali declared in front of his followers that I was the teacher of the future and that therefore I had to teach the ladies. "Why should it be the ladies?" I exclaimed. "Because the men are too distracted and concerned with work and money, so the future lies with the women who seek knowledge and their children. In our time, most men are misled and will mislead," he replied. He honoured his confidence in women by leaving his centre and charitable works in the hands of his adopted daughter, Anees, rather than any of his male descendants.

In spite of all the setbacks and difficulties, especially with his own family, he maintained an infectious sense of humour. He adopted the role of the jester and did not give much attention to the outer events that surrounded him. The wave of fundamentalist Islam was going through Pakistan. Faisalabad was one of the places affected, as there were a number of Arab students at the nearby training airbase, as well as at army training colleges. What saved him from criticism was his genuine disposition and compassion to all human beings and strict adherence to the basics of *shari'a*, which included constant recitation of the Quran, *salat* and other rituals. The other characteristic was generosity and feeding everyone who came to him, as well as gifting them with a specially designed cap. All the fruits from the surrounding orchards – mangoes, guavas, mulberries, kinnoos – were distributed to the needy.

He had started on the Sufi path as a Chishti, but in later years he was attracted to a multitude of *tariqas*. It seemed as if he was saying there is one transformative Islam, do not focus too much on the unimportant differences between various approaches to *Haqq*. It also befitted his spiritual state, as he was perpetually traversing two zones of consciousness and retained only some hazy memory concerning his former identity.

Sufi Barkat Ali's whole lifestyle was a challenge to everything that was going on around him. He lived according to the Prophetic model, surrounded by youngsters piecing together fragments of the Quran. Nearby, a feudal society co-existed with industrial agriculture. It was rather like someone dressed up in some folkloric costume dancing in the middle of an armament factory.

Sufi Barkat Ali was one of the few people I have met who radiated spiritual humour. Ordinary humour relates to relief. A person is frightened, threatened or challenged, then the problem disappears and they are relieved. This is mostly to do with the realm of conditioned consciousness and survival. The cartoon character is smashed, yet he lives on and you laugh. Spiritual humour is subtler, deeper and more potent as it touches upon the realization that the real "you" is boundless and eternal. It is so subtle that it can only be hinted at and is only relevant to those who are at the gateway of their inner Kaaba. Spiritual humour is the ultimate relief from the illusion of the separate existence of the individual's life, bracketed between birth and death. Most people are frightened, clinging to identity and remain like animals on two legs. Sufi Barkat Ali was a rare exception, as he did not take the earthly zone of existence seriously. He considered life on earth as preparation for the hereafter. He did not deny it but equally never allowed it to affect him. These are the signs of a true *wali*.

> *The energy at his shrine was very different from many of the other ones on our trip – there was lightness and I felt his presence very strongly. I was standing at the women's side and saw Shaykh Fadhlalla smiling. It was almost as though they were having an actual conversation, as though they had never parted. There is a picture in Shaykh Fadhlalla's study of him and Sufi Barkat Ali and that image kept coming to me. I could almost see them sitting there next to each other, in the same pose. When I left the shrine I was completely overwhelmed and could not hold back tears. I kept thinking about the love that they shared for each other, which was based on nothing but a complete love for HIM. It was a connection that was based purely on recognitions of another heart that was yearning only for HIM. This was the kind of bond that was beyond time and space, the hidden and the manifest. I could not help but think what our world would look like if we based all our relations on such a bond. There would be no real issues.*
>
> *A student's description of our group's 2010*
> *visit to Sufi Barkat Ali's shrine*

While riding on a train in Pakistan, one of my friends once saw a picture of a man on the back of a book, which was being read by a fellow passenger. He was shocked by the man's close resemblance to me, except for the different attire. When my friend asked his fellow passenger whom the picture was of, he was told that he was an Indian Muslim journalist called Seyyed Muhammad Azeem Barkhiyya. He was the founder of the Azeemiyya Sufi order and otherwise known as Qalandari Baba Auliya.

Although I never met Qalandari Baba Auliya (1898–1979) in this world, our connection in the unseen had brought strong love and affection. During the early 1980s, I was discovering the immensely powerful transformative inner meanings of the Quran. For two years I had countless insights and openings to deeper meanings. Some of these I was sharing with the Western students who had been with me and getting them to record these unveilings. On occasion, the insights were so powerful and personal that I was not sure whether sharing them would be beneficial to beginners on the path or detrimental. Naturally there was a temptation to say it all but equally I was restrained by remembering the caution of the classical masters of transcendent truth.

Qalandari Baba was a direct descendant of the eleventh Shiite imam, Hasan al-'Askari. Originally from Uttar Pradesh, his first teacher was his maternal grandfather, Tajuddin Baba Auliya. In 1947, after Partition, he settled in Karachi with his wife and other family members. On his arrival he repaired electrical appliances until he could get work on a newspaper. In 1956, he was initiated into the Suhrawardiyya order by Hazrat Abdul Fiaz Qalandar Ali Suhrawardi, who was visiting Karachi. It is said that Hazrat Abdul Fiaz had asked him to come to his hotel at 3am on a bitterly cold morning. As soon as Qalandari Baba arrived, the shaykh opened the door. He blew on Qalandari Baba's forehead three times. After this initiation, he received spiritual instruction in the unseen from Shaykh Najm ad-Din Kubra (540–618 AH/1145–1221 CE) of Khwarizm (Khiva), from whom many Sufi orders, some still in existence and some defunct, sprang, including the Firdawsiyya, Nuriyya, Rukniyya and Nurbakhsiyya.

Qalandari Baba wrote three books, *Loh-o-Qalam* (*On Treasure of Divine Knowledge of Mysteries and Secrets of Nature*), *Rubaiyate-Qalandar* (*A Collection of Mystic Verses*) and *Tazkira-e-Tajuddin Baba* (*A Scientific Interpretation of Divinations and Wonder-workings Performed by Spiritual People*).

One week before his death, he told the people around him that "I am a guest here a maximum of one week." He then appointed Khwaja Shamsuddin Azeemi as his successor. An imposing shrine has now been built over his tomb.

One day in Karachi in 1981, we set out to visit this new shrine in the Shadman Town, a subdivision of Karachi. After numerous stops we eventually reached an open space between poor houses, where considerable construction activities were going on. The shrine already had visitors and there was one room next door to it from which a well-dressed caretaker emerged to greet us. We found that he had been a successful contractor until meeting Qalandari Baba, who, in his words, "totally connected the seen and unseen beyond miracles and magic".

When I asked this man to give me an example, he said one day they had visitors and he asked Qalandari Baba if he could go and buy some prepared food. Qalandari Baba replied, "Wait a while." Within a few minutes, two ladies arrived with trays full of dishes of freshly cooked local foods. The shrine keeper said we were astonished as to whom these people were but Qalandari Baba greeted them and asked them to come back within an hour. There had been two chickens in the alleyway in the morning and they remembered that he had pointed at them and said, "There goes lunch." It was those two chickens that had been cooked by the ladies without any verbal communication between them and Qalandari Baba. There were, of course, numerous other stories. It is a great thrill to witness the seamless connection between the material world and its original essence.

According to the shrine keeper, Baba Munir, I really did look a lot like Qalandari Baba. I asked him if he could send a message to Qalandari Baba with a request. He smiled confidently and said every morning before the dawn prayer Qalandari Baba would visit him and sit at the base of his bed. He pointed out a steel single bed in the corner of the room. During these visits they would have conversations, especially if he had questions for him. I asked if he had any advice to give me regarding the insights I was getting from the Quran and to what extent I could share with others. Although I was cautious I did not want to be too cautious and keep these treasures to myself. I noticed in one corner of the room that there was a dusty telephone and, like all the poorer parts of Karachi, dozens of wires emerged from the door and disappeared toward a bent pole, which carried all kinds of connections, electric and otherwise.

The man gave my companion his telephone number and asked if he could be called at 8am the following morning. My friend also gave him my number before we left after an exchange of pleasantries. As we were leaving the compound, we could hear the shrine keeper's booming voice giving more instructions to the builders who were casting wide concrete steps at the entrance.

The next morning, at 7 o'clock, my friend called to say that the shrine keeper was asking urgently to talk to me. A most excited voice greeted me with much friendliness and announced that Qalandari Baba had come to him even earlier than usual and before any question was asked was already giving the answer. He told the shrine keeper that I should be even more cautious in disclosing these insights. His advice was that there would always be a time and a place for profound spiritual disclosures, but I should never rush. He said this knowledge was like rain water and the human heart is like the dam that can contain them. I was to be patient and allow the water to fill up the dam. At the right time it would overflow in its own way and create channels that would make their way to bring life downstream and not by excitement and concern to share it with others. Patience would bring more goodness to my unveilings. This resonated with me because the Quran says the two oceans do not overcome each other, the world of mind and matter is different to that of the heart and soul. They do connect but each has its own domain and this is courtesy of the path of transcendence. Your duty is firstly toward yourself and the soul within your heart; after that is your service to others. Good intentions can otherwise cause more confusion than assistance. They are only good in the appropriate context.

I visited the shrine again in 2010, accompanied by a few friends and family. It was now highly decorated, with quality marble everywhere and was exceptionally well maintained. A fountain at the entrance was a favourite spot with birds of all kinds. Baba Munir, the original shrine keeper, was now buried near his master.

On our 2010 visit, Muhammad Ahmad, a follower of Qalandari Baba, was present and told our group the following story:

He used to visit the shrine and slowly gave up his business to open a shop nearby for feeding people. He had developed knee joint pain, so it became difficult for him to visit the shrine. One night he dreamt of Qalandari Baba, who told him to continue visiting. His family had to carry him there. One day, while meditating, he noticed some children picking mangoes from a tree. He longed to have a mango and when a mango fell in front of him, to his surprise, he was able to get up and take it before the others. He was mobile from then on!

The Messenger of Allah has said, "If a man relies solely on Allah, Allah will guarantee him all his provision and in such a way as he had not expected; but if a man devotes himself to the world, then Allah will make him rely solely on it."[40]

Samandari Baba ("Man of the Sea") was one of the liveliest and most eccentric of the Sufis I met in Pakistan. Within a few decades, Karachi had grown rapidly from a small fishing village in the early years of the 20th century to a commercial metropolis. Toward the end of the 20th century, semi-governmental building societies developed sprawling housing estates located toward the Arabian Ocean (the Defence Housing Authority or DHA). The few old fishing settlements were all pushed further away from these urban sprawls. Samandari Baba had resented all of these encroachments and decided to establish his home in what became DHA Phase Eight. It was made of a few wooden crates and orange boxes with a beautiful jewel of a little mosque under construction next door.

Initially his shack was right at the edge of the sea. As his place was so close to the sea, he was visited a few times by the land inspectors and given a warning to move on. The few followers he had and the several cats refused to move, determined to complete the mosque in anticipation of the arrival of the Mahdi. Eventually an army Brigadier in charge of the housing estate had to pay him a visit and give him a final warning. Samandari Baba told him in response he was under instruction to stay there and build this mosque as evidence and a reminder of the atrocities and injustices of the officialdom of Pakistan, especially that of Karachi. The Brigadier, with his three accompanying jeeps and about a dozen troops, left in anger and sent the next day a contingent that literally took away Samandari Baba with two of his followers to detention, minus the cats, who had scrambled away amid the chaos.

Within two days he was visited by the Brigadier's wife, who pleaded with him to pray for their child, who had had an accident at the same time her husband was telling Samandari Baba to move. The child was now in a coma. She said that she was inclined toward the Sufis and decided that she must herself come and put right what had gone wrong. Samandari Baba told her his prayers would not do anything and that she must beseech Allah that if there was still some life in the child to bring him back to consciousness. However, he would pray for the child, if she wished. The Brigadier's wife later thought that it was at the moment when Samandari Baba raised his hands in prayer that the child came out of the coma.

The Brigadier became one of Samandari Baba's closest devotees. Later on, when he was working for the National Logistics Company, the Brigadier was instrumental in helping Samandari Baba dig wells for villages in the outlying areas around Karachi.

During my second visit to him, Samandari Baba tried to explain to me how inspirations would come to him from the unseen. He said one day he could almost hear Imam Ali telling him to go to the hills some 100-odd kilometres away from Karachi and help the people there to dig a well for water. He often heard a clear voice emanating from a light that appeared above him. He was also in communication with other living Sufi masters in Pakistan and India. When he knew that I had been friendly with Sufi Barkat Ali, he told me, "We are aware of each other's movements and activities all the time." They knew each other in the seen and unseen. People that are less encumbered by ego have their own channel or frequency!

Samandari Baba would sit up in his wooden box, which was about six feet by three, perched on a *charpoy*, often with a cat on his lap, sipping his tea cheerfully. His helper would bring countless cups of hot tea throughout the day, and was puzzled by why I didn't drink. I couldn't tell him that I could not stomach the boiled tea, which was thick like treacle with all the condensed milk.

One day, my companion asked him why the mosque he had built was locked up, and he answered that he wanted it to be new when the Mahdi appeared. He asked me if I wanted to go inside the mosque. We walked the 20-yard distance to this jewel of a place and we prayed inside on the gleaming tiles. It was like diving into a timeless celestial ocean of light. He then told my companion that the place would remain firmly shut, except when it was swept, until the Mahdi came to rescue them from dreadful Pakistani officialdom. I was told that some of the Shiites of Karachi had claimed that the Mahdi was theirs and therefore they should be allowed to pray in his mosque. As a result, he put a large notice at the entrance of his compound that read, "No dogs or Shiites are allowed".

Samandari Baba readily expressed his shock at the huge gap between the reality of light and generosity that emerges from the unseen and day-to-day misery. He would react angrily when he saw how everything gets distorted by human ignorance and mischief.

On my last visit to him, he revealed to me some of his numerous communications with Imam Ali and the other imams and said he may be the only real Hanafi Shiite in the land. I was told that a year later he had gone to a remote village north of Karachi to help them with their water well, where he died on 8 November 1992. There is a shrine for him there, which has become well known as a refuge for the destitute.

His beautiful little mosque is now managed by the Defence Housing Authority. It is surrounded by a growing network of roads, a power plant and some construction sites, but the mosque and its surrounds remain like an oasis. The Mahdi may still not have come, but people do pray there daily. My daughter Muna took Muneera there for a visit in 2012.

Both were impressed by the serenity of the compound and the simplicity of the dwellings where Samandari Baba once lived. A kindly caretaker served them lemongrass tea as they enjoyed the uplifting atmosphere and sense of peace at the edge of bustling Karachi. It was such a magical experience that Muna was moved to return again.

On this occasion, she met with former students of Samandari Baba, who gave her a book in Urdu on his life which told us more about his background. His name was Seyyed Ghulam Nabi Shah Qalandar and he belonged to a Seyyed family of Jammu, Kashmir. He was a trader and married with a wife who was three months pregnant at the time when a holy man came to their door. The sage told Samandari Baba that if he wanted God he would have to leave the things of the world, including his wife. Although his wife was beautiful and devoted to him, he left her and set out into the world in pursuit of *Haqq*. This search took him to Lahore and a meeting with Baba Chattri Sarkar, whom he found on the banks of the Ravi River. Baba Chattri became his teacher. In 1973, after many spiritual adventures, he walked all the way from Lahore to Karachi, where he settled.

Life begins with outer awareness and development of sound mind and intellect. For a few that earthly start leads to a heavenly awakening to the higher zone of timeless consciousness – the light of the soul radiating from a purified heart.

Seyyed Usman Ali Shah, former Chief Justice of the High Court of Peshawar and briefly, during 1986, Governor of the Khyber-Pakhtunkhwa province, was one of the most delightful and unassuming individuals I met in Pakistan. He lived very simply, refusing to use the Chief Justice's official residence. There was a containment and light about him. On one occasion I asked him what gave him pleasure in life. His reply was that every few months the police went to a remote valley, near the Afghan border, where drug traffickers and other criminals would be found, and arrested likely suspects to put in jail in Peshawar. He would then go to the jail, identify those who were Sufi ecstatics, give them some money and release them. Their company gave him great joy. He promised to take me to this valley, which was the home of many wandering *dervishes*, but the opportunity never arose.

> *Two Gnostics were trying to outdo each other in boasting and arguing about the secrets of gnosis and the stations of the Gnostics. One said, "You see the man who's coming on a donkey – I see him as God." The other said, "I see his donkey as God."*[41]

Along with the many uplifting encounters I had in Pakistan, there was one with a *tariqa*-proud shaykh which reinforced my belief that the days of traditional Sufism are coming to an end. Islamabad is a city of technocrats and bureaucrats. Other than government-related work, there was very little culture or entertainment during Zia-ul-Haqq's rule, which promoted Islamic austerity, so visiting scholars or Sufi shaykhs became big attractions in the city. My friends and hosts thought it might be of interest if I too visited a respected, popular old shaykh from an established *tariqa*, who had come to the city to bestow his blessings upon those who visited him.

He was staying in the house of a senior government official. The house had the usual large staircase that ascended to a spacious entrance hall leading to the main reception area. The shaykh was placed on a sofa near the wall, where the staircase curved around. There were dozens of people hanging around the banisters and sitting near where the shaykh was reclining. All together there may have been over 100 people in the house and a few more in the garden. As I entered, everyone was listening attentively to every word the shaykh uttered. I was ushered quietly to sit near his bed on a chair that was brought for me.

When he had completed his pronouncements, we exchanged greetings and someone introduced me in Urdu as a Shadhili shaykh on a visit to Pakistan. He perked up and uttered the word Shadhili a couple of times. He then announced that it was strange that on a recent visit he had made to the Prophet Muhammad in the higher realm, there were several other shaykhs who had initiated well-known *tariqas*; Shaykh Abd al-Qadir Gilani, Shaykh Baha ad-Din Naqshabandi, Shaykh Ahmed Rifaʻi and Shaykh Muin ad-Din Chishti, amongst others.

He then lapsed into silence. Everyone was holding their breath, waiting for the next sentence. Finally he spoke, expressing some surprise that there was no Shaykh Shadhili in that higher realm. Then again silence fell over the entire crowd. Some of the members of the audience made sounds of anticipation.

I then realized that many of these long-bearded fellows were looking at me in anticipation, waiting for an explanation or perhaps a defence of the Shadhilis. Without much thought, I felt the humour of the situation, realizing how religious people can take worldly competition into the sacred realm. I then heard myself saying, "Of course, Abu'l Hasan ash-Shadhili was not with the Prophet anymore because he was called to be with Allah only and not with any of his creation." The silence that followed was markedly different and seemed to have disturbed the entire atmosphere. Two of my hosts who were nearby quietly approached me and said gently, "It may be time we should leave." I immediately agreed and, greeting the shaykh, made a speedy retreat.

At the door I felt the relief of leaving such a heavy atmosphere, where superstitious and ignorant people imagine the presence of the sacred. I almost muttered to myself the Prophetic teaching that Allah is not subject to distance or closeness. He is before everything, after everything, permeates everything and He is the No-thing from which everything emanates and returns to. There is none other except the One. This was my shocking encounter of Sufi oneupmanship in such a blatant way. I had never been inclined to favour any one Sufi path over another or concern myself with such rivalries.

After we had left the house, I told one of my companions, "Now you understand why I think the traditional way of the Sufi *tariqas* is almost over. During the early years of Islam, there were neither schools of thought nor Sufis. It is now the time to return to that original Islam and to accept these outer differences as cultural and of historical interest, rather than spiritual divisions. The Cosmic Spirit is One and all souls emanate from that Oneness."

The most distinguishing feature of Islam is the declaration that there is none other than the One and all else in the universe is a mere shadow, which at best only indicates or reflects the One; the quest and purpose of human beings is to realize that truth and awaken to its magnificence. This awakening is one of the meanings of resurrection.

Men of wisdom who seek the truth have achieved the true state of the dervish, which is the state of total need. Not needing anything but Allah, they leave everything, except the search for truth.[42]

Abd al-Qadir Jilani

The Qadiriyyah is one of the most popular and widely spread of the Sufi orders which are still active today. Abd al-Qadir Jilani, the founder of the order, was born in 470 AH/1077 CE in the Persian city of Gilan (also spelt as "Jilan"), which lies to the southwest of the Caspian Sea. He came to Baghdad at 18 and studied to be a Hanbali *'alim*. It is unlikely that he received any Sufi teachings until he went to the school of Abu'l-Khair Hammad ad-Dabbas, after which it is reputed that he spent many years (20–25) wandering in the Iraqi deserts. After his return to Baghdad, he gained a reputation as a preacher in a *madrasa* built for him adjacent to his home.

There is a legend that says when Shaykh Abd al-Qadir reached the gates of Baghdad, he sent his servant along to the established religious authorities requesting permission to enter the city – as a gesture of courtesy. He had given his servant a pitcher of water as a message. A senior religious head understood the message to mean, "I come with water which is the source of life." He took the pitcher from the servant and filled it up to the top, implying that they had all the knowledge and guidance that they needed. When the servant returned to Abd al-Qadir, he dropped a rose petal on top of it, which added beauty and perfume to the water without letting it spill over. He was then welcomed as a true teacher. A similar tale has also been told in reference to several other great Sufi masters.

During the first two centuries after his demise, the shaykh was remembered more as an inspired and learned preacher than a Sufi master. Taqi ad-din Wasiti (d. 1343 CE) wrote that

> *Abd al-Qadir was renowned during his lifetime for his sermons and religious discourses, and not for tasawwuf [Sufism]. But after his death, two of his children who did not pursue a secular career, 'Abd ar-Raazaq (d. 603 CE) and Abd al-'Aziz (d. 602 CE) set to work to propagate their father's way. Soon they were assisted by a few sympathetic associates of their father.*[43]

The natural human desire for evidence of the supernatural and saintly miracles is well catered for in Sufi stories and anecdotes. A century after the death of Shaykh Abd al-Qadir, many stories about him gained authority due to books like *Bahjat al-Asrar* by Ali ibn Yusuf ash-Shattanawfi. Some of these claims were considered excessive even by the standards of those days. The shaykh was a sober Sufi, whose orthodox way of life and serious approach to religion was well known. But stories of miracles hold special appeal and become more exaggerated with time.

The shrine of the shaykh soon became a pilgrimage point for Sufis, as well as for conventional Muslims. Stories about miraculous events around the shrine gained popularity in public imagination. I had read numerous descriptions of events which at best I accepted as apocryphal. It is a pity that the true legacy of a great man should be obscured by superstition. Shaykh Abd al-Qadir's writings have been of great assistance and inspiration to countless Muslims over the years. They are profound yet accessible and can only benefit the reader.

> *Your heart is a polished mirror. You must wipe it clean of the veil of dust that has gathered upon it, because it is destined to reflect the light of divine secrets.*
>
> *Abd al-Qadir al-Jilani*

When I came to South Africa, I learned of an interesting connection between the shaykh and the Indian Memon community. According to the ancestors of today's Memons, they owe their Islam to a fifth-generation descendant of the shaykh: Seyyed Yusuf ad-Din Qadiri. Seyyed Yusuf was inspired by a dream to travel to Sind in present-day Pakistan, where he influenced the ruler, Markab Khan, to embrace Islam. Manekji, the leader of the Lohana community, with over 6,000 of his followers, also became a Muslim. Seyyed Yusuf renamed this group Mumin ("believer") instead of Lohana. Over the years "Mumin" became "Memon". They are a strong business community and played a key role in the establishment of Pakistan.

What touched me was the reverence given to Shaykh Abd al-Qadir's memory by this community and how particularly the Memon women still, after many centuries, call upon his light. I encouraged a group of my Memon students to collect an anthology of the shaykh's writings. This was published under the title *Sublime Gems*.

During the centuries following Shaykh Abd al-Qadir's death, the Qadiri order found a new home in Damascus (at the end of the fourteenth century CE) and soon spread to Egypt, Turkey, India, Sub-Saharan Africa, Russia, Indonesia, China and elsewhere.

The popularity of the Qadiriyya in India grew in the 17th century CE due to the translation into Persian of Shaykh Abd al-Qadir's famous *Futuh al-Ghayb* (*Victories of the Invisible*) by an Indian scholar, Abd al-Haqq Muhaddith of Delhi (d. 1624 CE).

The seeker cannot do without a leader and guide, for he is in a desert full of perils and savage beasts. He therefore needs someone to warn him of these dangers and guide him to the oasis of water and fruit-bearing trees.

If left to his own devices, without a guide, he would stumble into wild and rugged terrain, surrounded by lions, scorpions, snakes and all kinds of perils.

O traveller on the path of the Hereafter, stay with your guide until he leads you to the encampment. Serve him along the way, be on your best behaviour and never lose sight of him. Then, when he beholds your nobility, honesty and skilfulness, he will delegate responsibility to you as his lieutenant.[44]

Abd al-Qadir al-Jilani

In our time there are many thousands who claim descent from the shaykh and are called Gilani or Jilani. In the Baghdad shrine, the most senior direct descendant presides as the main shrine keeper.

During the 1980s, Pir Tahir 'Ala ad-Din was considered the worthy acknowledged heir. Several members of his family at that time were prominent in business, as scholars, and in government affairs. When Saddam Hussein wanted Pir Tahir 'Ala ad-Din's support for some of his despotic acts, the latter had no option other than to go into self-imposed exile to Pakistan, where his brother was at the time the ambassador of Iraq. As there were numerous Qadiri Sufi enclaves in Pakistan, he soon became the focal point for thousands of devotees and religious preachers. The last ruler of Kalat gave him his daughter in marriage and a new home was built for him in Karachi. His brother became a land owner in the middle of Pakistan in southern Punjab, where the best of date palms were grown in a locale reminiscent of Iraq. In today's Pakistan, the Jilani or Gilani name is seen regularly in higher circles of learning, the army or the government.

During my early visits to Pakistan, I often visited Pir Tahir 'Ala ad-Din and enjoyed delightful conversations with him. When I asked him to suggest a place for me to migrate to, as I was not happy to remain much longer in Europe, he said it must be a country that is furthest from the Middle East, and where the Muslims were a minority and had no chance to come to power. At that time I had bought a beautiful beach property in Sri Lanka and was planning its development into a house and a centre. Pir Tahir Ala ad-Din was firmly against that due to Sri Lanka's proximity to the Middle East and its own potential instability. A few years later, the civil war in Sri Lanka was at its peak. Until that time I never thought that Buddhists and Hindus could act so inhumanely and with such ferocious brutality.

One Friday morning, Pir Tahir 'Ala ad-Din had invited me with Abbas, my son-in-law, to lunch at his home. Soon after the end of the midday prayers in the local mosque, a large crowd of people was waiting outside the garden gate to greet him. Soon the garden was swarming with policemen and eager, devout-looking people rapidly rushing in and out after they had kissed his hand. After about an hour, the last person left. The servant then brought a pitcher for Pir Tahir 'Ala ad-Din to wash his hands. He looked at me with a relieved smile on his face and said softly, "The old tree of Islam is atrophied in its original land. Men of Allah must migrate literally, as well as within their hearts. You must go far to a land where there is nothing beyond it."

> *I came to all the doors of Allah and found crowds of people*
> *around the doors, until I reached the door of humility and*
> *poverty. This door was not crowded, so I entered. I turned back*
> *to look and found all the other doors still crowded.*[45]
>
> *Abd al-Qadir al-Jilani*

Many years later, on a visit to South Africa, I recalled Pir Tahir 'Ala ad-Din's counsel. Looking across from Cape Point, I could feel the cold wind from Antarctica – there was no more land beyond there. Maybe this was the right place. My companion, Shaykh Hosam Raouf, agreed that South Africa could be my next base. Unless one goes to the end, there will not be a new beginning!

At an earlier time, Shaykh Hosam had accompanied me on a visit to Shaykh Ahmad Bin Abdul Aziz al Mubarak (d. 1988), the head of the *shari'a* court of Abu Dhabi, who was a Maliki scholar. According to Maliki, *fiqh* Muslims should not stay under a non-Islamic rule. I asked him if European converts to Islam wanted to migrate to a Muslim country, in which they could work and live freely, and learn their *deen*, where could they go? Shaykh Ahmad told us to come back the following week for an answer, which we did.

Shaykh Hosam recalls his reply: "As we entered the *diwan*, Shaykh Ahmad asked all the people in the *diwan* to leave and asked us to sit close to him. He seemed to be in a predicament; he was upset and crying. His answer was one verse from a poem from Imam Ali, which said, 'When I open my eyes, I see a lot, but in fact I do not see anybody.'" The answer was painful – nowhere, nowhere. He apologized and said this was the situation.

Chapter 5
SHRINE CULTURE

SOMEWHERE NEAR MULTAN

All roads come from eternity.
The bullock carts, and the goats,
sad little donkeys with hanging ears
In the fields, near the thatched huts;
Camels, carrying cotton bales, day after day.

From the colourful trucks
Blossom the dreams of the poor,
And the reed longs to sigh of man's fate.

The nameless heroines of poverty,
Lifting their pitchers, await
The water of life.

All roads point to Eternity.
And their centre rests
Under the sky-like dome
In the heart of the saint.

Annemarie Schimmel

Sacred places and temples have played an important role in religions, culture and human development since early times. Saints, emperors and other important human beings were buried ceremoniously in sites which then acquired a reputation for sanctity. In most cultures, death and burial were considered the end of the journey on earth and the beginning of another phase.

Remembrance of and prayers to ancestors reflect a deep human need for continuity. Early man believed, for example, that a father who was no longer in this world might send a message of guidance and possible descriptions of life after death. For survival and a quality life we want to have knowledge of the future in order to be prepared. Human intercession and other communications between the seen and unseen are sought by most beings. The ancient Egyptians mummified the Sacred Ibis and placed them in their graves, as it was considered helpful on one's journey to the afterlife.

A European Muslim once exclaimed to me that the thousands of dead saints all over the Muslim world highlight the scarcity of living ones! From early on, pious Muslims found that most rulers were not good representatives of the Prophetic conduct, so they were inclined to flock to where a holy man had settled. Most old cities as a result grew around a tomb or mausoleum. As time went by, buildings would cluster next to the shrine of the deceased, often including a mosque, teaching centre, hostel and a cemetery close by.

Aden in Yemen is a good example of this. It is said that some centuries ago a saintly Sufi arrived at the shore where the old passenger liners' hall in Aden was later to be built. He had left his rebellious people in the Hadramaut, vowing to travel as far away as he could from them. After weeks of travel he reached the sea, stopped there and built himself a simple shelter. He prayed and recited Quran there for several days and was soon joined by a few fishermen. Within a year there was a small hamlet of local seafarers. Eventually it became the port area of colonial Aden.

When I visited Aden in the early 1990s, I was walking down the street by the old Victorian Customs Hall and was drawn to a small blue shrine across the road. Through the window of the shrine I saw two elderly men praying next to the tomb. As I stood by the doorway they looked up from their supplications and invited me in. The men in the shrine told me that thousands of ships had come and gone, politicians and rulers had risen and fallen, but the light of the departed shaykh lived on.

Fear is the guardian of hearts, and hope is the intercessor of the self. Whoever has knowledge of Allah has fear of and hope in Allah – they are the two wings of faith by which the slave flies to the pleasure of Allah.[46]

Imam Jafar as-Sadiq

The most celebrated *wali* of Aden is Seyyed Abu Bakr al-Aidarus (1447–1508 CE), a descendant of Imam Jafar as-Sadiq through the imam's youngest son, Ali al-Uraidhi, from whose line came many men of light. His family was from Tarim in the Hadhramaut but he spent most of his adult life in Aden, where he became the city's religious leader and oversaw the construction of the main mosque. He was revered for his high moral conduct and sense of justice to all. He travelled widely after he settled in Aden and is credited with bringing the Qadiri *tariqa* to Harar in Ethiopia.

The shaykh was responsible for the introduction of coffee to the Hadhramaut. He was so impressed by the strong stimulating berries of the coffee bush when he encountered it on his travels that he brought some back to Yemen and gave it to his disciples to keep them awake on night vigils. Many of his descendants were Sufis and they brought his teachings to India, Indonesia and the East African coasts, maintaining a family *tariqa*.

It can be helpful to visit shrines if the supplicant has faith and trust in the *wali*, just as confidence in a doctor is important for physical healing to take place. Spiritual ambience, faith and belief are all helpful to reduce the exclusivity of body and mind. The human journey is from physics to metaphysics and from body and mind to heart and soul. The notion of a spiritual or uplifting ambiance is a mystery of the soul, which is a mysterious package of primal energy, radiating at numerous levels of consciousness and containing strands of qualities and knowledges that emanate from an imprint of a sacred reality within that soul. In most cases the innate power of the soul is dimmed by the body/mind/ego. The reverse is true when the self and its veils have been thinned out so the sacred bundle emits all its potential radiation. The light from such evolved beings can be compared to nuclear radiation, where many years after the original explosion traces of radioactive material can still be found. This is the case with the burial grounds of enlightened men or women, where the impact of their light permeates the atmosphere long after the passing of their physical body. Since all souls are potentially the same, people who have faith in a deceased may have the possibility for their hearts to resonate with them and, thus, insights, contentment and peace may be experienced. Anything that helps in this journey is desirable.

My heart has become capable of every form; it is a pasture for gazelles and a convent for Christian monks and a temple for idols and the Pilgrims' Kaaba and the tablets of the Torah and the book of Quran. I follow the religion of Love: whatever way Love's Camels take, that is my religion and my faith.[47]

Ibn al-'Arabi

Sometimes tombs are discovered many years after the departure of the religious figure buried there. One such example was the tomb of Ibn al-'Arabi, north of Damascus. Ibn al-'Arabi (1165–1240 CE), a native of Spain who was of Arab origin, is commonly referred to as Shaykh al-Akbar and considered by many to be one of the greatest exponents of Sufi metaphysics. Many of the traditional teachers at his time and in the centuries that followed his passing considered his works to be confusing or even heretical. Over the past 100 or so years, however, there has been a serious revival of interest in his teachings. *Al-Futuhat al-Makkiyya* (*The Makkan Openings*) and *Fusus al-Hikam* (*The Bezels of Wisdom*) are generally considered his most important works. Ibn al-'Arabi wrote extensively about his personal spiritual experiences. He claimed that the metaphysical unveilings of the *Futuhat* were directly inspired by unveilings from Allah and that the *Fusus al-Hikam*, which looks at the message of all the Prophets revered in Islam, came to him through a vision of the Prophet Muhammad.

> *God – there is nothing Apparent but He in every similar and*
> *every contrary*
> *In every kind and every species, in all union and all separation.*
> *In everything that the senses or the intellect perceive*
> *In every body and every form.*[48]
>
> *Ibn al-'Arabi*

Legends and facts become entwined and we do not know for certain the real story about the discovery of his tomb. One popular account is that the Ottoman Sultan Salim entered Damascus triumphantly after a battle and enquired about Ibn al-'Arabi's tomb. After considerable investigation it was discovered that the tomb was surrounded by the city's rubbish dump, as it lay outside the built-up area. It is said that Ibn al-'Arabi had antagonized the established religious authorities when he had put his leg up on a side step by the main Umayyad mosque in Damascus and declared to the imams that the God they worshipped was under his feet. Even if this story is apocryphal, it is known that Ibn al-'Arabi's mystical insights did not endear him to the conservative Muslims of his time. Out of his hundreds of books, only a few have survived. Most of these manuscripts were only discovered and reproduced during the past 150 years or so. *The Makkan Revelations*, for example, was not accessible until Shaykh Abd al-Qadir Jaza'iri, the celebrated leader of *jihad* against the French in Algeria, arranged for its reproduction around the mid-19th century. Subsequently it has gone into many printings.

To continue with the story, Sultan Salim announced that he wished to meet all the shrine keepers and imams in and around Damascus at midday on Friday. The town criers and soldiers then went around the entire city with this order. At midday, which was the usual time for Friday prayers, the assembled few thousand religious dignitaries awaited the Sultan's audience at his palace. When he appeared, he was accompanied by attendants carrying sacks of gold to be given to all the religious leaders. When the distribution was complete, Sultan Salim told them that all of this gold came from a treasure trove found under the main gate of the Umayyad mosque, where Ibn al-'Arabi had placed his foot. He then reminded his audience that they had all forsaken their prayer for the sake of gold and this is what Ibn al-'Arabi meant when he said, "Your God lies beneath my feet."

Once, when I was in Egypt, I expressed disapproval at the shrine of one of the Mamluk sultans, as it was embellished like a saint's. The shrine keeper was too old to contradict me and sent his daughter to put my mind at rest that this sultan had been a pious person; being impatient, I dismissed her reproach, adding that I could not see much benefit in the culture of indiscriminate shrine keeping. The lady humbly responded that one of the more obvious benefits was that she and her father were living off that. They swept the place and welcomed visitors. Out of gratitude for their services, people would pay them. She completed her speech by saying, "All of this is *baraka* (blessing)," and went away grateful for my tip and change in attitude!

Important Muslim shrines had a formal tradition as to who is to be the shrine keeper. In Persia and related cultures, he is called the *killidar* (keeper of the key), whereas throughout the rest of Subcontinent and parts of Central Asia it is *sajjada nasheen* (he who sits on the prayer mat). Often family members would compete for important positions in the shrine-keeping business. In some cases, many pretenders might claim the position.

In Karbala, the last shrine keepers of Imam Hussein were Seyyeds whose origin was traced to the town of Astrabad in northern Iran. Their main responsibility was the upkeep of the shrine (cleaning, security, welcoming visitors, etc.) and the safeguarding of the donated treasures, as well as disbursement of salaries to the dozens of workers and guardians. There were several tiered ranks amongst the staff. The most significant was the role of special prayer reciters for the visitors. There was a special prayer for each of the buried saints and their family, which was about half a page long, but took several minutes to recite in a funereal tone. The *khadim* (servant of the shrine) was a well-dressed man with a distinctive turban – fez-like but with a cloth wrapped around it. The visitors would throw money and other valuables into the shrine, which was swept every night after they had left. Personal items were often donated as part of the belief that the imam would answer their supplications. The habit of tying strings or knots to shrines is prevalent throughout the Muslim world, to symbolize a wish or intention, as is throwing coins into wells, ponds or pools of water near shrines.

In some places, like the shrine of Shaykh Muin ad-Din Chishti in Ajmer and Shaykh Nizam ad-Din Awliya in Delhi, there are many of the descendants of the shaykh or his family who collect donations from visitors. In Karbala, the shrines of Imam Hussein and that of his brother Abbas have been managed by descendants of two well-known families for many generations. Large donations often fund major expansions or renovations. In Mashhad, in the northeast of Iran, the mausoleum of Imam Reza has grown more than tenfold in size over the past 30 years. Thousands of peasants from the surrounding area spend weeks, if not months, in and around the shrine when there is not much work for them in the villages during winter.

The majority of shrine keepers claim to be descendants of the Prophet, and in countries like Morocco, this claim has to be substantiated and registered at a special office. In the rest of the Muslim world, the claims to this illustrious lineage may not always be valid. Politics play a major role in whether it is advisable to claim to be a Seyyed or not. During the Ottoman rule, there were several attacks on the shrines in Iraq, Iran and elsewhere. At this time, many of the Seyyeds (including my mother's ancestors) had to hide their lineage. In one major raid in Karbala it is claimed that nearly 10,000 Seyyeds were killed and buried in the rubble of the devastated districts, where the Ottoman soldiers' orders had been to cleanse the place completely within three days.

In many parts of the Subcontinent, the *sajjada nasheen* ends up being a landlord of significance, as the poor peasants would consider it an honour to work for him. In their role of guardians for the shrine, they would often have several depositories of old manuscripts in their possession, to be sold to a generous buyer or manuscript collector.

In Pakistani Punjab, there are several old villages which were developed centuries ago because of the fertility of the land and their positions on trade routes but were subsequently abandoned for different reasons, including soil erosion, water shortages and unsustainably high populations. Uch Sharif is one such town where there are many mausoleums and tombs, mostly neglected and in ruins. There are, however, two famous and still frequently visited tombs, each managed by families with the surname Gilani. I visited the most scholarly of the two shrine keepers, who was jovial, hospitable and well-connected to the government. When I commented on the lavish reception we received and the food he was offering us, he assured me that as soon as we had finished eating there would be many poor people who would benefit from the leftovers.

Pseudo Sufis, charlatans and other shady pretenders to spiritual status have their role alongside the legitimate Sufi folds. In old Muslim cities there are local guides who earn their livelihood by taking visitors to different living saints, as well as special shrines and burial sites. In Cairo, one such guide showed me the alleyway where, during one night nearly two centuries ago, Mohammed Ali massacred several hundred of Egypt's dignitaries and men of power to consolidate his authority. My companion on this tour cursed Mohammed Ali for his atrocious act. Instantly, our female guide lifted her hands to heaven with loud prayers for Mohammed Ali's soul. She then looked at me reproachfully and said, "I owe my livelihood to him, so how can I accept any curse on his name?" Once again, I was shown how people's perceptions of past figures are coloured by their relevance to the individual's life!

In North Africa, where almost every old town or village has its shrine, there would generally be some descendants of the saint who would maintain the shrine. It is also a custom for there to be an annual festival in and around the shrine to celebrate the day of the saint's death. In Urdu this is referred to as 'urs ("wedding", from the Arabic word). It is only with the death of the physical body that the soul triumphs and soars to its heavenly state – a lasting celebration – a union. One very famous 'urs is that of Sultan Bahu, whose shrine is located in the west of the Punjab.

*So what if love's idol is hidden? One's heart will never be
far away
My guide lives many mountains away, but he is visible
before me.
Whoever has one grain of love is drunk without wine.
They are the true mystics, Bahu, whose graves are alive.*[49]

Sultan Bahu

Sultan Bahu (1039–1102 AH/1629–90 CE) was born in Shorekot in
the Punjab. His father, Bayazid Muhammad, had been given land by
the Mughal Emperor Shah Jahan as a reward for military services. The
family belonged to the Awan tribe, who claimed descent from Imam
Ali through his son, Muhammad ibn Hanafiyya. Sultan Bahu's mother,
Raasti, gave her son the name Bahu, which means "with Him". He
studied in Delhi under Hazrat Abdul Rahman Qadiri. He afterwards
returned to his birth place where he lived for the rest of his life. Deeply
influenced by his mother's spirituality, he was a prolific writer of
religious texts, but it is for his mystic poetry written in Punjabi that he
is remembered today. They remain a beautiful and accessible source of
teachings on key issues.

He came from a prominent family but fled the material world in the
search for his inner awakening.

*Half the curses on the world, and all of them on the worldly,
Whoever does not sow in the path of the Lord will reap the
lashes of torment.
Burn, evil world, which causes fathers to sacrifice their sons!
Those who give up this world, Bahu, will gain gardens
in bloom.*[50]

Sultan Bahu

There is often a homely touch to his verses.

*Only such a soul as my companion that is with me all
the way...*

*One that makes strict scholars bow down when they see a
scrap of food.
Whoever rides forth upon this soul has learned the
name of God.
The mystic path is hard, Bahu, not mother's home cooking.[51]*

Sultan Bahu

Like all the great Sufis, he emphasized the limitations of scholarship in the quest for inner unveilings and the importance of love uniting mind and heart.

*Having learned wisdom from a thousand books, they
become great scholars.
They cannot learn one letter of love – the wretches wander
in ignorance.
If a lover glances just once, he can swim a hundred million
rivers.
If a scholar looks a hundred million times, he cannot reach
the other bank.
Between learning and love is an arduous journey, with
many miles of distance.
Whoever does not gain love, Bahu, is a loser in both worlds.[52]*

Sultan Bahu

Sultan Bahu cut across all outer manifestations of what many people perceive as spiritual behaviour, pointing only to the essence and putting interest in the miraculous in proper perspective.

*Being a faqir is not dancing and whirling, waking up
sleeping people.
Being a faqir is not crossing glowing streams without
getting wet.
Being a faqir is not suspending a prayer mat in the air.
They are the real faqirs, Bahu, who nurture the Friend in
their hearts.[53]*

Sultan Bahu

He was saddened by pointless sectarian disputes, which are major causes of destructive distraction.

> *Neither am I Sunni nor am I Shia – my heart is bitter with both of them.*
> *All long, dry marches came to an end when I entered the sea of mercy.*
> *Many non-swimmers tried and lost; a few climbed the other bank.*
> *They made it across safe and sound, Bahu, who clung to the guide's hem.*[54]
>
> *Sultan Bahu*

At the time of my first visit to Sultan Bahu in the early 1980s, the road was thick with mud due to heavy recent rains. The *'urs* at Sultan Bahu was a music festival with singers from all over the country competing with each other and reciting his spiritual love poems. Some of his descendants are senior government officials and have businesses in Lahore and elsewhere. On several visits to Lahore and to their ancestor's shrine, I have enjoyed their hospitality.

When I was in his shrine listening to all these intoxicating renderings, the place thick with smoke from incense, the idea occurred to me that it would be enjoyable to stay the night there. The mud was so thick by the time we tried to leave that the car was completely stuck and no one could move it. The saint must have answered my subconscious wish!

> *This body of yours is the True Lord's dwelling, so mystic, look inside!*
> *Don't beg favours from Master Khizr, the water of life is within you.*
> *Illuminate the darkness with the lamp of longing, then perhaps You'll find what you have lost.*
> *They die before they die, Bahu, those who understand the Riddle of Truth.*[55]
>
> *Sultan Bahu*

Bari Imam (1616–1705 CE), or Shah Abdul Latif Shah Kazmi Mashhadi, is buried on one of the Silk Road routes, at the foot of mountains near Islamabad. From a Seyyed family, he is regarded as the patron saint of Islamabad. During his lifetime he visited Kashmir, Badakhshan, Bukhara, Mashhad, Baghdad and Damascus, as well as performed *Hajj*. Bari Imam is said to have meditated in the beautiful Neelam Hoto valley for 25 years. A local historian told me that at that time there were many Buddhist monasteries in the area and Bari Imam engaged with the monks and respected their traditions.

He eventually settled in Nurpur Shahan in the Margalla foothills, where his shrine now is, and many of the local Hindus became Muslims through his teachings. The title of Bari Imam ("Leader of the Earth") was given to him by his teacher Hayat al-Mir, known as Zinda Pir. The original shrine was built by the Mughal emperor Aurangzeb and in recent years there has been considerable expansion and renovation.

Some of Bari Imam's descendants were living nearby as caretakers, but the precinct of the shrine had become a sprawling informal bazaar for all kinds of illicit drugs and other immoral activities. Raja Akram was a dynamic follower of Seyyed Anwar Ali Shah, a Qadiri shaykh whose centre was at Manser, Attock, about an hour's drive from Islamabad. Seyyed Anwar had originated from Kashmir, as had his own teacher, Baba Rustam (known as Kalu Baba). Before his Pir's death, Raja Akram was told to go to Bari Imam and clean the place up.

Over the many years I visited him, I found his influence spreading effectively to an ever-widening area. His modest centre also became a regular destination, especially in the afternoons, visited by senior government officials and bureaucrats. As time passed his reputation grew considerably, as did threats to his life from whoever was adversely affected by his sweeping-up of corruption. He was most generous and welcoming on every visit that I paid but I never managed to get a clear picture as to his mission, other than cleansing the area of drug trafficking and illicit shrine profiteering.

Raja Akram was murdered in February 2005 after attending a funeral procession. He and his party were sprayed with bullets by a group of assailants who had positioned themselves on a rooftop behind the shrine. Raja Akram always refused security when in the vicinity of the shrine as a mark of respect to the *wali*. There had been disputes with rival groups over local land and the custodianship of the shrine. After his death it was said that Raja Akram had predicted his end and chosen his place of burial. He is buried in the middle of Seyyed Anwar and Kalu Baba's graves at Manser, Attock.

It is also said that the man behind his assassination was so haunted by guilt that he committed suicide shortly after the murder. The old shrine is now at the centre of extensive buildings and halls administered by the government. Raja Saheb had done his work!

In May 2005, there was a suicide bombing at the shrine during the *'urs* celebrations. Worshippers had been waiting for a well-known Shiite cleric to give a talk when the bomb exploded. Sadly shrines are often targeted because they are venerated by both Sunnis and Shiites and form a harmonious bridge between the two groups. Over the past 50 years, due to *Wahhabi* influence, the *Ahl al-Bayt* ancestry that is common to many of the Sufi masters is downplayed or ignored.

There is an interesting story about the lady who was the nursemaid of Bari Imam. Her name was Mai Khattian and she is known as *Ghakraan wali mayee*, which indicates she came from the Ghakrar tribe. Her grave is on a residential plot in the F-10 sector of Islamabad. In recent years, a local building contractor, who owned the land, tried to develop it. It proved an impossible task as machines would break down on site and progress could not be made. All the time the owner of the land was having repeated dreams in which a lady came to him and said, "You cannot build on my land."

Eventually, the owner asked a friend whose opinion he respected for advice. This man suggested that they see whether there were any graves on the land. Sure enough, about 30 graves were discovered. Then the owner had a dream in which Bari Imam appeared and said he could not touch the land because his nursemaid was buried there. The owner went to the government authorities to have it formally declared as a graveyard, so even in the future no building can take place on that area. There is a peaceful atmosphere around the graves, and the surrounding bushes and trees have been festooned with brightly coloured cloths – a little oasis surrounded by suburban developments.

Pir Meher Ali Shah Gilani (1859–1937) was a great saint living nearer to our times, whose coming was said to have been predicted by Bari Imam. He was a descendant of both Imams Hasan and Hussein, and on his father's side from Shaykh Abd al-Qadir Jilani. Pir Meher Ali was a shaykh of the Chishti Nizamiyah order who was famed for his erudition and powers of transmission as a teacher. His most famous book is *Saif-e-Chishtiya* (*The Sword of the Chishtis*), in which he attacked the Qadyani or Ahmadiyah movement of Mirza Ghulam Ahmad. His shrine complex is located at Golra Sharif, about 20 kilometres from Bari Imam.

Dr Khalid Iqbal took a group of us to the shrine in 2010. He had a prior arrangement with Fazlullah, the main shrine keeper, to take us round. On our arrival, Fazlullah was nowhere to be seen and was eventually found in his room in a state of collapse. He had been in a bad car accident that morning when his son was bringing him to the shrine. When Dr Khalid told him I was from Karbala he immediately came to life and started singing a *manqabat* (eulogy) for Imam Hussein. Fazlullah told us that his whole life from childhood had been centred around the shrine. He was in charge of the maintenance, accounts and administering the extensive daily feeding programme. There was an otherworldly quality about him and he seemed to live in a state of spiritual intoxication.

*I am burning with divine love every moment. Sometimes I roll
in the dust. And sometimes I dance on thorns. I have become
notorious in your love. I beseech you to come to me! I am not
afraid of disrepute. To dance in every bazaar.*[56]

Lal Shahbaz Qalandar

On the occasions when I wished to visit the saints of the interior of
Sindh, such as Lal Shahbaz Qalandar and Shah Abdul Latif Bhitai, I
was warned against *dacoits* (robbers) and unrest in the area. My visits
to Sindh often coincided with times of political turmoil and unrest,
and friends expressed fear for my safety. Despite these concerns, I did
eventually manage to visit the shrine of the Red Sufi, as Lal Shahbaz
Qalandar is commonly known.

The arid landscape of Sindh, with its desert wastelands and occasional
patches of agriculture, has historically been an area resistant to central
government, a fiefdom for tribal leaders and a shelter for unorthodox
religious sects. It had also acted as a melting pot for Hindu and Muslim
devotional practices. In Islam, the term *qalandar* is given to wandering
mystics who tend to be so completely absorbed in their ecstatic state
that they often ignore *shari'a* and reject the religious establishment. It is
appropriate that an ecstatic *qalandar* like Lal Shahbaz should be buried
in such terrain.

The shrine has always been under attack from the orthodox and never
more so than today, with the increasingly rigid external influences on
Pakistan. Drums, song, dance and the use of narcotics contribute to a
wild revelry that causes offence to conservative Muslims. Visiting Hindus
are welcome at the shrine and regard Lal Shahbaz as one of their own.
The atmosphere lends itself to tales of miracles and unexpected events.

The saint's name at birth was Usman Marwandi. He was born around
1178 CE near Tabriz in Azerbaijan and was a descendant of the sixth
Shiite imam, Jafar as-Sadiq. He was thus also directly descended from
Imam Ali and many of the visitors to the shrine feel a strong connection
with Ali, venerating him in song and verse. Lal Shahbaz is said to have

travelled in his youth extensively through Iran and Iraq, visiting Makka and Madina before journeying through the Punjab and Multan and finally settling in Sehwan in Sindh.

The nickname *Lal* (red) was given to him because of his fondness for wearing red garments, while the name *Shahbaz* (the noblest species of falcon) was bestowed on him by Baha ad-Din Zakariyya, the celebrated Suhrawardi shaykh of Multan, who was his contemporary. Legend claims that Lal Shahbaz turned himself on one occasion into a falcon in order to fly to Multan and rescue Baha ad-Din Zakariyya from the persecution of the Sultan of Multan. Normally Baha ad-Din Zakariyya disliked *qalandars*, but Lal Shahbaz was the exception. The shaykh took the wild *qalandar* as his disciple and tolerated his ecstatic states and predilection for whirling dance. To this day the trance dance is performed at Lal Shahbaz's shrine. Legend says that his grave was built over a Shivaitic temple. Shiva is known for his cosmic dance, and the old name of Sehwan is "Siwistan" (or "the town of Shiva").

Passing through the main covered veranda of the shrine, I noticed there were rows of ladies with toy-size cradles in front of them, which they diligently kept swinging. My friend whispered from behind me that it was a special occasion when women who wished to bear children hope the toys will help manifest real babies. I found later on that there is a thriving business of renting these cradles and the dolls that go with them. Here indeed was a Sufi shaykh with a wide range of influence and an attraction for people of different religious and ethnic origins. There was a welcoming atmosphere permeating the exuberant revelry.

After the evening prayers, there was spontaneous chanting, singing and dancing with women on one side and men on the other. I wondered to myself how long this would last as the influence of austere, sometimes grim, organized Islam was sweeping the whole country.

There were several Qalandari types sitting or praying around the shrine and one particular man with immense dignity attracted my attention. I signalled to my companion and we sat quietly next to him, exchanging greetings. He told my friend how attractive this part of the country is to spiritual seekers. Many people around the shrine had come from faraway lands and somehow managed to stay for years on end. He then told us stories of miracles, some of which have become well known. I asked him whether there was anything I could do for him. He pointed at my feet and said we must have the same size shoes and as he could not find any comfortable ones around here, perhaps I could give him my shoes. We carried on talking as we walked toward the car. When I got into the car I took my shoes off and gave them to him. As the car was driving off, I saw his handsome face looking very pleased at his new shoes. He waved to us and recited prayers for our safety.

Who die before death never will destroyed by dying be. –
Who live ere second life they see will live eternally.[57]
Shah Abdul Latif Bhitai

The shrine of Shah Abdul Latif Bhitai at Bhit Shah, Hyderabad District, is about two hours' drive south across the desert from Sehwan. Pilgrims visiting Lal Shahbaz Qalandar will often also pay their respects to this 18th-century saint. There is not the same wild majesty as found at Sehwan but the popularity of Shah Abdul Latif's poetry, written in Sindhi, ensures streams of visitors to the shrine. He is beloved of Hindus as much as Muslims.

Shah Abdul Latif Bhitai was born in 1690 CE and died around 1752 CE. He kept away from the political intrigues of the day and lived quietly, composing his poetry. His *Risalo* expresses man's yearning for the divine in the universal sense, but the homespun idioms he uses celebrate the cultural life of the simple folk of 18th-century Sindh.

Shah Abdul Latif was born into a conventional Muslim family, but after a broken love affair he joined a group of Nath yogis and roamed with them through Sindh and Rajasthan. He recognized no distinction between the

Hindu and Muslim seeker and the Sur Ramkali in his *Risalo* celebrates his years of travels with the yogis.

> *The glorious yogis in this world, some "fire" bring, some "light" –*
> *Who kindle themselves to "ignite", I cannot live without them!*
> *O nothing with themselves they take, with "self" they parted company –*
> *And those within whom such traits I see, I cannot live without them.*[58]
>
>

Shah Abdul Latif Bhitai

Shah Abdul Latif described his poetry thus: "These that you think to be poetic verses are signposts that give you glimpses of eternal beauty and set your heart in motion to seek the Divine."[59]

> *The echo and the call are same, if you sound's secret knew –*
> *They both were "one" but "two" became, only when "hearing" came.*[60]
>
>

Shah Abdul Latif Bhitai

LOST IN LOVE

> *I have got lost in the city of love,*
> *I am trying to know my self.*
> *I cannot lay my hands on the substance.*
> *I have rid myself of ego,*
> *And discovered my true self.*
> *All indeed has ended well*
> *O Bulleh, I find the Lord pervades both worlds,*
> *None now appears a stranger to me.*
> *I have got lost in the city of love,*
> *I am trying to know myself.*[61]
>
>

Bulleh Shah

The poetry of Bulleh Shah (1680–1758 CE), whose shrine lies in Qasur in the Pakistani side of the Punjab, resonates with love of Oneness. Though attracted to his poetry, I have not yet had the opportunity to visit his shrine. He lived beyond the confines of orthodoxy. He was not concerned with the establishment, or any structure that was considered to be sacred. He was constantly connected and energized by the Essence and this propelled him to a zone that most considered unorthodox and even heretical. He saw everything through the lens of unity and cared l for differentiation and duality.

Bulleh Shah's denunciation of empty rituals laid him open to attacks from the orthodox:

> *Accursed be prayers, to hell with fasts, and let confession of faith be damned.*
> *O Bulleh, I have found the Lord within, and the world wanders in delusion![62]*

He was particularly vehement in his opposition to acts of hypocritical outer piety:

> *You have wasted your life in mosques. Your heart is still filled with impiety, never did you realize the unity of God. Now why do you raise a hue and cry? Ever new, ever fresh is the spring of love![63]*

Bulleh Shah's passion for his master, the Qadiri Shaykh Inayat Shah (d. 1728 CE), was part of his path of *tawhid*. Inayat Shah came from the agricultural class, whereas Bulleh Shah was a Seyyed. He had to suffer much ridicule from his insistence that spiritual knowledge was not the sole prerogative of the Seyyeds. Bulleh, like many other seekers, followed the line that sacred love begins with a human love. Unless you love the visible human master, you will never dissolve in the absolute cosmic master – the force of connectedness. You connect with whatever is appropriate at the time – student to teacher, painter with his brushes, dancer merging with the dance – until it ends with pure passion beyond physicality, the cosmic source of connections and continuations. You must begin with the terrestrial if you wish for the celestial. The whole business is the unison between humanity and divinity.

> *Go and love first.*
> *Then come to me and I will show you the way.*[64]
> Nur ad-Deen Jami

> *If you haven't tasted the ultimate miracle of Divine presence,*
> *then you will naturally be seeking lesser miracles.*
> Ahmad Ibn 'Ajiba

From the earliest days of human consciousness, there has been the tendency to desire a better understanding of forces or powers beyond our control or expectations. Early human groups resorted to shamans, seers and prophet-like figures for guidance and glimpses of the future. Every society in history has had its particular religious, supernatural or spiritual dimension. Humans are obsessed with life, connection and confirmation.

In the monotheistic religions, especially Islam, there is a clear emphasis regarding the essence of Oneness in the universe. Truth is eternal and One but there are also many cultural habits and traditions that relate to other human needs and ideas. Talismans, special sacred objects or recitations, as well as religious offerings and promises, are a part of devotional practices throughout the Muslim world. The less formal the religious leader, the more likely that these aids will be used.

People often go to a shaykh asking for favours, as well as to remove curses which they believe have been placed upon them. The removal of different types of possession, especially by *jinn* (creatures made out of fire, who exist in a parallel universe to man), is another important function for some religious practitioners and Sufis. Quite often superstition and even deliberate abuse accompanies these strange and obscure happenings. The human tendency to exercise power can lead people perceived as having spiritual authority to try to assist. Yet, it is impossible, when dealing with such complex fields of energies, to get it right in any reliable way.

Dream interpretation is also common and can be a useful tool in the hands of an evolved master. The dream will reflect the overall state of the dreamer, reflecting as it does a wide vista of their hopes, aspirations, fears and pains. Whatever the subject of the dream, the dreamer will be the key character. The teacher, who uses dream interpretation for guidance, will probably ask about the inner feelings experienced, rather than the events themselves, and who the dreamer asks to help them in the dream. People are advised to be selective in asking for interpretations because any interpretation may lead to some actualization.

> *The one who is ruled by Mind,*
> *Without sleeping, puts her senses to sleep,*
> *So that unseen things may emerge from the world of the*
> *Soul.*
> *Even in her waking state, she dreams dreams,*
> *And opens thereby the gates of Heaven.*[65]
>
> *Jalal ad-Din Rumi*

It is common for people who are seeking signs and signals from the unseen regarding their earthly situation to have dreams or visions. We all look for signs on the horizon to minimize regrets or mistakes. This is an aspect of human psyche and consciousness that extends beyond the mind and imagination. Following any of these signs is like consulting an oracle; the outcome is never clear as to from which point of view events will unfold.

> *Looking out for the faults hidden within you is better than*
> *looking out for the invisible realities veiled from you.*[66]

It is the intelligent seeker who watches for and deals with his faults, shortcomings and veils, gross and subtle. The obvious faults of the self relate to desires, attachments, expectations and all imbalances in body and mind. The heart's sickness is due to inner desires for acknowledgement, hate, greed, lack of sincerity and other veils which deprive the heart of freedom from otherness. The Unseen is veiled from us precisely because of our faults, veils and cracks of our minds and hearts.

Ibn 'Ata' Allah

It is common for Sufis to have visions of the Prophet Muhammad, an imam, saint or a founder of one of the traditional Sufi lineages. They may be given a Quran, turban, cloak or sword by him or some instruction, sanction or blessing.

Illuminated hearts do not seek after occult powers;
but occult powers, by themselves, come to them.[67]

Hazrat Inayat Khan

I once asked Shaykh Bashir Uthman, an accomplished Sufi healer and expert on talismans, to explain how this power works. He said it is due to belief and trust. If you believe this piece of stone empowers you to be healthier and happier, then you may naturally look more positively upon your situation. This hopeful state will invariably lead you to better health than before. He described how the awakened, qualified teacher through focus and dedication can connect an appropriate energy field with some herb, tincture or talisman.

Bashir Uthman had over many years collected talismans, numerous formulae, symbolic writings and designs for access to higher realms from well-known masters. In the latter part of his life, he mostly used *Surat Fatihah* with tongue and heart while thinking of the person in need of help, irrespective of the details of the ailment or the request.

As Bashir Uthman was known to be a healer for both the body and mind, as well as for having access to the power of *jinn*, he was often asked how these abilities can be acquired. His stock answer was always not to seek personal power but always to surrender wholeheartedly to the Divine universal power. He would say, "Give in to Allah and you will be given the power suitable for you, otherwise there is a greater possibility to go astray with what you acquire." He warned against connection with the *jinn*, even for assistance in doing good deeds, as they are unpredictable entities and can give what is wanted to begin with but one is obligated to do what they wish at a later time. Temptation to gain power is the slippery path toward distraction and destruction.

Shaykh Bashir Uthman had been living in Madina for many years and was the closest companion to a venerable shaykh from East Africa called Shaykh al-Bukhari. Shaykh Bashir was from a prominent Eritrean tribe, settled around numerous coastal towns. He was a teacher and journalist with the first newspaper in Eritrea and also had some successful businesses. Later the main focus in his life was studying and practicing Islam with a strong orientation toward Sufi healing, which involved the use of herbs, oils and talismans. Shaykh Bashir was an accomplished herbalist, who used minerals as well as plant materials in his complicated concoctions. He was well known to Somalis and East Africans in Europe, America and the Middle East and would often be requested to provide remedies for the needy.

Once, he had invited me to visit Madina to meet with Shaykh al-Bukhari, but my travel arrangements changed so I arrived a few days later and had to find a different hotel from that previously agreed upon with him. It had not been possible to convey to him this change in plan. An hour or so after arrival, I could hear from my room on the first floor, which had a corridor open to the atrium, a serious discussion in the lobby. After a while I could discern Shaykh Bashir Uthman's voice insisting that I must be in the hotel. The confusion arose because he was using the first part of my surname and the hotel was using the last. Soon I joined him, along with Shaykh Hosam Raouf, who had accompanied me on this trip.

He expressed the importance of us departing soon for the Prophet's mosque to be there in time for the sunset prayers, as Shaykh al-Bukhari would be there. Nearing the precinct, I could already see the teeming crowd and wondered how on earth I would have the chance to sit quietly next to Shaykh al-Bukhari. Inside the mosque, the crowd was even thicker, and he told me that Shaykh al-Bukhari would be sitting right in front, facing the Prophet's tomb. I should make my way rapidly as the prayers were about to begin. I could only describe it as a miracle that I ended up in the front row and recognized Shaykh al-Bukhari, although I had not met him before. He had motioned me to go to his left side where he had reserved some space. After the prayers, he looked at me with gentle kindness and pointed out to a bookcase at the side of the wall, full of Qurans and books of supplications. He held my hand and whispered gently, "Do you see all of these manuscripts and their content? They are all of secondary importance to the realization of *La ilaha illallah* (There is no god but God), knowing there is none other than the One, the eternal light – Allah." Shaykh al-Bukhari looked deeply at me and said, "If you make this knowledge as your *qibla* (direction Muslims face when praying toward Makka), then truly wherever you turn is the face of Allah. This is liberation from existence by obsession with the One."

When Shaykh Bashir Uthman visited England he often stayed at our centre in London. On one of these occasions he was looked after by one of my close students, who later told me the following story. He had knocked on Shaykh Bashir's door after dawn but received no answer, so he entered the room to find the covers lifted over the shaykh's body. He rolled back the blanket to find his entire body was wrapped in a burial shroud, encircled with a *tasbih* of 1,000 beads. He wondered if the shaykh had died in the night, then the shaykh opened his eyes. Seeing how perturbed the visitor was, he greeted him, and requested him to leave the room for ten minutes before returning for an explanation. Shaykh Bashir then explained that every night before he slept he made *ghusul* (ritual ablution) in preparation for death. He would then wrap himself in his shroud and recite his litanies with the 1,000-bead *tasbih*. This *tasbih* would often end up circled around him as he moved in the bed.

The stranger is not who is lost in Syria or the Yemen, the stranger indeed is he who is not friendly with the shroud or the grave; for when my time comes my clothes will be stripped and I will be laid down to rest and cover me with a new cloth called the shroud and then placed under the earth and then leave me with sadness and even tears that will not help. Learn contentment in this world and witness He who owns it all, for victory will only come by contentment with the shroud and the grave.

Imam Ali Zaynalabidin

The same student had a most uplifting experience when staying with Shaykh Bashir in Madina in 1981. He had developed a high fever upon arrival and was unable to visit the Prophet's mosque with his companions. He had a vision that night that four young men entered the room. They did not speak but lifted him onto a wooden stretcher and carried it out of the house, as if he was on a flying carpet. As the student gazed in front of him, he saw he was being carried into the Prophet's mosque. They circumambulated the whole mosque over and over again until he was overwhelmed with bewilderment and lost consciousness of what was happening. When he regained consciousness, he was being held in the arms of Shaykh Bashir on the floor of his home, surrounded by the shaykh's family and his travel companions. They were all looking at him with concern, except for Shaykh Bashir. The shaykh then related a tradition from the Prophet Muhammad that when a traveller enters Madina for the sake of visiting the Prophet and becomes ill, the Prophet will come to visit him.

On one visit to America, Bashir Uthman had arrived at our centre there in search of a person to be given a complicated remedy that had taken him a few months to process. After the right person was found, I asked why he thought that there was a person that needed that particular remedy. He then told me the story of some close followers of his in New York who had asked him for this particular medicine, but on his brief visit to New York he found were out of town. He had still carried the bottle of medicine with him. As he was going to return to Jeddah from his visit to us he said the real person this remedy was made for must be with us and the person in New York was simply a connector. He then said reflectively, "If you do anything with the name of God upon it, then it is the light of God that will lead you to its proper purpose and destination. If you truly live by *Bismillah* (in the name of Allah), you will only experience the light of Allah that will lead and guide you. Allah is ever present and it is us who need to come back from our absence."

Bashir Uthman saw only goodness in everything. Once, a group of us were comparing notes as to the negative effects Arabic television programmes had on the quality of life in Madina. Bashir Uthman listened quietly and surprised everyone by declaring that he was most grateful for the television programmes in Madina and how much they have helped to improve the quality of his life. Then he went silent. A young friend in the circle asked him to explain. Bashir Uthman said that in their Sufi *dhikr* circle they used to be interrupted regularly by the religious police, but now they are too busy watching television, so the Sufis' quality of life has improved!

Bashir Uthman gave me a special supplication to do after the morning and evening prayers. He told me that these verses would save me from serious illness. I was also given permission to give this recitation to anybody whom I thought would treat it with commitment. Ever since then I have been following this prescription and have benefitted from it. Then one day I had a surprising letter from his son in Jeddah, which said that his father was ill in hospital and he felt I ought to know. A temporary doubt as to the potency of these verses came to my mind. A few days later, I learnt that many of his relatives and friends had gathered in Madina to be with him. After that I received a more detailed communication that he had passed away most peacefully with his extended family and friends around him, after a brief illness. During his last days, everyone received what they had hoped for and he had completed all of his duties and obligations. The last illness had been a gift for his family to get together.

The amazing story of how he was buried was given to me in detail both in letter and through telephone conversations. He had passed away late at night and the next morning, when they were preparing for his burial, an official government car arrived at his humble house with two distinguished Saudis who came in and announced that they were instructed by a higher authority to take the body to the Jannat al-Baqi graveyard for burial. This is the most famous ancient cemetery in the centre of Madina, where from the time of the Prophet until some 80 years ago the family of the Prophet, followers and famous Muslim personalities were buried. *Wahhabi* puritanism does not allow for marked graves, therefore the entire cemetery of the Baqi was razed to the ground and a perimeter was erected to restrict visitors. No one in recent times had been buried there. It was considered impossible to get permission from the government. There was the perfect connection from the unseen to the visible when Shaykh Bashir's body was carried with dignity and honour to be placed in the sacred precinct.

> *He whose beginning is illumined, his end will also be illumined.*[68]
>
> Ibn 'Ata' Allah

A life's journey which starts with clear conviction and sincere yearning for Truth, and continues on this path, will most likely end with success and illumination. That which begins with light will end with light and delight, while that which is born in darkness belongs to the darkness of ignorance.

Chapter 6

INDIA

LIFE'S OPPORTUNITY

Every moment presents us
Numerous levels of truth.
The most obvious is sensory,
Then concepts and ideas,
Insights and lights of delights,
Connecting the eternal with the transitory,
Unifying the limited with boundlessness.

The opportunity is to connect
Personal life with timelessness
Experienced in every aspect
Before all, after all,
Hidden in all,
Apparent in all.[69]

Shaykh Fadhlalla Haeri

During several visits I had made to Bombay during the 1970s, I had been curious about a shrine at the end of a narrow causeway linking the city precinct of Mahalakshmi to the Bay of Worli. The shrine can only be visited at low tide. I had postponed visiting it due to the precariousness of the causeway, which was about a kilometre long, with its line of beggars squatting along the entire length leading up to the shrine. Furthermore, I had been told that many of them were lepers, that others had had limbs amputated and there were mothers carrying deformed babies.

Eventually, one afternoon on this visit, on the way to a dinner engagement with Indian friends, I asked the driver if we could stop for a visit to the shrine. The driver told me it was known as the Haji Ali Dargah. It was built in 834 AH/1431 CE in memory of Seyyed Haji Ali Shah Bukhari, a wealthy merchant who had come to present-day Mumbai from Bukhara after extensive travels through the Muslim world and who had decided to settle there to spread Islam. One legend says that he gave away all his worldly possessions before going on pilgrimage to Makka, then died on the journey there, having instructed his followers to cast his coffin into the Arabian Sea. The coffin floated back to the shore of Worli Bay and was found on the rocky islets, where his shrine is now located.

The tomb became a popular place of pilgrimage for people of all faiths and today it is visited every Thursday and Friday by thousands of pilgrims – some reckon about 40,000.

The driver strongly advised that I carry a lot of change on me for the beggars. I was already out of the car when I was struck by concern about the unavoidable lengthy transactions with so many beggars. A few steps from the pavement, I was approached by several moneychangers and soon found myself with pockets full of rupees. The causeway was indeed precarious, with very uneven stonework, and the beggars were strongly expressing their sense of entitlement. I decided to commit myself fully to the act of giving to everyone attentively.

Halfway along the causeway, the change ran out, but there were numerous money changers sitting between the beggars. I thought to myself that they must have been ex-beggars who had done well and would soon end up as local bankers. By the time I got to the entrance of the shrine, the last beggar had received my last coin and I was feeling very pleased with myself for having endured this taxing journey.

The surroundings of the attractive, white-washed structure, which contains the tomb within a mosque, were pleasant and cheerful. The location itself was magical, perched in the middle of the sea, away from the noise and pollution of Bombay. As I exited the shrine having felt that my wish was fulfilled, I came face to face with a mendicant with beautiful shining eyes and plaited hair, with several strings of large beads around his neck. He was sitting on the ramparts overlooking the sea and thus was a couple of feet higher than myself. I went toward him, greeting him with folded hands and bent head. Then, without much thought, I put my hands in my pocket to give the mendicant an offering. Since all my change had run out, I could only give him a 100-rupee note, the equivalent of ten days' wages in those days.

With a contagious smile, the charismatic mendicant took the note from my hand between his thumb and forefinger, lifted it up in the air and let the breeze carry it into the sea. As he did so, he muttered, "Omm, Huu, Omm, Huu" (God). The smile was still on his face when I felt engulfed by an immense presence, a sense of absence from everything that was around, just a void of stillness. These are moments when measurable time becomes like eternity. For when I came back to consciousness, the beautiful face was right there in front of me again as though transfixed eternally. He then lifted his forefinger toward the sky and waved repeatedly as though indicating that all that is here is from there.

I, too, reciprocated these gestures, which resonated in my heart so deeply that at a point I felt there was nothing more to say or do. I gently withdrew, taking a few steps backward away from him and then walked toward the causeway. This trance-like state remained with me until dinner time.

When my host heard that I had visited Haji Ali's shrine, he surmised that his soul must have manifested to greet me, as he is said to appear on occasions to visitors. I was so taken by this all-absorbing encounter that it became clear to me that for higher consciousness we need to leave behind our worldly, normal mental state. Obviously the walk along the causeway and my intentions had prepared me to taste the very edge of oblivion.

SELF-KNOWLEDGE

To know yourself
Stop seeing yourself
Step beside yourself
Beyond the self
Where shadows and light merge
Where the universe submerges
Where Original Light emerges.
To know yourself
Forget identity
Face the Cosmic Reality
Radiating from the Sacred Soul –
Allah.[70]

Shaykh Fadhlalla Haeri

Oh God, may this shrine of the Beloved exist till the last day,
may this refuge of the poor remain for ever!
Invocation recited during the week before the
'urs of Shaykh Muin ad-Din Chishti in Ajmer

In 1985, I requested Seyyed Ikram to accompany me to the shrines of the Chishti shaykhs in India. This was following the Sufi custom that when you go to a new land, you take a guide from the people of the land. During this visit, Seyyed Ikram gave me some insights into the different Chishti saints in Ajmer and Delhi.

Ajmer is the burial place of Shaykh Muin ad-Din Chishti, otherwise known as Hazrat Gharib Nawaz, the founder of the order in India, and considered the most important and popular of all the Chishti shrines. The shrine lies at the centre of the town and is surrounded by buildings that house both permanent residents and the transient pilgrims. There is a mosque, several other tombs and the inevitable abundance of stalls selling stones and other trinkets that exist in most shrine complexes. The activity of everyday life continues all around and outside the intricately carved doors, which are the gateway to the tomb; outside, *qawwals* chant. The attendants of the shrine seem to be forever tossing sweetly scented rose petals on top of the tomb itself, while the visiting supplicants encircled it. Many Muslim shrines do not permit women to enter the tomb area but there are no such rules at Ajmer. Gharib Nawaz was accessible to all during his lifetime and this pattern has continued after his death.

It is said that one of Gharib Nawaz's first acts when he settled in Ajmer was the establishment of a *langarkhana* (kitchen feeding the poor, attached to a shrine), from which both Hindu and Muslim poor were fed daily. This is a practice that has continued up to the present day and contributes to Gharib Nawaz's reputation as a universal saint.

> *Conversation turned to the virtue of giving food to others. On the blessed tongue of the master [Shaykh Nizam ad-Din Awliya] came these words: "There is no merit attached to providing food for your own people." Then he began to talk of Khwaja Ali, the son of Khwaja Rukn ad-din, the venerable Chishti saint – may God bestow His favour upon both of them. He was taken captive during the onslaught of the infidel Mongols. They brought him before Chinghiz Khan. At the time one of the disciples of that noble dynasty [of Chishti saints] was present, not only present but in a position of authority [at the Mongol court]. When he saw that Khwaja Ali had been taken prisoner, he was dumbfounded. To himself he thought, "How can I procure his release? In what way should I mention his name before Chinghiz Khan? If I say he comes from a noble family and is himself a saint, what will Chinghiz Khan care? And if I mention his obedience and devotion, that, too, will have no effect."*
>
> *After pondering a long time, he went before Chinghiz Khan and announced, "The father of this man was a saint who gave food to people. He ought to be set free." "Did he give food*

to his own people," asked Chinghiz Khan, "or to people who were strangers?" "Everyone provided foods for his own people," replied the courtier, "but the father of this man gave food to strangers." Chinghiz Khan was very pleased with the reply. "A saint," he noted, "is someone who gives food to God's people." And immediately he ordered them to set Khwaja Ali free."[71]

The shrine benefitted from the patronage of the Mughals. Akbar donated silver candlesticks and cauldrons to feed visitors to Gharib Nawaz's shrine. His successors, particularly Jahangir and Shah Jahan, and Shah Jahan's daughter, the Sufi Princess Jahanara, also made regular visits to Ajmer and gave generous gifts. Gharib Nawaz is so venerated, not only in India but wherever in the world the Chishti teachings have spread, that he is also known as Sultan-i-Hind ("Ruler of India").

On one memorable occasion during our visit to Ajmer, I was sitting with Seyyed Ikram by Gharib Nawaz's tomb and noticed a Hindu semi-naked *faqir* circling and making noisy vocalized gestures, while pointing at the shrine. Seyyed Ikram had placed his shawl on my head and his own to improve our meditations but I was so disturbed by this fellow I asked what he was saying. Seyyed Ikram replied, "Do not call him a *faqir* (poor one, someone in need i.e. on the Sufi path). He is penniless, we are the *faqirs*." He went on to answer my question, "He is asking for a hundred rupees." In my annoyance, I muttered, "Who would be foolish enough to give this fellow a hundred rupees?" Very softly, Seyyed Ikram said, "You never know."

After numerous attempts to go into a state of mental peace and meditation and having reasoned that as this trip was a once-in-a-lifetime event, I didn't want it adversely affected because of this disturbance. I finally got up and gave the beggar the 100 rupees. As I sat back, I saw the satisfied smile on Seyyed Ikram's face. He seemed to be saying, "Didn't I tell you? There will always be someone…"

The legacy of Gharib Nawaz has been one of love and compassion for all humanity. The Chishtis have always interacted with people of other faiths with respect and tolerance. This is why their shrines are as much visited by Hindus as Muslims.

> *Oh, Allah, till the time there is sun spreading light in the sky and there are fish in the ocean, keep the lights spreading from the lamps of the Chishtis.*

During the trip to India with Seyyed Ikram, we visited the shrines of Gharib Nawaz's most prominent spiritual heirs in Delhi. Shaykh Qutb ad-Din Bakhtiyar Kaki, commonly known as Qutb Saheb (d. 633 AH/1235 CE), carried his master's work to Delhi, which was then the new Muslim capital. The ruler, Sultan Iltetmish, was known for his love of men of knowledge and gave Qutb Saheb a warm welcome. Iltetmish was one of the rulers of the Slave dynasty, so-called because they had been enslaved in their youth and gained their freedom and later power through military prowess.

The Sultan offered Qutb Saheb the post of Shaykh al-Islam, which would have made him responsible for all official donations to men of religion. He refused it, preferring to separate himself from the affairs of state in the Chishti tradition. The position then went to Shaykh Najm ad-Din Sughra, who was jealous of the popularity of Qutb Saheb and used every opportunity to harass him. When Gharib Nawaz visited Delhi, Najm ad-Din confessed his jealousy of Qutb Saheb to him and Gharib Nawaz promised that he would take his pupil back to Ajmer with him. When the two masters started their return journey, they were followed by crowds of people headed by Iltetmish himself. People were collecting the dust on the road where Qutb Saheb had trod as relics. Gharib Nawaz was so touched by the love and respect they had for his pupil that he allowed him to stay, saying that he would not make the whole city sad for the sake of one person.

Qutb Saheb, who originated from Central Asia, was, like Gharib Nawaz, a Seyyed. He was known for his ascetic outer life and inner intoxication.

Legend says that he received his nickname of *Kaki* ("Man of Bread"), because he used to borrow money from a neighbouring grocer to buy food. He would repay the grocer when he was given some *futuh* (unsolicited gifts). He decided to stop doing this, as he disliked borrowing. From that point on a piece of bread would appear daily under his prayer mat. The grocer wondered why he had stopped borrowing and asked his wife to find out the reason from Qutb Saheb's wife. The latter told her what was happening. After this, the bread never appeared again.

This is a warning to the seeker not to discuss their spiritual openings with others at an early stage in their development. It will only encourage arrogance and reduce the potency of what comes to them. There is a story told of a follower of the Prophet Isa (Jesus), who, when the master told him that he too could walk on water, did just that. Then the thought came to him that he was as powerful as Seyyedina Isa, and at that point he sank!

> *Once the Holy Prophet gave a woman a utensil full of flour, telling her that she should take out as much as she needed but she must never look inside it, nor ever turn it upside down and empty it. She did this and the flour lasted her all her life. In fact, her sons also ate it all their lives right down to her grandson. He also ate from it for a while. But one day he thought he would see what was inside the pot. The moment he emptied the flour from the pot, it lost its baraka [blessing].[72]*
>
> *Hazrat Zauqi Shah*

Like Gharib Nawaz, Qutb Saheb recognized the importance of devotional music. Historically, there had been much controversy concerning *sama'*, a term used to describe a spiritual recital where the participants would either participate in or listen to singing or repetitious recitations of verse or phrases with a spiritual significance. There might also be dancing and the use of musical instruments. The *'ulama* and the more orthodox Muslims were critical of this practice. Many of the Sufi *tariqas*, particularly the Chishtis, used it as a method to reduce agitation and mental distraction. Its use was governed by set rules and the intention had to be for spiritual upliftment, not entertainment.

Sultan Iltetmish, who was sympathetic toward the Sufi viewpoint, called a gathering for *'ulama* and Sufis to debate its legality. The Chishtis were the ones principally under attack for their use of music. On this occasion, the ruling was in favour of its permissibility.

The historian Isami, writing some 100 years after the event, recorded that it was a learned *'alim*, Qazi Hamid ad-Din Nagauri, who encouraged the Sultan to allow *sama'* for mystics but forbid it for the ordinary people. The Qazi reminded Iltetmish that when the Sultan had been a slave boy he had served the Sufis all night long by cutting the burnt wicks of the candles at a gathering of *sama'*, which was held in his master's house in Baghdad. The Qazi himself had been present at this gathering and had blessed Iltetmish.

Qazi Hamid ad-Din belonged to the Suhrawardi Sufi order. The Chishtis and Suhrawardis were at that time the main Sufi brotherhoods in India. The Suhrawardis tended to be more sober in their approach than the Chishtis, less inclined to *sama'*, and were willing to accept court positions. The great contemporary Suhrawardi master, Shaykh Baha ad-Din Zakariyya of Multan, was a man of immense outer wealth. He justified his material riches on the grounds that he controlled them, they did not control him. Often the Chishtis, who laid great importance on poverty, would dispute the Suhrawardi stance on this issue. Equally there was mutual respect and friendly exchanges between their masters.

The early Chishtis, who did not have religious texts written by their own masters, would teach from the *Awarif al-Ma'arif* (*Bounties of Divine Knowledge*) of Shaykh Shihab ad-Din Suhrawardi (539–632 AH/1145–1234 CE) of Baghdad. Shaykh Shihab ad-Din was considered one of the most inspired teachers of his time and his writings impacted on generations of Sufis. The Chishtis also used the *Kashf al-Mahjub* of Ali al-Hujwiri extensively.

Qutb Saheb is reported to have died while reciting a popular couplet, written by Shaykh Ahmad of Jam (d. 556 AH/1141 CE). He recited it continuously for four nights and days, breaking only to make the obligatory prayers. On the fifth night he expired. The couplet was:

Whoever has died by the dagger of surrender
Has at all times renewed life from the unseen.

Death and life are two sides of the coin of existence; the root of each is drawing nourishment from the other. For the people on the path, any reduction in sensual appreciation is often accompanied by increase in inner delights – sight to insight. The death to all senses leads one to the door of the inner Essence. So annihilation to a Sufi, while still alive, signals awakening and rebirth into the zone of the Everlasting Essence.

Qutb Saheb is buried at Mehrauli, near the Qutb Minar, one of the earliest Islamic monuments built in India. It is a small, peaceful shrine filled with light, a far cry from the crowds of Ajmer. Here the visitor can sit and reflect without the outer disturbances that are prevalent at the major shrines. The peace is only broken by the occasional monkey. As an important area for the early Muslims, it was a much-visited place for hundreds of years. After Partition, the majority of the Muslim population left and today the shrine is mainly frequented by Chishti devotees and locals who know a holy man is buried there.

> *Your love is ever dwelling in the centre of my heart and the spider has woven its web around it. I die when You are remembered and I come back to life and all the time I swing between those states and it surprises me when someone says, "I remembered my Lord." How can you forget that which is the source of all remembrance? I drink from the cups of love one after another and all the drinks have finished but my thirst continues.*
>
> *Imam Ali*

Almighty Allah has given thee knowledge, wisdom and spiritual thirst and he alone who possesses these three qualities is qualified to discharge the duties of the khilafat of saints.[73]

Baba Farid Ganj-i-Shakar
on Shaykh Nizam ad-Din Awliya

The premier shrine of Delhi is that of Shaykh Nizam ad-Din Awliya (636–725 AH/1238–1325 CE). He was a Husayni Seyyed on both his father and his mother's side. Shaykh Nizam ad-Din numbered amongst his direct ancestors the first ten of the twelve imams of the *Ahl al-Bayt*. He was the successor of Farid ad-Din Ganj-i-Shakar, whose shrine in Pakistan I had already visited with Seyyed Ikram. The time of Nizam ad-Din was the Golden Age of the Chishtis. The impact of his teachings on the Muslim population of Delhi was considerable. A contemporary historian, Barani, who often visited the *zawiya*, wrote, "Owing to the influence of the shaykh, most of the Muslims of the country took an inclination toward mysticism, prayers and aloofness from the world. The hearts of men have become virtuous by good deeds, the very name of wine, gambling and other forbidden things never came to anybody's lips."[74]

We know more about the life and teachings of Shaykh Nizam ad-Din than his spiritual forefathers because he permitted his pupil, Amir Hasan Sijzi, to record the discourses he gave. *Fawaid al-Fuad* (*Morals for the Heart*), skilfully translated by the distinguished American academic Professor Bruce Lawrence, brings to life the *zawiyas* of Baba Farid and Shaykh Nizam ad-Din, as the latter shared with Amir Hasan his memories of the time he spent with Baba Farid.

The picture of Shaykh Nizam ad-Din that comes from these writings is that of a man of deep insight and spiritual wisdom. In answer to the accusation of indiscrimination in the choice of his disciples, he replied, "It has repeatedly been reported to me that my disciples refrain from indulging in sin, and offer congregational and non-obligatory prayers. If I impose on them difficult conditions, they would be deprived of even that level of piety."[75]

On another occasion he was watching some Hindus perform their acts of worship and commented, "Every community has its own path and faith, and its own way of worship."[76]

He said about *sama'*, "It is neither absolutely forbidden nor absolutely permitted but dependent on what is heard and who is hearing."[77]

The area around the shaykh's tomb is teeming with life; devotees, beggars and shopkeepers throng the vicinity. Nobody around the *dargah* (shrine, implying sanctuary) goes hungry because of the volume of food distributed daily. The keepers of the shrine have always maintained the custom of Shaykh Nizam ad-Din to feed all the poor who came to him.

It is customary for all supplicants to pray first at the tomb of the shaykh's most celebrated pupil, the poet Amir Khusrau (d. 725 AH/1324 CE), who is buried near to his master. Khusrau's verse celebrating the deep connection between him and his shaykh is often sung by *qawwals* (singers of devotional songs) today:

> I have become you, you have become me.
> I have become soul, you have become body.
> From now on let no one say that
> I am other and you are another.[78]

This story is told illustrating Khusrau's devotion to his master. One day, Shaykh Nizam ad-Din had no alms for a beggar, so he gave him his shoes. Khusrau met the beggar as he came out of the city gates. He went up to him and said, "I feel some aroma from my spiritual guide. Do you have anything belonging to him?" The beggar showed him the shoes. Khusrau had just been paid five lakhs of silver tankas for some verses he had written and he gave all of it to the beggar in exchange for the shoes. Khusrau then put the shoes on his head and returned to Shaykh Nizam ad-Din's *khanqah*.[79]

Shaykh Nizam ad-Din recognized his pupil's sincerity, commenting that, "When on the Day of Judgement God will ask what I have brought for

Him from this world, I will say, the fire of divine love which consumed the heart of the Turk-Allah [i.e. Khusrau]."[80]

It is said that on his deathbed Shaykh Nizam ad-Din commented that Khusrau would not long survive his death and should be buried near him, for he was the keeper of his secrets. When Amir Khusrau heard of his master's demise, he fainted and, upon being revived, said, "I dare not weep for such a king. I weep for myself for I am not destined to live after *Sultan ul-Mashaikh*."[81] He then distributed all his worldly goods to the poor and died a few months later. He has always been considered the gatekeeper of the *dargah*.

Amir Khusrau is one of India's most beloved poets, celebrated as much for his secular as his spiritual verse. He created by his verse a sense of cultural identity for the Indian Muslim, eulogising the new capital of Delhi, "the Refuge of religion! Refuge and paradise of justice!", and was full of praise, not only for the flora and fauna of India, but for the quality of its people:

> *If a Khurasani, Greek or Arab comes here,*
> *He will not face any problems,*
> *For the people will treat him kindly, as their own,*
> *Making him feel happy and at ease.*
> *And if they jest with him,*
> *They do so with blooming smiles.*[82]

Khusrau was of both Turkish and Indian descent and proud of being an Indian Muslim:

> *I am a Turk of Hindustan, I answer in Hindavi.*
> *I don't have Egyptian sugar to speak Arabic.*[83]

He also described himself as "the parrot of India, ask me in Hindavi so that I can answer you correctly". Amir Khusrau's verses are sung continually at the shrine. The *qawwali* singers consider him to be the father of their art. He is believed to have invented the sitar and wrote some of the first verses in the Urdu language, which blended Persian and Arabic with the popular form of Hindi.

> *Shaykh Baha ad-Din (d. 1038/1628) was a prominent Chishti master who followed in the classical musical traditions started by Amir Khusrau. He encouraged meetings between Muslims and Hindus and would even invent new tunes for Vaishnavites to accompany verses of Kabir. One of his closest friends was Das Ghanun, a guru of prominent Hindus. At one gathering the shaykh commented that Hindu taboos against socialising between Hindus and Muslims increased the gap between them. Das Ghanun, then, took a meat samosa brought for the shaykh and started to bite into it. The shaykh took it from him to the Hindu's irritation; the latter retaliated that he was just responding to Baha ad-Din's comment. The shaykh responded that he had never doubted his friend's sincerity and that the differences in eating and drinking between communities were relevant only for people of the outer, for people who believed in the Unity of Being were one. When Das Ghanun was dying he sent a message to Shaykh Baha ad-Din: "Das Ghanun is like an ocean wave which rises from the ocean, then merges back into it."[84]*
>
> *Saiyid Athar Abbas Rizvi.*

During this visit, Seyyed Ikram commented that Shaykh Nizam ad-Din, like the other great Chishti masters, had during his lifetime performed special practices of *'ibadat* (worship). The effects of these practices had engulfed the surrounding environment and permeated their tombs. Visitors to these shrines may find the goodness and light in their hearts is enhanced and takes them to the horizons of knowledge and *'irfan*. In Seyyed Ikram's own words, "The fountain of these blessings will continue for ever but only those who believe will have access to their *baraka*." You need the potential to awaken, the readiness and appropriate time, before you take the light to be illumined!

He never liked that anyone should consider him a great man. He has suppressed his ego to such an extent that if I call him a shaykh, he is not pleased; and if I attribute miracles to him, he resents it and remains in silent contemplation.[85]

Hamid Qalandar
on Shaykh Nasir ad-Din Mahmud

The last shrine we visited was that of Shaykh Nizam ad-Din's successor, Shaykh Nasir ad-Din Mahmud (d. 757 AH/1356 CE), commonly known as *Chiragh-i-Delhi* (Lamp of Delhi). Dusk was falling as we neared the area around the shrine. There were two young attendants laying white roses on the tomb and a passing cow in the background. I have never been in the Subcontinent to so empty a shrine. The neighbouring vicinity had, like the case of Qutb Saheb's shrine, been largely Muslim before Partition. Once, too, this had been a popular visiting place for both Muslims and Hindus. Durga Kuli Khan, an earlier chronicler, visiting the grave, wrote of Shaykh Nasir ad-Din that he was the lamp not only of Delhi but of the whole country.

Shaykh Nasir ad-Din longed for a life of solitary asceticism but Shaykh Nizam ad-Din gave him the prescription: "To live amongst the people, submitting to their cruelties and blows, and responding to them with humility, generosity and kindness"[86] – advice he followed faithfully as he dealt with the difficult times that lay ahead for the Sufis of Delhi. In as much as the times of Shaykh Nizam ad-Din had appeared as a Golden Age, the years that followed brought many challenges. The new Sultan, Muhammad bin Tughluq, was determined to bring the Sufis under state control and get their assistance in a most ambitious scheme, the substitution of Daulatabad as the capital in place of Delhi and the Islamization of the Deccan area. He hoped to use the Sufis as missionaries, creating a bridge between Hindus and Muslims as had happened in the past. Much of the population of Delhi were forced to migrate to the Deccan, including many Sufis. This led to the spread of

Chishti influence to distant parts and a decentralization of the order. Chiragh-i-Delhi refused to go and was subjected to severe harassment from the Sultan. Eventually, the Sultan expired and the shaykh was able to live more peacefully in his *khanqah*.

One of Chiragh-i-Delhi's pupils, Hamid Qalandar, was permitted by his master to record 100 conversations that took place at *majalis* (assemblies) during the last three years of the shaykh's life. *Khair ul-Majalis* was revised by Chiragh-i-Delhi and allows us glimpses of his spiritual wisdom.

On one occasion, the master warns Hamid about half-hearted commitment to progress on the path:

> *If you are idle and still hope to reach the goal, you will not reach it. Striving is the precondition to success. "Those who strive in Us, surely we will guide them to our paths." (Quran 29:69) Afterwards he added, "And what is the fruit of this endeavour? Through striving you obtain the purification of the heart from any object other than Allah and you become totally absorbed in the task of aligning your will to His." Then he added, "This is the true meaning of 'There is no God but Allah.' Purify the heart from anything other than Allah is the denial ('there is no God…') while absorbing oneself in obedience to Allah is the affirmation (…but Allah)."*[87]

About three years before his passing, the shaykh survived a knife attack from a *qalandar* who entered Chiragh-i-Delhi's room and inflicted 11 wounds. His pupils saw blood flowing from the water hole and rushed in to save him. Chiragh-i-Delhi insisted that the man be escorted out of the city and set free, so the angry mob would not attack him.

He continued his gruelling schedule of attending to visitors during the day and spent his nights in prayer and contemplation. Despite the outer difficulties he may have experienced, he would have chosen no other life, saying:

Happiness is only found in the house of faqr [inner wealth].
In the house of worldly men, there is only sorrow and sadness.
There is, of course, sorrow and sadness in faqr also, but it is
due to the search for Haqq [Reality], not to the affairs of this
world; and in consequence of this sadness, there is joy and
delight. The Prophet of Allah (blessings on him) was a man of
prolonged sadness and deep reflections.[88]

He refused to name an heir, leaving his pupils a message that they had to bear the burden of their own faith, there was no question of them bearing the burden of others. The patched garment, staff, prayer beads, wooden bowl and shoes which he had inherited from Shaykh Nizam ad-Din were buried with him.

It seems fitting that a master who had longed for tranquillity and a life of peaceful contemplation but whom destiny had forced to serve his fellow men in times of great outer difficulty should finally be surrounded by the outer silence denied him in life.

Toward the end of his life his work reached perfection; he
became a pure soul. When I saw this miracle, I said to myself,
"Since he has reached perfection, it would be strange if they
allowed such a pure existence to remain in this world."[89]
    Amir Kurd on Shaykh Nasir ad-Din Mahmud

The Chishtis enjoyed a second Golden Age due to the patronage of the Mughal rulers. Shaykh Salim Chishti (897–979 AH/1479–1572 CE) was a descendant of Baba Farid. He had travelled extensively throughout the Middle East, making *Hajj* on several occasions, and had a reputation for asceticism. He chose to live simply on the ridge of the Sikri Hills, near Agra. The Emperor Akbar asked the shaykh to pray that he might have sons, as he had no heirs. The shaykh promised he would have three sons and when Prince Salim, the future Emperor Jahangir, was born, Akbar saw it as a direct result of the shaykh's prayers. In his gratitude, Akbar ordered a satellite town to be built at Sikri to connect with Agra. Fatehpur Sikri became the new capital of the Mughal Empire.

I have visited Fatehpur Sikri on several occasions and found its haunting beauty arresting. The mosque and *khanqah* complex were built under Shaykh Salim's personal supervision, with some of the calligraphy executed by his pupil, Shaykh Hussein Ahmad Chishti. The mausoleum of Shaykh Salim, a square pavilion faced in white makrana marble, is considered one of the most beautiful examples of Mughal architecture and shines out pearlescent amidst the red sandstone pavilions. The city, with its many Hindu motifs, displays Akbar's syncretism and intention to show that he was as much the Emperor of the Hindus as the Muslims.

On my first visit, I was particularly struck by the enormous gateway, which bears the inscription: "The world is a bridge; pass over it but do not build a house on it." This well-known saying is attributed to Seyyedina Isa (Jesus). It is an appropriate reminder, as construction started around 1571 CE and by 1585 CE Akbar had moved his court to Lahore. A few years later, the city was abruptly deserted, probably due to water shortage.

When I first visited Fatehpur Sikr in the mid-1970s, it was fairly desolate and difficult to reach. The roads from Delhi were poor and full of potholes. Now it is a popular tourist destination and access has been much improved.

> *Turn to none save God. The rosary and sacred thread are*
> *means to an end.*
> *Whatever thou beholdest except for Him,*
> *Is object of thy fancy;*
> *Things other than He have their existence like a mirage.*
> *The existence of God is like a boundless ocean –*
> *Men are like forms and waves in its water.*[90]
>
> *Dara Shikoh*

In spite of the centuries separating us, the spirits and legacy of these great masters resonated within me. The connection I felt with them in the unseen had made them familiar to me.

Hazrat Shah Manzoor Alam is a recently deceased Sufi master who had windows into the unseen. During a visit to Kanpur in the early 1980s, my host had arranged for my visit to this well-known and popular master. He was referred to by all his friends and followers as Huzoor. His centre was more of a meditation hall than a teaching centre. For years, Hindus, Muslims and others would congregate in this incense-smoke-filled room and experience different levels of trance and transcendence.

The afternoon that I visited him was obviously a special occasion because so many bundles of incense were burning within a few metres of each other and my headache only faded after a few days. There were very poor Muslims with the usual beards and semi-naked Hindu *fakirs*. The atmosphere was most benign, friendly and very intoxicating. I felt a most powerful charismatic transmission from Huzoor, who exuded extreme gentleness and friendliness.

The entire atmosphere seemed like a floating state from nowhere to nowhere and I could believe the rumours that some of his people communicate with each other telepathically, wherever they are. Indeed, my journey to Huzoor was perhaps half an hour by car, yet on every street corner there were people waiting to point out to us the direction to his place. Only the most advanced traffic police could have performed such a feat. I remember smiling when the thought occurred that to be a real superman you have to leave behind your human limitations and be exposed to what is beyond it. This zone of consciousness is there all the time but our minds block it. You need spiritual presence. The name Huzoor means presence.

Muneera and our daughters, Zahra and Fawzia, visited Huzoor in 2008. He made a big impact on all of them, mesmerising the girls with his striking appearance and penetrating gaze. Huzoor's eyes seemed to look right through them, as if he knew their innermost secrets. The girls were struck by how simply he lived and the access he gave to all comers, Hindu as well as Muslim. The sense was of a universal master, open to all seekers. While they were sipping a delicious, aromatic chai and chatting with him, a beggar woman came unannounced into the room crying out for alms. Huzoor explained she was a poor Muslim widow, who often asked for assistance. He instructed everybody to give her whatever funds they had on them.

When Huzoor heard of Muneera's interest in Dara Shikoh (1615–59 CE), he presented her with a book on Sarmad, who had been one of Dara's teachers. Dara was the eldest son of the Mughal Emperor Shah Jahan and heir apparent to the Empire. The Prince was a Sufi, a prolific writer on the *awliya* (friends of God) and responsible for the first translation into Farsi of the Upanishads. He was unpopular with the Muslim establishment because of his liberalism and interest in Hindu spirituality. Dara was defeated in the War of Succession by his brother, Aurangzeb, who had him executed on trumped-up charges of apostasy.

Sarmad (c1590–1661 CE) was born into a Jewish merchant family in Armenia. He later converted to Islam and travelled to India, which he made his home. He was originally a trader in fine arts but when he adopted the Sufi path he gave up this work. Sarmad grew his hair, stopped cutting his nails and wandered naked around the streets of Delhi. He was a controversial character, with his eccentric behaviour and unorthodox poetry. An obsession with Abhai Chand, a beautiful Hindu boy who lived with him, also fuelled the gossip.

> *Why seekest thou His abode in the chapel and the mosque?*
> *Seest not thou His creation above and below?*
> *Wherein does He not abide?*
> *The whole universe made by Him sings His praise,*
> *He alone is wise who for Him is mad.*[91]
>
> *Sarmad*

Dara, ever seeking connection with interesting mystics, invited him to court and often took counsel with him. It is said that Sarmad had predicted that Dara would succeed Shah Jahan on the Mughal throne. Sometime after Dara's execution, Sarmad was brought before Aurangzeb, who questioned the accuracy of this statement. Sarmad replied that God had given Dara eternal sovereignty so his prediction was not false! Aurangzeb then ordered he be beheaded on grounds of apostasy. Legends of his head reciting Sufi verse post-execution abound.

Huzoor died in October 2015 after a long illness. We remained in touch through one of his close devotees till close to his passing. I had requested him to record some of his reflections on the spiritual path but it was not to be. Huzoor very much typifies a special genre of Indian mystic who welcomes devotees of all faith. Yet, in his teachings to his Muslim pupils, he maintained a traditional flavour. There were frequent pilgrimages to Chishti shrines, particularly that of Gharib Nawaz at Ajmer. He often recommended that supplicants greet the Prophet, Imam Ali, Fatima, Hasan and Hussein and lose themselves in their illustrious company at the beginning of their *dhikr*.

> *The rays of insight make you witness His nearness to you. The eye of insight makes you witness your non-existence because of His existence. The truth of insight makes you witness His Existence, neither your non-existence, nor your existence.*[92]
>
> Ibn 'Ata' Allah

Insights lead to higher realities and truth, whereas outer sights relate to images, forms, causal relationships and realities. Higher and subtler than the ever-changing world of cause and effect are the Divine Qualities and Attributes and Names which are His only, and thus the seeker's awareness of his own existence vanishes. The ultimate, highest insight leads us to being immersed in the blazing light of Absolute Truth with nothing beside it. In this state one cannot talk of human consciousness or lack of it.

Chapter 7

NORTH AFRICA

*I pass upon doors without discernible need except within me
there stirs a deep desire to see You or to see those who have seen
You and it is all to do with the original love that has made
me drink from its pure cup. I wish I had not been served that
wine. What moves me at all times is Your memory, for if it was
not a love then my heart would not have moved at all.*

Abu Madyan Shuayb

My spiritual connection with the North African Shadhili-Darqawi
order inspired me to make several visits there over a period of 20 years.
I benefitted from the light of the great *awliya* of the past, as much as
from the companionship of the living men of knowledge. The following
impressions are of great figures, past and present, from that region, whose
lives and teachings have touched me.

Sidi Idris, a famous descendant of Imam Hasan, is considered by all
accounts to be the ultimate master of the Muhammadi followers in the
Maghreb. History records the immense persecution that the Prophet's
family had suffered in Arabia after the martyrdom of Imam Hussein, as
they were considered a potential threat to the Umayyad rulers. In fact, in
time they became an important rallying point for the revolt that ended
the Umayyad Regime, which lasted some 90 years and led to the Abbasid
rule. The Abbasids too felt threatened by the direct descendants of the
Prophet and there emerged another wave of fear of losing power!

Sidi Idris was the great-grandchild of Imam Hasan. He escaped from
Syria after the defeat of the 'Alids by the Abbasids at the battle of Fakhkh
in 787 CE. Sidi Idris, accompanied only by a companion servant, landed
amongst the Berber tribes of North Africa, who soon acknowledged

him as their spiritual master. He married Kanza, who came from the Awraba Berber tribe, and emerged as the ruler of a large area of northern Morocco, including Tlemcen in what is now Algeria.

The Abbasid caliph, Harun al-Rashid, was concerned by the emergence of an independent 'Alid kingdom and is reported to have been responsible for the murder of Idris, who was poisoned in 791 CE. His son, Idris II, established the city of Fez, which his father had founded, as the capital of the Idrisid dynasty.

Sidi Idris's shrine and the town that grew up around it are held in great reverence by Muslims in North Africa. The numerous people who claim descent from him, and many of the poor people who inhabit the area, look forward to visitors and their donations. These come in various forms, particularly the sacrifice of animals. Most of the Sufis and shaykhs I met in Morocco and the surrounding countries took pride in their descent from Sidi Idris. Historically, rulers in these areas often claimed descent from the Prophet via Sidi Idris. This includes the present ruling family of Morocco. The *ashrafs* (from the root word *shareef*, meaning "of noble descent") constitute a large influential religious and respected class of the population. Most Sufi masters have been *ashrafs*.

It has been considered a great honour from the early days of Islam to be descended from the Prophet Muhammad or from Ali Ibn Abi Talib – the fourth caliph, his cousin and husband of the Prophet's daughter, Fatima, through their sons, Hasan and Hussein. During the next 200/300 years, especially after the martyrdom of Imam Hussein, people who could claim to be descendants of either Imam Hasan or Imam Hussein were regarded with special respect in society. Until today, at the end of many *Jummah* (Friday) gatherings, blessings and salutations are given to Imams Hasan and Hussein. They are often referred to as the Prophet called them "the masters of the youth in paradise".

In North Africa and especially Morocco, the descendants of the Prophet are referred to as *Shareef*, while the Arabs, Iranians and Asians use the name *Seyyed* (literal meaning of "mister" or "master") for the progeny of the Prophet through the sons of Ali and Fatima. In Iran and the Subcontinent, as in North Africa, much respect and attention is given to these lineages and the Seyyeds have exercised considerable influence on the culture of the people.

The message of Islam was carried by Seyyeds, Sufis and traders, as well as by conquest. Sufis spread Islam deliberately and accidentally. Sometimes they would be fleeing from despotic rulers; other times the message was transmitted through trading, exemplary conduct, marriage or fellowship. Examples of those fleeing authority are Sitt Nafisa, who is buried in Cairo, 'Abd al Rahman of Cordova and Sidi Idris in Morocco.

Marriage between Seyyed families and traders or the ruling establishment has been common throughout the Muslim world. These marriages bestow religious respect upon a "worldly" family and give support and honour to the Seyyeds.

In Morocco, there is a government department that keeps a registry and records of *ashrafs*' genealogy and lineage. The records and archives kept in this department go back many generations and include tens of thousands alive today. The department was housed in a modern building, close to the royal palace. King Hassan II, arranged for a few thousand young *ashrafs* to marry at the same time as his son, Mohammad V, the present King of Morocco. The cohesiveness of Morocco's religious authority has been traditionally based on the public's respect for the *ashrafs* and their knowledge and application of the Way of Muhammad.

Estimates of Seyyeds or *ashrafs* alive at the end of the 20th century vary from 20 to 50 million. In the Shiite world they are distinguished by wearing black turbans as opposed to white. In North Africa, green turbans prevail.

At the time of my visit to these archives, the director of the department in those days, Jafar Ibn 'Ajiba, whom the king had appointed, had a great knowledge about the lives of *ashrafs*, dead and alive. I asked him what he considered the most common characteristic to be found amongst them, both in historical times and the present. He replied that it was dedicated service to anybody in need, according to the Prophetic teaching and conduct. The selflessness, generosity and kindness of some of these saintly beings are sometimes publicly known, but more often enacted quietly. The Quran warns not to cancel the goodness of a generous deed by boasting. Of course, there have been some rascals over the ages of sharifian descent, but generally there is a strong accountability and tradition of service.

It is generally considered that Abu Madyan Shuayb (519–94 AH/1126–98 CE) from Seville, also known as Bu Madyan, was the first influential Sufi master in the Maghrib. Rulers throughout the Muslim world have often regarded Sufis with apprehension, mainly because their teachings touch the hearts of the masses and can inspire popular movements against the rulers. Abu Madyan's influence was such that he was summoned to the Almohad Court in Marrakech to be questioned about his teachings. He died on his way there. Ibn Tumart, the founder of the Almohad movement, had been influenced by the great Sufi scholar, al-Ghazzali (d. 1111 CE), but as his movement expanded it lost its original spark of Sufi influence. The later rulers came to fear the impact of Sufi teachings on the masses. Most rulers wanted religion to subdue the masses and Sufis were on the path of liberation from the self and worldly attachments. This teaching cannot be popular with kings, who desire control of the population, often at the cost of justice and human compassion.

> *True joy in this life is by companionship for the devotees, for they are the true masters and real rulers and then only witness faults within yourself because only by such insights will you be redeemed and realize that the path is based on insight and grooming the character. These companions are whom I love and I am honoured by their proximity. They are the ones wherever they go is like fresh air and clean rain.*
>
> *Abu Madyan Shuaib*

One of the greatest of the spiritual heirs of Abu Madyan was Abd as-Salaam Ibn Mashish (1140–1227 CE). My heart was deeply drawn to this unconventional being and I visited his shrine on two occasions. He reminded me in some way of Shams-i-Tabriz. Ibn Mashish's celebrated eulogy on the Prophet, *As-Salat al-Mashishiyya*, reputed to have been revealed to him while in mystic communion with the Prophet, resonated deeply with me and increased my determination to visit his shrine. My favourite line from it is, "Oh God, rescue me from the mire of (belief) in unity and drown me fully in the ocean of Oneness so none of me is left." This plea can be taken as a signpost between self and soul, taking the personal limited lake of the mind to the ocean of soul and spirit. The Sufis have always tried to demonstrate the truth of human make-up – self and soul!

After he received *idhn* from Abu Madyan Shuayb, Ibn Mashish dedicated his life to encouraging the population around him to practice and live Islam. Many of the Berbers in that area were still adhering to heathen practices, such as black magic. Legend says that his death in 622 CE was instigated by a local magician, Abu Tawajin, who claimed he was a prophet. One day some *jinn* controlled by Abu Tawajin were late in answering his call. They told him that they had been trying to harass a man praying on a mountain side but when they came close a great light radiated from him and they had burst into flames. The magician was so jealous of Ibn Mashish's light that he sent a band of men to murder him. One story relates that Ibn Mashish had a vision of what was going to happen. He spent the whole night in prayer and when his murderer came to his room, Ibn Mashish handed over his own sharpened knife and asked that it be used to cut his throat. The assassins all perished after they had killed the master, as a dense fog descended and they fell into a chasm in the mountain. When the local authorities heard of Ibn Mashish's death, the magician was killed by their soldiers.

Ibn Mashish's teachings emphasized the importance of fidelity to the *deen*, advocated peace and condemned militancy and aggression instigated under the pretence of religious objectives. He said, "Let your hearts get attached to the Creator, rather than the concerns of the creation, and purify them of doubt and vain thoughts with the Water of Certainty."[93]

He was known to have had only one pupil and that pupil was Abu'l-Hasan ash-Shadhili, one of the outstanding Sufis of all time. My acceptance of Ibn Mashish's position as first of the great saints of the Maghreb increased the intensity of my pilgrimage, while the starkness of the location of his final resting place accentuated the aura of saintliness that emanated from it.

The shrine of Ibn Mashish is perched right on top of one of the mountains in the Rif Range in northwestern Morocco. From ancient times this area was forested, mostly with cork trees. Until the 1970s, access was along a narrow, precarious path that would take the best part of two days of walking and half a day's mule ride from the city of Chaouen.

On my first visit in 1987, there was a gravel road. We started in the early morning. After an easy start with a gentle climb, we hit our first obstacle of the day, only to be followed by near disaster. This part of the Atlas Mountains is subject to continuous winds, and when they change direction strange local weather patterns set in. The fog and mist thickened, slushy snow melted as it reached the ground and the rented Fiat started to slide. My companion and I had convinced ourselves that it was the spirit of Ibn Mashish that had called us to visit his shrine, so we continued our precarious climb in the face of a protesting car and a near 3,000ft drop on our left-hand side. We also knew the tradition that pilgrims to Ibn Mashish's shrine are always confronted by difficulties and obstacles.

We were near to the top when we saw a figure coming out of the thick fog, gesturing for us to stop. Up until this point we had seen no sign of any life on the road. By now it was snowing heavily and the car was sliding in fresh snow. The man was clad only in a thin shirt, which was dripping with snow. As we unwound the window, he asked for a cigarette. He seemed surprised when we had none. We were non-smokers and disapproved of smoking.

The man was not impressed with this negative response and shook his head with an air of bemused puzzlement. From there on the car was only able to move backwards. So we had no option other than to return the way we had come. This forced us to follow another route, which was much longer but had a gentler incline and was less treacherous. In fact, these two roads joined 50 yards along from where we had stopped, but we did not know this at the time.

Six hours later, utterly exhausted, cold and wet, we had circled back to the same spot again. The man was still standing there with the same bemused smile on his face. We were shocked and invited him to ride with us for the remaining short distance.

As he entered the car, he informed us that his home is the shrine and he cannot live away from Moulay Abdul Salaam. He again asked for a cigarette and advised us to make sure that we carried cigarettes with us in the car in future. Once again my companion and I expressed our disapproval of tobacco. He only shook his head in surprise.

The simple mausoleum of Ibn Mashish is like an eagle's eyrie. The entrance is some 3,000ft high with a spectacular vertical drop to the valley below. The entire ground is carpeted with a thick cushion of cork. There were all kinds of people milling around: devoted believers, bedraggled beggars, children, old women, people reciting Quran, unemployed youngsters, donkeys, goats and a few mangy dogs.

We paid homage to the *wali* and performed our prayers. Just as we were leaving, we saw our friend, the smoker, surrounded by a gang of hangers-on.

The snow had stopped falling but the wind was bitterly cold. As I shivered through my cashmere sweater, the smoker's gentle eyes kept their gaze on me while totally oblivious to all around him. I gave him a fistful of paper money and asked him to buy himself some clothes. He looked at the notes in the palm of his hand, as though he neither recognized their meaning or value, nor indeed his need for clothes. I requested him to put the money in his pocket, as I was sure the human vultures around him would grab them away.

If it was not for our desert crossing three days later, I would probably have forgotten this incident. As it was, we were driving on a sandy, desert road paved with shingles when we were overtaken by an army lorry, which sprayed us with clusters of sharp stones as it sped by. Within minutes, steam poured out of the engine and we stopped, only to discover that the small stones had made holes in the radiator. Water as well as steam was pouring out. We had to wait by the side of the road for the next car to come along. It was a long wait.

When the driver of the passing car inspected the radiator, he smiled at us and said that the cure was cigarettes. We were puzzled and told him that we had none. He went to his car and brought out a pack. He then broke half a dozen cigarettes into a container of water and let it stand for a few minutes before pouring it into the radiator. The driver explained that dry tobacco leaves expand in water and as they circulate around the radiator they plug the holes. The next 30 miles to the nearest town was only made possible courtesy of the cigarettes. My companion and I laughed as we remembered the knowing smile of the *majdhub* (ecstatic) at Ibn Mashish, when he insisted we should carry cigarettes with us.

AS-SALAT AL MASHISHIYYA

In the name of Allah, the Benevolent, the Compassionate
O Allah shower blessings on him, from whom the secrets emerge,
And from whom stream forth the lights,
And in whom the realities are contained,
And in whom descended the totality of the Adamic knowledges, and all creatures find themselves in utter bewilderment, and comprehension is altogether rendered unto naught before him.
None of us could attain his station in the past, nor will be able to in future.
The gardens of the Spiritual Kingdom blossom ornately with the resplendence of his beauty

*And the reservoirs of the World of Dominion overflow with
the emanation of his lights.
There is nothing that is not existentially connected to him;
If there were no intermediate, that, which is linked to it
— as it has been said —
Would cease to exist.
A Blessing becoming of You, from You to him — to which
he is entitled.
O Allah he surely is Your gathered Secret, indicating You,
And Your greatest Veil, established before You.
O Allah attach me to his kinship, and realize my nature
through his noble descent,
And grant me true cognizance of him, to be safe by it from
the springs of ignorance,
And make me drink by it from the springs of Grace,
And carry me on his path to Your Presence, bounded by
Your Support,
And hurl at me that, which is false, and grant me to rout it,
And plunge me into the seas of Only-ness, and pull me out
of the quagmire of rationalized unification,
And drown me in the source of the one singular ocean,
Until I neither see, nor hear, nor find, nor sense, except by it.
O Allah let the Great Veil be the life of my spirit,
And let his soul be the secret of my reality,
And let his reality assimilate the realms of my being,
Through the realization of the First Truth.
O First! O Last! O Manifest! O Hidden!
Listen to my call as You listened to the call of your bondman
Zachariah
And help me by Your Self for You, and support me by Your
Self for You
And join me to You, and sever me from other than You.
Allah — Allah — Allah!* [94]

Abd as-Salaam ibn Mashish

This beautiful prayer has been shortened in more recent years to suit the needs of contemporary devotees.

If you see your nafs dominating you,
And it leads you into the fire of desires,
Then avert its desires with the prayer, persisting in it,
And especially with the Dalail al-Khayrat
Hold fast to the Dalail al-Khayrat,
And calling to its recitation and you will obtain what you
wish.
The radiance of lights shines by it,
O brother, leaving it is not proper.[95]

Muhammad al-Jazuli

The devotional focus on the Prophet Muhammad, with expressions of love and veneration for him, evolved into an important aspect of Muslim life with another North African master, Abu Abdullah Muhammad ibn Sulayman al-Jazuli (d. 869 AH/1465 CE or 875 AH/1470 CE), a Berber of sharifian descent from the Sus region of southern Morocco. He followed the Shadhili *tariqa* and was the author of *Dalail al-Khayrat* (*Proof of the Blessings*). Al-Jazuli lived for a time in Madina and recited *Dalail al-Khayrat* twice daily at the Prophet's grave. His intense outpouring of love for the Prophet influenced many branches of North African Sufism in his lifetime and spread throughout the Muslim world. Embellished manuscripts were given as gifts, pilgrims wore it on their way to *Hajj* and its popularity has remained to this day.

Al-Jazuli was supposedly poisoned by the Governor of Asfi, a supporter of the Marinid dynasty, who was concerned about his charismatic influence on the populace. Al-Jazuli's movement became politicized after his death by his pupil, al-Sayyaf, who led rebellions in revenge for his master's murder against the Marinids and later Wattasids. He was also active in battles against the Portuguese in the coastal areas. Al-Sayyaf carried al-Jazuli's remains with him everywhere, even into battle. Thus, al-Jazuli was only buried in Afughal in the Haha district, when al-Sayyaf died around 1485 CE. By that time the Sadiyans, a new dynasty, had arisen who were supported in their climb to power by the successors of al-Jazuli. The Sadiyans, as *shareefs*, favoured the Jazuliyyah, who taught an orthodox Sufism that focused on veneration of the Prophet. One of the first acts of the Sadiyan ruler, Ahmad al-Araj, was to bury his father next to al-Jazuli. Once Ahmed had conquered Marrakech, he moved al-Jazuli and his father's body there. Just as the Mughals took the Chishtis as their patron saints, the Sadiyans adopted the heirs of al-Jazuli as the spiritual props for their dynasty.

Legend says that Imam al-Jazuli was late for his morning prayers and couldn't find any pure water to perform *wudu*. As he was looking he encountered a young girl who expressed surprise that he could not find any pure water. The girl spat into a well, which then overflowed with pure water. The imam was able to do his ablutions. He asked her how she had achieved such a high spiritual station. The girl said it was by "making constant prayer for God to bless the best of creation by the number of breaths and heartbeats".

This encounter inspired al-Jazuli to compose *Dalail al-Khayrat*, asking for blessings on the Prophet Muhammad.

Today al-Jazuli is known as one of the seven saints of Marrakech. The visitor is supposed to walk in a certain order from shrine to shrine to pay their respects. Not all of these saints were originally from Marrakech but the Sultan Moulay Ismail ibn Sharif in the 17th century ordered that their remains be placed in the old city to bring prestige to Marrakech. Apart from al-Jazuli's tomb, there is Sidi Abdul Aziz, who was the spiritual successor of al-Jazuli, and Sidi Abdullah al-Ghazwani, the successor of Sidi Abdul Aziz. These three saints belong to the Shadhili-Jazuli Sufi order. Sidi Bel Abbas al-Sabti has the largest and most popular *zawiya*; he was known for his care of the poor and sick. Qadi Iyad was a Maliki scholar who wrote *al-Shifa* (*The Cure by Means of Expounding the Rights of the Chosen One*) on the sublime nature of the Prophet and the duties his followers have toward him. Sidi Youssef bin Ali was a leper, renowned as a teacher and preacher. Sidi al-Suhayll, the last of the seven saints, was originally from Andalusia and is known for his commentary on Ibn Hisham's *Seerah*. In 2005, seven towers were erected to honour each of these seven saints and the shrines are an important feature on Morocco's map of religious tourism.[96]

Some years before the towers were built, I had been on this one day of intense shrine visitation. My guide was an Italian convert, who called on me early in the morning at my hotel and enthusiastically led me to the seven shrines with erudite descriptions and influences of the buried saints. I lingered especially long at the al-Jazuli tomb and mosque. The atmosphere was very sweet and pleasant and there were several groups reciting melodiously *Dalail al-Khayrat*. At the end of the tour, my companion took me to his beautiful home, where I was plied with refreshments and more stories about the saints of Marrakech.

> *Peace be upon a grave which is visited from afar.*
> *Peace be upon the Rawda where Muhammad is.*
> *Peace be upon the one who visited his Lord in the night and*
> *reached the desire in every aim.*
> *Peace be upon the one who said to the lizard, "Who am I?"*
> *And it replied, "The Messenger of Allah. You are*
> *Muhammad."*
> *Peace be upon the one who is buried in a good land*
> *And who the All-Merciful singled out for excellence and glory.*[97]
>
> Muhammad al-Jazuli

> *Muhammad is the most honoured of all people and is the best*
> *that has ever walked on feet. He is the being of honour and*
> *the perfect wisdom for his light is from before time. He is the*
> *glory and joy in this life for the All Merciful brought him out*
> *of generosity.*[98]
>
> Imam al-Busiri

Shaykh al-Jazuli was following in the footsteps of the earlier Imam al-Busiri (608–95 AH/1212–96 CE), whose "Qasidat al-Burda" ("Poem of the Mantle") in praise of the Prophet is recited all over the Muslim world, particularly on the occasion of the birthday of the Prophet. Al-Busiri was a Sanhaji Berber and followed the Shadhili order. He lived in Egypt, where he wrote poetry under the patronage of the Vizier, Ibn Hinna.

Al-Busiri was inspired to write this hymn before asking the Prophet's intercession to cure his paralysis, which had left him bedridden following a stroke. After intense supplications to the Prophet, he slept. In his dream, he saw the Prophet wipe his face and cover him with his *burda* (mantle). When he woke up he could walk again.

Al-Busiri wrote that after his miraculous recovery he left his house and met a Sufi on his way. The Sufi asked for the poem he had written in praise of the Prophet. As al-Busiri had written several verses of this nature he asked which one and was told, "The one you wrote when you were sick." The Sufi then recited the first verse unprompted and told al-Busiri that he had heard the poem being recited in front of the Prophet in a dream he had had the previous night. The Prophet was pleased with the invocation and covered the person who sang it with his mantle.

Verses from "al-Burda" have been used as amulets up to the present day. It has been engraved on the walls of many mosques and shrines, including the poet's own tomb in Alexandria and on the walls of the Prophet's mosque in Madina, where it remained for centuries until the *Wahhabis* erased it, leaving only one line:

> He is the beloved whose intercession is hoped for as arms
> against a host of relentless calamities.

Al-Busiri's "al-Burda" is one of earliest examples of stylized praises on the Prophet. The veneration given by Christians to Jesus must also have encouraged celebrations for the Prophet's birthday. It has also been suggested that "The celebration of the Prophet's birthday seems, at least in part, to be a compensation for the suppression of Alid demonstrations after the destruction of Shiite regimes."[99] It was certainly not a practice in the earlier years of Islam, but Ibn Jubair (travels between 1183 and 1185 CE) refers to it in his travelogue as an established ritual. During the peak period of Ottoman rule during the 16th and 17th centuries, even more elaborate recitations and festivities began to take place to mark the event.

When He alienates you from His creation, know that He wants to open for you the door of intimacy with Him.[100]

Ibn 'Ata' Allah

The heart can only have one direction at a time. If it is attracted or attached to creation then it is distracted from the Creator. The heart reflects what it faces. With creation there is both pleasure and displeasure, change and uncertainty. With Allah there is constant solace, peace and contentment. Fleeing from creation to the Creator is the first major move for the fortunate seeker of truth.

Abu'l-Hasan ash-Shadhili is one of the key figures in the history of Sufism. As the founder of the Shadhili order, from which the Shadhili-Darqawis and many other orders come, his impact has been immense. The four masters whose writings influenced me the most, Ibn 'Ata' Allah, Ahmed al-Zarruq, Sidi Ali al-Jamal and Ibn al-'Ajiba, were all connected to his *silsila*. Shaykh Abu'l-Hasan's biography, written by 'Abd al-Nur al-Imrani, who had interviewed pupils of Shaykh Shadhili, shows that as a young man he had been torn between the life of an ascetic, living in the wilds, and studying in an urban environment under the tutelage of religious scholars. When he heard about a *wali* living in isolation on the mountain, Jabal al-Alam in the north of Morocco, he decided to visit him. As he reached Ibn Mashish's cave, he heard a voice from within, reciting,

O God, there are people who ask You to give them power over your creatures, and You give them that. But I, O God, beg You to turn Your creatures from me so that I may have no refuge except in You.[101]

These words resonate with the future Shadhili teachings on the importance of total God-centeredness and inner withdrawal from creation in times of both difficulty and ease.

Shaykh Abu'l-Hasan's prescription for his pupils was to

Arm yourself with ritual purification, fasting, prayer, dhikr, reciting the Quran and renouncing all claims to strength and power and you will be safe. Should you be overwhelmed take faith as your fortress, if you are overcome surrender the affair to God. Remain steadfast with divine unity [tawhid], faith, and the love of God. Drown the mundane world in the ocean of Tawhid before it drowns you.[102]

After his brief stay with Ibn Mashish, Shaykh Abu'l-Hasan settled in Tunisia, where he gained a reputation as a great master. He emphasized the importance of the pupil's complete submission to the authority of his spiritual master. The local *'ulama* there were hostile to his teachings and eventually he was forced to leave for Egypt. He died on his way to *Hajj* in 1258 CE and is buried on the old pilgrims' route near the Red Sea. The *tariqa* which was called after him, was founded in Egypt after his death but came back to the Maghrib. It is considered to be the forefather of many great Sufi movements, including the Shadhili-Darqawi. The Shadhili path is balanced between outer sobriety, service, Prophetically based conduct, and inner intoxication with divine presence and guidance.

Shaykh Abu'l-Hasan's teachings have inspired seekers through the centuries, fulfilling his promise to the pupils of the future: "I have companions born of men and women that have not yet been created. Their spirits have already made the pact with me."[103]

The lights of the sages precede their words. Thus, wherever illumination occurs, expression arrives.[104]

Ibn 'Ata' Allah

Men of wisdom have transcended the veils of the self and thus their lights are reflections from Him through their purified hearts. The illumined ones therefore speak from their hearts and hence the power and effectiveness of their expressions. What is transmitted from a pure heart will resonate in other hearts.

Sufism is a science by means of which you learn how to behave in order to be in the presence of the ever-present Lord through purifying your inner being and sweetening it with good actions. The path of Sufism begins as a science, its middle is actions and its end is divine gifts.

Ahmad ibn 'Ajiba

Shaykh Ahmad Ibn 'Ajiba (1160/61–1224 AH/1747/48–1809 CE) was a Shadhili-Darqawi shaykh who wrote over 30 Islamic Sufi books. He was born in a village near Tetouan to a sharifian family, who originated from an Andalusian mountain village called Ayn al-Ruman ("the Source of Pomegranates"). He showed from an early age an aptitude for the religious sciences and became a traditional *'alim*. His orientation changed when he read *The Hikam* of Ibn 'Ata' Allah with the commentary by Ibn Abbad al Rundi (d. 792 AH/1390 CE). The latter had been largely instrumental in the spread of the Shadhili teachings in Morocco.

I came across Ibn 'Ajiba through his commentary on *The Hikam*, which I found in an old bookshop in Marrakech. It made such a profound impression on me that I bought up every copy I could find to give to friends. Later I was to translate and comment on *The Hikam* myself.

On reading the following lines written by Ibn 'Ajiba, I knew he was enlightened due to his total reliance to *Haqq* and the Divine decree:

> *Then I owned myself and became a slave, my life was exalted and I lived in glorious contentment and I owned my land by generosity of my Lord and that is why I left everything else to be in my contentment.*

I have come to realize that if you want inner enrichment you must take on the attributes of impoverishment; if you want openings of the higher horizon you must accept restriction, loss of personal will or power, and then you will taste glory. If it is the sacred precinct you are after, disappear from anything else and you will perceive Truth within everything that exists. If you always bear in mind that there are two realms, earthly and heavenly, you will have clarity in whatever you look at and you will witness that the great attributes of God are like the fabric that holds the universe.

Ibn 'Ajiba described the impact *The Hikam* had on him:

> *After this reading, I abandoned exoteric knowledge and dedicated myself to devotional practice, to the remembrance of God, and to the invocation of blessings upon God's Messenger. Then I felt a desire to practice retreat and I began to detest the world and its denizens: when someone approached me, I fled...[105]*

Although he wanted at this time to follow the Sufi path, a vision at the tomb of Sidi Talha, a *wali* of Tetouan, encouraged him to continue with his studies of the exoteric sciences. A decade later, when he was in his late 40s, he met the great Moroccan Sufi master, Moulay al-'Arabi al-Darqawi, who entrusted Ibn 'Ajiba's spiritual training to one of his closest *khalifas*, Sidi Muhammad al-Buzidi.

> *The Sufi is the one who is not saddened when he lacks something, great or small.[106]*
>
> *Moulay al-'Arabi al-Darqawi*

Shaykh al-Darqawi was born near Fez in 1130 CE to a sharifian family. His early studies were with Islamic scholars of law but when he wanted to find a spiritual guide he went to the shrine of Moulay Idris in Fez. There he settled down to recite Quran and pray in the hope of gaining direction to the right master. After 60 recitations, he left the shrine in despair, as he had not received any sign. His eyes were red with weeping and in this state he encountered a *shareef*, Sayyidi Hamid, who asked him what was wrong. On hearing of his search for a teacher, Sayyidi Hamid directed him to Sidi Ali al-Jamal (d. 1194 CE), a hidden Shadhili master. It is reported that upon meeting Sidi Ali, Shaykh al-Darqawi said, "O, master, I have been looking for a shaykh for a long time." Sidi Ali al-Jamal replied, "And I have been looking for a sincere follower for a very long time." Shaykh al-Darqawi is said to have been his only really devoted follower, but from him hundreds of people of knowledge sprung.

> *Know that there is nothing more beautiful than the assemblies of the fuqara and those who are seeking the face of Allah. Whoever considers himself independent is at a loss. Allah guides those who are guided by Him. Those who are content with themselves have no entitlement to increase. Whenever increase is absent, decrease appears.*
>
> *Sidi Ali al-Jamal*

Sidi Ali al-Jamal's book, whose original Arabic title translates as *'Advice to the Seeker on the Path of Asceticism'* or *'Beautiful Rubies in Understanding the Meanings of Man'*, was a book I loved and benefitted from. It was particularly helpful for understanding the meeting of opposites in creation, but the style of writing is free-flowing and repetitive, with long paragraphs and sentences covering several ideas in a charmingly quaint fashion. Its only English translation was difficult for a contemporary seeker to understand. Shaykh Hosam Raouf and I worked on an abridged translation, from a photocopy of a handwritten version of the book that came down through the family of Shaykh Ibn 'Ajiba, to make the teachings more accessible. Shaykh Mustafa al-Basir, a Darqawi shaykh, told me that Sidi Ali al-Jamal had written a few pages at a time and dropped them in the courtyard of his house. It was Shaykh al-Darqawi who collected the papers and put them together in the form of a book.

> *Would that You were sweet*
> *While this life is bitter.*
> *Would that You were pleased while people are angry,*
> *Would that what is between You and me*
> *Were filled and flourishing, and that*
> *What is between me and the world were a ruin.*
> *If Your love proves true,*
> *Then all is easy, and all which is on earth is earth.[107]*
>
> *Sidi Ali al-Jamal*

Shaykh al-Darqawi was to refer to himself as the Sufi reformer of his age. His emphasis on asceticism and the importance of poverty, combined with his criticism of the contemporary Sufi orders' involvement with worldly matters, laid him open to attack from the Sultan, Moulay Suleman, and the traditional *'ulama* of Morocco. His followers embraced the life of the wandering *dervish*, wore patched clothing and carried large prayer beads. They also used musical instruments and songs to enhance *dhikr* and access states of transcendence. The new order was called Shadhili-Darqawi and the teachings spread rapidly through the urban poor and the rural areas. Inevitably there were protests about reprehensible innovations from the authorities.

The Sultan closed the Darqawi *zawiya* in Tetouan and had Ibn 'Ajiba, by then its *muqaddam* (senior Sufi), and other *fuqara* temporarily imprisoned. One of the charges against them was allowing women to attend *dhikr*, albeit in a separate room! However, the movement's impact amongst both lowland and mountain Berbers and in western Algeria forced Moulay Sulayman to reduce his opposition.

Shaykh al-Darqawi spent his last years in a mountain village north of Fez. He died when he was about 80 in 1823. His shrine is popular with visitors and there is an annual festival there every year, celebrating his earthly departure.

*There is a knowledge beyond written transmission which is
finer than the ultimate perception of sound intellects.
Books do not contain the cure of the hearts.
Hearts are cured by the company of masters of hearts.
The knowledge of books is a residue from the knowledge of
hearts.
It is impossible that it be contained by books.
The knowledge of books is an indication of the knowledge of
hearts.
None contains what the hearts contain except for the Knower
of the Unseen worlds.
Man is helped by books while he does not see the Beloved
When he sees the Beloved, books are helped by him.*

Moulay al-'Arabi al-Darqawi

Sidi Muhammad al-Buzidi prescribed that Ibn 'Ajiba put on a patched cloak, beg at the entrance of the mosque and sweep the market place. He had been a respected *'alim* but in his new guise he was ignored by passing members of that fraternity. The master was wearing away any sense of pride or arrogance Ibn 'Ajiba might have had. Soon Ibn 'Ajiba was walking the mountain roads of Morocco barefoot with other members of the Darqawi order, calling villagers to join the brotherhood.

There is a story told in this context of an early 20th-century Moroccan *wali*, who had a considerable following. One day the Sultan visited his town and went to the local baths. The *wali* came and took the Sultan's gold embroidered brocade robe and wore it in the bazaar. There was a huge hue and cry when the theft was discovered. When the *wali* was brought before the Sultan, the latter expressed his astonishment at the theft, saying he would have gifted it to the *wali*, if he had asked. The *wali* confided in the Sultan that he needed to lose his reputation. His fame and popularity was such that he was not left in peace for his prayers and meditation. The people who had been running toward him were now running away!

After his brief imprisonment, when the Sultan became concerned that

Darqawi teachings might negatively impact on his control over his kingdom, Sidi Muhammad sent him to travel for five years in other areas of Morocco. He instructed Ibn 'Ajiba to write Sufi commentaries on *The Hikam* of Ibn 'Ata' Allah, the *Khamriyya* of Ibn al-Farid and the *Tasliyya* of Ibn Mashish. Any one of these great Sufi transformative elixirs could produce the desired spiritual gold for the serious follower.

It was Ibn 'Ajiba's commentary on the Quran, *Al-Bahr al-Madid Fi Tafseer Al-Quran Al-Majeed* (*The Vast Ocean in Expounding upon the Glorious Quran*), written during the last part of his life, that most interested me out of his works. This was also written at the instruction of his teacher. Shaykh al-Buzidi had told him to write a comprehensive commentary on the Quran to include historical aspects of the revelations, as well as linguistic and grammatical expositions, and to explore the different levels of meaning with reference to other commentators. Ibn 'Ajiba found the task very daunting and doubted whether he was up to it. His teacher indicated that he should move to an area southeast of Tangier, which was quite wild at that time and populated by unruly Berbers.

He had enormous difficulty in settling because the tribes there were often engaged in raiding and had little interest in religious matters. After a few years, people from near and far came to recognize his qualities and the extent to which his presence had helped to bring about a higher quality of life. *Al-Bahr al-Madid* was completed after about seven years work, three years before the shaykh's death. It is remarkable that a work of this complexity, which reflects on both the outer and inner meanings of the Quran, should have been composed at such a difficult period in the life of the shaykh. Northern Morocco suffered from outbreaks of plague during these years and Ibn 'Ajiba lost most of his family to the pestilence. His commitment to Truth was clearly such that no outer disturbances diverted him from his spiritual calling.

Before Ibn 'Ajiba's death, considerable tracts of land and settlements were placed at his disposal and the tradition of good neighbourliness and good human contact pervaded the whole area. He is buried in a beautiful little white shrine on the top of one of the hills in the village of Djimmij, sloping away to the valley below. There is a branch of the Shadhiliyya-Darqawiyya Sufi line that is named after him, al-Tariqa al-Darqawiyya al-'Ajibiyya, and every August hundreds of followers of this path gather together for the yearly *mawsim* (annual gathering commemorating a *wali*'s death).

Ibn 'Ajiba endeavoured to separate the classical commentary from the Sufi interpretation, but because of his own state at the time of writing, about a fifth of it focuses on the inner meaning. I had enjoyed the similarity between Ibn 'Ajiba's work and that of the earlier Persian Sufi, Ruzbihan al-Baqli (d. 606 AH/1209 CE), whose Quranic commentary, *Ara'is al-Bayan*, had been one of my favourites. Recently it has been discovered that one of the sources Ibn 'Ajiba quoted for his work was Ruzbihan, although another name, probably that of a scribe or manuscript owner, had been attributed to it. The *isharat* or signs of Ibn 'Ajiba's commentary is to do with inner transformation and reflects the similar lights of the work of Ruzbihan.

From Ibn 'Ajiba's introduction to *Al-Bahr al-Madid*:

> *Of all the religious sciences, the science of tafsir is the greatest and the most excellent object of thought and understanding. None, however, should approach this vast undertaking other than an accomplished scholar who has achieved a profound knowledge of the exoteric sciences of the religion and has then directed thought and meditations toward the Qur'an's beautiful meanings. In other words, to explain the Qur'an, one must first have mastered, under the tutelage of the learned, the Arabic language, its morphology, semantics, and rhetoric, then jurisprudence [fiqh] and hadith. If one then becomes immersed in the science of Sufism and attains therein a genuine spiritual taste [dhawq], then state, and then station through companionship with experienced people of the Way (it is permissible to mention as well the Qur'an's inner meanings), but if not, then it is better to remain silent concerning them and limit oneself to the exoteric dimensions.*[108]

When my friend Bashir Uthman visited America, he had asked me to make available Ibn 'Ajiba's commentary. In my search for a complete manuscript of *Al-Bahr al-Madid*, I met in Tangier Abdul Qadir Qassimi, one of the shaykh's descendants, and we became good friends. Abdul Qadir found several old manuscripts, including a couple of handwritten ones, of this commentary on the Quran. There was one full set in the king's archives, one with the descendants of Ibn 'Ajiba, and another in a famous private library. Work was started to produce a printable commentary but after a year we discovered that a well-researched edition was about to be published in Beirut, so our edition was never completed. I acquired photocopies of several thousand pages of handwritten commentary of Ibn 'Ajiba.

During a visit to Morocco in the late 1980s, I met through Abdul Qadir Qassimi the then living shaykh also named Ibn 'Ajiba and his three other brothers, who were all prominent and well-respected scholars and jurists in their own right. The shaykh was not the oldest of the brothers, but was considered to be the enlightened one amongst them.

The shaykh's house and *zawiya* was about an hour's drive from Tangier toward the southeast, some 15 kilometres south of the sea. Close to the *zawiya* there were several hills and clumps of cactus plants in full bloom and bearing fruit. Shaykh Ibn 'Ajiba's compound was a few acres of land on high ground, fenced by impenetrable cactus plants except for one main entrance. The spacious courtyard was surrounded by several mud-brick buildings. They included one large hall which acted as a reception area and was located next to a *zawiya* on the right-hand side of the main entrance. From another building I could hear young voices reciting *Surat Yaseen*.

Shaykh Ibn 'Ajiba was waiting in the main reception area, where his frail body was reclining in one corner on the cushioned floor. With his sharp eyes and kindly gestures he welcomed us and offered the customary sugared mint tea. I expressed my personal indebtedness to his ancestor's Quranic commentary and asked his personal permission and blessing for my attempts to publish it. He expressed blessings without hesitation.

Grace seemed to engulf him and his presence was comforting. As the day progressed there were numerous visitors from different parts of Europe, especially Spain and Moroccans who were working abroad.

Then came a new visitor: a wealthy merchant from Saudi Arabia who had brought his disturbed daughter whom he had taken to America and elsewhere without achieving a cure. He had already been to visit the shaykh a few days earlier. The shaykh turned quietly to me and said, "Some people think they can bribe God and carry on the way they are. God wants to show this family His power but they cannot acknowledge it and submit to His will. They look everywhere except at Allah." He turned to Abdul Qadir and said, "The Almighty catches us where it hurts most so that we take notice." Then he quoted a verse of the Quran that says that most men are in denial.

As we were leaving in the late afternoon, I could hear the cheerful voices of the young resident students chanting *dhikr*. As the car was hurtling down the hill, there were a few children on the side of the road selling cactus fruit from a basket. I questioned them as to how they pick them without being pricked. The little girl picked up the thorny fruit in one hand, rubbed it in the palm of her other hand and gave it to me. Her beautiful brown eyes told me that the small thorns simply fall off when rubbed in her rough hands.

The shaykh's eldest brother had a house on a slope which went all the way down to the Atlantic with a view of Gibraltar. On a few acres of land he had cultivated a lush orchard of the best of figs, pomegranates, grapes and a wide variety of seasonal vegetables and herbs. On the same land there was a mosque near the entrance and a well-attended Quran school. His little reception room was stacked with books, most of them in manuscript form.

That evening I asked the eldest brother of the shaykh, who was in his own right an acknowledged scholar, teacher and theologian, as to why the younger brother was the shaykh. He said it was clear that the shaykh was more illumined than all of them, as his station was that of a transformed being. Age and other considerations were secondary. He also emphasized to me the importance of an enlightened teacher, if the seeker is to progress consistently and be awakened to truth.

> *I heard the master Abu Ali say, "The tree that grows by itself without a gardener puts forth leaves, but it does not bear fruit. Similar is the disciple who has no master from whom he can learn his path, one breath at a time. He remains a worshipper of his own desire and does not attain success."[109]*
>
> *Abu al-Qasim al-Qushayri*

> *When the veil was removed, revealing her beauty all reason crumbled into confusion and my heart emptied with passion causing my entire being to be on fire. How can anyone keep such a secret when the mere mention of the Beloved makes you fly and if only they understand the power of the love of Layla they will be all-forgiving and it is not the love of the lovers that has overwhelmed my heart, it is the love of the in-dweller.*
>
> *Muhammad al-Harraq*

On my first trip to Morocco in 1979, I visited the *zawiya* and tomb of Shaykh Muhammad al-Harraq al-'Alami in Tetouan. It was attached to one of the old gates of the town, where the piles of charcoal and bunches of green fodder for goats for sale looked exactly as we would have seen them in Shaykh al-Harraq's time.

Shaykh al-Harraq (1772–1845 CE) was a pupil of Shaykh al-'Arabi al-Darqawi and a younger contemporary of Ibn 'Ajiba. He was of Andalusian origin and is remembered as a great scholar who combined depth in *shari'a* with Sufism, as well as being a sublime poet of *Haqq*. *Harraq* means "he who sets others on flame", for without passion for truth the spiritual journey may be sidetracked. The Arabic word *fu'ad* (innermost of the heart) comes from the root "to burn and perish". Passion fuels the path to Reality. Shaykh al-Harraq wrote three *diwans* of ecstatic poetry which are sung to this day at many Sufi gatherings, especially in North Africa. Yet, in his lifetime the shaykh's knowledge of *shari'a* protected him from criticism from the religious authorities. A few years later, I found Sultan Bahu of the Punjab was the Indian version of al-Harraq: the parallels in flavour were striking as both were given to ecstatic song and both also used a number of musical instruments to encourage inner spiritual zest.

The *zawiya* was on top of one of the entrance gates of the old city and overlooked a large graveyard. We climbed up the steep steps that led to the entrance, an old man, who was the *muqaddam* of the *zawiya*, met us there and escorted us to the tomb, where he made a supplication for us. There was an intense atmosphere of joyfulness emanating from the shrine. The *muqaddam* invited us to come back for sunset prayers that evening, when there would be a usual weekly gathering for *dhikr*, accompanied by violin and a few other musical instruments. The classical Andalusian cultural influence gave sobriety and calmness in contrast to the more explosive ambiance at other North African *dhikrs*.

Tetouan was founded in the early fourteenth century. Sometime just before or after the fall of Granada to the Spaniards in 1492 CE, a group of Andalusian refugees arrived in Tetouan. The town, which had been destroyed by the Portuguese earlier, was rebuilt in the Andalusian style by the new settlers. The Moriscos, as Andalusian Muslims were called, were harassed by local tribes but managed to get some support from a local ruler, friendly to their cause. They were soon joined by increasing numbers of immigrants from Spain. Later on, Tetouan became a centre for attack against the Christians.

Initially the Moriscos were expelled from the province of Granada but not from the rest of Spain. There had been the hope that they would become assimilated, but from 1609 to 1614 CE Philip III passed decrees expelling all those Muslims and Jews who would not convert to Christianity. They mainly settled in the north of Morocco and north of Tunisia. Tetouan was a popular destination for many and has maintained an Andalusian flavour to this day. The treatment of the Moriscos had been so harsh that the refugees were more violently anti-Christian than the native North Africans and were often involved in piracy against the Christians. The loss of their homeland and possessions was devastating but many also had their children torn from them. These children were then given to Christian priests and nuns to be brought up in Spain and never saw their families again.

There had been Morisco immigration since the 12th century to the Maghrib. Up till 1492 CE, these settlers had come in small numbers and often obtained important government positions. The situation was not so easy for the later migrants, who considered themselves superior to the native Maghribis and compared living conditions and cultural standards in their new homeland unfavourably with what they had enjoyed before their persecution in the Iberian Peninsula. It is noticeable that numerous great Sufi masters were of Andalusian origin; Ibn al-ʿArabi being one example.

Shaykh al-Harraq had brilliantly echoed his feelings of the overflowing generosity of Allah's Mercy in his illumined verses. His complete trust in his Lord enabled him to experience and express perfections.

> *And when I woke up and began to witness what was not clear,*
> *before I realized that death was none other than an illusion,*
> *which had distracted me, as all illusions do, and I began to*
> *see that I am other than what I had thought as I have been*
> *transformed to this new state where there is no otherness. For*
> *if I was not in truth One I would not have realized whatever*
> *else emanates from the One. Thus write on my grave: here lies*
> *a lover, who simply burnt in his passion.*
>
> *Muhammad al-Harraq*

A few years later I went on a tour to Morocco with a Lebanese friend. As we neared Tetouan, the traffic was diverted due to the king's visit and we found ourselves forced into a dusty narrow road, cutting through orchards and palm groves. A haunting voice was reciting the Quranic verse:

Say: O my servants who have acted extravagantly against their own souls, do not despair of the mercy of Allah; surely Allah forgives the faults altogether; surely He is the Forgiving, the Merciful. (Quran 39:53).

Following the source of the voice, we saw the reciter, a blind man, who was sitting by a mud wall. He seemed oblivious of the material world around him. Any disappointment at missing visiting the *zawiya* disappeared into the perfection of the moment. Mercy permeates all times and places. It is due to our lack of attention that we miss Allah's messages.

No quest which you seek by your Lord is ever withheld [from you], nor will any quest be easy if you rely upon yourself.[110]

Ibn 'Ata' Allah

If you sincerely and truly rely on Allah's Generosity, Guidance and Perfection, persist in steadfastness and confidence in His Mercy; then the answer will be most satisfying. All personal endeavours will lead to disappointment and failure unless they are part of progress toward knowledge of Allah and His Will.

The Sufis of Morocco attracted many Western converts to Islam. Over a period of nearly 20 years I had visited Morocco several times, learning about living and dead Sufis, sometimes accompanied by European Muslims.

The Moroccan Sufis of the past were not quietists or unconcerned about their rulers. This explains how a few bands of people managed to cause so much resistance to the French forces around the mid-19th century. The Shadhilis, Qadiris and Tijanis were amongst the most prominent Sufi groups that fought both the outer and inner *jihad* most valiantly.

I had heard about Sidi Saleh being the last survivor of those who had been in active armed resistance. By the time I traced him, he was perhaps in his mid-80s, living in the most inaccessible and barren part of the Middle Atlas Mountains. My driving companion was exhausted after several hours of navigating winding dirt roads, which were occasionally completely washed out, as we continually climbed toward the mountain peak. Near the rocky top, a spread-out hamlet curved around the rocks and scrubland. It was the day of *al-'Eid al-Adha* (the Hajj Eid) and there were a dozen or so visitors from different parts of the country paying homage to the great hero of a bygone era.

Along the route toward the hamlet, we were intercepted on two occasions by a few of the younger men of the community to establish our credentials. When we came out of the car, six tough-looking young men surrounded us, while chanting a very powerful incantation. Once we had joined in their standing, swaying and chanting, a communal resonance between us grew to the point where we all hugged and greeted each other as long-lost brothers. The men then sent us on our way up the mountain. *Hadra* was their customary way to distinguish friends from foes: its literal meaning is "presence". The devotees link hands in a circle and call on the name of God, usually swaying in a rhythmic manner. *Hadra* as a greeting belongs to a specific culture. When it becomes a spiritual exercise adopted by Western Sufis without skilled guidance, it can be dangerous, sometimes leading to hyperventilation and collapse.

Word had already reached Sidi Saleh. As we arrived at the top, there were men in flowing *djellabas* (traditional Moroccan robes with hoods) greeting us and showing the way to the main reception building. This was a rectangular courtyard with visitors' rooms on two sides, a large hall for reception and prayers with a *dhikr* room on the other side. As it was nearly noon, we joined in the midday prayers, after which the Moroccan fare of roast meat and tagine were served on large trays for nearly 50 people, visitors as well as the extended family of Sidi Saleh, except for the very young ones. He had over 30 children, no less than 50 grandchildren and a few great-grandchildren all living around him. When I presented him with a tin of chocolates bought at Heathrow Airport, he clapped his hands to summon the children. Within minutes, there was a long line of children, aged between four and seven, to receive the sweets.

The land was harsh and raising mountain sheep or goats was probably the main economic occupation. Clumps of wild mint grew on the side of the mountain. One of his sons in his mid-30s asked me shyly if he could accompany us down to town. He was looking for a way out of life being stranded up a barren mountain with a young wife and children without much comfort or hope for a better future.

During the feast I conjured up the image of a king from ancient times, taking rest after a battle. Sidi Saleh would offer chunks of meat to the visitors around him. He caught my eye and then threw a piece at me, about 2 metres away. Thankfully it was grabbed by my neighbour and placed on the tray in front of me to eat. The atmosphere was very cheerful and everyone was in a celebratory mood. When the meal was over, I asked my companion to ask Sidi Saleh if I could put to him some questions about his life.

With a gentle and friendly voice, he started telling me that throughout his life he had fought the foreign invaders wherever he could. He pointed out the many bullet scars on his neck, chest and arms, where he had been injured on numerous occasions. He said that in those years he aimed his rifle at anybody he considered a colonialist. Sighing, he continued to say that some 40 years ago he realized the futility of this resistance, as some of his children began to wear European-style jackets. Until then such attire represented the enemy. Soon after this realization, he decided to go into self-imposed exile, and as this part of the mountain was totally barren and uninhabited, he came there with his family.

He said he knew that most of the young people were unhappy, but he could not show them a way out for a decent future, as he had not found it for himself.

Muslims love to eulogize about the simplicity of life at the time of the Prophet and dream about recreating those times and living an easy and simple life. The reality today is that even in remote areas the youth are aware of what is happening in the outside world and long to be a part of it. The challenge is to go forward to the future without losing sight as to the essential meaning of the purpose of human life.

Before we left I asked him what his advice might be to me and others who want to live their *deen*. He held my hand gently and said, "It was much easier in the olden times when outer mobility was restricted and people were dependent on the land near them. We now have to learn how to live our *deen* in totally different circumstances." He then sighed and said, "The *jihad* of my time was easy and your *jihad* will be very difficult. Outer *jihad* is much easier than inner transformation." As we were about to take leave, he added softly with his husky voice, "But equally the rewards in the future will be greater than following the old traditions."

> *The seeker of this path will only succeed if he is brave, resolute, and does not care about profit or loss. As for the fearful and cautious, there is no place for them on this path.*
>
> *Sidi Ali al-Jamal*

Sidi Muhammad Al-Sahrawi was the great-grandson of a 19th-century Sufi master, Sidi al-Arabi al-Hawari. He was called by the few people who knew his spiritual station "the Wali of Bahlil". The old settlement of Bahlil is nestled in the foothills of the Northern Atlas Mountains, outside Fez. He was far more acknowledged away from this village where he lived than by the people close by. The man of knowledge is often denied by his own people.

The Wali of Bahlil was probably in his 80s when I first met him. I guessed his age from his stories of the many spiritual masters he had served over the last 60 years of his life. He recalled them as vividly as though it happened yesterday. Amongst the people whom he had served were the most famous Shadhili-Darqawi shaykhs, including Shaykh Ahmad al-'Alawi. There were also Qadiris, in addition to others, who did not belong to a *silsila*. When I met him he was blind, but he could read my mind. Quite a few Westerners had found their way to his humble abode near the village square and close to the mountain beyond the poplar trees. His little house had two bedrooms on each side of a short corridor and a long living reception room to one side. There was a small kitchen between the two rooms. The main tap and toilet was on the roof.

I had encouraged a group of new converts to Islam to travel to Morocco to meet him. Upon their return, they told me of their surprise when a member of the party had asked the *wali* about *sadaqa* (charity, payment to the poor). He said he was worthy of it and that now they must all empty their pockets. When all the money was presented, he pointed out two of the visitors who had not fully emptied their wallets and told them to do so. They were all shocked that he knew where their money was kept. They then asked who else was worthy of *sadaqa* and he mentioned my name. This shocked them even more, as they had regarded me as a wealthy patron. The visitors remained in a state of fear and anxiety as to how they could manage the rest of their tour without funds. At the last moment before their departure, he told them to go to the *zawiya* of Sidi Bukhorshid in Tafilalet and they would be replenished. My informant told me that they were well-compensated there.

On another occasion, the *wali* asked the visitors about me and then said, "You may think I am blind, but consider Shaykh Fadhlalla as my eyes."

The *wali* was very forthright in his manner. On one occasion a few members of my own family were visiting him and he instructed them to give gifts of money to him only and nothing to his daughter, who was living with him and looking after him – he did not consider her worthy to receive any *sadaqa*.

> Know that money is connected to the self as the self is connected
> to money. Disposing of the self is like disposing of one's money.
> He who can spend his money liberally is not the same as he who
> is enslaved by it. Similarly, the one who can give of himself is

*not the same as the one who is obsessed with himself. What a
difference between the one who controls himself and the one
whose whims (and desires) control him.*

Sidi Ali al-Jamal

The Wali of Bahlil's suggestion that I was worthy of receiving *sadaqa*
reminded me of an occasion when I was visiting the *Masjid al-Hussein*
(Mosque of Hussein) in Cairo. A regal-looking man came into the
mosque, accompanied by an assistant and a few followers, who helped in
distributing money to the poor. The man stood quietly in the centre of
the mosque, taking in the atmosphere. He then walked deliberately over
to me and said, "It is you who deserve the *sadaqa*." He stood facing me for
a few intense moments with a deep smile and pleasure. He presented me
with a packet of notes with such grace I could only feel the invisible hand
in this gift. Within a minute they had all disappeared and I remained
alone in my quiet corner of Imam Hussein's mosque.

*The heart is the house of Allah – from it come the actions of the
world, whether good or evil. If beauty appears in your heart, in
the outer existence will confront you with beauty.*

Sid Ali al-Jamal

Sidi Bukhorshid had been told by his shaykh to go to the deserts of
Tafilalet and plant sweet dates and let goodness overflow to whomever
comes to him. The area also grows roses planted by the French for the
perfumery industry. The *zawiya* was a little haven for whoever visited
it. There was always an overflow of generosity to all. The sweet potent
prayers and *dhikr* day and night gave a tangible atmosphere to this
blessed outpost.

When I reached this Sufi caravanserai after a long journey through the
arid countryside, I found 100 or so people living a simple life in an
isolated oasis. On the way to the *zawiya*, I was drawn to visit a cemetery

by the side of the road. There I was attracted to a simple grave where I sat communing with a tangible presence. I was later told it belonged to a *wali* who had never in his life sat with anyone if the talk was not about truth or its earthly manifestation.

Sidi Bukhorshid gave us a warm reception and heaped provisions on us for our return journey. The shaykh radiated goodness and his hospitality was legendary. When we departed, he stood at the gate of the caravanserai praying for our safe journey and assuring us there would always be places of light on earth providing refuge for the sincere seeker. He had plied us with provisions for the trip and nothing could dissuade him from sending us off with sacks of sugar, dates and other foodstuffs.

We afterwards learnt that he was planning to send some of his disciples a few hundred miles further south to be further away from the distractions of civilization. Sidi Bukhorshid passed away at the age of 110 in 2012.

It is common for illumined people to live longer than others. Their inner light conserves energy and protects against the usual dramas and afflictions of life that trouble most people. A simple lifestyle, good thoughts, appropriate actions, clean food and no drugs or stimulants encourages longevity.

After one of my public talks in Hamburg, I met a few young Moroccan Sufis in the audience who asked me to join them for a night of *dhikr*. Their songs and *diwan* were familiar and enjoyable. The meeting left a big impression on me and I promised to visit Sidi Mustafa al-Basir, their teacher, on my next trip to Morocco.

The centre or small village was some two hours' drive out of Marrakech on the road to Fez. We travelled for half an hour toward the mountains after leaving the main road, passing olive groves and date palms, before we reached the hamlet. The *zawiya* of Sidi Mustafa was perched on a hill overlooking the valley, which stretched for many kilometres. It was a rectangular *zawiya*: at one end of it was the *madrasa* for the young and the other end led to a courtyard with rooms around it, where the gatherings and *dhikr* took place.

As we arrived, Sidi Mustafa was at the gate to greet us; probably some people had told him that cars were approaching. He was a most jovial, smiling man with boundless energy, in spite of a noticeable limp in his right leg. I was told the story that a mad man had come with a gun to the school, where the young Sidi Mustafa was teaching. Everybody fled but Sidi Mustafa refused to move. The man pumped him full of bullets but he survived the attack.

After the customary embrace and pleasantries, we settled in and met his many visitors, students and relatives. At prayer time the *adhan* (call to prayer) was called by a man who had been calling it regularly for over 50 years. He was a friend of Sidi Mustafa's grandfather and probably over 100 years old. Sidi Mustafa was five years old when his father died, as an old man. Sidi Mustafa had initially chosen a higher spot on the mountain for peace and tranquillity but many of his followers and friends had managed to persuade him to come lower down to make it easier for them to visit. The *zawiya* had been his base camp and he ended up looking after the land owners and the peasants in the village along the valley. This area stretched north along the main road for about 100 kilometres and was some 30 to 40 kilometres wide. There were camels, goats, sheep and chickens roaming around everywhere. Palm trees and olive orchards also dotted the area.

Like most of the other *zawiyas* in North Africa, the members were elderly, except for the young resident students at the *madrasa*. I learnt later that many of the dozen or so students were orphans. The young people had gone away in pursuit of a livelihood or career. The traditional *dhikrs*, night vigils and celebrations were open to all the people, although the younger members participated mostly in recitation and singing rather than *hadra* and Sufi dances. The *zawiya* was the hub of activity for much of the surrounding land and traffic in and out was constant.

A few years later, Sidi Mustafa visited me in South Africa and relayed to me many stories about his own explorations and visits to Sufis in different parts of the world, especially in Egypt and Turkey. Members of the Moroccan communities in Europe had invited him a few times and had exposed him to Western ways. His beautiful cherubic son, who was then a small child, reminded me of Sidi Mustafa himself, as he was about that age when his father died and his older brother had taken charge of him.

I recommended that a couple, who were students of mine, visit Sidi Mustafa during their trip to Morocco in 2004. They were given a warm welcome at the *zawiya* and joined in the Thursday night's *dhikr*. The wife had a wonderful time with the ladies of the *zawiya*, who insisted on dressing her in a *burnous* (cloak), Moroccan-style, put *kohl* (traditional eye cosmetic) in her eyes and festooned her with colourful beads and bangles. The ladies participated in the *dhikr* from a next-door room, clapping and singing in unison with the men's more vigorous incantations. On the face of it, life in the *zawiya* did not seem much different to how it would have been at Ibn 'Ajiba's time. Yet, in the background, cell phones tinkled and the people talked of Dar al-Bayda (Casablanca) with a mixture of hushed excitement and apprehension.

The next day, the wife was given a lesson in the underground kitchen on how to make flatbreads soaked in honey. The young girls confided in her their desire to broaden their horizons and possibly travel. She concluded that these people were at a real crossroads between the traditional and unchanging and the fast pace of contemporary life.

Sidi Mustafa passed away in his *zawiya* on the night of mid Shaban 1427 (7–8 September 2006), at the age of 67. Like many other Sufi paths, it is unlikely for the old momentum to continue with its past vigour. The law of supply and demand is operative in all of life's endeavours. The Sufism of today cannot survive by imitating the old ways. It will have to adopt a different style. Sidi Mustafa's family, headed by his eldest son, Sidi Ismail, are now active in organising seminars on Sufism, which are supported by the Moroccan government. They invite overseas guests to these events but as yet I have not been able to accept their invitations.

The influence of the Shadhili-Darqawis had been widespread for more than 200 years. They were living proof of the original Muhammadi way of life, based on the Quran's multi-dimensionality. I have heard Shadhili shaykhs singing on the coast of the Red Sea, as well as in Sri Lanka. The atmosphere I felt in my visits to shrines as well as the *zawiyas* was friendly and hospitable to outside visitors and new converts to Islam. They are resistant to so-called *jihadi* Islam. The traditional form of *zawiya* life, with a teacher as the focal point, may be coming to an end, but I am sure for years to come the sublime *diwans* of the Shadhili-Darqawis will be sung and Morocco will retain the flavour of its glorious tradition of Sufism. In my estimation, it remains the best country for Western Muslims to visit and learn their *deen*.

> *The sea of light, which separates the illuminated seeker from his Lord, destroys whoever enters it without a guide. Whoever finds the doorkeeper will reach Allah.*
>
> Sidi Ali al-Jamal

> *Do not accept any love other than passion for Allah, for everything other than Him is a mere mirage. Look at those who are drinking of that nourishment, they are not veiled from effulgent truth, so if there is a desire for you to know more keep company with those, for that will give you the direction.*
>
> Ahmad al-'Alawi

If part of the focus of my trips to Morocco was to visit the shrines of the *awliya* connected with the Shadhili order, there was one great being belonging to this tradition whose impact on me had been considerable but whose tomb was in Algeria.

Soon after the end of the Algerian War of Independence, I went on a motoring tour through Algeria as part of a longer journey right through North Africa to Iraq. At that time I had little interest in Sufis, but during a stay in Mostaganem I felt drawn to a part of the old town. It was a difficult walk, as I was often stopped by curious, idle townsfolk. The chanting sound of *dhikr* drew me and I found myself at the *zawiya* of Shaykh Ahmad al-'Alawi. There were only a few elderly people present but the atmosphere was sweet and compelling, reminding me of my younger days in Karbala. There was a powerful, uplifting energy in the air. I walked around the area, imbibing the atmosphere, which left a deep impression on me.

Years later, I was introduced to his *diwan*, which I enjoyed singing, and learnt about the life of this great master, one of the most influential figures in 19th-/20th-century Sufism. Shaykh Al-'Alawi was born in Mostaganem, Algeria in 1869, and was interested from his youth in the study of the religious sciences.

As a young man he had joined the 'Isawiyya Sufi brotherhood, whose practices had degenerated into knife-swallowing and snake-charming activities. According to his memoirs, Shaykh al-'Alawi was attracted as a youth by the miraculous, but one night at a *dhikr* he saw a *hadith* written on the wall which made him question this orientation. He withdrew from the 'Isawiyya and stopped performing any of their magical tricks, except for snake charming.

Muhammad al-Buzidi, a local Shadhili-Darqawi shaykh, told him that he had heard of his ability to charm snakes and asked him to bring one to demonstrate his talent. Shaykh al-'Alawi was only able to find a small snake to show Shaykh al-Buzidi, who asked him whether he could charm a bigger snake than this. When Shaykh al-'Alawi replied that size made no difference, Shaykh al-Buzidi said, "I will show you one that is bigger than this and far more venomous, and if you can take hold of it you are a real sage." When asked where it was, the shaykh continued: "I mean your (lower) self which is between your two sides (earthly and heavenly). Its poison is more deadly than a snake's, and if you can take hold of it and do what you please with it, you are, as I have said, a sage indeed." Shaykh al-Buzidi then forbade him ever to be involved with snake charming or any such practices again.[111]

After Shaykh al-Buzidi's death, Shaykh al-'Alawi took over the direction of his master's *fuqara*. It is common that two or three generations after the lifetime of an inspired master the teachings become diluted and diverted as the order starts to serve social or other functions. At this point, a fresh branch may grow from the old tree. Shaykh al-'Alawi called his new order *Al-Tariqa al-'Alawiya ad-Darqawiya ash-Shadhiliya*. It is said that Imam Ali had appeared to him in a vision and gave him the name "*Alawiya*" for the order. The shaykh's announcement of his own *tariqa* was a declaration of independence from the principal Darqawi *zawiya* in Morocco and the various Algerian branches of this *tariqa*. The great-grandson of Shaykh al-Darqawi took the shaykh as his teacher, recognising in Shaykh al-'Alawi a worthy successor to his own ancestor. This helped to reduce objections to his new *tariqa* from fellow Sufis.

Shaykh al-'Alawi laid particular emphasis on the practice of *khalwa* or spiritual retreat and the constant invocation of the Divine Name. The Shadhilis had customarily made their retreats in remote areas, whereas Shaykh al-'Alawi supervised his pupils closely, which required his physical proximity to them.

Shaykh Al-'Alawi travelled extensively throughout Algeria and would give an "initiation of blessing" to the general supplicants as well as guidance to serious seekers. He had numerous representatives who also journeyed through the country spreading the teachings. The shaykh's impact was immense, not only on the committed spiritual seekers but on the larger population, by encouraging the latter to pray and adhere to traditional Muslim values, such as abstaining from alcohol and the ego-enhancing Western dress of their French colonial rulers.

'Alawiyya *zawiyas* were established for Algerians in France and for Yemenis in Wales. Shaykh al-'Alawi also inspired many Europeans to embrace Islam. He visited France in 1926 to inaugurate the first mosque in Paris and led the opening communal prayer. This action was widely criticized at the time but years later this mosque was used as a meeting place for negotiations that led to the independence of Algeria.

Despite the shaykh's generally conservative outlook, he encouraged the translation of the Quran into French and Berber, which was controversial in his time. He also supported sending Muslim children to school to learn French. He showed respect for Christians and studied their beliefs, as well as those of other faiths.

Shaykh al-'Alawi believed that Muslims were constantly misinterpreting Islam and founded two newspapers, *Lisan al-Din* (*Language of Faith*) and *Al-Balagh al-Jazairi* (*Algerian Messenger*), using them to air his views. At one time, he wrote:

> *If Islam could speak, it would complain to God, enumerating all the evils that assail it.*[112]

He particularly saw the danger of the Salafis, who claimed to be reformers and whose attacks on Sufism in the press on one occasion prompted him to quote from the Quran:[113]

> *And when it is said to them, "Do not make mischief in the land", they say, "We are but peace-makers." Now surely they themselves are the mischief makers, but they do not perceive.*
> *Quran 2:11–12*

Equally, he was a fierce critic of the secular Kemalists in Turkey.

Shaykh al-'Alawi firmly believed that it was the *zawiyas*, not the *madrasas* or mosques, which had kept Islam alive in the hearts of the people throughout the years of colonial occupation. He conceded that there were those amongst the Sufis who deserved censure but protested strongly against attacks on all Sufis because of the mistakes of some who claimed that name. Secular opposition against the French may have been more effective in terms of the outer struggle but those people mirrored the French in their behaviour and would only achieve ultimately the illusion of independence, as their government and culture would retain the same materialistic orientation of the colonial regime without the cultural roots of the colonialists. Indeed, so many Muslim governments mimic Western-style democracies to retain the political and commercial support of their former masters.

> O France! You have left [Algeria], but in reality you have not;
> for in the name of cooperation you undermine.[114]
>
> Contemporary Algerian poet

There are many descriptions of Shaykh al-'Alawi's charisma and light by Europeans, as well as Algerians. One of his pupils wrote that

> He spoke to everyone according to his intellectual capacity and
> particular disposition, and when he was speaking it seemed as
> if the one he was speaking to was the only one he cared for in
> the world.[115]

This is not unusual with enlightened teachers. Marcel Carret, the French doctor who attended the shaykh during the last years of his life, described him as bringing to mind the representations of Jesus. It is said that when Dr Carret died in Tangiers, he was found with the Quran Shaykh al-'Alawi had given him open on his chest. The doctor was buried as a Muslim.

The *zawiya* in Mostaganem, which I visited as a young man, had been built according to the shaykh's instructions, without an architect. Relays of voluntary labour received only food and daily spiritual instruction from the shaykh in return for their work. Shaykh al-'Alawi was buried there in 1934.

He left behind him various writings, the best known of which are probably his *diwan* and memoirs. His warnings about the danger of misinterpreting Islamic teachings by Muslims, in particular the extreme Salafis, are equally relevant in our times. He saw danger coming to

Islam from Muslims, rather than from Christians. The hypocrisies and ignorance of the former are potentially more deadly than the known limitations of the latter.

Shaykh al-'Alawi was an ecstatic, so his *diwan* was controversial because it glorified the gnostic state.

> *Oh you, who desire the wine of Oneness, you must leave otherness aside and dive into the highest of attributes and disappear from the universe and dive into the ocean of timelessness that is the sacred ocean, then travel along the sea of lights and witness meanings and insights and vanish into Whom you worship. You will come to taste the meaning of witnessing and come to know that all existence emanates from the Nur [light] of Allah, which brings about attributes and colours which are none other than colours journeying from your Source and back to it. All of creation is a mirror where all the attributes appear, such as the guidance of Muhammad, who brought the light of the Essence near for the seekers of truth.*
>
> Ahmad al-'Alawi

> *No matter how much the teacher strives,*
> *No matter how much the close follower wants,*
> *No matter how sincere he is, spending days and nights [in worship],*
> *Ultimately enlightenment is a gift from Allah.*
>
> Muhammad al-Fayturi

Once, while I was living in the Gulf in the early 1980s, I received a call from Shaykh qadir recommending that I visit Damascus to meet with his second teacher, Shaykh al-Fayturi. The shaykh lived in Libya but was currently visiting Damascus. He was then a very old man and this might be the last opportunity to see him. Shaykh Hosam Raouf accompanied me and recalled the visit thus:

Shaykh Fadhlalla and I went to Damascus to receive the blessing and baraka of Shaykh al-Fayturi. The murid who had accompanied the shaykh from Libya met us at the airport and took us to see the shaykh.

He was very weak and confined to his bed, but he was kind enough to see us. We were thrilled to kiss his hand and be in his presence. He kept on apologising that he could not serve us because of his physical weakness, but to us to be in his presence was wonderful and more than enough. He was in dhikr throughout our visit.

While we were there, the adhan was called for the afternoon prayers. He made his tayammum [ritual ablution using sand, dust or a stone, instead of water] using a smooth stone big enough to fill his two hands. He stroked the stone and then wiped the part that needed the water.

It was moving to see the shaykh perform his tayammum with ease in spite of his confinement to his bed. He managed to perform his prayers from his position sitting in his bed. It was a really wonderful experience visiting him.

Soon after our visit, the shaykh insisted on returning to Libya. He had a premonition of his passing, which happened shortly after his return. We had met him a week before his death.

Muhammad al-Fayturi was born in al-Janina on the western border of the Sudan. His father was a Sufi shaykh of Libyan Bedouin origin and his mother was from a Gulf tribe which traced its descent back to the Prophet Muhammad. He had studied Islamic sciences, philosophy and history at al-Azhar University in Cairo, then literature at Cairo University. He worked as a journalist and writer, publishing various collections of poetry, including *Songs of Africa*, *Sunrise and Moonset* and *Lover from Africa*. He was inspired by his experiences as an African, living amongst the Arabs, and dealt with issues of race, class and colonialism.

The driving passion of his life, however, was Sufism. As a young man, he became the pupil of Shaykh al-Chinguet, a master who only taught masters. He followed Shaykh al-Chinguet on his travels across the Jordanian desert. After the shaykh's passing, he met with Shaykh al-'Alawi in Damascus, after which his quest was satisfied.

Shaykh al-Fayturi was a man of light, whose outer sobriety veiled inner intoxication. His *diwan* gives glimpses of how beauty and majesty in him combined.

> *My Beloved called me from the presence of my nearness – I*
> *stood up to answer the call of Allah.*
> *I came to the door without hesitation and I found the lovers*
> *in the presence of Allah.*
> *I drank cups from the wine-jars of joy, and so the forms*
> *quivered out of rapture with Allah.*
> *A timeless drink whose value is immense, a straight path for*
> *the one who desires Allah.*[116]
>
> *Muhammad al-Fayturi*

Before his death in 1972, Shaykh Muhammad ibn Habib had told his *muqaddam*, Abdalqadir as-Sufi, to find his *murids* in England. Initially, Shaykh Abdalqadir thought there were people connected already, but soon realized that his job was to discover potential beings and become their teacher. After a few years, he felt the need to be with Shaykh al-Fayturi and be put into seclusion with him. Upon his arrival at the *zawiya* in Libya, the shaykh asked him whether he had any possessions on him of value or attachment, whereupon Shaykh Abdalqadir produced his leather-bound collection of odes and songs of six great masters, including those of Shaykh al-Fayturi. Shaykh al-Fayturi asked him to give it to him as a gift so he would no longer own anything of value. After a few days the shaykh returned it to him. Years later, Shaykh Abdalqadir gave it to me after my *khalwa*.

> *Oh murid! Abandon your self and what it wants if you desire*
> *increase from the secrets of Allah!*

Enter the path and cling to the friend – he will give you an ancient vintage of the wine of Allah to drink.
The Beloved will give you His wondrous secret – thirst with love for him and withdraw into the lights of Allah.[117]

Muhammad al-Fayturi

On Sufism: Its foundation is the knowledge of unity, and you need thereafter the sweetness of trust and certainty, otherwise you will not be able to bring about the necessary healing of the heart.

Ahmad al-Zarruq

As happened with Shaykh al-'Alawi, I passed by the shrine of one of the earlier great Shadhili masters, Shaykh Ahmad al-Zarruq, long before I knew anything about his life and teachings. This took place while driving through Misrata, in Libya, in my early 30s.

Ahmad al-Zarruq (1442–93 CE), like so many Sufi shaykhs, was also a prominent Muslim scholar. Born in the mountain area near Fes, of Berber descent, he had been orphaned as a baby and brought up by his grandmother, who was recognized as a jurist and became his first teacher. He was called Zarruq (blue) because of his blue eyes.

Shaykh Ahmad is considered one of the greatest Maliki scholars and wrote commentaries on Maliki jurisprudence. He is also known for his *Qawa'id al-Tasawwuf* (*Principles of Sufism*) and his commentary on *The Hikam* of Ibn 'Ata' Allah. He spent time in Makka and Egypt before settling in Misrata, where he died.

He is the founder of the Zarruqiyya branch of the Shadhili order and in his *Principles of the Path and the Foundations of the Truth* he laid down the foundations of the Shadhili path based on the original teachings of Shaykh Shadhili:

> *God awareness inwardly and outwardly, accordance with sunna in speech and deed, withdrawal from expectations of creation, in prosperity and adversity, contentment with God in scarcity and plenty, and turning to God in joy and sorrow.*

He described Sufism as

> *The science by means of which you can put right the "heart" and make it exclusive to Allah, using your knowledge of the way of Islam, particularly jurisprudence and its related knowledges, to improve your actions and keep within the bounds of the Islamic Law in order for wisdom to become apparent.*

I felt a strong attraction to Shaykh al-Zarruq after seeing part of a long poem he wrote on the sicknesses of the *nafs* (self, ego). Every line described a specific disorder, commented on how the sickness manifests and grows, then gave the cure for it. In the case of pride and self-concern, for example, the cure was adopting deliberate humility and preferring to serve others in preference to oneself.

He considered blameworthy behaviour to be nourished by three main roots. One is to be content and pleased with one's own self – from this root all desires arise, like distraction and forgetfulness, as well as rebellion and disobedience. The second root is fear of creation, and from it anger, disappointment, discord, rancour, jealousy and envy come. The third root is fear for provision, and this gives rise to greed and covetousness, expectations and avarice. It took some effort for me to finally obtain a copy of the whole poem, which I found succinct and instructional. I tried to popularize it with friends and students.

Shaykh Ahmad al-Zarruq's influence spread far and wide, continuing long after his lifetime. His shrine was often visited by seekers of guidance. One of these was Shaykh Muhammad al-Sanusi (d. 1859 CE), commonly known as the Grand Sanusi, who prayed by Shaykh Ahmad's tomb before commencing his work to create a network of cooperativeness and trade between dispersed oasis spots in the Libyan desert. After some years, towns were built with *madrasas* and libraries. Opportunities for legitimate outer livelihood were provided for impoverished tribes, who had previously made a living from banditry.

After the recent mayhem in Libya, many displaced folks sought refuge in the areas around Shaykh al-Zarruq's shrine. At 3am on 26 August 2012, extremist Salafis came and dug up his body and desecrated the tomb. Later it was posted on the internet that his body had been found intact and is being kept in a secret location.

Faced by extremist desecration of many graves, Libya's Mufti, Sadiq al-Ghariani, issued a *fatwa* (legal opinion, issued by a canon lawyer), which condemned such action. These vandals are influenced by the *Wahhabi* rulings that it is heretical to build over graves, and praying by the side of graves leads to *shirk* (polytheism, worship of other than Allah), hence it is meritorious to level anything over a grave to the ground. Sufism is sometimes condemned for malpractices, one of which is the accusation that it encourages worship of the dead saints.

So long as you have not witnessed the Maker, you are amongst created beings. But when you have witnessed Him, created beings are with you.[118]

Ibn 'Ata' Allah

The seeker is chasing illusory worldly harmony and security and as such is caught in creational change, confusion, aspiration and ambition. It is only when you begin to awaken to the divine presence that you journey away from creation to the Creator. And it is only when you are confined to your Creator that creation seeks you, rather than you seeking creation. This is the station of inner joy and contentment that all creation aspires to with or without a path to follow.

Ibn 'Ata' Allah al-Iskandari (d. 709 AH/1309 CE), the third shaykh of the Shadhili order, has previously been mentioned with reference to Ibn 'Ajiba's commentary on his *Hikam*. After translating *The Hikam*, it was time to visit his shrine.

Ibn 'Ata' Allah's mausoleum is located in Cairo's famous City of the Dead. It was nighttime when I paid my respects to this illustrious being; this gave me a window on life in the vast necropolis, which is inhabited by hundreds of thousands of Cairenes, dead and alive. Originally located outside the city walls, the Mamluk rulers used this desert space to build their mausoleum complexes. Inspired doubtless by the ancient Egyptian traditions, the mausoleums were always intended to house living visitors, praying for their family and friends, as well as the deceased. From medieval times to the present day, it has been customary for people to picnic amongst the graves, as they remember the close ones who have gone before.

The homeless of Cairo from Mamluk times have squatted amidst the tombs. Today the municipality provides water, gas and electricity; there is also a post office and police station. The living and the dead co-exist together in an organic manner; there are streets running through the tombs and suddenly you will come across two- or three-storey buildings by the domes that designate the more famous or wealthy amongst the departed. The city comes alive at night, full of the hustle and bustle of human activity, not to forget the scrawny stray dogs and cats that infest all the streets of Cairo. I particularly noticed people feeding the poor; all over the Muslim world food is distributed from mosque and shrine areas.

Ibn 'Ata' Allah was a pivotal figure in the development of the Shadhili order. The popularity of his written works, particularly *The Hikam*, *Miftah al-Falah* (*A Sufi Manual of Invocation*), a treatise on *dhikr* and his biographies of Abu'l-Hasan ash-Shadhili and his successor, Abu'l-Abbas al-Mursi, encouraged the spread of the Shadhili teachings in North Africa. *The Hikam* had a profound effect on many great Shadhilis, such as Ibn Abbad al-Rundi, Shaykh Ahmad al-Zarruq and Shaykh Ahmad Ibn 'Ajiba, who all made commentaries on it. *The Hikam* offers in today's religious confusion a blessed rose garden, where serious seekers of truth can meet with love and harmony.

Ibn 'Ata' Allah was also a Maliki jurist and earlier on was not attracted to Sufism, preferring the study of the religious sciences. His father had been a follower of Shaykh Shadhili but his grandfather had written books hostile to Sufism.

> *Shaykh Abu'l-Abbas al-Mursi said, "This path of ours can only be travelled by people who will sweep the dung from the roads with their souls." The song says, "Humble yourself before the One you love, for passion is not easy. If the Beloved is pleased, then arrival is assured. Humble yourself to Him and you will come to see His beauty."*
>
> *Sidi Ali al-Jamal*

Ibn 'Ata' Allah's first meeting with Shaykh Abu'l-Abbas al-Mursi came about because he wanted to verify for himself the claims made by one of the shaykh's followers. He was attracted to the shaykh and felt something had moved in him. Later he was to return and, in the shaykh's presence, he felt as though all his troubles faded. He followed him devotedly from that day and was acknowledged as his spiritual successor. Ibn 'Ata' Allah became a much-loved teacher, as respected for his spiritual insights as for his command of *fiqh*.

> *What the heart experiences as worries and sadness is due to being barred from inner vision.*[119]
>
> *Ibn 'Ata' Allah*

Worries and anxieties relate to past losses or future uncertainties. Thus, grief and concern relate to pleasures and pains. When He is witnessed as the essence and cause behind all situations and when one is content with His grace, then spiritual vision is opened. In this state, sadness and afflictions become purifiers of the heart and causes of higher insights regarding His presence.

Another celebrated inhabitant of the necropolis is Umar Ibn al-Farid (1181–1235 CE), commonly known as *Sultan al-'Ashiqin* ("King of the Lovers"). He is considered by some to be the greatest of all Arab mystic poets, known best for his "Al-Khamriyya" ("Wine Ode"), which celebrates the "wine" of divine bliss.

The most quoted and studied is his *Regulator of Conduct*, which comprises about 761 lines covering about 40 pages. He writes about how he was given this immense dose of love, which gave him comfort. His cup revealed to him the cause of this love so he gave the illusion to his friends that drinking from their cups was the secret of witnessing intoxication. Even the mountains when exposed to this energy crumble. He wept so much that he knew what Noah's Floods were. By his death he realized what had been returned to him. He understood that his mental death was the way to gain everything. He declared his incapacity on so many affairs that he could not even count them. Part of being cured from his sickness was the understanding that nobody is different in their cry. The acknowledgement that everyone is the same is one of the biggest spiritual healing gifts. He became content with the least, for without restriction no unveiling would have taken place.

Ibn al-Farid was a native of Cairo and was studying Shafi'i *fiqh* in a *madrasa*, when one day he came across a greengrocer performing *wudu* outside the *madrasa*. The man was not performing the ablution in the prescribed order, so al-Farid pointed this out, whereupon the greengrocer told him that he would not receive enlightenment in Egypt, he would only wake up in Makka. Al-Farid retorted that he could not go to Makka at that time, and then a vision of Makka was revealed to him. He realized that the greengrocer was a man of inner knowledge, who had been sent to him as a guide. He departed to Makka forthwith. Ibn al-Farid wrote that as soon as he entered Makka, "enlightenment came to me wave after wave and never left".

After 15 years in Makka, Ibn al-Farid had a vision of the greengrocer calling him back to Cairo. When he arrived, he found the latter on his deathbed. After his return, the people of Cairo treated him as a saint and followed after him in the streets.

> *Ibn al-Farid says, "The most wondrous thing is that whenever I increase in my abasement to the people, my power amongst them rises."*
>
> *Sidi Ali al-Jamal*

Although he was an ecstatic given to spells of dancing and spiritual intoxication, he taught *Hadith* at Al Azhar and appears to have been tolerated by the religious establishment of his day. A couple of hundred years after his death, this was not the case. Ibn Khaldun, then a *qadi* (judge) in Egypt, issued a *fatwa* calling for the banning of his poetry. The keeper of Ibn al-Farid's *waqf* (religious endowment) sought the assistance of the Sultan of the day, al-Ashraf Qaytbay. The Sultan wrote to a respected religious figure asking, "What do you say about those who claim that our lord and master, the sheikh, the gnostic of God, Umar Ibn al-Farid, may God protect him with His mercy, is an infidel?"

The rulers of Egypt, past and present, have often managed to manipulate the religious authorities, as they are usually the salaried employees of the state, to give the opinions they required. This shaykh was no exception. The annual *mawlid* (birthday) celebrations for Ibn al-Farid have thus continued to this day, although attended by lesser numbers than the thousands of past years. The procession goes through the City of the Dead toward his tomb, which is at the foot of the Muqattam hills. The celebrants dance in a trance-like state and put skewers through their cheeks, believing that the spirit of Ibn al-Farid protects them.

FROM HIS LIGHT

From his light,
The niche of my essence enlightened me,
By means of me,
My nights blazed morning bright.

I made me witness my being there
For I was he,
I witnessed him as me,
The light, the splendour.

By me the valley was made holy,
And I flung my robe of honour –
My taking off of sandals –
On those summoned there.

I embraced my lights
And so was their guide,
How wondrous a soul
Illuminating lights!

I set firm my many Sinais
And there prayed to myself;
I attained every goal,
As my being spoke with me.

My full moon never waned,
My sun, it never set,
And all the blazing stars
Followed my lead.[120]

Umar Ibn al-Farid

Whoever tastes the world will realize that purity and goodness is accompanied by affliction and harshness, that in truth it stinks, attracting all the dogs and wild beasts and thus if you avoid it you will be safe from its distractions and if you are attracted to it you will be torn to pieces by its beasts. Great fortune is for whoever can be safe behind doors and drawn curtains.

Imam ash-Shafi'i

On the other side of the City of the Dead, divided by the rocky outcrop on which the Citadel of Cairo is built, lies the Southern Cemetery, where the tombs there date from Fatimid times. One of the most visited is that of Imam ash-Shafi'i (d. 820 CE), the pious founder of the Shafi'i *madhhab*, who grew up in Makka and became a *hafiz* (one who has memorized all the Quran) at the age of nine. This distinguished *'alim* tried to forge a compromise between the teachings of Imam Malik (716–95 CE) and Imam Abu Hanifa (d. 767 CE) on questions of jurisprudence. He considered Imam Malik to be too narrow in his interpretations and Imam Abu Hanifa too broad. He also encouraged study and scrutiny of *Hadith* and the Prophetic Path. Egypt mainly follows the Shafi'i *madhhab* to this day, although there has always been a Maliki influence and many of the great Sufis have been Malikis. Imam Shafi'i left a legacy for his followers of his great love of the Quran and veneration of the Prophet and his family.

There are those who have woken up to the nature of realities and have thus left behind the attractions of this world for they realize they are not for those who desire life beyond limitations. They have regarded it as a tumultuous ocean and they rode upon it in their ships of good deeds.

Imam ash-Shafi'i

Shaykh Fadhlalla at the grave of Baba Farid, Pakpattan

Outside the shrine of Baba Farid, Pakpattan

Shaykh Fadhlalla and Seyyed Ikram

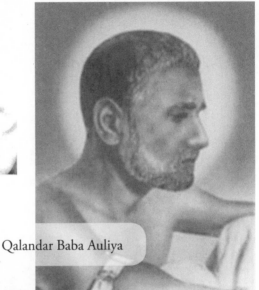

Qalandar Baba Auliya

Samandari Baba

Shaykh Fadhlalla, Sahibzada Sultan Hameed and Haroun Ebrahim outside the shrine of Ali Al-Hujwiri, Lahore

The main entrance to the shrine of Sultan Bahu

Shaykh Fadhlalla and Dr Khalid with Fazlullah,
the shrine keeper, at Pir Mehr Ali Shah

Babaji at the shrine of Baha ad-Din Zakariyya, Multan

Shaykh Fadhlalla and Shaykh Hosam Raouf

Shaykh Abdalqadir as-Sufi

Shaykh Bashir Uthman

Shaykh Muzaffer Ozak al-Jerrahi

The shrine of Abd as-Salaam Ibn Mashish,
near Chaouen

The shrine of Shaykh Ahmad Ibn Ajiba,
near Tangier

The shrine of Khattian Wali Mai,
nursemaid of Bari Imam, Islamabad

The Wali of Bahlil

The authors at Mian Mir, Lahore

Bibi Fadhila, Shaykh Fadhlalla's mother

Muna and Abbas Bilgrami

Chapter 8

SUFIS IN JIHAD

*Religion consists of two parts, the leaving undone what
is forbidden and the performance of duties. Of these the
setting aside of what is forbidden is weightier, for the
duties or acts of obedience are within the power of
everyone, but only the upright are able to set aside the
appetites. For that reason Muhammad ... said, "The true...
Hijrah [emigration] is the flight from evil, and the real...
Jihad is the warfare against one's passions."[121]*

Abu Hamid al-Ghazali

At a time when the concept of *jihad* (literally "intense striving") has been
tragically misinterpreted, causing immense suffering and confusion, it
seems appropriate to look at this issue and see how some of the Sufis
of the past engaged with it. Human struggle (inner and outer *jihad*)
begins with birth and ends with death. The Sufis emphasize the need
to purify the self, awaken to Truth and soul consciousness. When the
Prophet's companions returned from a battle, he reminded them that
now that they had returned from the lesser (outer) *jihad*, they needed
to focus upon the greater *jihad* (against one's own lower self). Up to
now, the Sufis and a minority of Muslims followed the path of inner
jihad for experiencing the purpose and meaning of life. The masses
followed contradictory and confused versions of the outer *jihad* and
literalistic ritualistic practices. Despite the present darkness in much
of the Islamic world, we may be now moving toward a new era where
Muslims and others will embark on the inner struggle and evolvement
to realizing the Truth, guided by the light of Quran, the eternal mercy
upon all creation.

Islam has often been considered as a militant, proselytizing faith which was spread by the sword. This may have been the case on occasions, but the Sufis were responsible for more conversions to Islam by conviction than any army, particularly in the Subcontinent. In the first and second centuries after the death of the Prophet Muhammad, and in the power vacuum left by the exhausted Byzantine and Sassanian Empires, the Arab Muslim armies were concerned with the subjugation of the people of conquered territories, rather than forcible conversions. The new overlords were happy to collect tax from the *dhimmis*, as the non-Muslims were called, in lieu of the *zakat* (mandatory charitable contribution or tax) levied on the Muslims. Islam was associated with an Arab identity and non-Arab converts were often treated as lower-class citizens; a far cry from the teachings of the Prophet Muhammad.

The concept of a Muslim Empire became a reality at the time of the Abbasid caliphs (750–1258 CE). The differences between the lifestyles of the Muslims and non-Muslims became more clearly delineated and the advantages of conversion obvious. The population was not forced to convert but if they did not they would remain lower-class citizens, paying a higher tax and forbidden to marry Muslim women, as well as other limitations and discriminations. Practicality as well as genuine attraction to the faith motivated conversion in increasing numbers.

In today's world, the Arabic word *jihad* is commonly associated with militant action from extremist Muslim groups, with little understanding of the broader implications of the term. The root of the word is "energy" or "expending it" – to act appropriately. *Jihad*, expending energy, is always balanced between the self and others, the inner and the outer. Personal well-beingness mirrors that of society, so to be self-accountable and correct involves giving assistance to others. *Jihad* in the universal sense is for humanity to exert energy to one's utmost capacity, to align one's will and actions with the will of God and thus a better destiny.

The outer *jihad* or war is governed by rules, which were developed and established in early Islam. However, it is important to note that the majority of Muslim scholars would agree that there should be no coercion or force used to convert people to Islam.

There is no compulsion in religion; truly the right way has
become clearly distinct from error

Quran 2:256

There are a number of Quranic verses that are used to justify warfare to establish a caliphate, particularly the much-quoted *ayah* (Quranic verse; sign or mark) of the Sword:

So when the sacred months have passed away, then slay the
idolaters wherever you find them, and take them captives and
besiege them and lie in wait for them in every ambush, then
if they repent and keep up prayer and pay the poor-rate, leave
their way free to them; surely Allah is Forgiving, Merciful.

Quran 9:5

In its historical context, it was revealed when hostilities were already underway against people who had broken a treaty and instigated warfare against the early Muslims. It is not a ruling that justifies aggression against all non-Muslims at all times. Verses in the Quran can only be properly interpreted in reference to the Quran as a whole, not viewed in isolation. Historical perspective and context are essential foundations for a proper understanding of the original Islamic teachings and the Quran. It is also important to acknowledge that there have been many occasions when so-called Muslims have acted in a manner that blatantly contradicts the Islamic teachings they may have claimed to profess.

During the early centuries of Islam, there were situations when *jihad* was invoked mainly to defend the Muslims. It was soon used by despotic rulers as a justification for wars of conquest. The real objective in these cases was acquisition and control. The armies of Mahmud of Ghazna in 11th-century India were under the command of his Hindu general Tilak and had more to do with territorial expansion and looting than conversion. It was convenient for Muslim rulers to justify their conquests under the banner of *jihad*. It was also popular with the fighters due to the material rewards expected. Tamerlane devastated the Islamic East at the end of the fourteenth century under the pretext of *jihad*. He sacked

Delhi, a great Muslim city at the time, and slaughtered Indian Muslims claiming they were infidel Hindus!

Context, as it relates to time and place, is the key deciding factor in action or inaction. There are times when fighting is the correct action and times when it is wrong. Imam Ali chose not to fight for the position of caliph after the death of the Prophet because to do so would have weakened the young Muslim community. Equally, his son, Imam Hasan, decided that an open battle against Mu'awiya would have negative implications for Islam and the masses of confused people. The destiny of Imam Ali's second son, Imam Hussein, was completely different.

The martyrdom of Imam Hussein at Karbala became an early historical reference for Muslims revolting against despotic, dynastic rule. The imam could not pay allegiance to the dissolute Caliph Yazid, who was a disgrace to humanity, let alone Islam. As Yazid would not allow him to depart in peace to distant lands, the imam had no option but to fight in self-defence to the death, against all hope for outer success. His victory was that of the soul.

> On the day of Ashura the people of Aleppo gathered at the Antioch gate until nightfall. Men and women in a great multitude kept lamentations for the Prophet's family. The Shiites of Aleppo wailed with tears on account of the massacre of Karbala and the oppression and tribulations of the Prophet's family and their suffering at the hands of Yazid and Shimr. The whole desert was filled with the cries of their grief and lament. A traveller from afar asked the reason for this sorrow and the occasion for mourning. Someone answered that this tragedy can only be appreciated by the true lovers of the Ahl al-Bayt. The traveller thought to himself that these people must indeed mourn for themselves for they seem to be in deep ignorance. Here is a royal spirit [Hussein] escaped from an earthly prison as a monarch of truth and thus it must have been joyful to break loose from the earthly bondage toward the ultimate source. Now they are the true kings and sovereigns

but if you do not perceive it in this way you only weep for yourself. So mourn you people for your own corrupt heart and religion for you only judge things from the worldly view. Those who have gone past all bravery and self-sacrifice, are they not fully content.

Adapted from writings of Jalal ad-Din Rumi

The martyrdom of Imam Hussein and the battle of Karbala, which may have seemed more localized in its early days, began to grow as a rallying point against mainstream Muslim rulership and its deviation from the original transformative path of the Prophet. Ever since then, the Muslims still ask themselves as to why the grandson of the Prophet and 70-odd family members and companions were slaughtered mercilessly in the plains of Karbala, barely 60 years after *hijra*. It is this question that also increased the division between Shiites and Sunnis, as the latter tended to acquiesce to the rulers, while the former objected to dynasties and kingships.

Authentic Sufis represent the people who want to combine the rituals and laws of the religion with the promise of transcendence to the light of truth at heart. Some Sufis of the past were more oriented toward outer action, using those arenas to purify their inner, while others adopted a quietist approach. The balance between the outer and inner state is necessary before perceiving the prevalence of the original light of Oneness.

Whoever has the outer Law without the inner Reality has left the right way;
Whoever has the inner Reality without the outer Law is a heretic;
Whoever joins the two of them has realization.

Imam Malik

When I reached the age of thirty-six, God stripped the veil from my sight, the imperfection from my hearing and sense of smell, the flatness from my taste, the knots from my hands and the heaviness from my feet and body. I saw things far away like near things and heard distant sounds like close ones. I smelt the good smell of the worshipper of God, sweeter than any sweetness, and the bad odour of the sinful man, more repugnant than any putrefaction.[122]

Shehu Uthman dan Fodio

As I live in Africa, it seems appropriate to refer to the Fulani *jihad* of Shehu 'Uthman dan Fodio (1168–1232 AH/1754–1817 CE) in West Africa. This arose out of the Shehu's desire to purify a hypocritical, pseudo-Islamic society and provide a kingdom where *shari'a* was adhered to and animist beliefs purged. The Shehu was Maliki, belonging to the Qadiri Sufi order. He had visions before his *jihad* of both the Prophet and Abd al-Qadir Jilani encouraging him in the struggles to come. The latter crowned him with a turban and gave him a sword to use against the enemies of Islam. He also used a *wird* (litany) that was revealed to him by Abd al-Qadir Jilani.

From the Shehu's youth he had protested against so-called Muslim rulers, who still followed pagan rituals and permitted black magic to be practiced. Assisted by the military expertise of his son, Muhammad Bello, he defeated the rulers he considered irreligious and abusive and founded Sokoto, which became the capital of the new Fulani Empire. His authority became accepted by all neighbouring Muslims, even by those in areas he did not directly rule.

The Shehu was the first African leader of *jihad* to insist on Muslims making *hijra* (migration) from an unbelieving country to one under Muslim rule, unless they were physically unable. The Muslims who chose to stay with the unbelievers were no longer treated as fellow Muslims but regarded as collaborators. This concept was later adopted by some future leaders of *jihad* against the colonial powers. It was practical at a time when there were still Muslim lands to migrate to.

He was ahead of his time in questioning certain aspects of Islamic practices. There are only minor differences between the four Sunni schools of law in their interpretations but historically there has been antagonism between *madhabs*, so the Shehu proposed that they merge in one.

> *Whatever came from Muhammad was not known as a "school of law"; it was called His Divine Law... Does God in His Book or His Prophet in the Sunna make it necessary to rely on a single law school or one mujtahid [practitioner qualified to make ijtihad] in particular? We have not heard of a single person amongst the learned men of the past who directed anyone to follow a specific school of law.* [123]

The Shehu always claimed that his *jihad* was not motivated by territorial acquisition and worldly power. He lived seven years after his final victory but spent almost all of them in retirement, engrossed in mystic contemplation and religious teachings. There was an element of disillusionment behind his retreat, as he saw that many of his followers did not follow in victory the high standards that had motivated his struggle. The kingdom he forged was divided between his son, Muhammad Bello, and his younger brother, Abdallahi. The Shehu also had a remarkable daughter, Nana Asmau, who is mentioned later in the chapter on female Sufis and whose work for the spiritual upliftment of women he inspired. He was a sincere, committed seeker, who believed he was called upon to be the *mujaddid* (reformer) of his age. Numerous Sufi masters all over the world have claimed this title when creating new revivalist movements.

The Shehu had completed his outer *jihad*, so he spent his last years in quiet contemplation and worship. It is a natural progression to move from the outer exertion of youth to the inner contemplation suited to the latter period of life. Most people miss this evolvement and refinement in perception. In the words of Muhammad Bello, his father was "an upholder of the Right, a man of sound vision practiced in the teaching of enigmatic things, the carrier of the flag of study ... Greatly liked by high and low, the Renewer of the turn of this (Muslim) century, an eloquent speaker and accomplished poet." [124]

Empty your heart of other than Allah and it will be filled up with Gnostic knowledges and insights.[125]

Ibn 'Ata' Allah

The heart can only reflect higher knowledges when it is clean and clear like a polished mirror reflecting light. Subtle inspirations and openings are always available, but they will only be relevant when the heart receives them, relates to them and acts upon them. The wholesome heart contains nothing other than His love, trust in Him and contentment with His Will.

The colonial period was the time when the Sufis were most actively involved in outer *jihad*, which they justified on the grounds that their lands and livelihood were threatened by invaders. In some cases the freedom to practice Islam openly was also at risk. The foreigners were not always non-Muslims. The Qadiri, Tijani and Darqawi *tariqas* rose up against the Turkish rulers of Algeria in protest against the punitive taxation and poor treatment meted out to their population at a time of famine and plague. They were fellow Muslims, but still guilty of abusing the populations they governed; although suffering under the Turks was minimal when compared to the French onslaught that was to follow.

The *jihad* of Amir Abd al-Qadir of Algeria (1222–1300 AH/1808–83 CE) against the French is a unique story in the annals of *jihad*. He was able from 1832–39 CE to establish an indigenous state in Algeria and for this reason came to be regarded in the 20th century as the father of Algerian nationalism. His power base was the Sufi Qadiri order and the tribes of the interior. He was to some extent successful in persuading Arabs and Berbers to fight together under the banner of Islam, in spite of historical animosities. As magnanimous in betrayal and defeat as in success, Amir Abd al-Qadir represented for Westerners, by his noble behaviour and spiritual qualities, the finest characteristics of the followers of Islam.

The Amir was far ahead of his time in the treatment of prisoners of war. One French commander wrote, "If our troops knew how well he treats his prisoners we would never persuade them to fight him." Years later, in exile in France, Abd al-Qadir was delighted to receive the thanks and good wishes of former captives who came to visit him.

> At a time when French commanders were offering rewards for the ears of Arabs, the Amir issued a proclamation saying that "Every Arab who captures alive a French soldier will receive as a reward eight duros for a male and ten for a female. Every Arab who has in his possession a Frenchman is bound to treat him well and to conduct him to either the khalifa or the emir himself, as soon as possible. In cases where the prisoner complains of ill treatment, the Arab will have no right to any reward."[126]

Another story that illustrates the Amir's compassion was his sending of goats' milk to the Bishop of Algiers for the Christian orphans in his charge, at a time when the two sides were engaged in military hostilities. Bishop Dupuch was later to become a friend of the exiled Amir and entreat the French government for his release from prison.

His French opponents were understandably mesmerized by the Amir. General Buguead, whose successes forced his surrender, was to write that the Amir "is pale and somewhat resembles the way that Jesus Christ is often portrayed".[127] He described him also as a "kind of Prophet, the hope of all fervent Muslims".[128]

Abd al-Qadir did not receive the support he needed from either his fellow countrymen or the Sultan of Morocco. Historical differences between his Qadiri order and other Sufi brotherhoods, specifically the Tijaniyya and Tayyibiyya, against whom he also fought, further weakened his position. He realized that the success of the earlier years of his *jihad* had meant that the French now waged war with increased ferocity and had adopted a scorched-earth policy. By continuing to fight a foe he would in the long term be unable to vanquish, he would bring more devastation upon his people. In 1847, he surrendered to the French on promise of safe conduct to a Muslim land. This promise was broken and he was imprisoned for several years in France until Napoleon III released him.

In his years of exile, Amir Abd al-Qadir was able to take on a life of spiritual contemplation, teaching and writing. He wrote a book, *Hints for the Wise: Instruction for the Ignorant,* which was primarily instructing Christians about Islam but also dealt with political economy, history and ethnology. He arranged for the publication of the *Futuhat Makkiya* of Ibn al-'Arabi. *Kitab al-Muwaqif (The Book of Stops),* the esoteric writings of the Amir, makes frequent references to his indebtedness to Ibn al-'Arabi.

There have been many outstanding resistance fighters against colonial oppression, but Abd al-Qadir is unique amongst the leaders of *jihad* in being instrumental in saving the lives of thousands of Christians. This happened in Damascus in 1860 at a time of sectarian violence. The Amir, who had settled there some years after his surrender to the French, rallied his private army to evacuate the foreign embassies and shelter thousands in his compound and those of his friends. The angry mob asked why he was trying to save these people, as he had fought and killed so many Christians during his years of *jihad* in Algeria. His reply was, "If I slew the Christians it was in accordance with our law – Christians who had declared war against me and were ever arrayed in arms against our faith."[129] It is estimated that his intervention saved the lives of around 15,000 people. In gratitude, the French government awarded him the *Legion d'Honneur.*

Of the many people who wrote to congratulate the Amir on his conduct in Damascus, one of the letters that touched him most was from Imam Shamyl of Daghestan, the defeated leader of a *jihad* against the Russians. Imam Shamyl expressed his astonishment at the behaviour of the people of Damascus who had behaved in a manner unworthy of Muslims and had forgotten that the Prophet Muhammad had said that he would testify on the Day of Judgement against any Muslim who had been unjust to a Christian.[130]

Toward the end of his life, the Amir was to spend two years in Makka, Madina and Taif. During this period he became a pupil of the Shadhili Shaykh Muhammad al-Fasi, who put him in seclusion. Thus, the leader of the outer *jihad* yielded to the inner or greater *jihad* and awoke to the light within his heart – the sacred soul that lives within every heart.

On the necessity of a spiritual master:

> *Oh, you who believe! Fear Allah, and seek a means of access to Him, and struggle on His way; perhaps you will succeed!*
> Quran 5:35

> *"And struggle on His Way": this is an order to do battle after having found a master. It is a matter of a special holy war [jihad], which is carried out under the command of the master and according to the rules which he prescribes. One cannot have confidence in a spiritual combat carried on in the absence of the master, except in very exceptional cases, for there is not a unique holy war carried on in a unique manner. The dispositions of beings are varied, their temperaments are very different one from another and something which is profitable for one can be harmful for another.[131]*
> Amir Abd al-Qadir

Imam Shamyl (1211–87 AH/1797–1871 CE) waged guerrilla warfare for 25 years against the Russian invaders of the Caucasus. He fought, like Amir Abdul Qadir, his country's invaders with courage and determination, striving to maintain the Islamic way of life he treasured; like the Amir, he had no bitterness toward his enemies and accepted his destiny of exile with the same faith that had sustained his *jihad*.

Imam Shamyl established an austere, theocratic state that governed the whole Chechen region and much of Daghestan. There had been three major imams before him who had called for *gazavat* (a sanctified attack) against the pagan tribes of their region, as well as the Russians. Their campaigns became known as the Murid Wars. All had demanded the absolute obedience of their *murids* and had based their teachings on the Naqshabandi model. This concept of the unquestioned obedience of the *murid* to the shaykh's instructions in traditional Sufism worked especially well when transposed to the battlefield. Eventually, however, the Russians by systematic deforestation and population deportation weakened the *murids'* resistance. Shamyl was taken as a prisoner to Russia and eventually allowed to go on *Hajj*, where he died. His name still lives on amongst the Chechens of today.

The fight for the freedom of the Caucasus has continued almost unabated to present times, and often with a strong Sufi element underpinning the struggle. There have also been Qadiri fighters joining the Naqshabandis. Kunta Haji Kishiev (d. 1867), a Daghestani shepherd, was a Qadiri leader who allowed vocal *dhikr* and dancing amongst his followers. Former followers of Shamyl joined his ranks and Chechens today still remember the 1864 dagger fight of Shali, where Russian troops fired at over 4,000 Qadiri *murids*, killing many. The Qadiris and Naqshabandis combined under the leadership of Shaykh Uzun Haji (d. 1920) to fight both White and Red Armies for eight years in a struggle to gain an independent North Caucasian Emirate. Stalin ordered the deportation of large numbers of Chechens to Siberia. The Sufi brotherhoods provided the organizational structure that enabled these communities to survive in exile.

Contemporary fighters against Russia may have been supported by *tariqa* allegiance, but in the absence of an illumined leader the outer struggle will generally take over and the spiritual element will be overshadowed by worldly conflict. Indeed, the Chechen Muslims with their Sufi orientation faced from the 1990s the challenging presence of Salafi fighters from other parts of the Muslim world, whose ideology was not compatible with their own. Initially, the young Chechen fighters welcomed assistance from the well-armed foreign combatants against the Russians and were influenced by their perceptions of Islam. However, their government and religious establishment could not tolerate the propaganda of the outsiders. Nationalist aspirations, rather than Muslim terrorism, disguised as *jihad*, came to the fore. These underlying tensions remain in the overall area to the present day as local governments try to prevent their citizens from going to fight in the Middle East or importing terrorism into their own countries.

Muhammad bin Ali al-Sanusi, generally known as the Grand Sanusi, was like many of the great *awliya* of North Africa of sharifian lineage and claimed descent from the Moroccan dynasty of Idris. He was born near Mostaganem, Algeria around 1787, spent some years in Arabia under the tutelage of Ahmad ibn Idris (c1749–1837 CE), the founder of the *Tariqa Muhammadiyya* (The Muhammadi order), a revival and reformist movement (sometimes referred to as the Neo-Sufi movement), whose mantle he inherited. The Grand Sanusi is largely remembered for the *zawiyas* he set up in Libya, which created a complete tribal network for the interior.

The *Tariqa Muhammadiyya* kept much of the organizational framework of traditional Sufism, with a strong emphasis on Quran and *Sunna* and criticism of the superstition, saint worship and sometimes charlatanry that the old orders had fallen into. Both Ahmad ibn Idris and the Grand Sanusi, as his closest pupil, strove to imitate the Prophet Muhammad. Through constant prayers and glorification of the Prophet, they hoped to find themselves in his presence and be taught directly by him. Ibn Idris wrote that he had received the prayers and litanies he used for his new order, the Idrisiyya, in a vision whereby the Prophet Muhammad first recited prayers to Khidr, who then taught Ibn Idris the prayers.

Khidr ("the Green Man"), the ever-green, ever-living guide, sometimes associated with the Prophet Elijah of the Old Testament, is a legendary figure who appears in many cultural traditions in modified forms and with slightly changed capacities. In the Islamic traditions he is seen as the guide of the Prophet Musa (Moses) and Alexander the Great. Islamic writers identify him with the figure who taught the Prophet Musa by showing him three situations where the correct action was not what would have been the conventional response (Quran 18:65–82). He is described as "one from amongst Our servants whom We had granted mercy from Us and whom We had taught knowledge from Ourselves" (Quran 18:65).

In some Sufi orders he becomes the initiator for those who do not have a living teacher in the Uwaysi tradition. Uways al-Qarani from the Yemen was unable to visit the Prophet in person but the teachings were transmitted to him in the unseen. In the Naqshabandi tradition, the Quranic reference to Khidr meeting the Prophet Musa where the two seas meet is interpreted as the meeting point of past and future, the transient and eternal, the entry for the spiritual seeker into the inner realm, seen and unseen, earthly knowledge and reason and direct revelation. Khidr can be seen as a being able to cut across the norms of space and time; he is neither born nor dies. The idea of Khidr represents the ever-present messenger beyond history and denomination.

Ahmad al-Tijani (1737–1815 CE), a North African master and a contemporary of Ibn Idris, similarly claimed he took the inspiration for his order, the Tijaniyya, directly from the Prophet and not from the past masters of traditional Sufism. The Tijani *silsila*, which has been active since its formation throughout Africa, thus goes back directly to the founder of the order, rather than through the traditional lineages.

Ibn Idris was originally a Shadhili shaykh, and like many Shadhilis made extensive use of *The Hikam* of Ibn 'Ata' Allah in his teachings. In these aspects he could be said to follow the conservative Shadhili model, but controversially for his time laid great emphasis on the importance of *ijtihad* (independent reasoning) and for Muslims to take personal initiative for their spiritual education. He never advocated an outer *jihad*, although he was in Egypt at the time of Napoleon's invasion; nor did the Grand Sanusi. They created a new ideological platform for Sufism, which their spiritual heirs were to use as a basis for mass movements, some of which were militant. Their times coincided with increased European invasions of Muslim lands, so the eventual move to military action in what were ultimately unsuccessful attempts to drive the foreign invaders from their countries is understandable. The Sufi shaykh was sometimes a tribal leader and also a natural figure for a beleaguered populace to turn to in times of crisis.

The Grand Sanusi always claimed that he was a man of peace, following in the footsteps of the Prophet Muhammad, trying to reform Islam through peaceful means, not through bloodshed. After his lifetime, the reputation of the Sanusis as a military force came from a chance skirmish with the French in western Chad in 1900, in which the French mistakenly identified the Sanusis as their enemies and a major threat to their colonizing aspirations. The Sanusis ended up being involved with the local tribes in the Saharan war and gained a reputation as successful fighters. When the Italians invaded in 1912, Ahmad al-Sharif al-Sanusi, the Grand Sanusi's grandson, was approached to lead the resistance. He overruled those tribal leaders who cautioned against war; the elders realized that the Sanusis would then become a military, rather than a spiritual, organization. Eventually, Ahmad al-Sharif's cousin, Idris, ended up with British support becoming King of Libya. Idris was later deposed by a young, hot-headed army officer. This officer, Muammar Gaddafi, ruled Libya for many years but was eventually brutally killed in 2011 during the vicious break-up of the country. Violence continues unabated in Libya up to the present time.

Muhammad Al-Sanusi's mission was to bring the teachings of Islam to the nominally Muslim tribes of the Saharan interior and create sustainable agricultural communities where there had previously been impoverishment and banditry.

His community-building successes in Libya were in part due to the veneration given to him by the desert tribes who revered holy men. He was equally successful with the notorious Banu Harb, a Bedouin tribe which raided caravans between Makka and Madina. They were encouraged to practice Islam and set up agricultural settlements, while previously they had considered it unmanly to farm. He was never as effective in urban communities, despite his reputation for scholarship and prolific literary output.

The Sanusi capital at Jaghbub, near the Egyptian border, housed a university *zawiya* with a vast library. From this stronghold they sent teachers out to assist the tribes of the interior and created a powerful network based on spiritual and commercial collaboration.

The Sanusis were on friendly terms with the Turks, who ruled the coastlands of Libya. As their influence expanded throughout the Sahara, the Turkish representative in Cyrenaica, Rashid Pasha, visited al-Mahdi, the Grand Sanusi's son, in Jaghbub to enquire about the supposed cache of arms stored there. He was shown their library and assured that the brotherhood's only weapons were their books!

The Grand Sanusi resisted being involved with the Mahdi's rebellion in the Sudan and refused the latter's offer to make him one of his four *khalifas*. He did, nevertheless, see the difficulties of his time and the increasing encroachment of Europeans as being the precursor of the advent of the Mahdi. He named one of his two sons and heirs al-Mahdi. Although the son never claimed he was the Mahdi, the Sanusi brethren of the Sahara will have considered him as such and this will have prevented them giving allegiance to any other Mahdi. Humans are naturally disposed to follow a guided, powerful or illumined leader. In the absence of such a being, we either await a saviour or find lesser alternatives to follow.

Wanting to know the original driving force behind the Sanusi movement, I sent an American Muslim to the Libyan interior to research their history. My conclusion was that a highly evolved being had been inspired to work amongst a difficult and violent people, as though trying to grow an orchard on a rubbish heap. He turned highwaymen into hospitable, peaceful beings, sustained by a network of trade and agricultural enterprise, competing in virtuous conduct. The Quran describes this grace as bringing the living out of the dead.

⤚⤛

The Mahdi will be my progeny, his name will be as my name, his title as my title; he will resemble me in his build and his disposition more than any other person. He will go into a period of occultation and the various nations will fall into confusion and evil ways. Then he will appear as a shining torch and will fill the earth with equity and justice as it once was filled with oppression and tyranny.[132]

Prophet Muhammad

Mahdi means "he who is well guided". There has been a strong belief amongst Muslims that near the end of our world, at a period of great hardship and difficulty, a descendant of the Prophet Muhammad, bearing the name Muhammad ibn Abdullah, would appear to restore the Muslim community. He will rule briefly over a just society, with Sayeddina Isa (Jesus) by his side. This is an important belief in Shiite Islam, where the twelfth imam, Muhammad al-Mahdi, is in occultation awaiting the time when he will reveal himself again. The belief in the coming of the Mahdi also exists in Sunni Islam and has been particularly prevalent throughout the centuries, especially amongst the poor in Africa. At times of plague, famine, wars and social injustice, there was within the hearts of the oppressed the hope that divine justice would manifest on earth in the form of a saviour. Mahdis invariably appear more at turns of the Islamic millennia.

There have been many so-called Mahdis throughout Islamic history; most of them have brought bloodshed and suffering upon themselves and their followers, although the occasional few have disappeared gracefully from the pages of history. One such character was the son of a shepherd from Kurdistan, who put himself at the head of a few thousand men and was eventually brought before the Ottoman Sultan, Muhammad IV around 1666 CE. When the Sultan questioned him about his claims, he renounced them with such grace and pleasant manners that Muhammad IV pardoned him and retained him as his page. The same ruler was also presented with a handsome Jewish boy from Smyrna, Sabbatai Zevi, whom the Rabbis of the Empire had hailed as the new Messiah, who would build Jerusalem again on earth. The Muslims believed that the advent of the Mahdi would be preceded by an Antichrist, so Sabbatai's arrival may have precipitated the shepherd's uprising. Sabbatai too was captured, chose conversion over death and became one of the doorkeepers to the Sultan's harem!

Sufis were sometimes reluctantly dragged into supporting Mahdis, as their support was actively sought to give legitimacy to such uprisings. This was the case with Shaykh Abd al-Hafiz of the Rahmaniyya, who initially used withdrawal as a means of protest against the French occupation of Algeria. He retired to his remote *zawiya* and lived in a coffin. His followers took this as a symbolic rejection of foreign rule, which gave him great moral authority. The shaykh was reluctant to accept the Mahdist claims of Bu Ziyan but popular opinion eventually forced him to join the revolt. After the rebellion was put down, the French, in view of the shaykh's age and the prestige he had amongst the masses, allowed him to return to his *zawiya*. Having decided that *hijra* was now incumbent on him, he left for Tunisia, only to die shortly afterwards in a cholera epidemic in 1850. His body was repatriated and entombed in his *zawiya*. Popular belief was that Shaykh Abd al-Hafiz had not died but was again alive in the tomb; his sons were not his spiritual heirs but the representatives of a living master.

The most celebrated of all Mahdis for Westerners is Muhammad Ahmad of the Sudan (1844–85), linked forever in British memory with the killing of General Gordon at Khartoum.

Muhammad Ahmad ibn Seyyed Abdullah was the son of a boat builder of sharifian origin. He studied the religious sciences, was attracted to Sufism at an early age and became a shaykh of the Sammaniyya Sufi order. He quickly gained a reputation for holiness and asceticism. Even his enemies often referred to his pleasant demeanour and soft-spoken manner. He smiled often, displaying a gap similar to the Prophet Muhammad between his front teeth – an auspicious sign!

In 1881, Muhammad Ahmad declared he was the Mahdi. This met with an enthusiastic response from the poor, oppressed people of the Sudan, who had suffered over 50 years of corrupt Turkish rule and the decline of the slave trade on which they depended. The Mahdi considered the Turks and their Egyptian soldiers to be the enemies of Islam and tainted by Western influence. The Sudanese, who collaborated with these foreign oppressors and enjoyed an affluent lifestyle, were little better.

> *Do not follow the example set by your oppressors the Turks, who live in luxury and exultation, and who fire their guns and rifles through pride and haughtiness. The following has come down to us through the traditions of our Prophet Muhammad: "Tell my brethren, live not the way my enemies live, wear not what they wear; if you do not obey this, then you become my enemies as they are my enemies."[133]*

Muhammad Ahmad wanted to return to the Quran and *Sunna* and recreate life as it had been at the time of the Prophet. He appointed four *khalifas*, who each represented one of the first four successors to Muhammad. He then banned the four *madhabs* and all Sufi orders, forbidding even the pilgrimage to Makka, because the Holy City was under Turkish control. Many of the *'ulama* and elite of the Sudan refused to recognize him as the Mahdi, but this did not stop the co-operation of powerful tribes and an amazing sweep of victories through the land, including against British-led forces. Despite his ban on the Sufi orders, he maintained a close relationship with his former teacher, the Sammaniyya shaykh, Abdullahi al-Dufari, who had initiated him into the teachings of Ibn Idris.

It is understandable why Muhammad Ahmad behaved in an autocratic and high-handed manner that was unacceptable to the Muslim establishment. At an early stage on the path, more than one teacher can confuse the novice. The Mahdi was dealing with fractious, ignorant tribes; only by subjecting them to the most arduous discipline and simple prescriptions could he be effective. In trying to emulate the Prophet in every way, he gave them a role model and a belief that they were in some way reliving the inspirational early flowering of Islam. The Mahdi told them that this world was for the infidels, while the next world was for them. The result of this teaching was an army willing to fight fearlessly to the death.

Victorian England took their defeats, particularly the sacking of Khartoum and the killing of Gordon, to heart. The Mahdi had instructed his army that Gordon be brought to him alive but these orders were not followed. It took some years for the Anglo-Egyptian army to re-assemble and defeat the Mahdist State at Omdurman in 1898. It was then under the rule of the Mahdi's successor, Abdullahi. The Mahdi died probably from typhus in 1885. He had set up a theocratic state, which as the Mahdi is not supposed to have a successor, was deprived by his death of its divine sanction.

After the battle of Umm Diwaykarat (and death of the Mahdi's successor, Abdullahi) Sir Reginald Wingate (future Governor-General of the Sudan) had telegraphed his wife: "Hurrah Mahdism finished." But Mahdism did not die, it only grew respectable. The man primarily responsible for keeping it alive and for making it respectable was Abdel Rahman el Mahdi (the posthumous son of the Mahdi). He was knighted by the British and created a Pasha by the Egyptians. On a visit to London, Abdel Rahman called at No. 10 Downing Street while a cabinet meeting was in progress. A cabinet meeting is rarely interrupted, but a private secretary thought Sir Winston should be advised. The Prime Minister told the private secretary that the Mahdi would have to wait, but added, "Unless you think he will go off and make another revolt."[134]

Winston Churchill had been present at Omdurman, when the armies of Abdullahi were defeated. The enemies of yesterday are often the friends of tomorrow!

In Sub-Saharan Africa, the Tijaniyya and Muridiyya exert great political and social influence. Initially in West Africa there had been opposition to the French, but the founder of the Muridiyya, Ahmadou Bamba (1853–1927) of Senegal, was eventually wise enough to concentrate his effort on community-building and improving the lives of his followers rather than hopeless warfare against superior forces. Unlike many of the Tijani leaders, he never waged war against the French but instead encouraged a pacifist resistance. However, the French were so afraid of his huge following, which included local rulers and tribal leaders, that they exiled him. He was freed in 1907, and in 1912 wrote to his followers urging them to accept French rule, as it had brought peace, stability and equality to Senegal.

Ahmadou Bamba preached the importance of the work ethic and good *adab* (courtesy, appropriate conduct) as a means to spiritual fulfilment. In 1887, he had founded the city of Touba, which he designated as his spiritual capital. The French gave the Muridiyya some internal autonomy, particularly in religious affairs, and supported their development projects. The understanding, commonly called an *échange de services*, that existed between the Muridiyya and the colonial government continues to exist in the brotherhood's tacit understanding of mutual support with the modern Senegalese state.

The shaykh was considered by his devotees to be a *mujaddid*. Today there are about four million Muridiyya followers in Senegal, plus some thousands working as migrant workers abroad. They contribute earnings to the brotherhood, which gives social services, loans and business opportunities in return. Appropriate behaviour has to be judged against the context of the times. Waging war against a colonial power was no longer practical by the time of Ahmadou Bamba, but his emphasis on personal responsibility for spiritual development within a brotherhood of like-minded people has left an enduring and positive legacy for his people.

A present Muridiyya master, Shaykh Ali, has visited me a few times at the Rasooli Centre with his followers, who sung for us from their *diwan*.

> *Jihad does not mean wielding a sword and fighting for God's cause. Jihad is taking care of your parents and children and being free from depending on others.*[135]
>
> Prophet Muhammad

The current wave of extremist movements and the terrorist activities of al-Qaeda and so-called Islamic State (IS) are anathema to Sufism. However, in the years that followed the Russian invasion, Sufis and other religious groups in the country were actively involved in Afghanistan. During the latter years of the Russian occupation, foreign Muslims, often of Arab origin, flocked to Afghanistan to join the fighting. After the Soviet withdrawal, there were considerable numbers of these nomadic fighters looking for new battlegrounds. They found them in other parts of the world – in Bosnia, Chechnya, Dagestan, Kashmir, Philippines and wherever an oppressed Muslim population existed. Al-Qaeda sprung from these roots; IS from the US invasion of Iraq and its aftermath. The war in Syria, disturbances in many Muslim countries and the current refugee crisis ultimately come from the dual standards of Western powers in their dealings with the Islamic world. The West rightly condemns terrorism but continues to support oppressive rulers, whose confused, ignorant and disenfranchised populations have spawned the inhuman movements of today. Disturbing events and worldly tragedies will continue until people wake up to the purpose of life and act with reference to higher consciousness.

Every entity in existence has an identity and appears separate outwardly, yet is very much connected inwardly with other creation. When it comes to issues of survival, personal concerns will dominate over spiritual fulfilment. With enlightenment, one views the outer and the inner with the eye of Oneness and it is only in the interplay of space and time that we can distinguish the outer and the inner. *Jihad*, both outer and inner, begins with birth and ends up with the consciousness of death, while the soul consciousness, which was there at the beginning of one's life, continues after.

> *My heart is veiled with melancholy and sadness*
> *for my followers.*
> *Truly I ask forgiveness of God many times a day.*[135]
> Prophet Muhammad

My only personal exposure to Sufi fighters came from a strong, fiercely knit group, who were the followers of a Naqshabandi shaykh during the early days of Afghani resistance to the Russians. His book, *The Telescope of Quran*, had become popular with the educated classes in the country. In this small book he suggested his followers look through the lens of the Quran at any situation and discover its real nature, like a telescope that brings better definition to remote objects. The light of Quran brings reality near, whereas human influences tend to mask every situation.

On a visit to Pakistan during the 1980s, I had the opportunity of meeting some of this group. A friend of mine, who was a professor at Peshawar University, invited me to visit an area in Pakistan near the border with Afghanistan, where many of the fighters were based. The main compound was protected by a high mud wall and located in the outskirts of a modest town in the Northwest Frontier of Pakistan. It was a large rectangular compound with the main entrance leading through numerous buildings and homes belonging to Prince Daud and his relatives. He was the last member of the royal family to remain behind when his uncle, the king, had fled to Italy. In the middle of the courtyard there were numerous trees, shrubs, some herbs and vegetables. At the other end of the compound there were a dozen or so large rooms where the Sufi fighters would be staying for rehabilitation, medical treatment and rest. On average there would be about 50 of these fighters who would stay for a week or two, before returning back to the front line. One of the people accompanying me was a Swedish doctor whom they adopted that evening and placed in the middle of their circle of *dhikr*. Toward the end of our stay, they declared him *Rafi'ullah* (elevated by Allah).

I emerged from the intense periods of *dhikr* exhausted physically but uplifted by the sheer energy and devotion of these people. A senior member of the group tried to describe to me in Pashtun how their shaykh had been killed in battle just a few weeks previously. He showed me the picture of the teacher and gave me a copy of his book, *The Telescope of Quran*. Before leaving, I asked them whether there was anything I could do. A thin, tall man answered that they were totally in God's custody and that they prayed for me to feel the same as they did, as a guest of Allah on earth.

It was a cold night and Prince Daud insisted that I should have an additional blanket as I was sleeping outdoors under the stars. In the morning before leaving, his mother emerged from the ladies quarters to greet me and gave me the light-brown fur blanket as a gift. I was really touched because I am sure it was a legacy from their past. It stayed with me for a few years until the moths of Pakistan decimated it.

> *And whoever strives hard he strives only for his own soul; most surely Allah is Self-Sufficient, above [need of] the worlds.*
> *Quran 29:6*

Chapter 9
FEMALE SUFIS

If all women were like the one we have mentioned,
then women would be preferred to men.
For the feminine gender is no shame for the sun,
nor is the masculine gender an honour for the moon.[136]

Nur ad-Din Jami

Women are far more receptive to accepting a path, a teacher or *tariqa*, and are tenacious in persevering. Men are the reverse: reluctant to take to a path and easily disposed to leave it. The idea of "Sufi women" is a misnomer: all women are Sufis! The archetype of the mother equates to being selfless. Women all have the natural propensity to be selfless. When it comes to preserving life, they are the guardians of it. When they are denied, therefore, they take on the opposite qualities, becoming formidable adversaries to deal with.

Women have not only featured in the literature of Sufism as metaphors for divinity, but also as its transmitters and teachers, and this chapter takes a look at several outstanding ones, including those who have affected me most deeply.

Before the advent of Islam, it was customary for the Arabs, as well as other tribes in Asia and Africa, to debase women, much as they have been in predominantly patriarchal societies throughout history. Traditional Arab tribesmen, for example, feared the birth of girls in case they brought dishonour to the family; hence the common practice of female infanticide.

One of the early difficulties the teachings of Islam confronted was the Quran's declaration that men and women were equal in the eyes of God. This revolutionary social message, however, did not develop into the full, equitable participation of women in life at every level of society. If Muslims had fully lived the path of Prophetic Islam and evolved with it, I believe the position of women – socially, economically, politically, as well as in matters of religion – would have been very different to what it is now in most Muslim societies.

In discussing the status of Muslim women, it is important to note the differences between those from urban and rural backgrounds, as well as varying socio-economic backgrounds and ethnicity. With the rise of dynastic Arab rule and exposure to the Iranian Sassanian culture, the practice of segregation of the sexes and veiling began to be adopted and acquired a social status. Within 100 years or so, the new nations that embraced Islam developed different versions of *hijab* or veils. These new styles, especially those of the Hindu converts to Islam, became fashionable in cities. However, the women of the nomadic tribes, whether Arab or from other racial groups, continued to participate fully in day-to-day life, working alongside their menfolk. Practical reasons meant that they could not wear *hijab*, despite the status it conferred.

The story of Adam's creation is entwined with that of Eve's. This is at the foundation of unity and duality. From pre-historic times, matriarchy and patriarchy co-existed and interchanged. Man was often more of the initiator and destroyer, the agent of change; while the female was connected to nurture, maintenance, stability and continuity. During life's journey, we differentiate between male and female, along with all the other natural orientations, potentials and complementary differences in existence, yet we all emanate from Unity, are sustained by it within the field of duality and return back to it.

For the past several thousand years, most human settlements and civilizations were led by males. God is therefore commonly referred to as male. Earlier on, before agricultural settlement, women's status was on some occasions higher than men's. Female goddesses dominated in parts of the ancient East. Then, with the plough and need of stronger physical strength, patriarchy emerged. Gendered language has also contributed to the "masculinity" of God.

In most modern societies, male dominance extended even into childbirth and the predominance of male gynaecologists. Initially this came about with the use of forceps, which required physical strength, followed by more surgical intervention, rather than midwife-assisted natural childbirth.

The historical supremacy of males in the worldly sense, in the zone of survival, also extends toward the religious and spiritual spheres. I am often asked why there are not many known female teachers. Part of the reason why we do not hear much about spiritually accomplished women is cultural. Women tend to remain in the background and only under exceptional circumstances push themselves to the forefront. Yet, every mother is her child's first and most influential teacher.

The tirade of Seyyeda Zainab, the sister of Imam Hussein, against the tyrant Yazid in Damascus, following her brother's martyrdom at Karbala, is an example of this. All the men in her family and their supporters had been killed at Karbala, except for her nephew, Imam Ali Zaynal-'Abideen, whose sickness saved him from a certain death. She publicly called Yazid and his followers to account for their actions because there was no male to do this.

The different physical and hormonal make-up of men and women dictates their separate spiritual development. Man's ego has to be curbed deliberately, whereas that of a mother is naturally diminished by the act of birth and having to bring up children. In theological terms, men are given the advantage in order to practice selflessness, while women have already done this through their feminine roles as mothers and wives. Men go to the outer world for growing up; unless they are given a head start on women, they would have no chance!

Men generally gain wisdom with maturity, but a woman usually has signs of it from childhood, while the full blossoming of intellect and the heart comes after the menopause. In her earlier years, she will usually be involved in child-rearing and domestic issues, while a man may have more time for his spiritual development.

Ibn Khaldun (1332–1406 CE), in his *Muqaddima*, wrote about the repetitive cycles of nomadic invasions followed by urban civilizations, which degenerate and are then conquered again by new waves of nomadic forces. He believed that the ease of urban living undermines the virility of a people; certainly it leads to excessive restrictions and confinement of women. The more a society was exposed to nomadism, the more likely you were to see freedom of expression and action of women.

Only one woman is mentioned in the Quran by her first name. This is Maryam, the mother of the Prophet Isa (Jesus), who had no husband. She is greatly revered by Muslims and one tradition says that she will be the first person to enter Paradise. Asiya, the wife of Pharaoh, disobeyed her husband to rescue and bring up the Prophet Musa. These two women, along with Khadija, the first wife of the Prophet Muhammad, and their daughter Fatima, are considered the most blessed of all women. Khadija was an independent businesswoman who employed the Prophet Muhammad. Out of the four ladies, only Fatima can be seen to fulfil the traditional role of a woman as a daughter, wife and mother.

Fatima Umm Hani was a cousin of the Prophet Muhammad and sister of Imam Ali. She was one of the most respected women from the Household of the Prophet. Umm Hani was well known for her intellect and wisdom and what she related from the Prophet is considered of great value.

She is reported to have prayed, "Oh, Lord, I am weak, confused and uncertain but I am hanging on to the Prophet of Allah expecting relief. Thus whenever I remember my troubles are over, I am content and I have discovered all the wealth and treasures in that remembrance and prayers upon You."

The discovery in 1991 at the University of Riyadh of a lost work, *Dhikr an-Niswa al-Muta'abbidat as-Sufiyyat* (*Early Sufi Women*), by the celebrated Sufi scholar Abu 'Abd ar-Rahman as-Sulami (937–1054 CE) allows the Western reader, through the translation of Rkia Cornell, windows into their lives. This book indicates that the effulgence of the first 300 years or so of Islam seems to have provided more conducive arenas for the intellectual and spiritual upliftment of women than the later periods.

While these pious women were often defined by their relationship to learned men (daughters, wives, sisters etc.), it is clear that in some cases their spiritual station was considered to be higher.

> *When Hasan ibn Ali ibn Hayyawayh took his wife, Malika, on pilgrimage to Makka, they visited the great spiritual master, Abu Bakr ash-Shibli. When ash-Shibli saw her, he said to al-Hasan, "You are a man and this is a woman, but she is greater than you in her spiritual state".*[137]

Sulami makes it clear that in the early period (late Umayyad to early Abbasid), women were acknowledged as teachers and learned men took advice from them. By the 10th century CE, they appear to have been the pupils of male shaykhs rather than teachers.

There were female mystics, such as the celebrated Rabi'a al-'Adawiyya of Basra, who chose a life of asceticism and celibacy. Rabi'a was born around 714 CE and may have been a freed slave who converted to Islam. She is supposed to have lost both of her parents when very young. Sulami concentrates on her intellectual prowess and the spiritual counsel she gave to some of the great jurists and transmitters of *hadith* of her day, especially Sufyan ath-Thawri and Shuba ibn al-Hajjaj. However, she became universally perceived as the founder of Sufi love-mysticism.

Sufyan ath-Thawri is said to have asked her, "What is the best way for the slave (*abd*) to come close to God, the Glorious and Mighty?" She wept and replied, "How can the likes of me be asked such a thing? The best way for the slave to come close to God Most High is for him to know that he must not love anything in this world or the Hereafter other than Him."[138]

O Sustainer,
If fear of hell prompts my devotion, let hell burn me.
If hope of paradise moves it, let heaven spurn me.
But if I worship you only to feel your nearness,
don't hide your beauty from me.[139]

Rabi'a al-'Adawiyya

Rabi'a is the symbolic female seeker who shuns husband or family, focusing only on love of the Divine. Farid ad-Din al-Attar writes of her suffering in search of God, as does Rumi. Ibn al-Jawzi of Baghdad (d. 597/1201) wrote *Sifat as-Safwa* (*The Nature of the Elect*), borrowing much from Sulami's descriptions of Sufi women but adding something of his own interpretations, particularly in the case of Rabi'a, who he portrayed more as a recluse. Al-Jawzi also writes that the first school of women ascetics was founded by Muadha al-'Adawiyya of Basra, who lived about 100 years before her. Rabi'a, therefore, personifies a flowering of a female school of asceticism, not its beginning.

A Beloved unlike all others:
He alone has touched my heart.
And although absent from sight and touch,
He is ever present in my heart.[140]

Rabi'a ash-Shamiya

As-Sulami gives us snapshot portrayals of a variety of other types of female seekers. There was Maryam of Basra, a companion of Rabi'a: "She used to lecture on the subject of love and whenever she listened to discourses on the doctrine of love, she went into ecstasy. ... Shabaka of Basra had 'underground cells' (*saradib*) in her house for her female students and disciples, where they learned the ways of self-denial and spiritual practice." Al-Wahatiyya Umm al-Fadhl lived in the 10th century CE. She visited Sulami's maternal grandfather in Nishapur. He describes her as "unique in her age, in her speech, her knowledge and her spiritual state. She was a companion of most of the spiritual masters of her time."[141]

Umm Ali of Nishapur was personally known to As-Sulami. He said of her that "she attained exalted spiritual state and was highly esteemed. The Sufi shaykhs used to honour her and recognize her status." It was reported that she said, "One who is confirmed in his knowledge of true servitude will soon attain the knowledge of lordship." Her brother was a noted preacher of his day and had his own *madrasa* in Nishapur. Many female mystics came from families steeped in Sufism.[142]

For Sulami, Fatima of Nishapur was the most outstanding female gnostic of her time. According to Sulami, Abu Yazid al-Bistami praised her and Dhu an-Nun al-Misri sought her advice on doctrinal matters. She used to spend time devoted to worship in Makka, where she died in 223 AH/838 CE.

Abu Yazid al-Bistami said, "In all my life, I have only seen one true man and one true woman. The woman was Fatima of Nishapur. Whenever I informed her about one of the stages of spirituality, she would take the news as if she had experienced it herself." I asked Dhu an-Nun about her and he said, "She is a saint from amongst the friends of God, the Glorious and Mighty. She is also my teacher (*ustadhi*)."[143]

Many of these women seekers appear to have used devotion to husband or teacher as a means of purifying their lower self and assisting their spiritual evolvement.

Umm Ali (Fatima) was one of the daughters of the leaders and the high elites. She was wealthy and spent her fortune on the Sufis. She helped Ahmad ibn Khadrawayh, her husband, in all matters pertaining to his spiritual practice. Her husband was well known as a practitioner of Sufi chivalry (*futuwwa*). Abu Yazid al-Bistami said, "Whoever practices Sufism should do so with the spiritual motivation (*himma*) of Umm Ali, the wife of Ahmad ibn Khadrawayh, or with a state similar to hers."[144]

Ali al-Hujwiri tells a well-known story about how her husband went with Umm Ali to visit Abu Yazid al-Bistami and became jealous of the rapport between them. She told Ahmad that "you are my natural spouse, but he is my religious consort; through you I come to my desire, but through him to God. The proof is that he has no need of my society, whereas to you it is necessary."[145]

The more traditional Aisha of Merv, the wife of Abd al-Wahid as-Sayyari, was described as the "most excellent of the Sufis and specialists in self-denial. No one exceeded her spiritual state in her time, and no path in Sufism equalled hers in subtlety. She spent more than 5,000 dirhams on the needy Sufis. I was informed that a professional invoker said to her, 'Do this and that and an unveiling of divine secrets will be granted to you.' She said, 'Concealment is more appropriate for women than unveiling, women are not to be exposed.'"[146]

> Amma, who was the sister of Shaykh Abu Said ibn Abu'l-Khayr (d. 441/1049), compared his teachings to an ingot of gold. He is reported as replying that her silence was an unpierced pearl![147]

Sitt Nafisa is one of the most celebrated of the female descendants of the Prophet Muhammad. She was married to Ishaq, the son of the sixth Shiite imam, Jafar as-Sadiq. Sitt Nafisa was born in 760 CE and brought up in Madina. She was well versed in knowledge of the Quran and *Hadith* and studied when young under the great jurist Malik ibn Nas. After her marriage, she went to live in Cairo. There are many stories of her life of piety and continual fasting, of the miracles she performed and the great love and veneration she was held in by the people of Cairo.

One of the miracles she is said to have performed was curing an epileptic child through bathing her. Her reputation spread and when there was a drought she was asked to help. So she tore her scarf in pieces and told the people to spread it on the dry bed of the Nile. Within a few days water came and the pieces from her scarf floated to the top. Allah was the Doer, Sitt Nafisa just read the signs. No human being can do more than respond to His decrees. Sometimes enlightened beings are so attuned to what is happening that it appears as if they are performing miracles. It is the same thing if a saint appears to be cursing someone. He is merely indicating that if the person continues on that path, the end will be a disaster. The Prophet

Muhammad taught that even if the entire of creation wanted to harm you, nothing would harm you unless it was the will of Allah.

It is said that Imam ash-Shafi'i, the founder of the Shafi'i school of law, would listen to her discourses and held her in great esteem. He was descended from an uncle of the Prophet Muhammad and was known for his love of the Household of the Prophet.

> *Oh, family of the Prophet, your love has been made a condition*
> *from Allah in the Quran. It is an honour for you that whoever*
> *does not acknowledge you is outcast.*
>
> *Imam Shafi'i*

Whenever Imam Shafi'i was sick, he would send a messenger to request Sitt Nafisa's prayers. By the time the messenger returned to him, the imam would have recovered. When the messenger came to her during his final illness, Sitt Nafisa told him to inform Imam Shafi'i that "God has blessed him with the pleasure of seeing His Noble Face." On hearing this, the imam prepared for death and requested that Sitt Nafisa perform his funeral prayers. When he died, his body was taken to her, because she was so weak from her constant fasting and vigils that she was not able to leave the house.

Munawi, one of their biographers, records that she had dug her grave herself in her own house. She would regularly spend time in her grave, where she is said to have recited the Quran 6,000 times before her death.

When Sitt Nafisa was dying, people tried to persuade her to break her fast. She refused, saying that for 30 years she had been praying to Allah that she should meet Him while fasting, so how could she break her fast now? It is said that she recited from Surah al-An'am, and when she reached the verse, "For them is an abode of peace with their Lord" (6:127), she took her last breath. Her mausoleum in Cairo remains to this day a popular place of pilgrimage, particularly for women. Sitt Nafisa was known for her ability to heal diseases of the eye and today there is an eye hospital near her shrine.

A true union in marriage comes about when both partners share common spiritual goals and assist each other in their journeys of transcendence. The history of Sufism gives us many examples of pious women who supported great men of light and through a path of service found their own fulfilment. A touching marriage is recorded in the autobiography of Hakim al-Tirmidhi (d. 255 AH/869 CE), a mystic from Central Asia. Hakim al-Tirmidhi is known principally for his doctrine of sainthood, whereby the *awliya* uphold the universe, are capable of miracles and act as intercessors for the common man. He also believed in the teaching potential of dreams. He records how, in his own spiritual unveiling, he was much assisted by his wife, who through her dreams brought him guidance from the unseen, and how she too was guided to experience light upon light by revelations in dreams.

The part played by pious mothers, sisters and aunts in the lives of men of knowledge is often chronicled. Many spiritual masters are seen to have lost their fathers early and been raised by devout mothers, grandmothers or aunts. Examples of mothers as teachers are Umm Khair Fatima, mother of Shaykh Abd al-Qadir Jilani (d. 561 AH/1166 CE), and his aunt, Umm Muhammad. The Chishtis remember the mothers of Shaykh Farid ad-Din Ganj-i-Shakkar (d. 663 AH/1265 CE) and Shaykh Nizam ad-Din Awliya, in particular. The well-known Punjabi mystic poet Sultan Bahu paid this touching tribute to his mother: "Bliss of God for Raasti be, for with truth is gifted she." When Sultan Bahu first decided to embark on his spiritual journey, he wanted his mother to be his guide. She directed him toward a male teacher.

Wives and daughters play their part in Sufi history. Both the wife, Rabi'a bint Abi Bakr, and the daughter, Zaynab, of Shaykh Ahmad Rifa'i were known for their sanctity, as was Bibi Aisha, the daughter of Shaykh Farid ad-Din Ganj-i-Shakkar.

Ibn al-'Arabi, Shaykh Al-Akbar, wrote in his *Futuhat al-Makkiyya* that women could attain the highest mystical rank, saying that 'both men and women participate in all of the levels, even in being the axial saint (*qutb*). ... In other words, everything that a man can attain – spiritual stations, levels or qualities – can be attained by women if God wills, just as they can be attained by men, if God wills."[148]

Two of his early teachers in Andalusia were women: Fatima bint Ibn al-Muthanna and Yasmina (or Shams) Umm al-Fuqara. Fatima was over 90 years old when he knew her and Ibn al-ʿArabi says of her in his *Ruh al-Quds* that "she was a mercy for the worlds." He wrote of Yasmina that "amongst people of our kind I have never met one like her with respect to the control she had over her soul. In her spiritual activities and communications, she was amongst the greatest. She had a strong and pure heart, a noble spiritual power, and a fine discrimination."[149]

When he travelled to Makka, he met a young Persian woman, Nizam, who was the daughter of the imam of Maqam Ibrahim. Ibn al-ʿArabi first met her when he was circumambulating the Kaaba in a state of ecstasy, reciting verse. She heard him and gave an interpretation of the verses. She inspired his collection of verses, *Tarjuman al-Ashwaq* (*The Interpreter of Longing*). They are written in the style of Arabic love poems, and are accompanied by the author's Sufi commentary. Nizam symbolized the personification of Divine Love and Beauty, rather than an object of physical desire.

Ibn al-ʿArabi also met another woman in Makka, Zaynab al-Qaiyya. She was known for her devotions and her ability to levitate when meditating. He travelled with her to Jerusalem.

The relationships Ibn al-ʿArabi had with all the women in his life – mother, sisters, wives, teachers and pupils – seem to have been honourable, respectful and at a higher level of consciousness. Of the fourteen *khirqas* (patched cloak of the Sufis) he bestowed on his pupils, 13 were for women. He allowed women to listen to his teachings.[150]

Following in the footsteps of Ibn al-ʿArabi with regard to his recognition of a woman's spiritual potential, but in the 20th century, Sufi Barkat Ali had male descendants yet called himself Abu Anees, after his adopted daughter. When he passed away, he left Dar al-Ehsan, his charitable foundation, under her control.

The Mughal princess Jahanara (1614–1681 CE) was known for her spiritual dedication and devotional writings. Her Sufi name was Fatima. To this day there is a mosque in Agra where every Thursday night the women devotees remember her at their *dhikr*. Jahanara wrote a biography of the great Chishtis masters, *Munis ul-arwah* (*The Confidant of Spirits*) and expressed lyrically her spiritual devotion to Shaykh Muin ad-Din Chishti, the founder of the Chishti order in India. She experienced such unveilings by the tomb of the master that she wrote,

> *The Beloved has placed a noose on my neck,*
> *And He pulls me wherever He wishes.*[151]

She also wrote a biography of her living teacher, the Qadiri Shaykh Mullah Shah, and refers to him as "the keeper of the treasure of God".

Jahanara never married, but she became the first lady of the Mughal Empire after the death of her mother, Mumtaz Mahal, in whose memory the Taj Mahal was built. She was very close to her brother, Dara Shikoh, who shared her love of Sufism. Aurangzeb, her third brother, who imprisoned their father, Shah Jahan, and ordered the execution of Dara Shikoh on trumped-up charges of apostasy, was also devoted to Jahanara. She chose to share her father's imprisonment in Agra, but after his death she forgave Aurangzeb, who respected her greatly. She was then reinstated in her position as first lady of the realm.

She is buried near the shrine of Shaykh Nizam ad-Din Awliya in Delhi. Her grave is covered only with grass at her request: "For this very grass suffices as a tomb cover for the poor." She describes herself in the inscription on her tomb as "the annihilated *faqir*, Lady Jahanara, disciple of the Lords of Chisht".

Mortals we are, and fashioned thus of earth,
Makhfi, vain is this world in which we trust,
Dust is the rank of kings, the pride of birth,
Yea! Know then that thou thyself art also dust.[152]

Princess Zebunissa

Zebunissa (1638–1702 CE), the niece of Jahanara and daughter of Aurangzeb, was an accomplished poetess who wrote under the pen name of Makhfi ("The Hidden One"). She was Aurangzeb's favourite daughter but incurred his wrath by assisting her younger brother, Akbar, in a rebellion against Aurangzeb. Akbar escaped to Persia, while the hapless Zebunissa, only 43 years old, was imprisoned for the rest of her life. She had from youth been exposed to Sufism through her Aunt Jahanara and Uncle Dara Shikoh, so the orientation was probably there even before her fall from grace. Her poetry deals with the transience of life and its travails, loves which may have been worldly, as well as spiritual, are alluded to and, finally, piercing through her miseries, is the hope of salvation:

O Makhfi, for thy fate
Be not fearful nor be disconsolate.
Higher, upon the day of reckoning
Fakir than king, there shall be none lovelier nor great
Lo! The fakir's torn clothes shall appear to be
More regal than the robes of majesty.[153]

In the end, she consoles herself that, despite all her sufferings, "in my soul the feast of God is laid, within the hidden chambers of my heart."[154]

O love, I am in thy thrall.
As on the tulip's burning petal glows
A spot intense, of deeper dye, withal,
And see the dark stain which within it blows,
Of its intensity, more acute than all,
My heart is torn to pieces in its throes.
As for the shining diamond of the soul,
I pine in vain, Beloved one, my goal.[155]

Looking toward more recent times, Adile Sultan (1826–99) was another Sufi princess. Shaykh Muzaffer Ozak al-Jerrahi had such high regard for her memory that he would offer prayers for her soul. She was the daughter of the Ottoman Sultan Mahmud II and sister of the Sultans Abdulmecid I and Abdulaziz. After the death of her husband and young children, she entered the Naqshabandi order and devoted the rest of her life to philanthropic causes. She wrote Sufi poetry, published under the title of *Adile Sultan's Diwan*, as well as arranging for the publication of the *diwan* of her ancestor, Suleiman the Magnificent. She bequeathed her palace to the state, stipulating that it be used for a girls' high school.

> *In the way of Truth they all forsook –*
> *Cause the dervishes no harm.*
> *The Beloved's way was the way they took –*
> *Cause the dervishes no harm.*
>
> *For dervishes Truth is the way*
> *To neither left or right they sway*
> *Attain the Truth as Saints they may –*
> *Cause the dervishes no harm.*
>
> *The dervish cannot be described*
> *To meet the Friend they have arrived*
> *Say those to whom perfection is ascribed –*
> *Cause the dervishes no harm.*
> *This worldliness they would decline*
> *To extreme hardship they'd incline*
> *Of Unity they'd drink the wine –*
> *Cause the dervishes no harm.*
>
> *Adile! Let talking be*
> *The dervish way is calling thee*

The face of Truth thyself to see –
Cause the dervishes no harm.[156]

Adile Sultan

Let us dwell there and drink milk and honey
And enjoy bliss together with Ahmada.
For there is no illness, no ageing, no poverty
No death; we remain forever
Forever in enjoyment, relaxation and pleasant talk
We walk in Paradise, we have seen Muhammada.[157]

Nana Asmau

Nana Asmau (1793–1864) is regarded as an iconic figure by African Muslim women today. She lived a full life as a Qadiri Sufi, writer of spiritual elegies (including one celebrating Sufi women) recited to this day in her native Nigeria, and was an educator of both men and women. Interestingly, her poetry tends to be addressed to humanity, rather than exclusively to either men or women. Her father, Shehu Uthman dan Fodio, led the Fulani *jihad* and founded a Muslim kingdom. He was succeeded by his son Muhammad Bello, who relied on his sister's counsel in matters of state, as well as education and social reform. The Sokoto caliphate was concerned with bringing newcomers to Islam, as well as teaching ignorant Muslims, and Nana Asmau dedicated her life to achieving this vision. Both the Shehu and Muhammad Bello considered the education of women essential for a healthy Muslim society – a far cry from today's events in Nigeria.

Nana Asmau set up a network of women teachers called *jajis*, who journeyed into the rural, as well as urban, areas. The *jajis* trained groups of women, who were called *yan-taru* ("those who congregate together", "the sisterhood"), to spread Islamic teachings throughout the caliphate. Nana Asmau was able to communicate to both scholarly and illiterate alike; her teachings left a profound and enduring impact, showing the dignity and upliftment that Islam could bring to women. She encouraged learning through her verse, using the enlightened Muslim women of the past as role models. Many schools and women's institutions in northern Nigeria are named after Nana Asmau, and her tomb in Sokoto remains a popular place of pilgrimage.

EULOGY FOR THE GREAT WOMEN SAINTS OF ISLAM

For their majesty will wipe away my sins
And because of them I will escape the burden of my
wrongdoings.
In this world and the next, where souls await judgement
I will rely on them for my salvation.[158]

Nana Asmau

Women throughout the ages have reflected the Higher Truth and the Absolute. More often than men their loyalty has been to that Truth. Thus, in Muslim societies in times of ease and difficulty they have played a big role in maintaining the connection to the Real, and through female rituals kept alive that remembrance. Razia Sultanova's informative *From Shamanism to Sufism: Women, Islam and Culture in Central Asia* shows how, even during the Communist years, the women of Uzbekistan maintained the traditions of their faith through music, *dhikr*, recitals of poetry and celebrations of events such as the Prophet's birthday, the martyrdom of Imam Hussein, the anniversaries of the passing of saints and rites of passage like birth, marriage and death. These events are led by female teachers, called *otin-oys*.

LAMENT FOR IMAM HUSSEIN, READ IN MONTH OF ASHURA

He has left this world, the noble Hussein,
His clear light has left this world,
Where, my friends, is the flesh and blood born of Fatima's
flesh and blood
Whom can I tell of my unhappiness?
What can I do in this suffering?
I would rather go blind, my friends,
Oh, how I wish I could see him!
My heart is broken, Hussein, oh Hussein,
What can I do, I am destined to live this fate,
I cry on this day when he suffered from the hands of his yazids.
On the Judgement Day you will rise and stand next to your
stern Lord.
Oh, Imam, oh Hussein where are you, my soul?
You left here me and departed, oh victim of Karbala.[159]

Women, like men, must find the way appropriate to their roots and circumstances to achieve spiritual fulfilment. It seems patronising that when male writers talk about the phenomenon of gnostic women they describe them as "no longer women". In reality, as Attar implied, when a woman has awoken, she is neither a woman nor man, for in the realm of *tawhid* (Divine unity) there is only the One. Equally, at the end of his ode to a nameless Egyptian female ascetic, the poet Jami prays for access to the station of *tawhid*, where duality has been transcended and there are no differences in essence between the sexes.

The spiritual objective of both sexes is to go beyond the individual, egotistical identity. In ascertaining a person's station, one would consider not whether they are male or female, but the degree of their material desires, whether good or bad.

The spiritual journey may be regarded broadly as covering two phases: the first is denial of falsehood, which leads to witnessing an assertion of truth. This phase is easier for women than men; the latter need to fight against visible injustices and their egos. The second phase requires qualities of nurturing, supporting and giving protection. This is part of the overall female make-up, which contains within it a steadiness and constancy that will mature with time. Women's spirituality can be compared to a perpetual ocean, rather than the dramatic highs or sparkling waterfalls that enlightened men may achieve.

> *The master [Shaykh Nizam ad-Din Awliya] then declared that dervishes who ask saintly women and saintly men to intercede on their behalf invoke saintly women first because they are so rare. "When a wild lion comes into an inhabited area of the forest," he explained, "no one asks, 'Is it male or female?' Similarly, the sons of Adam, whether they be men or women, must devote themselves to obedience and piety."[160]*
>
> *Amir Hasan Sijzi*

> *God purifies the heart of a person according to the measure of the sincerity of a person in remembering Him.*
>
> *Imam Junayd*

Amongst the spiritual women I have met, Mrs Junaid from Sri Lanka made a deep impression on me. Shaykh Hosam Raouf and I, along with some other friends, had initiated various projects for human development in Sri Lanka. In the 1980s, when we were setting up activities, there was a small but well-respected Muslim community comprising about 8 per cent of the total population. They are called Moors because, some hundreds of years ago, North African Muslims en route to China landed near the city of Galle, in the south of the island. "Galle" is a corrupted version of the Arabic word *galaa*, meaning "castle". They needed repairs to their ship and so, impressed by their ethical behaviour, the local ruler invited these Muslims to stay on in his country. They became the ancestors of the present-day Muslims.

The agent for our affairs in Sri Lanka, Saheed, a fine man, came from this community. On one of our visits, he found us a well-run boys' orphanage to assist. The plan was then to visit a girls' orphanage in a poor suburb of Colombo. As we approached the home, we could hear the sweet voices of girls chanting "*La ilaha illallah*". Mrs Junaid, an elderly lady who was the matron of the home, came to the door to welcome us. She apologized for the building rubble outside the entrance. The roof of the house had recently collapsed and they had run out of money while repairing it.

When I in turn apologized for interrupting their *dhikr*, she explained with her radiant face, wreathed in smiles, that they had all been waiting for us. Their orphanage had received no donations, although Eid had just passed, and there was no money for sufficient food or the customary new clothes for the girls. Mrs Junaid had instructed them to make a rota and do constant *dhikr*, asking God to assist them in their plight. They had been doing this for two days without stopping. Our visit was for them literally an answer to prayer. We all emptied our pockets and with the money on us were able to provide each of the seventy-odd girls with food, new clothes and sandals. Later on, we returned to make arrangements for further assistance to the home.

> *Allah says, "Call on Him humbly and sincerely." Dhikr is the greatest 'ibada. For he who is aware of what is in the hearts, the Most Generous gives His rewards without measure.*
> *Sidi Ali al-Jamal*

Mrs Junaid, who had dedicated her life to service, exemplified for me the concept of *baraka* (grace) and the deep rewards of serving based on trust with no expectations. She had done what she could to repair the fallen roof and fulfil her girls' needs. When her personal actions failed to bring about the desired for assistance, she had called upon the unseen. In turning away from a cul-de-sac, she gave in to the unseen, allowing nature to bring in its bounty. *Baraka* follows pure intention and reliance upon God. It implies an x-factor which brings a greater power than expected to a process or activity. Much of the outcome will depend on the good will, intention and attention of the people involved. When an activity is potentized by the correct intention of the participants, and it takes place at the right time and in the right place, the outcome is likely to be a great success. People are most fortunate if, like Mrs Junaid, they have direct experiences of how the seen and the unseen connect. When a person unifies their personal will with God's, there is no longer any blockage and there will be an immense potency in their actions, even though the outcome may not appear to others as significant. Potency sometimes appears immediately and carries on indefinitely.

During the past decades, there have been many cases of Western women converting to Islam due to their marriages to men from Muslim backgrounds. Sometimes there is already a prior attraction toward Islam, but in other cases there may be an element of convenience in the decision. Whatever the initial motivation, the women often develop more commitment to the *deen* than their born-Muslim husbands.

During a trip to Norway some 20 years ago, I was giving talks at Oslo University on Sufism and spirituality. I became curious about the presence in the audience of a large number of Norwegian ladies in *hijab* – maybe two dozen or so. Many of them were young mothers pushing prams. During a tea break, I asked an Iranian political refugee about them, who told me these girls were mainly divorcées who had been married to men from the Middle East and other parts of the Muslim world. He himself was married to a beautiful blonde who had become a fervent Muslim after their marriage. He now had a strict Ayatollah in the home and he feared that divorce was inevitable!

I asked one of the mothers about her attraction to Islam and she said it gave her dignity, as well as a "clear direction" in life. We all seek respect, honour and equitable treatment.

The Loved One within makes the lover's life thrive,
The veil of Self-Knowledge he finds his way past.
In Unity's circle, if he's all alive,
His drop becomes sea, then he finds Oceans vast.
Who drinks love's goblet from the perfect guide
Straightway finds himself the Beloved beside;
Comes love, and the lover's will is set aside,
Then, bidden "Return!" he finds his Lord at last.

This transient world's basis and frame is love;
Here and Hereafter the lover's aim is love;
He serves, obeys and works to proclaim his love;
Who lives with love, to Paradise comes at last.
From East to West, whichever the way you do,
That lovers are legion experience will show;
For man in our age is longing Truth to know,
In the depths of his heart he'll find it at last.[161]

Muzaffer Ozak al-Jerrahi

Allah has a garden in this world. Whoever enters it does
not yearn for the garden of the next world.

Ibn 'Ata' Allah

Attached to the household I grew up in was a venerable lady called Umm Hussein. She had all the attributes of an enlightened and humble being. Umm Hussein was one of several women who had lived in our compound ever since I could remember. She had a small room with a little kitchenette at the end of it. Occasionally the children were given some nuts and raisins produced from ancient-looking tins in her larder. She would always be helpful for us children, with bits of sewing, mending or fixing buttons that were about to fall. Like several other ladies of her age, who were considered ancient in my childish eyes, she never refused the children anything.

I often remember her leaving at dawn every morning to go to the shrine of Imam Hussein. The door of my aunt's house was of the old variety, where the lock would make a loud clonk when it turned. One day, I complained that, sleeping on the roof as we did in summers, you could hear the "battle" of the door early in the morning. My father quietly said to me that it might take 40 years for me to change the way I heard this sound as Umm Hussein did: as the opening of the doors of Heaven.

Three nights before she passed away, she told my mother that she had dreamt of having moved to the next world: she had been taken to this ethereal vista where there were all kinds of homes and gardens, hills and waterfalls. She asked where her home was and was shown a pleasant cottage, which had no roof on it yet. Her guide to the hereafter told her that the roof would be fixed in three days and then it would be ready for her. So she asked my mother if she could be with her on that night. Obligingly, my mother went to Umm Hussein's room after the night prayers. She was shown various parcels to be given to the other ladies, as well as small sacks of rice and lentils to be cooked for distribution to the needy after her death. Umm Hussein was in no pain, nor was there any sign of imminent death, and she apologized to my mother for the inconvenience.

Sometime after midnight, my mother felt the change in her breathing pattern. After giving her some water, she sat quietly next to her head reciting the Quran. She said it was as though she lost track of time or place for a while, then she realized that Umm Hussein had passed away. My mother said that all she was able to describe of the event was that it was one of peace, ease and angelic lights.

The next morning, most unexpectedly, a large congregation of well-known religious scholars and pious people gathered behind her coffin. It happened to be a special day and all of these people had gathered when her coffin was carried for the customary circumambulation around the shrine of Imam Hussein. I can say that at no time did I or any of the children in that household have any negative thoughts or opinions about Umm Hussein, alive or dead. Like a quiet butterfly, she returned back to light.

Bibi Fadhila, my mother, was considered by many who knew her as an "unsung saint". Her faith and trust in Allah's decree was constant; even if an event distressed her, she would quickly accept it, saying, *"Allah raad"* (God willed it). Her positivity, unconditional reliability, good nature and desire to help all those who crossed her path influenced me greatly. Bibi was always clear about the importance of intention in all her actions. On the rare occasions that she criticized another's behaviour, it was always done in the spirit of compassion. Bibi was deeply loved, not only by her family, but by a wide circle of friends and acquaintances. Everybody who knew her benefitted from her presence and counsel. She had total trust and reliance on Allah's generosity, always believing in the best outcome even if her prayers were not immediately answered.

Generally we tend to extol the virtues of the departed, especially those whom we have loved, but even bearing this in mind I still do not think I am exaggerating my mother's qualities. Outwardly she always did her best for the benefit of whosoever concerned her, and her inner calm, open-mindedness and trust in the perfection of the Creator gave her presence a special light. Her scrupulous *adab* (courtesy, appropriate conduct) and constant reference to God encapsulated for me the role model of a spiritually directed seeker – a Sufi without the name!

MOTHER'S BEAUTY

My mother was most beautiful
I had always thought, quite rightly,
Always there to help, give and serve,
End of desires and special needs.
Beginning of endlessness.
Her long hair was plaited –
A ladder to heaven
I had often thought.
Her beauty absorbed me,
Leaving soul's light in my heart,
Past images or descriptions,
Sacred presence.
Pure beauty,
Unconditioned love and presence.[162]

Shaykh Fadhlalla Haeri

Chapter 10

SOUTH AFRICA

Now surely the friends of Allah – they shall have no
fear nor shall they grieve. Those who believe
and guarded [against evil].

Quran 10:62–63

Ever since my first visit to South Africa in 1993, I have made regular visits to Cape Town, a city full of Sufi shrines. On these occasions, I would always visit the *kramats* (burial places) of the first Muslim men of light to come to this country. These pious beings, who had reached a high spiritual station, have had a strong ongoing influence upon the population in Cape Town and the spread of Islam in the broader sense.

During the 17th century, a struggle took place between the Dutch and Portuguese for control of the coastal areas in India such as Bombay, Goa, Cochin, the Coramandel Coast and Bengal, Colombo and Galle in Ceylon, Medan and Padang in Sumatra, Batavia and Bali in Java and smaller islands in the Indonesian Archipelago, such as Macassar, Timor, Ternate and Tidore. Many of the rulers of these areas rose up to fight the European invaders. Amongst the leaders of the resistance were men of inner knowledge, some of whom were captured by the Dutch and sent in chains to the Cape. These exiled beings radiated goodness and encouraged those who had contact with them to take on the Prophetic Path.

When Jan van Riebeeck first established a station at the Cape of Good Hope after landing there in 1652, he hoped that the local "Hottentots" would provide the necessary labour force. When they proved unsatisfactory, he requested that the Dutch Council in the east send him slaves. The purpose of this station was to replenish Dutch ships sailing between Holland and the East Indies, which were carrying spices.

By this time, the Dutch had colonised several islands in the Indonesian Archipelago. They accordingly despatched to the Cape as slaves those who resisted their rule in the new colonies, as well as common criminals.

In May 1668, important prisoners arrived in the Cape from the west coast of Sumatra. Shaykh Abdurrahman Matebe Shah, the last of the Malaccan Sultans, was one of them. He and his religious advisor, Seyyed Mahmud, were banished to the forests of the Dutch East India Company in Constantia. The third prisoner was sent to Robben Island.

The shrine of Seyyed Mahmud has a special place in my heart. During that first visit to Cape Town, when I was considering moving to South Africa, I was invited for dinner at the home of an old business associate. He suggested that I might like to visit a well-known Sufi shrine, located within walking distance from his house in Constantia.

This turned out to be that of Seyyed Mahmud. The shrine stood in a small pine forest with an air of peace and grace about it. As I gently pushed open the creaking door, I made the intention of receiving some sign regarding my stay in South Africa. I sat in a corner by the dark, windowless shrine and proceeded to meditate upon the soul of the departed Sufi sage. When my eyes adjusted to the darkness of the interior, I could see three figures sitting motionless and in silence near me.

After a period of stillness, the person near me stirred, and when I opened my eyes I saw an old man removing the shawl that was covering his head. He moved gently toward me and said in a soft, clear voice, "If you move to South Africa, you will have the best of times and you will be honoured by the people here." Then he withdrew back under his shawl.

After a while, I got up and left, lingering outside in the hope of meeting this man again. Soon the door creaked open and the old man, a younger man in jeans and a young lady in *hijab* came out. The old man introduced his son, who was a doctor, and his daughter, who had been ill for a long time. She was revitalized once a week when they visited the shrine. The man told me that what he had said inside the shrine was not from him.

He had simply conveyed the message from the soul of the buried Sufi.

Years later, I heard through a friend that the old man was looking for me. We finally met again in 2009. I learnt he was known as the "keeper of secrets", and people claim that he has a special relationship with the *awliya* and knows the burial places of many unknown saints.

Shaykh Abdurrahman Matebe Shah, the last of the Malaccan Sultans, lies near Seyyed Mahmud in Constantia. After the Dutch capture of Malacca, he had continued to lead the Muslim resistance bravely from the fortress of Soerosesang. Eventually he was captured along with Seyyed Mahmud and his other religious adviser and banished to the Cape as the first political exiles. The Dutch decided that executing them would make them martyrs, and if they remained in the vicinity of Malacca, they would continue to be a rallying point for further resistance.

The Dutch authorities therefore exiled these popular leaders to remote areas where they could not influence the slaves of Muslim origin and other subjugated peoples working in Cape Town. Yet, despite these restrictions, it is said that Shaykh Abdurrahman befriended the slave population in the forests of Constantia and taught them about Islam. He died there around 1682 CE and was buried by the river at the place where he used to pray.

Today, families visit the shrine, have a picnic there and sit close by the burial site, surrounded by trees, running water and chirping birds, imbibing the atmosphere of peace and tranquillity.

Shaykh Yusuf of Macassar is probably the most famous of all the early men of light who came to the Cape. He belonged to the royal family of Goa, studied the religious sciences in Makka and was also a Khalwati Sufi shaykh. After he had completed his studies in Makka, he migrated to Banten in western Java due to the Dutch occupation of Goa. The Sultan Ageng of Banten recognized his outstanding qualities, appointed him as his chief *qadi* (judge) and married him to his daughter.

A civil war broke out in Banten between the followers of Sultan Ageng and his son, Pangeran Haji. Shaykh Yusuf fought until the last, only surrendering to the Dutch, who had backed the rebellious son, on a promise of a pardon. The Dutch broke their word, imprisoned him first in Batavia, then Ceylon, and finally sent him to the Cape in 1693 CE. Once in the Cape, Shaykh Yusuf, his family, 12 imams and other members of his entourage were sent to the remote farm of Zandvliet.

The Governor of the Cape, Simon van de Stel, treated him well, giving funds for his maintenance in keeping with his high status. This may have been because the King of Goa was tireless in his requests for Shaykh Yusuf to be sent back to Goa, where his spiritual knowledge was much needed. Shaykh Yusuf turned Zandvliet into a sanctuary for runaway slaves and his teachings of Islam spread in the Cape. He died in 1699 CE and was buried at Faure. The whole area is known as Macassar in his memory.

The story of early Islam in the Cape is one of courage, perseverance and dignity, where men of spiritual and worldly status, despite being prisoners of an alien power, managed to bring their Islamic faith and conduct to a disenfranchised population.

Sufis came to the Cape not only from Goa and the Indonesian Archipelago, but also from India, Turkey, Yemen and Arabia. In later years, the Indian Sufi contribution was largely due to a Chishti master, Hazrat Ghulam Muhammad Sufi, commonly known as Sufi Saheb. His teacher in Deccan, Hyderabad, Shaykh Habib Ali Shah, was inspired by a vision of the medieval Chishti shaykh, Nasirudin Mahmud Chiragh-i-Delhi, to send Sufi Saheb to teach the young Muslim community in Natal. He was assisted in his struggle to educate the traders and indentured labourers there by his brother-in-law, Moulana Abdul Latif. Sufi Saheb established a chain of mosques through Natal and was also inspired to purchase land in Cape Town. Maulana Abdul Latif took the first Juma *salat* in the Cape Flats in 1904 and the next year the Habibya Mosque was built. Sufi Saheb instructed him to develop the centre there, where to this day his descendants play a significant role in the spiritual life of the community, as is also the case in Durban.

When Ibrahim Rasool was Premier of the Cape, he had invited me along with some friends to dine with him. A portrait depicting Shaykh Yusuf of Macassar hung in a place of honour in an ante-chamber. During the dinner, Ibrahim said how privileged he and his wife, the descendants of slaves, felt to be in a position to serve the surrounding community, Muslim and non-Muslim alike. A circle had been completed.

> *Outer might can only emerge from inner humility and inner might emerges from outer humility.*
>
> *Sidi Ali al-Jamal*

> *The Prophet said, "If you find the meadows of Paradise, linger there." He was asked, "What are the meadows of Paradise?" His reply was, "Gatherings in remembrance of God."[63]*

After some years in South Africa, a few close students built a mosque and centre near Pretoria on land that belonged to friends. The mosque is generally referred to as the Rasooli Sufi Mosque. It was conceived as a place for all Muslims, regardless of whichever school of law they follow, to meet together and pray in the spirit of mutual respect and harmony. Sufism is neither Sunni nor Shiite, nor does it favour any *madhhab* over another. It is the heart of Islam, open to all. Women are welcome and can participate in the centre's activities. It provides a liberal atmosphere with a strong Sufi orientation and emphasis on Quran and Prophetic Islam. This has enabled the Rasooli Centre to host remarkable speakers and preachers from different denominations over the years.

For fourteen years the focal point has been an annual gathering, where a different topic is addressed every year and there are often distinguished visitors from overseas. These gatherings were all planned around themes that would honour the path of the Prophet Muhammad and his message and show its universality without denying cultures or communal habit. They covered the years between 2002, with the theme of "Living Islam", to 2015, addressing "Humanity's Connection to Divinity". Other titles included "Gnostics and Politics" (2007), "The Quran's Universal Message – A Mercy for All the Worlds" (2010) and "World Religions and Spiritual Illumination" (2014). It also afforded the opportunity for people from abroad to connect with the South Africans who are involved with the centre and enjoy the company of like-minded, like-hearted people.

A regular visitor has been Shaykh Hosam Raouf, my lifelong friend and companion. His friendly teachings and Friday prayers' discourses have been very popular as he speaks directly to the listeners. Shaykh Hosam personifies the characteristics of his name; *raouf* means gentle, kind and compassionate. His pure heart, unconditional compassion and illumined presence touch all those who meet him. It gives hope that there are still people like him, who can be trusted, respected and loved. Shaykh Hosam accompanied me on my first trip to South Africa and has been of immense help with my life's work here.

> *If kindness was a visible thing, nothing that God has created would be more beautiful than that.*[164]
>
> Prophet Muhammad

One delightful guest was Imam as-Sadiq al-Mahdi (b. 1935), who is a former Prime Minister of the Sudan (1966–67 and 1986–89). Imam as-Sadiq is the head of the National Umma Party, which his grandfather, Sayyid Abd al-Rahman al-Mahdi, founded, and is the great-grandson of Muhammad Ahmad al-Mahdi, who led the Mahdist War to free the Sudan from Anglo-Egyptian rule. Imam as-Sadiq has more than inherited the charisma of his forefathers. His education combined both the traditional religious studies with two degrees from Oxford University. He was thrust into politics at an early age, promoting Islamic democracy and co-operativeness with a strong international flavour. As well as his political affiliations, he is the imam of the Ansar, a Sufi *tariqa* that follows the teachings of his controversial forefather,

Muhammad al-Mahdi. Imam as-Sadiq is also the author of several books on Sudanese politics.

During his talk at our gathering, he highlighted how, in the early years of the Ummayad and Abbasid caliphates, the large number of Jewish and Christian converts to Islam affected the understanding of the *deen* and interpretations of Quran. He proposed that much of the clarity and purity of the original teachings were diluted and misinterpreted by these converts' influence. These confusions in understanding have had a negative impact on Muslims into the present day. They reduced the dynamics of transformative Islam into a religion that worships a remote god. I mentioned to him in relation to what he was expounding that rather than focus on human history, its dramas and what went wrong, we should return to the study of the Quran and be thrilled by the magical mystery of the Divine presence.

I enjoyed several pleasant discussions with Imam as-Sadiq during his stay with us. On the day of his departure, the imam was unable to say goodbye to me personally because of meetings with South African government officials. As he was being seated in the plane, he gave a beautiful swiss silver pocket watch to his South African host as a gift for me. This gesture will have been inspired by a previous conversation during which he asked me whether I had a watch. I had replied that my inner freedom lay in my lack of enslavement to time. He doubtless felt that, since I am involved in worldly activities, there should be some remembrance of time!

> *Imam Junayd was once asked, "Who is a Gnostic?"*
> *He replied, "The one who is not bound by time."*

The celebrated *ratib* (litany) of Imam as-Sadiq's ancestor, Muhammad al-Mahdi, had intrigued me because of the almost hypnotic effect it is recorded as having on his followers, who recited it on a daily basis. The teaching in the *ratib* is sequential and it defines a path of conduct that can only lead to higher spiritual states, as it aims for a being to be unaffected by outer events and more anchored in trust and reliance upon Allah. The communal recitation will also have acted as a bonding mechanism.

The original invocations were very long and I am not surprised that in recent times it has twice been shortened. The present *ratib*, in its comparative brevity, is more suited to our modern times.

> *The seeker of this path will only succeed if he is brave, resolute, and does not care about profit or loss. As for the fearful and cautious, there is no place for them on this path.*
>
> *Sidi Ali al-Jamal*

> *Open our hearts that we may hear Thy voice Which constantly cometh from within.*
>
> *Disclose to us Thy Divine Light, which is hidden in our souls, that we may know and understand life better.*[165]
>
> *Hazrat Inayat Khan*

Shaykh Saadi Shakur (Neil Douglas-Klotz) is an American Chishti master, religious and linguistic scholar, and writer. He holds regular workshops all over Europe, Russia and North America from his Scottish base. Shaykh Saadi expounds upon and transmits the eternal truths in a manner appropriate to our times. He and his delightful wife, Natalia, have been popular visitors at our annual gatherings. Natalia has shared with us an effective form of walking meditation from the Chishti teachings.

Shaykh Saadi has delved deeply into the Jewish and Christian mystical traditions, as well as the Islamic. His recitation of the Lord's Prayer in the original Aramaic has a transmittive resonance that reminds us of the power of the languages of revelation, like Sanskrit and Arabic. Two popular books of his are, *The Sufi Book of Life: 99 Pathways of the Heart for the Modern Dervish* and *Desert Wisdom: A Nomad's Guide to Life's Big Questions from the Native Middle East*. He weaves together guidelines for meditation with teaching stories from the Abrahamic traditions in an attractive and meaningful way.

Shaykh Saadi recently shared with me some of his insights on Sufism in the West. He particularly reflected on how the followers of Hazrat Inayat Khan (d. 1927), who brought the spiritual music of the Chishti tradition from India to Europe and North America, and whose message of love and harmony had captivated many Westerners, had adapted the traditional teachings.

In conversation Shaykh Saadi said:

Hazrat Inayat Khan came to Europe about a hundred years ago teaching his first mureeds the way he had been taught, with all of the prayers of the Prophet Muhammad and the outer rhythmic disciplines, which are necessary for freeing the inner life. He found that they were unable and/or unwilling to undertake the study of Arabic needed and deemed it absolutely necessary that they establish a rhythmic prayer life in some way. Most of his students began to do their prayers in English. While this was "adaptive", it also led to the work he brought being institutionalized almost as another religion, in form if not in name, with the result it was called by some "non-Islamic". This was never his intention.

There were many disputes over Hazrat Inayat Khan's "succession" after his passing, again evidencing the human mischief that often affects many institutional tariqas. One of his closest mureeds (with no claim to succession) was Sufi Ahmed Murad (Samuel L Lewis), who saw himself within what he considered the "real" or "original" Islam. His work in spiritual music, which I shared at the Rasooli Centre, is based firmly in the roots of prayer and devotion, rather than any kind of entertainment or performance. For him, all spiritual music needed to come from an experience of effacement in the One. Music in this sense is one of the highest non-verbal languages that can communicate the inexpressible.

Samuel Lewis was a unique mystic who followed both the Zen Buddhist path and that of the Sufi for most of his adult life. He introduced the Zen master Nyogen Senzaki to Hazrat Inayat Khan in 1923, and according to Sufi Ahmed Murad, they "sat down at a table, looked into each other's eyes and both immediately entered into that samadhi [complete absorption] which so may lecturers tell us about but do not experience themselves".

I find that in Europe and the USA, spiritual hunger is the greatest need and not only as a "personal growth" pastime. Unless this inner need is properly filled, the West will always be a burden on the rest of the world, both in terms of resources and cultural hegemony. Just as the Chishtis of old gave food freely to whoever came, as in those days physical hunger was a great need, the role of spiritual masters today is to try to do whatever they can, step by step, to fill what Camus called the "God-sized hole" of the Western psyche.

Toward the end of his life, Sufi Ahmed Murad had a very close connection with Sufi Barkat Ali in Pakistan, whom he visited in 1961–62. This relationship was continued by his khalifa, Moineddin Jablonski, after Sufi Ahmed Murad passed in 1971. Moineddin, who was my own Sufi guide, sent a number of us to visit Sufi Barkat Ali in Dar al-Ehsan in 1979. Afterwards, Murshid Moineddin wrote to Sufi Barkat Ali about the practices the mureeds followed:

"Hazrat Inayat Khan says, 'The Sufi method of realization – the study of shariat, tariqat, haqiqat and marifat, also the practice of zikr, fikr, kasab, shagal and amal is claimed to be the easiest, shortest and most interesting for spiritual accomplishment.' Our Murshid instructed us in the methods of tasawwuri, of akhlak Allah and, through divine grace, the mysteries of fana and baqa. And the phrase 'follow in the footsteps' has also been employed most joyously in the very sacred Dances of Universal Peace that Sufi Ahmed Murad Chisti gave to us, so that we might share the same spirit that inspired King David the Psalmist to dance in the presence of the Lord, Ya Hayyo Ya Qayoom, to share that spirit with those

*whose hearts are awakened through the Sacred Dance. There is
not one iota of frivolity in these Dances, for they are every one
based upon the repetition of the divine Name, upon the Name
of Allah, who is Rahman and Rahim.'"*[166]

*That heart which stands aloof from pain and woe
No seal of signature of Love can show:
Thy Love, the Love I chose, and as for wealth,
If wealth be not my portion, be it so!
For wealth, I ween, pertaineth to the World
Ne'er can the World and Love together go!
So long as Thou dost dwell within my heart
Ne'er can my heart become the thrall of Woe.*[167]

Hakim Sanai

Shaykh Jamal ad-Din was one of the most interesting converts to Islam
I have met, and was a welcome visitor to my home, Highwood Orchard,
and the Rasooli Centre. Born to a Roman Catholic father and Russian
Jewish mother, but raised as a Jew in his childhood, the tragic death of
his twin brother inspired him to convert to Catholicism in his teens.
He studied for the priesthood, joining the Dominican order and later
working in the Vatican. Shaykh Jamal was sent as a special envoy of the
Pope to South Africa to explore the possibilities of appointing a non-
white Roman Catholic bishop. While based in Durban, he received
permission to spend time with Ahmad Deedat and the Muslims around
him, as he wanted to find out about Deedat's activities and why he had
such a following. He intended to discover the weak points in the Islamic
teachings and expose them.

Over a period of months, Shaykh Jamal became increasingly challenged
as Deedat answered all his queries with quotes from the Bible. Then one
day he accompanied Deedat to an orphanage and school on the south
coast of Natal. Deedat asked him to make *wudu* with him, when the

time for prayer came. At first he refused, but was convinced when told that Jesus had also practiced a similar style of ablution. Then Deedat asked him to pray, and he again protested until Deedat explained that Jesus, too, had been described as going into *sajda* (prostration). When he prayed for the first time in the Muslim fashion, he experienced such a state that he repeated the prayer when he was alone in his lodgings in Durban. He once again accessed this state. He visited Deedat again and eventually took *shahada* with him. This was the beginning of a journey that took him from acceptance of Islam to excommunication from the Catholic Church, to the study of Quranic Arabic and mastery of Islamic jurisprudence. He had studied law at Cambridge and later practiced in Canada. After the tragic death of his wife and daughter, he returned to South Africa to undertake full-time studies of the religion of Islam for many years.

During the last two decades of the 20th century, South Africa had become a target for Islamic fundamentalism. Shaykh Jamal became one of their heroes. However, he emerged from this period of sterile narrowmindedness to the open horizons of original Islam and spiritual illumination. His honesty, courage and knowledge touched many hearts, while the bigoted amongst the professional preachers avoided him, leaving him contentedly at peace. I very much enjoyed his company and encouraged all my friends and family to visit him in Durban. He spent his last years there and passed away in 2008.

During the latter part of his life, he spoke openly about the light of Islam, the Sufis and the disastrous darkness that had engulfed many ignorant Muslims. It is noticeable that many converts begin by being very zealous about the *shari'a* aspects of the *deen*, which is appropriate when it ends up like Shaykh Jamal in leading to inner openings. Several of his friends and students have tried to keep his memory alive by establishing a centre bearing his name in Durban.

THE WINDOW WITHIN THE SOUL

During prayer I am accustomed to turn to God like this:
That's the meaning of the words of the Tradition,
"the delight felt in the ritual prayer."
The window of my soul opens,
And from the purity of the Unseen World,
The Book of God comes to me straight.
The Book, the rain of Divine Grace and the Light
Are falling into my house through a window
From my real and original source.
The house without a window is Hell
To make a window is the foundation of true religion.
Don't thrust your axe upon every thicket:
Come use your axe to cut open a window.[168]

Jalal ad-Din Rumi

Translations of the works of Jalal ad-Din Rumi (d. 1273 CE) enjoy a widespread popularity in the United States. Shaykh Kabir Helminski and his wife, Camille, have translated many works of Mawlana Jalal ad-Din Rumi, as well as authoring books on Sufism. They are also co-founders of the Threshold Society, an education foundation in the Mevlevi tradition based on the teachings of Rumi. Their international tours with the whirling *dervishes* of Turkey has brought the spiritual culture of the Mevlevis to thousands. It was delightful to see such a collaborative partnership and welcome them to the Rasooli Centre. Aside from her work on Rumi, Camille has also written *Women of Sufism: A Hidden Treasure*, which celebrates the contribution made by women through the ages to Sufism.

The inner light of Islam has illumined Kabir and Camille deeply and propelled them toward sharing the universal path of love of Rumi and passion for divine awakening. Their books have contributed to Rumi's public exposure in many countries and have brought authenticity to it. This has given a lot of help and hope to people of a spiritual orientation.

Modern Muslims who are looking for more than the *shari'a* part of Islam find in Rumi an encouraging and uplifting reference. His writings address the higher self, giving hope irrespective of circumstances. This makes a popular tonic in these times of outer restrictions and oppressions. A love for poetry and music can help in transcending the limitations of structures. Rumi's cheerful and illumined sonnets are most helpful and durable for those who have a sufficient foundation to receive them; a candle needs the wax and wick for it to be illumined, otherwise it will not last.

THE SEARCH

Past time, past space I sought Him,
Where space and time were not –
For I came to the day where was no day,
And no thing a name had got.

No "ego" then existed,
There was no "I", no "we",
All was forlorn, till creation was born
And names were assigned by me.

The curl of my Beloved
Methought its tip I saw;
Yet 'twas but a sign for this hope of mine:
The curl I saw no more.

I sought Him in congregations
Where Christians knelt in prayer.
"O surely He is on Calvary,
On the Cross?" He was not there.

I sought Him where heathen worship
In temple and in shrine –
But wherever I'd turn, I'd only learn
How fruitless this search of mine.

I journeyed to the distant
Herat and Candahar,
Through hill and glen I'd ask of men –
None knew Him, near or far.
I scaled the toilsome mountain
And gazed from Qaf's lone peak.
The birds of the air had nested there:
All else was bare and bleak.

'Mid the press of the pilgrims I quested,
Thronging black Kaaba's stone,
The old and the young, men of every tongue,
But not there had HE gone.

I asked of the Sage of Sina,
He knew not where He'd stay;
In Gabriel's court in Heaven I sought –
And empty, turned away.

Silent and still, my searching eyes
Within my heart did roam,
And lo! The light of His Presence bright;
'Twas there, 'twas there His Home.

With wine the drunkard staggers,
Blind, wild, with tottering knees;
Yet wilder to see is the ecstasy
Of the enraptured Sun of Tabriz.[169]

Jalal ad-Din Rumi

Mawlana Jalal ad-Din Rumi was born in Balkh in 1207 CE. His father, Baha ad-Din Veled, was an acknowledged theologian, Sufi master and the son of a princess of Khorasan, according to legend. The Mongol threat to Balkh forced the family to migrate, and they eventually settled in Qonya, then the capital of Rum, a province in central Anatolia. The Sultan, 'Ala ad-Din, extended a warm welcome to Baha ad-Din Veled, and Rumi was brought up amidst the elite of that society. After his father's death, Rumi studied under a Sufi master, Shaykh Burhan ad-Din Muhaqiq al-Tirmidhi. Shaykh Burhan ad-Din supervised the spiritual retreats which led to Rumi's awakening. Before he retreated from the world, the shaykh told Rumi he would meet someone who would be his dearest friend and open the innermost doors of the spiritual world to him. They would be each other's mirror.

Rumi took over his father's work as a traditional Sufi master and *'alim*. He was the much-respected professor of four colleges with a large following. Then, in 1244 CE, he met the "dearest friend" that his teacher had told him of. Shams ad-Din Tabrizi was an itinerant *dervish* who was roaming the world seeking someone to share his knowledge of divine love. He had travelled through many lands in search of the best spiritual teachers and had been given the nickname Perenda ("The Flier" or "Bird"). According to the *Menaqibu' al-Arifin* (*The Acts of the Adepts*) of Shams ad-Din Ahmed al Aflaki (a pupil of Rumi's grandson, Chelebi Emis Erif), he prayed to be led to the man most favoured by Allah. A voice then asked him what he was prepared to give for this introduction. Shams replied, "My head." It was then revealed that Rumi was the man he sought.

They had encountered each other years previously in Damascus, but Rumi had turned away when Shams had addressed him. This time Shams met Rumi while he was riding a mule, surrounded by a crowd of his disciples, who accompanied him on foot. Shams took hold of the mule's bridle and Rumi was so moved by their exchange that he took Shams home. They stayed together, inseparable for months, lost in spiritual communion. Rumi's pupils were overcome with jealousy. Shams must have been aware of this, for he suddenly disappeared. A distraught Rumi adopted as a sign of mourning the hat and wide cloak that Shams used to wear. This has been worn by the Mevlevi *dervishes* from that day on. It was from this time that Rumi started the whirling dance that is characteristic of his order. Many people said he had gone mad due to Shams's evil influence. People in Makka said the same about the Prophet Muhammad. We are always afraid of what we do not understand, especially when a human being accesses higher consciousness.

It is said that one day Rumi sent his son, Sultan Veled, to Damascus to bring Shams back to Qonya. This he did. Rumi and Shams became once again inseparable. The pupils again felt neglected and full of jealousy. They were unable to understand why Rumi was so enraptured with Shams. Rumi had enjoyed his status as an acknowledged master but his higher self was attracted to Shams, who tried to demolish the edifice of that self-image. He mirrored for Rumi his soul, showing him the source of his own life and how it was at one with the source of Shams's life and all human beings.

Shams came from a traditional scholarly background, but as a man of *tawhid* he could not tolerate the hypocrisies of some of the religious establishment and erstwhile Sufis. This made him an uncomfortable companion for Rumi's pupils, whose platitudes he often deflated. Shams's lack of concern for social and cultural niceties was a genuine reflection of his spiritual station, but disturbing for those at a lower level of cognisance, who felt confused and threatened.

Rumi's *The Sun of Tabriz* gives in one of his poems, entitled, "The Man of God", a picture of an illumined being – his tribute to Shams. Sir Colin Garbett's translation of *The Sun of Tabriz* has been used as a token of respect for a sincere seeker and lover of Rumi. Sir Colin was a distinguished British colonial administrator and Farsi scholar who served both in Iraq and India. He was a devout Christian and freemason, but at the end of his Indian service he met Maharaj Sardar Sawan Singh, an enlightened master of Sikh origin, and followed his path of Sant Mat for the rest of his long life. Sardar Charan Singh Maharaj, the great master's successor, later became his teacher and gave his approval of the authenticity of this translation of *The Sun of Tabriz*. Sir Colin eventually settled in White River, South Africa. Although he had passed on before I moved to this area, we have friends in common. Sant Mat follows the teachings of the "ancient wisdom taught by all true masters since the beginning of time". They are lovers of Rumi and other Sufi poets, like Bulleh Shah. Their organization, Radha Soami Satsang Beas, has produced fine publications on Sufism, including my favourite on Shams-i-Tabriz.

THE MAN OF GOD

Intoxicated he – and yet no wine he sips.
Full surfeited – and yet no meat has crossed his lips.
The Man of God.

"Oh God," he cried, "Oh God" – bewildered and amazed.
No dreaming vision his, on Very Truth he's gazed.
The Man of God.

A King is he – and yet a beggar's robe his wear.
In lonely desert, lo, a market rich and rare.
The Man of God.

He is not of the Air, he is not of the Earth,
No element of Fire or Water gave him birth,
The Man of God.

He is an ocean, yet its source no one can tell.
He raineth pearls that never knew an oyster shell,
The Man of God.

His are a hundred moons, a hundred circling ones.
In his effulgence shine a hundred blazing suns –
The Man of God.

Who sought to learn of Truth, from him their learning took.
The lore that he imparts he learned not from a book.
The Man of God.

A heathen now he seems, and now a man of Faith,
But what is right? Who knows! And what is wrong?
Who saith!
The Man of God

He rides on earthly horse amongst the race of men.
He rides in Heaven on high above all human ken.
The Man of God.

The Son of Faith is he – bear ever this in mind.
Him seek with heart and soul, Him seek and thou
Shalt find.
The Man of God.

His are a hundred moons, a hundred circling ones.
In his effulgence shine a hundred blazing suns –
The Man of God.

Who sought to learn of Truth, from him their learning took.
The lore that he imparts he learned not from a book.
The Man of God.

A heathen now he seems, and now a man of Faith.
But what is right? Who knows! And what is wrong?
Who saith!
The Man of God.[170]

Jalal ad-Din Rumi

Shams disappeared once more, never to return. There are various legends about his death. One story says he was executed by the Vizier of Qonya's soldiers, another that Rumi's pupils murdered him. The distraught Rumi travelled to Damascus hoping to find him. It was then that he woke up and knew:

Why should I seek? I am the same as he.
His essence speaks through me.
I have been looking for myself.[171]

Rumi went on to write *The Diwan of Shams-i-Tabriz* in a format as if Shams himself was penning the verse. Rumi's love for Shams inspired his outpourings of intoxicated verse. After Shams' disappearance, Rumi had a close companion in Sala ad-Din Zarkub, a goldsmith and later his scribe, Hussam Chalabi. It is said that the *Mathnawi* was written in response to Hussam's suggestion that he follow in the footsteps of Attar and Sanai. The *Mathnawi* has become one of the bestselling poetry collections in the US, has been translated into many languages and is read all over the world.

Rumi was known for his love of music and dance as a means of transcendence. The ecstatic whirling, which mirrors the rotation of the heavens, and the musical recitals for which the Mevlevi *dervishes* are renowned have been controversial. However, the *fatwas* of the orthodox in Turkey through the centuries have generally been in their favour.

> *Watching the lovers whirling in worship as they remember and proclaim the Divine Unity, certain unperceptive onlookers may reach the conclusion that the dervishes are merely playing games or dancing. But it is known and accepted by men of real understanding that a grave sin is incurred by comparing the Remembrance of God to a game or dance, or by jumping to such superficial conclusions. To compare the Remembrance of God, and the whirling movements associated with it, to mere play-acting is an error as serious and unpardonable as equating lawful sex with adultery and fornication, or military service with murder. For while it is true that there is a similarity in each case from the point of view of the action, in meaning and nature they are utterly different and distinct. To pretend otherwise is certainly to invite the displeasure of God, Exalted is He.[172]*
>
> Sheikh al-Islam and Grand Mufti Ebu-Su'ud,
> *Official Ruling on the Sufi Practice of Whirling*

Rumi's stories and musings, as well as his poetry, continue today to enchant people of many languages and faiths the world over.

> *From the Lover and the Beloved Are One.*
> *In the early morning, a lover asked her beloved, "Do you love me more than yourself?"*

"More than myself
For sure I have no self anymore
I am you already.
The 'I' has gone, the 'you' has come about.
Even my identity is gone.
The answer is taken for granted 'You' and 'I' has no meaning.
The 'I' has vanished
Like a drop into an ocean of honey."[173]

Jalal ad-Din Rumi

There was a Bektashi dervish and a conventional Muslim travelling together. They stop for the night and tether their mounts. The Muslim asks Allah to protect his horse, while the Bektashi prays, "Oh, Shaykh, take care of my donkey during the night."

In the morning the horse had been stolen and the donkey was still there. The Muslim asked the Bektashi how he could explain this. The Bektashi replied, "Allah has many servants and he let the horse be taken from one servant and given to another. But my shaykh has only one pupil, he had no one to give my donkey to!"[174]

Professor Thomas McElwain (Haydar Ali), an American religious scholar, author and musician, has visited us on several occasions. Haydar Ali believes that his work, *The Beloved and I*, which translated the Quran and Bible in rhymed verse and includes some works from the New Testament, Apocrypha and the Hebrew Bible, is important at a time when there is increasing physical violence and misunderstanding between the faiths. He describes himself as a "Quaker hard-shell Baptist Sufi", who has practiced Islam for several decades. Equally intriguing is his link with the Bektashis, one of the most controversial of the Sufi orders.

His grandmother was descended from German converts to Islam through Turkish influence in the 17th century. She attended church in the Appalachians, where the family had migrated to from Germany, but had, in his words,

> *a robust family tradition based on their Islamic memory. What was passed down tended to be things Baptists and Muslims have in common. The devotional practice, both in the family and the individual, was the recitation of the Bible, specifically the Psalms of David, since no one had a Quran nor could have read it. The Psalms were given a strongly Islamic interpretation, not to say a Twelver Shiite interpretation, including the realization that the Psalms contained the names of Muhammad and others. There was a devotional focus on the names that were handed down, Muhammad, Ali and the imams. A dhikr that consisted of merely reciting: O Ali (Ya Ali!) was about as far as external practice went. The tradition maintained itself as merely the recitation of the Psalms while giving them an Islamic identity and intent.*

> *All down through Ottoman history, when the orthodox religious life of the people was under dominant Arabic influence, when the classic literature in vogue in palace circles was Persian, and when even a great mystic order, such as the Mevlevis, based its belief and practice on a book written entirely in Persian, the Bektashis consistently held to the Turkish language and perpetuated in their belief and practice some at least of the pre-Islamic elements of Turkish culture. A Turkish investigator in 1926, writing in the official magazine of the national culture society called the* Turkish Ocak, *makes the claim that the Turkish national ideal never was able to find its expression in the Arab internationalism, but did find it in the tekkes or lodge-rooms of the Alevi orders of which the Bektashis and village*

groups related to them are chief examples. In the secret practices of those religious groups alone was "national freedom" to be found. The very aim, he says, of the founders of these groups, was to preserve the Turkish tongue and race and blood.[175]

John Kingsley-Birge

Hajji Bektash Wali (d. c1297 CE), a Seyyed from Khurasan, is a semi-legendary late 13th-century CE figure who is credited with setting up *tekkes* throughout eastern Anatolia. He is the embodiment of the wandering holy man, spreading Islam throughout the Turkish-speaking rural areas.

Hajji Bektash initially followed the order of Ahmad Yasavi (d. 562 AH/1166 CE), founder of the first truly Turkish Sufi order, whose teachings facilitated the adoption of Islam by the nomads of Turkestan, as they retained some of the flavour of their pre-Islamic practices. Ahmad Yasavi made Yasi into a learning centre for the Kazakh steppes and was the author of the first Sufi work to be written in a Turkic dialect. At 63, the shaykh retreated to an underground cell, where he spent the rest of his life. Tamerlane considered him to be so significant a figure for Central Asian Islam that he built a magnificent mausoleum over the site of his grave in Yas.

By the late fourteenth century, the Janissaries, an elite military organization largely consisting of Christian prisoners of war or children taken from conquered parts of Eastern Europe and brought up as Muslims, upheld the belief that they had been blessed from their formation by Hajji Bektash. Their headgear and costume were authorized by the Bektashi order. Historically, the Janissaries were founded in the 1380s by Sultan Murad I, so the physical blessing by Hajji Bektash is suspect, but Bektashi *dervishes* certainly accompanied them on their military campaigns from early days. The Bektashis became their official Sufi protectors and the Janissaries believed their *dervishes* provided them with magical protection on the battlefield.

Although Hajji Bektash is considered the founder of the order, it was Balim Sultan (c1500 CE), known as Piri Sani ("Second Saint"), who was responsible for the formalization of their doctrine and rituals. He synthesized Sunni and Shiite beliefs and mixed Muslim with Christian devotional practices. The sixth Shiite imam, Jafar as-Sadiq, was taken as a patron saint, bread and wine were offered at initiation ceremonies and teachers had to be celibate. Turkish rural communities had historically been tolerant to the Christians in their midst, which facilitated conversions of Greeks and Armenians; while the Turkish Muslim presence in Albania and Bulgaria during the 14th and 15th centuries produced an Islam which incorporated Christian and pagan practices.

The Bektashis, like the Ismailis, believed the Quran had an outer and an inner meaning, and gave greater importance to the esoteric interpretation. There was secrecy surrounding their practices and accusations of infiltration by heretical sects, such as the Hurufis. Some within the order were said to have divinized Imam Ali, believed in the transmigration of souls and incorporated shamanic elements into their belief system. They are also known for the symbolism behind their calligraphy. The Bektashis were frequently under attack by the *'ulama*, as well as the more orthodox Sufi *tariqas*. Yet, their influence on the court elite of the Ottoman Empire, as well as the rural masses, was immense for hundreds of years. The government protected them against charges of heresy due to their doctrinal deviations.

In 1826, Sultan Mahmud II destroyed the whole Janissary corps and dissolved the Bektashis, executing thousands of their *dervishes*. All the order's property was taken and given to the Naqshabandis, including their vast salt mines. In their heyday, the order had distributed salt under the name of Hajji Bektash! The survivors went into hiding, operating as an underground movement. It is said that some Bektashis pretended to be Naqshabandis but continued their traditional devotional practices in secret. After 30 years or so, they had a visible presence again in Turkey. Kemal Ataturk closed the *tekkes* of all the Sufi orders in 1925 as part of his modernization policy and the Bektashis moved their headquarters to Tirana, Albania. Unlike the orthodox *tariqas*, they favoured secularism because it gave some protection against persecution from religious authorities.

They continue to have a strong presence in Eastern Europe, particularly in Albania and Macedonia, and there are Bektashi *tekkes* in the USA. They are particularly known for their jokes, which have an iconoclastic style and poke fun at the religious establishment.

Over the last year, I have much enjoyed recordings of Bektashi *dhikrs*. The singers are both men and women coming from the Kirkuk region of Iraq and Kurdistan. Their praises of Imam Ali reverberate in my heart, so intense are they in their passion. One day recently I asked Hajji Bektash to explain the popularity of their *dhikrs* now that we are living in an age where people do not have the luxury of years of training to live the *deen*, as had been the case with the seekers of the past. He said that basic self-awareness, accountability and acceptance of the Prophetic message are a necessary foundation for the love of an awakened being, as exemplified by Ali. The Bektashis lose themselves in their love of Ali and strive for perfection by emulating his outstanding qualities.

> *A Bektashi was praying in the mosque. While those around him were praying, "May God grant me faith," he muttered, "May God grant me plenty of wine." The imam heard him and asked angrily why, instead of asking for faith like everyone else, he was asking God for something sinful. The Bektashi replied, "Well, everyone asks for what they don't have."*[176]

Recent visitors to the Rasooli Centre have included a small group of serious seekers from Bangladesh, a land of Sufis past and present. Some years ago, one of them had bought a book of my Quranic *tafsirs* at an airport and later made contact. They have taken the teachings, especially those on the Quran, to their centre in Dakka, where regular gatherings have been established. The courtesy and commitment of these students has been a delight.

Dr Muhammad Abdur Rabb was a dear friend whom I used to visit whenever I was in Montreal. He was from Bangladesh but settled in Canada. A serious student of Sufism, he presented me with copies of his Masters' thesis on Imam Junayd and his PhD on Abu Yazid al-Bistami. We often talked about the possibility of touring with a group of friends around the Sufi shrines of Bangladesh, but the opportunity never arose.

The people of Bengal have always had a strong devotional orientation and there are many shrines spread throughout the country, particularly in the Chittagong area. The first Sufis probably arrived around the middle of the 11th century CE. They came from all over the Muslim world, including Turkey, Iraq, Iran, Central Asia and Yemen. Although some will have followed in the wake of Muslim armies, many will have been itinerant mystics more concerned with their own spiritual unfoldment than mass conversions. The locals will have come to revere the holy men in their midst and legends will have grown from memories passed down through the generations.

The sweetness and gentleness of the people of this area was not always accompanied by the necessary boundaries. The result has been a lot of superstition and deviation from the authentic Sufi teachings. This has laid them open to attack from fundamentalists in recent times.

Shaykh Badru'd-Din or Pir Badr-i Alam (d. 844 AH/1440 CE) is one 15th-century figure who has for centuries been revered as the patron saint of sailors, Hindu and Muslim alike, and is a good example of how stories get distorted through the ages. The historical figure is said to have come to Chittagong from Meerut via Bihar and was from an established Indian Sufi family. The area he settled in was considered haunted, so he won the respect of the locals, predominantly Buddhists and Hindus, for his courage in facing the demons. He later moved to Bihar, where he died and now has a mausoleum. He was known for his serious study of Sufism and doubtless would have been surprised by the cult that has grown up around his name.

The legendary Pir Badr-i Alam is said to have arrived in Chittagong on a floating rock and travelled by river on a fish to nearby Arakan. He is associated with Khidr, who also travelled by fish and whom the Hindu population will have equated with the fish incarnation of Vishnu. Local boatmen would always ask for his protection before embarking on a journey.

There are symbolic tombs of Pir Badr all over the area, generally located at river mouths. Joint ceremonies are held for the Pir and Khidr, whereby grass rafts carrying lighted lamps are floated on rivers or ponds. Pir Badr is also considered one of the Panch Pir or five masters revered locally. The others are Ghazi Miyan (Salar Mas'ud), Shaykh Farid and Khidr. All are held in great esteem by both Muslims and Hindus.[177]

"Islam began as a stranger and will return.
Blessed, therefore, are the strangers."
The Prophet was asked who the strangers were,
to which he replied, "The strangers are those who rectify
what people have corrupted of my laws, as well as revive what
people have destroyed of it."[178]

In past years I had often been invited by Sufi groups in Sweden and Denmark. The connections made then have continued and the interest in Islam and Sufism has grown considerably in those countries over the years, encouraged by the influx of Muslim refugees. The recent visits of Shaykh Muhammad Muslim, a Swedish imam, with some of his family, especially his son Yusuf, confirmed to me how Prophetic Islam will touch people's hearts irrespective of race or culture. Shaykh Muslim's command of Arabic and Urdu and the fact that he completely adopted his wife's Subcontinent culture meant that he is accepted by born Muslims. Historically, when Westerners have become Muslims, they have often had difficulties because prevailing cultural norms had taken a priority over the *deen*.

Shaykh Muslim has studied at Deobandi *madrasas*, which, despite the movement's Sufi origins, are more associated with a Salafi Islam than mysticism. Originally students at all Deobandi *madrasas* went on to study Sufism after they were qualified in the religious sciences, as was the case historically with most Sufis, who generally had a strong grounding in *fiqh*. Societal changes over the past 100 years or so have meant that it has become impractical for the graduating *'alim* to expand his studies into the inner dimension to balance that excessive concern with outer rules and regulations, which stifles the heart. Shaykh Muslim follows a Sufi *tariqa* that combines the Chishti, Kubrawi, Suhrawardi, Naqshabandi and Qadiri chains of transmission. Like the late Shaykh Jamal, he progressed from a solid background in *fiqh* to exploring the lights and delights of the way of the heart.

On Shaykh Muslim's last visit, he was accompanied by Abdul Salaam, a Swedish Muslim who works with him in running programmes teaching Swedes about Islam. Abdul Salaam's explanation that he had initially been attracted to Islam because he felt it was not a religion but a natural way of life heartened me. Islam's emphasis on the interconnectedness of everything in creation had particularly resonated with him. Increasingly there will be more and more Western converts to Islam, attracted to the clarity and simplicity of the Prophetic revelation.

The Prophet once spoke of his beloved brothers of a later time who would love him without having seen him. The challenge for new converts is to reconcile distracted or confused Muslims with Muhammadi Islam. Up to recently, European exposure to Sufism or Islam would have been through individuals visiting a Muslim country or through books, or marriage. Now, more people through internet access and ease of research will discover the benefits of the Quran and Islam without having to belong to a particular sect or group. As travellers, we all need a map that leads to the city. It is only those who have not arrived who argue about the map!

Shaykh Muslim told us that when he was 20 years old he had given up all his possessions and was living on a farm in rural Sweden. One day, there was an unexpected visitor from a stranger. The man was a Swedish convert to Islam and he had come looking for someone who was no longer staying in that area. Shaykh Muslim had had no previous exposure to Islam but was attracted to it when he saw the stranger make *wudu* and pray. He embraced Islam the next day and left with the man for a trip to Pakistan. Afterwards, he went with him to join a small community in Norway, some of whom later became Muslims. Shaykh Muslim eventually settled in Yorkshire, England, and began his serious studies of Arabic and *fiqh*. He later married and had a family there and only returned a few years ago to his native Sweden.

In this path, the foundation is built upon breathing.
The more that one is able to be conscious of one's breathing, the
stronger is one's inner life.[179]

Baha ad-Din Naqshabandi

There have been various Naqshabandi visitors and connections during my years in South Africa. The Naqshabandi *tariqa* has had an immense impact on the history of Sufism; it brought light to Hanafi Islam and is today one of the most popular of the Sufi orders. It is the only known Sufi *tariqa* that traces its lineage through Abu Bakr, the first caliph, back to the Prophet Muhammad, rather than Imam Ali. The order defines itself as the *Tariqat al-Sahaba* ("The Path of the Prophet's Companions"). The *silsila* does, however, connect indirectly to Imam Ali through his descendant, the sixth Shiite imam, Jafar as-Sadiq.

The origin of the Naqshabandi teachings, according to a history of the order, *Rashahat Ain al-Hayat* by Fakhr al-din Ali, can be traced back to Yusuf al-Hamadani (d. 1140 CE), who took both from the teachings of classical Sufism and the Malamatiyya. He was originally from Iraq but migrated to Merv in Khurasan. His *khalifas* spread into Transoxiana. His most celebrated *khalifa* was Ahmad al-Yasavi (d. 562 AH/1166 CE), from whom the Yusaviyya orders come, and who is noted for bringing Islam to the Turkic tribes of the steppes. He influenced the teachings of the Bektashis, who had a strong presence in the Ottoman Empire.

A later master, Abd al-Khalilal-Ghujduwani (d. 1220 CE), who lived at the time of the Mongol invasions, is said to have advocated the silent *dhikr* used by the Naqshabandis and formulated the eight rules, which are the basic teachings of the *Tariqat al-Khawajagan* ("The Path of the Masters"), the name given to his *silsila*. Baha ad-Din Naqshabandi (d. 1389 CE) was a Tajuk born near Bukhara who lived most of his life in that region. He built on the earlier teachings of the Khawajagan and it is by his name that the order is known.

Shaykh Baha ad-Din laid great emphasis on adherence to *shari'a* and simplicity of worship, with no complex or distracting rituals. He is reported to have said, *"Az-zahir li'l-khalq, al-batin li'l-Haqq"* (The exterior is for the world, the interior for God). The Naqshabandis became associated with Sunni orthodoxy, with a strong tradition of emulating the behaviour of the Prophet Muhammad. Their close association throughout the centuries with Muslim rulers and those in positions of power was justified as guiding those in authority toward a better way of living and thus improving society as a whole. This is a similar approach to the Suhrawardis and in complete contrast to the Chishtis, who always warned against association with rulers and their appointees.

The order was actively involved in spreading Islam amongst the Turks. Shaykh Baha ad-Din's mausoleum became an important pilgrimage destination in Central Asia. Ubaydallah Ahrar (1404–90 CE) of Tashkent, one of the early successors of Shaykh Baha ad-Din, was the spiritual advisor of the Timurid Amir of Samarqand, exerting considerable influence on government policy. He encouraged Naqshabandi expansion by sending his *khalifas* to Afghanistan, China, Iran, Anatolia and the Hijaz.

The Naqshabandi teachings travelled even further in successive generations into India, the Caucasus, Kurdistan and Syria. Amongst the most celebrated of its numerous sub-orders is the Naqshabandi-Mujaddadi, founded in India by Ahmad Sirhindi (1563–1624 CE), who had styled himself as a reformer of his times and strongly opposed the Mughal Emperor Akbar's policies of religious tolerance. He was committed to the concept of a Muslim state and against the introduction of Hindu practices into the Muslim way of life. He aggressively campaigned against the more cultic manifestations of Sufism, saint worship and Shiite influence on Sunni Islam.

Sirhindi's orientation was followed by Shah Wali-ullah (1702–63 CE), who advocated a Muslim state, modelled on the early caliphate and led by a caliph, whose virtuous example based on following the Prophetic model would lead his subjects toward an Islamic way of life. He also attacked the worship of saints. Shah Wali-ullah's teachings have to be seen within the context of a declining, permissive Mughal Empire and the popularity of Sufism amongst the Muslims, where Sufi shrines were equally visited and venerated by Hindus.

His contemporary Naqshabandi master, Mirza Mazhar Djan-i-Djanan (1699–1781 CE), in contrast, regarded the Vedas as a revealed book and advocated dialogue with the Hindus. He also stated that Shiite–Sunni disputes had no relevance with regard to basic Islamic beliefs. He regarded many popular theological disputes between Sufis as coming more from misunderstandings of Sufi terminology than real differences. One Muharram, however, he criticized the excessive respect shown to wooden models depicting the tomb of Imam Hussein and was shot by irate Shiites, dying shortly afterwards from his wounds. An ironic end for a man of moderation and balance.

The Naqshabandis were to play a prominent role in 19th-century *jihads* against the Russians and later against the Communists. They also figured in the history of Chinese Central Asia, where Chinese Muslim generals of the 19th century were generally affiliated with the order.

The Kurdish connection with Naqshabandis has been strong up to the present day, and generally associated with their nationalist aspirations. Shaykh Diya al-din Khalid (1776–1827 CE), a Kurd from the Shahrizur district of northern Iraq, became one of the most prominent Sufi masters in the 19th-century Ottoman Empire. He settled in Damascus at the end of his life, establishing the Khalidi branch of the Naqsbandiyya-Mujaddidiyya. His teachings were influential in the reformist movements of the time and continued to impact upon the Muslim community throughout the 19th century and into the 20th. He met the young Amir Abdul Qadir of Algerian Damascus before the latter's *jihad* against the French, and his teachings are also said to have influenced Imam Shamyl of Daghestan in his *jihad* against the Russians.

A recent Grand Mufti of Syria, Ahmad Kuftaro (d. 2004), was a Naqshabandi. In response to the Salafi attacks on Sufism, he advocated use of more Quranic terms in the place of traditional Sufi vocabulary. He used modern media to make his teachings on human rights, inter-faith dialogue and the environmental crisis accessible to a larger audience.

Shaykh Nazim al-Haqqani Qubrusi (d. 2014) followed the traditional line of Naqshabandi teachers. He was a gentle, fatherly figure who provided a welcoming haven to anyone visiting his centre in Cyprus. He established centres throughout Europe, North America and South Africa, which provided places of *dhikr* and worship for his followers, attracting many converts to Islam.

Shaykh Amanullah, Philippe de Vos, whom Shaykh Nazim al-Haqqani had appointed as the Naqshabandi representative in France, is from a distinguished French family and had converted in his teens to Islam. He has on several occasions visited the Rasooli Centre and shared with us Naqshabandi teachings, often effectively incorporated with music.

> *Give me the pain of Love, the Pain for Thee!*
> *Not the joy of Love, just the pain of Love,*
> *And I will pay the price, any price you ask!*
> *All myself I offer for it, and the price you will ask on top of it.*
> *Keep the joy for others, give me the pain,*
> *And gladly I will pay for the pain of love!*[180]

Irina Tweedie (1907–99) was of Russian origin. After the death of her British husband, she embarked on a spiritual quest in an attempt to come to terms with her grief. In India, she became the pupil of Radha Mohan Lal, a Hindu Sufi shaykh of the Naqshbandiyya-Mujadiddiya order, and the first Western woman to be trained in this order. Her master instructed her to keep a diary of her training with him and the unveilings that came to her along the spiritual path. An abridged version of this diary was published as *The Chasm of Fire* and is considered to be a most comprehensive account of the teacher/pupil relationship. Her sincerity and struggle for awakening reverberates on every page.

After Radha Mohan Lal's passing, Mrs Tweedie started a Sufi meditation group in north London, which spread through Europe and North America. When she retired in 1992, she appointed Llewellyn Vaughan-Lee as her successor.

> *The Realization that every act, every word, every thought of ours not only influences our environment but mysteriously forms an integral part of the Universe, fits into it as if by necessity, in the very moment we do or say or think it, is an overwhelming and shattering experience.*
>
> *If we only knew deeply, absolutely, that our smallest act, our smallest thought, has such far-reaching effects; setting forces in motion; reaching out to the galaxy; how carefully we would act and speak and think. How precious life would become in its integral oneness.*
>
> *It is wonderful and frightening. The responsibility is terrifying and fascinating in its depth and completeness, containing as it does the perplexing insecurity of being unique and the profound consolation of this wonderful meaning of life; one is quite simply part of it all; a single vision of Wholeness.[181]*
>
> *Irina Tweedie*

⌒

Our souls are made of a quality of light, a light that belongs to God and carries a knowing of its source. Through this light the soul sees its way, the path it follows, the destiny that needs to be lived. Without this light there could be no evolution, no meaning to life.

Spiritual life is a means to bring the light of the soul into the world. Spiritual practices give us access to our light and the teachings of the path help us live it in our daily life. The more our light shines in this world, the easier it is to follow a spiritual path and be guided from within. Through this light the inner meaning of the soul comes into our life, and the wonder of God becomes visible. In this light we see the oneness that belongs to God, that is a direct expression of His nature. Without it we only see the reflections of our illusory self, the shadows of the ego.[182]

Llewellyn Vaughan-Lee

After his move to California in 1991, Llewellyn Vaughan-Lee (b. 1953) founded the Golden Sufi Center to make the Naqshabandi teachings more available to Western seekers. Llewellyn is a prolific writer, has hosted many Sufi conferences, and is a specialist in dreamwork, where he combines the traditional Sufi interpretations with Jungian psychology. He has more recently taken on the mantle of highlighting the importance of the environment and reduction of waste. This concept of spiritual ecology brings in the universality of human beingness that takes us beyond family, clan or nationhood. I have had several pleasant communications with Llewellyn and respect his work.

LIFE AS AN EXPRESSION OF DIVINE LOVE

In the heart of the world the future is being written in the language of love. Our ability to read this language will determine whether we participate creatively in our own destiny and the destiny of the world or whether we are victims of fate, blindly reacting to the events that happen to us.

All of creation is a manifestation of divine love; every atom spins on an axis of love and every form from a butterfly to a bomb is an expression of a quality of love. Through our understanding of the primal language of how love manifests in creation, we can help to guide the world through the changes that are taking place; we can work with the ways He is revealing Himself to Himself.[183]

Llewellyn Vaughan-Lee

During my years in South Africa, there have been some memorable and uplifting visits to other African countries, particularly the mainland of Tanzania and Zanzibar. My visit to the Bilal Mission in Tanzania was one of these. Around two hours' drive inland from Dar as Salaam, some 63 inmates, all blind orphans aged between eight and late teens, including some albinos, lived in a Second World War railway station shed left over from the German occupation. The older orphans would help look after the younger.

There was some subsistence farming of coffee, bananas and maize. When our party arrived, we saw some of the orphans, all barefoot, emerging from the surrounding woods. The boys were called to come together to sing and recite the Quran for us. Their open-air school had no doors and was housed in a large corrugated iron railway shed. After they had been given their breakfast of a slice of bread and a banana each, I asked them if there was any special help they needed. My presumption was that they would request something to do with their education or quality of life. I had already arranged for them to have a water connection to a pipe about a kilometre away and 63 mattresses, as they were all sleeping on concrete.

Their spokesman stood up, thanked me and requested that I pray for them to remain content! He said what he prays for all the time is trust in Allah and purity at heart. He knew there were many more people in the world in a worse state than them, so they were grateful for what they had. He then thanked me for the visit. These poor children were rich at heart.

> *When He endows you with obedience [to Him] and contentment [with Him, from it], know that He has bestowed upon you His Graces both outwardly and inwardly.*[184]
>
> *Ibn 'Ata' Allah*

Submission, surrender and unconditional obedience are indeed the greatest gifts and doors given to human beings. The path of the seeker is smooth when he yields and submits to Allah's Decree cheerfully. The result is both joy and contentment with Him. This state is often described as living the Will of God. In this state, what is desired and the will and power to reach it are limited. The illumined seeker transcends the rewards of piety and asceticism and thereby is engulfed in the Grace of the Eternal One, beyond all experiential manifestations.

On one of my visits to Zanzibar, a friend took me to a non-touristic part of the island to visit an old blind man known for his piety. He lived in a small clean hut by the sea, surrounded by clove forests on one side and mangroves on the other. Young and old often came to greet him in search of blessings. They would find him sitting in his hut, reciting the Quran, connecting to the voice of Truth and the invisible world. When I was introduced to him, he said he had been expecting me, as sometimes he would get a clear signal from the unseen that someone is to visit him. Souls that have awakened to truth reflect each other.

Wisdom and certainty are only obtained by keeping the company of the Gnostics. Know that whatever your himma [yearning] connects to, will only be reached by the company of its people. A condition of this path is recognition of the people of sincerity and confirmation of those to whom the Beloved appears in tajalli [a divine manifestation witnessed by the inner eye of a seeker].

Sidi Ali al-Jamal

As a teacher and writer on religious and spiritual issues, there have been over the past few decades a number of occasions when I have reviewed and reflected on how useful my work has been. At one point two years or so ago, I had decided to leave behind this role of teacher. I am sure many other people in my position have also reached that point. The story of Hayy ibn Yaqzan ("The Ever Living Son of the Awake") came to me vividly, for he, too, realized that most people prefer their old habits and slumber rather than waking up to Higher Reality.

The Andalusian philosopher, Ibn Tufayl (1110–82 CE), known in the West as Abubacer, based his tale of Hayy, abandoned as a baby on an uninhabited island and raised by a deer, on an original story by Ibn Sina (Avicenna). Ibn Tufayl uses this allegorical tale to support his hypothesis that man's innate reason will allow him to develop naturally, even in the absence of societal programming, and that isolation is a prerequisite for spiritual awakening. The deer dies when Hayy is seven. He dissects her body in an attempt to find the reason for her demise. He decides that her death was caused by loss of heat and when he moves into a cave to escape maltreatment from the other animals, he inadvertently discovers fire. He then concludes that warmth is the animating force for all living things. Hayy has escaped the usual human development and exposure to culture and religion but by a series of logical deductions he develops a consciousness of an all-encompassing power that envelops everything in existence.

When Hayy is 50 years old, he encounters a man called Absal, who has come from a nearby inhabited island in search of solitude. Absal teaches him his language and tells him about the religious rituals and laws of his land. These are quite incomprehensible to Hayy, who has reached his inner awakening without any of these tools.

Hayy also represents the exception that proves the rule; a being who is enlightened without having had a spiritual master. The foetus emerges from the three darknesses of placenta, womb and stomach. The equivalent earthly darknesses after birth are genetic and racial affiliation, culture and habits, ideology and belief. Hayy has had none of the outer conditioning, so he lives by the light of his soul and has to learn from Absal about language, identity, mind and the other veils that cover the effulgent light of Reality. Hayy speaks the language of the heart; Absal that of men.

Absal has come with a consciousness of his identity and mind, looking for heart and light to rebalance the human state of earth and heavens, the individual identity and cosmic reality. He represents the best that can happen when a person uses mind and intellect to a point where you realize it is not adequate and you are searching for the light of your own soul. Once that happens, it is natural to want to share the knowledge with others, but the outcome is not predictable.

Absal persuades a reluctant Hayy to come to his island to teach the people there his techniques for self-unfoldment. The King Salaman and his people practice a religion that uses symbols, rather than inner truth; even the most intelligent amongst them cannot go beyond the literal meaning of their Holy Book. Hayy sees that the people are buried under their culture and illusions, and realizes that the process of awakening is an evolutionary one, so he leaves them to their old habits. Revolution rarely works unless it is personal, and evolution continues toward higher consciousness at its own pace. There are only a few who can straddle physics and metaphysics.

I have personally seen myself as a frustrated Hayy, trying to rid the mosque of cultural idols, and have naturally failed. As the soul is ever triumphant, when the self gives in to it, victory is by Allah; admitting to or seeing failure is proof of this ever-victorious light.

> *He who knows the Truth will witness Him in everything, and he who is annihilated in Him is absent from everything, and he who loves Him will prefer nothing else over Him.*[185]
>
> *Ibn 'Ata' Allah*

To know the truth is to see all existence emanating from Him and sustained by Him. Annihilation is transcending the veils of otherness to witness His Light behind every light and shadow. The seeker progresses from knowledge to love to annihilationf and to ongoingness by the One.

Chapter 11

IRAN

We are People who need to love
Because Love is the soul's life.
Love is simply creation's greatest joy.[186]

Hafiz

My links with Iran are both genetic and cultural. Until my teens, most of my friends in Karbala were strongly connected with the religious and cultural ways of Persia. I understood the different nuances and forms of social interaction. As a youngster, I recall the numerous Iranian *dervishes* visiting the shrine of Imam Hussein, reciting invocations at the entrance and sprinkling rose water. Even now, the fragrance of rose water transports me back to Iran and a way of life that strongly attracts me.

In October 2008, I visited Iran with a group of family and friends. Most of my companions came from South Africa and this was their first exposure to this rich and varied land. Everybody was impressed by the friendliness of the people and the simple but high-quality life they enjoy. We travelled extensively through the country, visiting many places of great beauty and historical interest. My daughter, Muna, afterwards wrote a short book, *Iran Through Our Eyes*, to commemorate the visit.

The area of Khurasan in northeastern Iran was one of the most fascinating from the Sufi perspective. It has been the centre for early spiritual interactions and movements, probably from 5,000 years ago and before Zoroaster. About half of the great Muslim scholars who are now considered as classical contributors, such as Imams Ghazali, Bukhari, Muslim, Tabari and many others, came from that area. It was the birthplace of the Sufi luminaries of medieval Islam – men like Bayazid Bistami (804–74 or 877/8 CE), Abu Abd al-Rahman as-Sulami (d. 1021 CE), Abu Qasim al-Qushayri (d. 1074 CE) and Ali al-Hujwiri (d. 1071 CE) from Ghazna, the author of the first Sufi manual written in Persian, *Kashf al-Mahjub*. The famous Central Asian scholar, Hakim al-Tirmidhi, lived the last years of his life in Nishapur. He was the author of *Khatm al-Awliya* (*Seal of Saints*), which describes the way to sainthood.

> *The heart is healed by the permanent remembrance of God.*[187]
> *Hakim al-Tirmidhi*

A remote mountain hamlet called Gonabad, southeast of Khurasan, has been known for its enlightened beings for several centuries up till the present day. Some of the great men of that region had become legendary saints in Iranian folklore. The teacher of my great-uncle, Shaykh Abdullah, was based in Gonabad. Shaykh Abdullah himself lived there for many years before moving to Tehran. There are various Gonabadi orders active today, including a Gonabadi-Nimatullahi branch which has had much exposure in Europe and America. Although I did not have the opportunity to visit Gonabad on this visit, I did meet Shaykh Muhammad Hasan Salih Ali Shah, a Gonabadi master. Relatives arranged for me to visit his home in north Tehran and I had a pleasant encounter with this most refined and welcoming teacher. He presented me with a well-presented book he had written on the refinement of conduct.

Prior to this meeting, my only contact with a contemporary Iranian master was with Pir Malikniya Nasir Ali Shah (d. 1998). He was a prominent Nimatullahi shaykh who lived between Paris and Istanbul after the Iranian Revolution. We exchanged greetings when my son-in-law, Abbas Bilgrami, met him on a visit to New York in the early 1980s, and later in Istanbul. Zahra Trust, the foundation I had established, purchased Books on Islam, a book-distribution business, from American converts to Islam Charles Ali Campbell and his wife, Maryam. Ali was the head of the American Heart Association and a pupil of Pir Malikniya. Ali arranged for Abbas to visit his Pir, who had only just arrived in the States, at a time when all his pupils were coming to pay their respects.

Abbas recalls a handsome, elderly man, small in stature with a light beard, who welcomed him warmly and suggested he might like to visit him in Istanbul. Abbas and Muna later went to see him at his home in the Asian side of Istanbul. The morning of his visit, Abbas had purchased a beautiful turquoise *tasbih*. He was surprised when Pir Malikniya asked him if he had anything in his pocket. When he brought out the *tasbih,* the master told him that his *dhikr* must be in the heart and not reliant on any crutches! This made a big impact on Abbas.

Nishapur in Khurasan has always fascinated me, and during my 2008 visit I was able to explore the city and environs. I can well understand why it was a natural haven for people seeking higher meaning. Sparkles of mystery still linger in the breezes that often blow through the city. Wonderful orchards are scattered around the area, fed by old underground canals, many of which are still operative today. Local mines traditionally produced the best turquoises until recent depletion. Its location on an earthquake belt meant regular natural disasters; a sense of the impermanency of life must have helped its inhabitants live more fully in the now. There were nine different cities built on top of each other over a period of 4,000 years. Nishapur was a city that was constantly reinventing itself through endless cycles of construction and destruction. These cycles are mirrored in the successive diverse spiritual movements that waxed and waned in this vibrant city.

Three of the major destructions were due to fire or warfare, specifically from the Mongols. The local religious leaders refused to trade with the Khans and arrogantly held their emissaries hostage. This prompted a savage reprisal by the Mongol hordes. In 1220 CE, Genghis Khan apparently rounded up all the notables of the city and asked whether they believed in the wrath of God. When they said they did, he declared that he himself was the ultimate manifestation of God's anger and put the city to fire.

The various rebuilds of the city are not exactly on the same site as the ones that preceded them. This makes serious archaeology difficult as the area has spread out widely. Human remains found in some strata show sudden onslaught of death, as people were performing various functions when disaster struck. This is like Pompeii, where volcanic ash froze everything in time after Vesuvius erupted.

In the medieval period, Nishapur was an important trade centre, with daily traffic from all over the Islamic world. After the decline of the Abbasid caliphate around the middle of the 10th century, local regimes took the place of centralized government. Khurasan was the first settled society to be conquered by the Turkish Ghaznavid dynasty at the end of the 10th century and by the Seljuqs in the 11th century. Each time the economic recovery was spectacular.

Each wave of foreign conquerors had to use the Khurasani *'ulama*, Sufis and bureaucrats to help them govern the newly annexed province. In exchange for their co-operation in providing the new rulers with legitimacy, the religious classes received salaries, and funds were made available for building *madrasas* and *khanqahs*. This mutual backscratching between government officials and religious elites was first put systematically into effect in Khurasan and later adopted in Baghdad and other states.

The spiritual history of Nishapur in the Islamic period tells us much about the development of Sufism and its links with the mystic schools of Baghdad. Until the middle of the 10th century, there was not much Sufi activity in Nishapur. The original popular mystic movements in the area had been the Karramiyya and the Malamatiyya. The Karramiyya was the most important renunciatory movement to come out of Khurasan, having considerable influence from the mid-9th to the 12th century. It was founded by Muhammad b Karram (806–69 CE), an ascetic preacher who had a large following in southern and eastern Iran, Transoxiana and Afghanistan amongst the working classes. They were the first group in the area to build *khanqahs* as centres for their missionary activities and were instrumental in converting many non-Muslim Persians to Islam. They were a fundamentalist sect who believed in the mortification of the flesh and living a righteous life. The poor of the area, particularly the weavers, flocked to their centres. The Karramiyya were always at loggerheads with the religious establishment.

Some scholars claim that the Malamatis were the forerunners to the Sufis. The root of the word in Arabic is "to blame" – humbling the self before transcending to higher consciousness. The Malamatis avoided anything that could be considered religious ostentation and encouraged self-righteousness. This was a deliberate way of renouncing the animal self and losing ego-identity. Their goal was always to avoid hypocrisy. Sometimes they would appear to be acting in an unethical manner so that they could give the ignorant a lesson in how to behave.

> *When Abu Yazeed al Bistami was asked how a Sufi could draw nearer to God, his answer was through that which was not a property (attribute) of the Almighty, "humility and indigence."*[188]

One of the most famous early Malamatis is Abu Yazid, or Bayazid al-Bistami (804–74 or 877/8 CE). The story is told that one Ramadan (Islamic month of fasting) he travelled to a neighbouring city. His fame was such that the locals came out to greet him and were disturbing his inner peace. So he went to the bazaar, took out a loaf of bread and began to eat. The people all ran away from him. "See," Bayazid said to his travelling companion, "whenever I obey the *shari'a* they reject me." The ignorant townsfolk were forgetting that the traveller is not supposed to fast.[189]

Bayazid was known for his ecstatic states. It is related that the famous Sufi Dhu'l-Nun al-Misri sent a man from his circle of devotees to report about Bayazid's circumstances.

The man came to Bistam, asked directions for the house of Abu Yazid, and went to visit him there. Abu Yazid said, "What do you want?" The man said, "I want Abu Yazid." He replied, "Who is Abu Yazid? Where is Abu Yazid? I too am seeking Abu Yazid myself." The man departed, saying to himself, "He's mad." When the man returned to Dhu'l-Nun and reported what he had seen, Dhu'l-Nun wept and said, "My brother Abu Yazid has gone the way of those departed to God."[190]

Bayazid enjoys much popularity in Sufi lore and stories about him are myriad. There is even a shrine for him in Chittagong in Bangladesh, where he is said to have visited.

> *The Chishti master, Shaykh Nizam ad-Din Awliya, used to tell the following story in connection with sincerity and honesty amongst Muslims: "There was a Jew who lived in the neighbourhood of Khwaja Bayazid Bistami. When Khwaja Bayazid died, they said to that Jew, 'Why did you not become a Muslim?' 'If Islam is what Bayazid professed,' he replied, 'then I cannot attain it, but if it is this that you profess, then of such an Islam I would be ashamed!'"[191]*

> *The people of the path of blame are "true men" who have assumed the highest level of walaya [being a friend of God]. There is nothing higher than them, except the station of prophecy. Their station is the one referred to as the "station of nearness".*
>
>

Ibn al-'Arabi

Hamdun al-Qassar (d. 883/84 CE), an eminent theologian of Nishapur, is said to have been the founder of the Malamati path. He described the objectives of the People of Blame "to renounce in all one's states and actions the need to please people, and to be at all times beyond blame in fulfilling one's duties to God." According to as-Sulami, he encouraged *dhikr* to be done silently, in case any audience for an audible recitation encouraged religious pride in the supplicant. His successor, Abu Hafs, followed by Abu Uthman, took a more moderate stance.

Most of the Malamatis belonged to trade guilds, did not beg or wear distinctive dress, took counsel from spiritual masters but did not pledge absolute obedience to the shaykh in the same way later Sufis did. In their interactions with others, they adopted a code of spiritual chivalry, known as *futuwwa*, which encouraged hospitality and co-operation with those around them. Above all they dedicated themselves to a rigorous monitoring of the lower self.

The use of the term "Sufi" in the context of Khurasan is first seen in religious chronicles of the 10th century CE. It is thought that Sufis from Iraq, like Abu Bakr al-Wasiti (d. after 932 CE), brought the teachings of the Baghdadi School of Junayd to the area. Moderate Malamatis, like Abu Hafs al-Haddad and his pupil, Abu Uthman al-Hiri, who were influenced by the Sufi teachings of Iraq, western Iran and Transoxiana, were able to fuse the two schools together. Both opposed the teachings of the Karramiyya, whose prohibition on working for a living and outer displays of piety contrasted strongly with Malamati beliefs, and whose simple fundamentalism would have had little attraction for the refined and educated Sufis.

The Sufis were mainly Shafi'i and their emergence by the late 10th and 11th centuries as the main mystic group in Nishapur was mainly connected with their affiliation to that *madhhab*. Contemporary biographical dictionaries show that no Hanafis or Karramis were listed as Sufis. The legal affiliation of all Sufis was Shafi'i.

First, flashes of lightning from an unknown horizon,
Then rays of light showing the path ahead,
Finally, light all around,
The full brilliance revealed
Only to those who turn their senses within.[192]
Abu Qasim al-Qushayri

One of the most famous early treatises on Sufism was the *Al-Risala al-Qushayriyya (Al-Qushayri's Epistle on Sufism)*. In it, the famous legal scholar and Sufi master Abu Qasim al-Qushayri defends the Prophetic roots of Sufism, discusses Sufi beliefs and practices as well as biographies of famous Sufis of the past. I consider this work to be one of the most important reviews of transformative Islam. He recommends that the *murid* joins the Sufi *madhhab*, that is to say the Shafiʻi *madhhab*, as it has secure foundations and its shaykhs are the most learned. He expressly advises imitation of such masters as Imam Shafiʻi (d. 820 CE), who is clearly referred to as a Sufi in this context, Junayd al-Baghdadi (d. 910 CE) and Abu Bakr al-Shibli (d. 946 CE).

> *Let the days for what they wish and be content when you see the hand of destiny and do not despair from events at night, for no worldly events ever last and be a man of courage with compassion, loyalty and generosity and do not ever expect goodness from a mean being for you never get your thirst satisfied by fire. As for your provisions, they will not diminish by quietness, nor will your provisions increase by struggle and know that neither sorrow, nor pleasure will ever last nor does difficulty or ease, if your heart is content. You and He, Who owns all of the world, are at one and whenever afflictions arrive at your courtyard, no earth or heavens will ever protect you, although the earth is spacious and wide but when affliction is your destiny the widest horizons become constricted. Let days do their turn and realize that at the end no medicine will save you from death.*
>
> *Imam ash-Shafiʻi*

As for the Malamatis, they seem to have completely merged with the Shafiʻi Sufis of Nishapur. Their teachings re-emerged later under the Hanafi banner, particularly in Central Asia and the lands of the future Ottoman Empire. It has been suggested that they inspired the Khwajagan forefathers of the Naqshbandis. Closer to modern times the Malamatis, often aligned to other *tariqas*, flourished in Turkey at the close of the Ottoman period. When Kemal Ataturk outlawed Sufism in 1926, those with Malamati tendencies did not protest but considered it a necessary move to deal with an antiquated religious establishment which had often attacked them. They continued to live their philosophy of inner intoxication and outer sobriety within the secular society that emerged in Turkey. Today, Turkey is enjoying a resurgence of interest in the Quran and Sufism. It has been suggested that an invisible thread of Malamati teachings has played a role in this revival. The way of the Malamatis has much relevance for seekers of our times. They focused on their own inner unfoldment, did not wear distinctive dress or do anything to attract attention to themselves and showed respect for their neighbours, who belonged to other faiths.

The Moving Finger writes; and having writ,
Moves on: nor all your Piety nor Wit
Shall lure it back to cancel half a line,
Nor all your Tears wash out a Word of it.[193]

Omar Khayyam

Omar Khayyam (1048–1131 CE) is one of the most famous sons of Nishapur. His fame in the West is mostly due to Edward FitzGerald's (1809–83) translation of some of his poetry into English, published as *The Rubaiyat of Omar Khayyam*. FitzGerald's poetic rendering of verses dwelling on the transient nature of life and the powerlessness of man appealed to his 19th-century European readership, but has been criticized for liberties taken in the English translation.

Tis all a Chequer-board of Nights and Days
Where Destiny with Men for Pieces plays;
Hither and thither moves, and mates, and slays.
And one by one back in the Closet lays.[194]

Omar Khayyam

On the face of it, much of the poetry attributed to Khayyam sounds fatalistic and lacks hope and delight. Yet to accept the visible world for what it is can be a powerful step toward witnessing the unifying power and force of God. You must act in life, but ultimately the outcome is not in your hands.

Omar was remembered for centuries after his death as a great astronomer and mathematician, rather than as a poet or Sufi. The beauty of the star-strewn night skies around Nishapur certainly made me sympathize with Omar's fascination with astronomy.

Leading Iranian scholars today agree that much of what has been attributed to Omar is probably not his work. The author's identity matters little, however, as whoever penned the original *Rubaiyat* taught that living in the now is dependent on loss of earthly ambition, and the drive to inner unveilings is fuelled by devotion, meditation and spiritual practice. In these verses, intoxication is taken as a symbol of a state of ecstatic transcendence that takes you to the edge of this temporary abode, and human life is shown to be futile unless it is based on contentment, joy and transcendence.

On our 2008 trip, we visited Omar's tomb outside Nishapur. As I wandered through the beautifully tended garden around the mausoleum, I felt the desire to go back to those days. They lived with a passion and intensity amidst the flowering of a great culture, despite constant threats of war, political change and potential earthquakes. The very uncertainties of the time must have contributed to the vibrant creative outpourings.

> *One Moment in Annihilation's Waste,*
> *One Moment, of the Well of Life to taste –*
> *The Stars are setting and the Caravan*
> *Starts for the Dawn of Nothing – Oh, make haste![195]*
>
> *Omar Khayyam*

Once one is one,
No more, no less:
Error begins with duality;
Unity knows no error.

Place itself has no place
How could there be place
For the creator of place,
Heaven for the Maker of heaven?[196]

Hakim Sanai

Persia has always been a rose garden of beauty and culture. This is reflected in the aesthetic sense of the people, whose love of harmony is displayed not only through their poetry, art and carpets, but in their overall way of being – even the manner in which they present their food and arrange flowers. Love of beauty is a love of harmony, which connects to gatheredness, which is Oneness or the essence of life itself. It is no coincidence that the names of several masterpieces of Persian poetry should depict the imagery of gardens, such as Sanai's *Walled Garden of Truth* and Shabistari's *Secret Rose Garden*.

The development of Persian poetry was much influenced by the *Hadiqatu'l-Haqiqa* (*The Walled Garden of Truth*) of Hakim Abdul Majid Majdud Sanai (d. c1131–50 CE). As the earliest of the great masters, Sanai is credited with being the first poet to use the *qasidah* (ode), *ghazal* (lyric) and *masnavi* (rhymed couplet) in a Sufi context. Rumi expressed his debt to Sanai and Attar as his main inspirations, saying that "Attar is the soul and Sanai its two eyes, I came after Sanai and Attar."

Sanai came from Ghazna, in present-day Afghanistan. Little is known about his life, but he was initially a court poet to Sultan Bahram Shah. The story goes that he was about to accompany the Sultan on a military expedition to India when he passed a walled garden where he heard the voice of Lai Khur, a local drunkard, who may have been a Sufi. Lai Khur was asking for a toast to the foolish Sultan for his greed at leaving beautiful Ghazna in order to plunder India; then he proposed a toast to the young poet, Sanai, who, despite his spiritual awareness, was too blind to see the futility of using his talents in the service of this earthly ruler. Sanai recognized the truth in these utterances. He gave up his position at court, even turning down a marriage with the Sultan's sister, and followed the Sufi master, Yusuf Hamadani. Shortly afterwards, he went on *Hajj*. On his return, he composed his masterpiece, *Hadiqatu-l-Haqiqa* (*The Walled Garden of Truth*).

Hakim Sanai's lines have inspired me on occasions to rewrite his themes in a contemporary style. Truth is eternal, but the message must be delivered in a manner that is meaningful to the present times.

> *When the sunlight falls on water,*
> *The ripples' movement is reflected,*
> *And throws a brilliant picture on the wall:*
> *Remember that this secondary reflection*
> *Is also from the sun.*

> *Whether you exist or not*
> *Is indifferent to the working of God's power.*
> *Everything is the work of God alone,*
> *– and happy is the man that knows it!*
> *Reason was the pen, self the paper;*
> *Matter was given form; bodies received their shapes.*
> *To love he said, "Fear none but me."*
> *To reason his words were, "Know yourself."*[197]

Hakim Sanai

> *Whoever lives, the wicked and the blessed contain a hidden*
> *sun within his breast –*
> *Its light must dawn though dogged by long delay.*
> *The clouds that veil it must be torn away –*
> *Whoever reaches to his hidden sun*
> *Surpasses good and bad and knows the One.*[198]

Farid ad-Din Attar

Farid ad-Din Attar (c1142–c1220 CE), one of the most revered writers and poets in the history of Sufism, was another native of Nishapur. He is most remembered for his *Mantiq al-Tayr* (*Conference of the Birds*), an allegorical tale in which the Hoopoe, as the leader of the birds in their journey of spiritual discovery, adopts the role of the Sufi shaykh. He relates stories of the *awliya* of early Islam in his *Tadhkiratu'l-Awliya* (*Memoirs of Saints*). Attar may well have been persecuted and stripped of his possessions for his so-called heretical writings and banished from Nishapur.

> *But who can speak of this? I know if I*
> *Betrayed my knowledge I would surely die;*
> *If it were lawful for me to relate*
> *Such truths to those who have not reached this state,*
> *Those gone before us would have made some sign,*
> *But no sign comes, and silence must be mine.*
> *Here eloquence can find no jewel but one,*
> *That silence when the longed-for goal is won.*
> *The greatest orator would here be made*
> *In love with silence and forget his trade,*
> *And I too cease: I have described the way –*
> *Now you must act – there is no more to say.*[199]
>
> Farid ad-Din Attar

It is thought that he returned to Nishapur after his exile and was beheaded during the Mongol invasion. Legend claims that, to the horror of his executioner, the body got up after being beheaded and walked to a point where Attar declared, "This is the right place to die." The head executioner is said to have built Attar's shrine on that location and remained as the keeper of the shrine. The mausoleum today is surrounded by a beautiful garden and is much visited.

There is an apocryphal story regarding Attar in which Rumi said that Attar had passed through seven cities of love and we (i.e. Rumi and his circle) are still meandering in the alleyways of the first city.

The home we seek is in eternity;
The truth we seek is like a shoreless sea,
Of which your paradise is but a drop.
This ocean can be yours; why should you stop
Beguiled by dreams of evanescent dew?
The secrets of the sun are yours,
But you
Content yourself with motes trapped in its beams.
Turn to what truly lives, reject what seems –
Which matters more, the body or the soul?
Be whole: desire and journey to the whole.[200]

Farid ad-Din Attar

The philosopher with his two eyes sees double,
so is unable to see the unity of the Truth.[201]

Mahmud Shabistari

Some of the most sublime Persian poetry is threaded through with imagery of gardens. Mahmud Shabistari (1288–1340 CE) is another of the most famous Persian Sufi poets, mainly remembered for his "*Gulshan-i-Raz*" ("The Secret Rose Garden"). It was written in response to 17 questions posed by another Sufi, Rukn al-Din Amir Husayn Harawi (d. 1318 CE). He came from the town of Shabestar, near Tabriz, and like Attar lived at the time of the Mongol invasions.

Early on in my search, "Gulshan-i-Raz" gave me delight and inspiration. Zahra Publications produced a good translation of it, but I still wanted to re-translate it myself, so I collected all the commentaries in Arabic, Farsi and English. Once I embarked on the project, I realized what a complex task it would be, as it is full of symbolism, reflecting the Quran and ancient traditions. Then I had a vision of Shabistari, joined by some of the other great luminaries of Sufism – Sanai, Attar, Rumi, Ibn al-'Arabi and Mulla Sadra – smiling at me, waving their hands and saying,

"What we did was perfect for our time but you must do something appropriate to your time and culture." Life within the flower remains the same, but the shape and fragrance change. This made me realize the necessity of seeing teachings and traditions in their proper context, if they are truly to be transmitted.

> *Know the world from end to end is a mirror;*
> *In each atom a hundred suns are concealed.*
> *If you pierce the heart of a single drop of water,*
> *From it will flow a hundred clear oceans*
> *If you look intently at each speck of dust,*
> *In it you will see a thousand beings.*
> *A gnat in its limbs is like an elephant;*
> *In name a drop of water resembles the Nile.*
> *In the heart of a barleycorn are stored a hundred harvests.*
> *Within a millet-seed a world exists.*
> *In an insect's wing is an ocean of life.*
> *A heaven is concealed in the pupil of an eye.*
> *The core at the centre of the heart is small,*
> *Yet the Lord of both worlds will enter there.*[202]
>
> *Mahmud Shabistari*

THE DIVINE ATTRIBUTES

> *The entities are many-coloured windows,*
> *Upon which fall the rays of Being's sun.*
> *Whether windows be red, blue or yellow,*
> *The sun will show itself in that very hue.*[203]
>
> *Nur ad-Din Jami*

Nur ad-Din Abd ar-Rahman Jami (1414–92 CE), one of the greatest Sufi Persian poets, was called the seal of the Persian Poets and ranks with Sanai, Attar, Shabistari and Rumi as communicators of the mystic state, although he is less widely read in the West today. He was highly accomplished in several disciplines, but is known mostly in the West for his allegorical love tale of Yusuf and Zuleikha. He was a committed Sufi, so his writings transmit his own inner state.

Jami was a polymath, who wrote commentaries on Ibn al-'Arabi's work, as well as ecstatic poetry that rivals Rumi's, and works on history and science. Astonishingly, his manual of irrigation design is still used as a reference in Herat for the irrigation department!

He included illustrations with his creative outpourings, which was not common in his time. Lines from works such as *Haft Awrang* (*Seven Thrones*), which has as its fifth book the famed story of Yusuf and Zuleikha, based on the Quranic version, and his rendering of *Layla wa-Majnun* (Layla and Majnun) were illustrated by painters, often in the style of exquisite miniatures. The cover of the recent edition of my book on *Decree and Destiny* shows, by permission of the Smithsonian, a scene from *Haft Awrang*.

Jami's family may have come originally from Iran, but he spent most of his life in Herat in Afghanistan. He had a prominent position at the Timurid court as a poet, theologian, historian and scholar, enjoying worldly success and recognitions, as well as spiritual openings.

> From all eternity the Beloved unveiled His beauty in the solitude of the Unseen;
> He held up the mirror to His own face, He displayed His loveliness to Himself.
> He was both the spectator and the spectacle; no eye but His had surveyed the universe.
> All was One, there was no duality, no pretence of "mine" or "thine".
> The vast orb of Heaven, with its myriad incomings and outgoings, was concealed in a single point.
> The Creation lay cradled in the sleep of non-existence, like a child ere it has breathed.

The eye of the Beloved, seeing what was not, regarded non-existence as existent.
Though He beheld His attributes and qualities as a perfect whole in His own essence,
Yet he desired that they should be displayed to Him in another mirror,
And that each of His eternal attributes should become manifest accordingly in a diverse form.
Therefore He created the verdant fields of Time and Space and the life-giving garden of the world,
That every bough and fruit might show forth His various perfections.
The cypress gave a hint of his comely stature, the rose gave tidings of his beauteous countenance.
Wherever Beauty peeped out, Love appeared beside it;
Wherever Beauty shone in a rosy cheek, Love lit his torch from that flame.
Wherever Beauty dwelt in dark tresses, Love came and found a heart entangled in their coils.
Beauty and Love are as body and soul; Beauty is the mine and Love the precious stone.
They have always been together from the first: never have they travelled but in each other's company.[204]

Nur ad-Din Jami

This world is a prison for the mumin [believer] and a paradise for the unbeliever.[205]

Imam Ali ar-Reza

There is an interesting little oasis about 20 kilometres east of Nishapur on the road to Mashhad. It is called Qadamgah, which means "the place of the footprint", purportedly that of Imam Ali ar-Reza, the eighth Shiite imam. There is a caravanserai nearby situated in gardens which are a popular picnic spot and recently a sizeable mosque has been added to the complex. The footprint of the imam is embedded in a slab of black stone and lies within a 17th-century octagonal shrine capped by a blue dome. I often wonder why there are so many footprints of revered saints and never handprints. During my travels, I have come across more than two dozen footprints but no handprints. One famous footprint, next to the Kaaba, is where the Prophet Ibrahim supposedly stood with his son at Makka, lifting the stones of the Kaaba.

Nearby the shrine of the footprint is a spring. The story goes that the imam stopped at the village to pray at midday and asked for water to make *wudu*. When no water was found, the imam scooped up some earth and a spring gushed out. It flows strongly to this day.

Imam Ali ar-Reza (148–203 AH/765–818 CE) was the son of the seventh Shiite imam, Musa al-Kazim, and the designated imam. He was considered outstanding both in his character and knowledge of the *deen*. Imam Reza, like all the imams of the *Ahl al-Bayt*, were able to convey and interpret the teachings of the Prophet for the people of their times.

> *Imamate is the rank of the prophets, and the inheritance of the spiritual guardians. Imamate is the caliphate of Allah and the Messenger; it is the station of the Commander of the Faithful [Imam Ali abi Talib] and the heritage of Hasan and Husayn. The Imamate is like the guiding reins of the din and the government of the Muslims; it is righteousness in this world and the glory of the believers. Truly, Imamate is the root of a flourishing Islam and its widespread branches. Through the imam is prayer, alms-giving, fasting and pilgrimage perfected, booty and charity become plentiful and the laws and punishments are executed. The imam makes lawful what Allah has made lawful, and forbids what Allah has forbidden.*[206]
>
> *Imam Ali ar-Reza*

Imam Musa al-Kazim, Imam ar-Reza's father, died during his imprisonment by the Abbasid Caliph Harun al-Rashid. Imam ar-Reza was equally harassed by the authorities. However, Harun's son, the Caliph al-Mamun appointed the imam as his successor in order to gain the support of the Shiites, who were frequently rebelling against the Abbasids. The imam accepted this position with reluctance. Iraq rose up in rebellion with his appointment as the caliph's designated heir. Al-Mamun insisted on Imam ar-Reza accompanying him to Iraq to subdue the uprising. The imam fell sick on the journey and was buried in Mashhad. His sudden death was helpful to al-Mamun and it is said that the caliph had poisoned him with a bunch of grapes.

The imam was buried near the tomb of Harun al-Rashid. Harun had personally selected the location for his own grave and even supervised the digging at the site. Yet, with the passing of time, nobody knows where the caliph is buried – one legend suggests his tomb was destroyed by the forces of Genghis Khan – and the shrine of Ali ar-Reza is one of the most visited in the world. It is a curious phenomenon that often the tombs of emperors and famous people disappear into obscurity, while those of men of light continue to attract visitors.

On my visit to Damascus to meet with Shaykh al-Fayturi, I had enlisted the help of the antiquities department to locate the grave of Mu'awiya, the first self-proclaimed Muslim caliph. He had forcefully assumed the role of a "prophetic being" through Machiavellian manoeuvrings and determination, using Arab tribal identity and affiliations to enforce iron-fisted controls upon the nascent Muslim masses. His grave, the officials informed me in a rather embarrassed fashion, is thought to be on the site of a popular ladies public bath and toilets!

There have been many prominent Sufis who claim direct descent or spiritual lineage through a *tariqa*, like the Nimatullahis, to Imam ar-Reza. He was considered by his contemporaries as a man of profound inner knowledge, who lived the meaning of his name, which is "contentment".

If a man is content with what satisfied him of the world, the least of things will be enough for him, but if a man is not content with what would suffice him of the world, there will never be anything which would be sufficient for him.[207]

Imam Ali

As a six-year-old, I accompanied my family on a visit to Iran to stay with our relatives. During this holiday we visited Mashhad, and I remember being awed by all the movement and activity, and particularly the sound of kettle drums around the shrine of Imam Ali ar-Reza. The shrine had been expanded over the years, but since the Iranian Revolution it has increased even more in size. The intricate mirror mosaic and other classical interior decorations are overwhelming in their glitter and vastness. It is like an enormous public palace for worship for the benefit of the people from the surrounding neighbourhoods, who often spend months at a time in the shrine. There is a vast underground hall where you can find families spread in different corners or next to pillars enjoying themselves. The library attached to the shrine is considered one of the richest in the Muslim world and many researchers visit it. There is also a vast feeding hall, where most of the visitors try to have a meal, feeding several thousand every day. The quality of the food and its reputation for *baraka* is well known. The meal I had there was simple, but one of the tastiest I had ever eaten. The ushers distinguish themselves by holding a coloured feather duster, about a yard long, in their hands.

There are many tales of miracles around the shrine. Kettle drums are traditionally beaten when any sick pilgrim gets miraculously healed. While we were there, the drums sounded to announce the healing of a blind girl of about ten whose sight had been restored to her.

As I had grown up in Karbala, next to the shrine of Imam Hussein, one of the most famous of all, I was never overly interested in the immense popularity of shrine visits for Muslims. When I was invited for an evening at the Governor of Khurasan's reception hall, he may have intuitively read my thoughts on the role played by shrines. He summed up his welcoming address by saying, "In Iran we have the culture of relating to the family of the Prophet in such a way that we converse with them and tell them everything that concerns us. People address their needs directly to the imams. By developing the shrine at Mashhad and making it available for people, it makes them feel as though they are living in the imam's household and can have direct access to him at all times." The Governor continued, explaining that this is an effective way of improving people's conduct and quality of thought. I found this explanation quite unique and I saw clear evidence of its veracity during my visit. Love of the Shiite imams in Iran takes the place of the veneration shown to the Sufi saints in Sunni Muslim countries.

> *The Messenger of Allah said, "O people! I have left amongst*
> *you two things, and if you take hold of them, you will never go*
> *astray: they are the book of Allah and my progeny."*[208]
> Prophet Muhammad

My 1989 visit to Iran was very different from the tourist meanderings of 2008. Seyyed Mehdi al-Hakim, who was a prominent figure in the Iraqi opposition to Saddam Hussein, insisted on me accompanying him to Tehran with other Iraqi exiles. There was a meeting in Ayatollah Khomeini's small compound north of Tehran. It was bitterly cold and the concrete floor of the meeting hall was covered with the thinnest carpets. Despite my attempts to avoid sitting in front of the TV cameras, I found myself a few metres from the Ayatollah. As I listened to the impassioned rhetoric of the Iraqi opposition, my heart prayed for some sign. Suddenly, in front of my eyes appeared the word *'irfan* (enlightenment) written on the rug at Khomeini's feet. The full sentence read *"Khanaqah Jamiran 'Irfani"*, or "the Jamiran Centre for Gnosis". The influence of Sufism on Khomeini is something that is not commonly known. It was a Sufism that was fully in line with the teachings of Shiite Islam and, as explained earlier, would have been called *'irfan* not *tassawuf.*

In the circle of the Sufis I did not experience purity.
In the high mountain retreat I did not hear the call.
In the seminary I did not receive the message.
Up in the minaret I did not see the light.
By collecting books the veils were not removed.
                                    Ayatollah Ruhollah Khomeini

Ayatollah Khomeini, in his younger days, had a Sufi master, Ayatollah Muhammad Ali Shahabadi (d. 1950), whom he acknowledged as the bridge that enabled him to cross to the ultimate light. He studied with Ayatollah Shahabadi the Sufi texts of Ibn al-'Arabi, Sadr al-Din Qunavi and Khwaja Abdullah Ansari. His state of gnosis is well presented in several books, which include his poems. My renderings of some lines of his Sufi poetry are included here:

I am drunk with the wine of Thy love, so from such a
drunkard
Don't ask for the sober wisdom of a man of the world.
In the party of the Beloved there is smoke and blood.
In the circle of the Sufis pain is blessing.
If you are looking for pleasure or grief get out.
In this place you will never find pleasure or grief.
                                    Ayatollah Ruhollah Khomeini

During the whole meeting with the Iraqi opposition, the Ayatollah never uttered a word, yet the next day the Iranian press claimed that he had given his support to the Iraqis. I have heard many stories that indicate he was frequently misinterpreted and his instructions disobeyed. Khomeini's depth of understanding of the world and the spiritual station he was at contrasted markedly with the people around him.

More than any other of Iran's glorious Sufis, Sadr ad-Din Shirazi (1571/2–1640 CE), commonly known as Mulla Sadra, has influenced me. Mulla Sadra is considered by many to be the most influential Islamic philosopher of the past 500 years. He synthesized the works of Avicenna, Shaykh al-Ishraq's Illuminationist philosophy, Ibn al-'Arabi and the Shiite imams to create his own school of Transcendent Philosophy or *al-Hikma al-Muta'aliya*. His commentaries on the Quran are like a collection of jewels and stimulate awakening to truth.

Like many original thinkers, he came under attack from the *ulama* for his unorthodox approach. He retired from public life to a village near Qom, where many of his books were written. Years later, the Governor of Fars invited him back to head a school of intellectual sciences in Shiraz.

Mulla Sadra's main work is *The Four Journeys of the Intellect*, which inspired my own collection of poetry, entitled also *The Four Journeys*. He was outstanding in the depth and breadth of his understanding. The Islamic establishment acknowledged him fully, as did spiritual seekers and masters. At the human level he knew the need for grooming, upbringing and boundaries, and at the spiritual level he had experienced perpetual reality.

In Mulla Sadra's *Four Journeys*, he describes the seeker's ascent into higher consciousness in four stages. The first journey is from the creation toward Truth. The second is by Truth in Truth. The third journey directly mirrors the first as it is from Truth to creation. The fourth journey is by Truth amongst creation.

Many people have had some experience of the first journey – especially when they want to escape affliction and discord. Epiphanies and special insights hint at the second journey. Helping and serving others with empathy and generosity reflects the third journey. The fourth journey is a rare undertaking where outer effort and sacrifice is balanced by inner reliance upon the origin of life – Allah. One hand gropes in darkness, while the other hangs on light.

It is inevitable that at times the sincere seeker will experience states that reflect different aspects of the journey. However, a *hal* (state) or an *ishraq* (momentary spiritual illumination) is different from a *maqam* (station), the latter being when one is firmly established within this condition and remains steadfast on the Path.

The need for a teacher, guide or mentor is essential throughout the journeys, especially the second. The boundaries between these stations are not rigid; they overlap and are hazy in the flow of time and sequence. An aspect of the fourth journey, for example, can be realized while on the first.

As for those intoxicated with His love, they start by witnessing Allah's essence in bewilderment, and then descend to attributes and existential realities. The wayfarer, on the other hand, is constantly concerned with Allah's manifestation and His relationship with creations, meanings and attributes, ending with witnessing the Essence. The God-intoxicated ones descend from Him toward creation while the normal wayfarer ascends from creation toward the Creator.

THE PARTY

The breeze of mercy –
An invitation to celebrate
Love, light and life,
To count blessings and then
Run out of numbers,
Inexpressible gratitude
For cosmic love,
Reminding earth
Of its heavenly origin,
Where our hearts had not yet descended
To bless the dead earth
With eternal life –
Here our party has no beginning or end.[209]

Shaykh Fadhlalla Haeri

Seyyed Hossein Nasr (b. 1933) is a modern-day commentator on the work of Mulla Sadra (*Sadr al-Din Shirazi and His Transcendent Theosophy: Background, Life and Works*). He is one of the most distinguished Iranian contemporary scholars and authorities on Islam and Sufism. He is currently Professor of Islamic studies at George Washington University. Seyyed Hossein was born into a distinguished Iranian family but educated in America from an early age, which has enabled him to bridge the gap between Western culture and the understanding of original Islam and Sufism. Before the Iranian Revolution, he was head of the Imperial Iranian Academy of Philosophy but was forced into exile due to political events.

I met him shortly after he had left Iran in 1979, before he embarked on a new academic career in America. He modestly remarked at that time, having been forced into exile by the Iranian Revolution, that now he must see what plan Allah had for him. Allah's plot was as always perfection; exile meant that his impact as an interpreter of Islamic philosophy and culture to the West has been far greater than it would ever have been had he remained in his homeland. Many professors and academics have benefitted from his generous guidance. He has been a prolific writer and amongst his most popular recent titles are *The Heart of Islam: Enduring Values for Humanity*, *The Garden of Truth: The Vision and Promise of Sufism, Islam's Mystical Tradition* and *Islam in the Modern World*. His most recent publication as editor-in-chief is *The Study Quran: A New Translation and Commentary*. Seyyed Hossein, like Llewellyn Vaughan-Lee, sees the present ecological crisis as a spiritual crisis.

Seyyed Hossein has repeatedly stated that there can be no Sufism without *shari'a* and expressed his personal indebtedness to Abu'l-Hasan ash-Shadhili and the great masters of the Shadhili *tariqa*. Seyyed Hossein and I are on the same life trajectory in our spiritual understanding. Our cultural backgrounds are similar and there is a shared connection with the Shadhilis. This has reinforced the many pleasant connections we have had over the years.

> *The heart that through gnosis has the light of God seen,*
> *Whatever it sees, it first does God see.*[210]
>
> *Mahmud Shabistari*

One pleasant encounter with a man of light took place during my 2008 visit to Tehran. Ismail Doulabi was a popular commentator on the Quran, whose recordings were distributed throughout the country. Friends recommended that I visit him at his home in Shimran, in the north of Tehran. I took a taxi to an alleyway near his house and by prior arrangement Ismail came on foot to meet me. He was an unassuming man who had not had much formal education, but over a period of a few years had emerged as a fully awakened being whose discourses were energized by profound insights.

During the years of attempted modernization, as a client of West, no one would have expected Iran to make a 180-degree turn to look for its future through Islam, which was out of fashion and neglected by most of the more educated people there. It is a miracle that Iran has survived as an Islamic Republic for nearly four decades, despite constant pressures and attacks from within and without. Their version of Islam, which has benefitted from nearly two centuries of teachings from the imams to reinforce and interpret the Prophetic message, has produced a different mindset to that of conventional Sunni Islam. The Iranian experiment of living Islam has been a considerable learning curve for all concerned and mistakes were made, but now we are seeing the fruits of their persistence. Iran is attempting to bring a form of democracy that does not jeopardize the moral and spiritual foundation of the *deen*. Certain boundaries and levels of morality and ethics pertaining to family life, alcohol, drugs, gambling and other societal issues have been maintained. It has been the only real attempt of living according to a true Islamic model, rather than copying Western-style governance.

> *Unless you are a lover unconditionally your worldly affairs will only confuse you, whereas the lover is ever engrossed with the Beloved.*
>
> *Ayatollah Ruhollah Khomeini*

Chapter 12

HERE AND NOW

*You contain the meaning of the whole universe. Every truth
tries to describe the Real and in truth there is only the Real.*
Niffari

During the past 5,000 years of human history, there have been a few
momentous events which brought about radical changes in human
evolvement and progress. Agricultural settlements, writing, the
establishment of law and order, religion, organized wars, paper, the
printing press, the engine and other systems and practices have preceded
the industrial and technological life of today. The global network of
communication and information exchange and the rise in the levels
of education and health are key factors in shaping the future. During
the past two decades, we have shrunk distances in the world and have
made intercontinental travel an everyday activity. The worldwide rise
in awareness of poverty, environmental degradation and demand for
human rights are factors helping to raise human consciousness.

It took human beings thousands of years to emerge from hunter-gatherers
to settled tribes and nations. Many experiments with different types of
governance led to the global acceptance of the essential sameness in human
potential, which is the basis of the practice of democracy. We can now say
that throughout the world most human beings desire the same outcome
in this life; safety, stability, health, education, opportunity for progress,
well-being and happiness. The young and educated people of today have a
better chance to attain realistic material, moral and spiritual goals.

We are driven in our lives to experience harmony and unity; so a baby
clings to a mother's breast to merge with her in oneness. The soul within
us is a reflector of the universal Oneness and therefore in its essence it

has utter security and perfection. Thus, at all times every human being desires access to an inner state of ease and contentment.

Up until a few decades ago, due to limitations of mobility and communication, the majority stayed very close to where they were born and lived according to the social norms of their society, religion and culture. Even in urban environments people simply belonged to the established culture and way of life.

The Sufi orders were a response to the religious and spiritual needs of a time and place, and thus reflected the dynamics of the prevailing situation. The type of clothes, scarves or turbans that were worn varied considerably, as did the culture of hospitality and expected conduct. The different incenses and perfumes that were used varied from place to place. In South India, sandalwood and other aromatic smells were prevalent; in the north of Iran it was mostly rose water; in Morocco, orange blossom. In the northern and cold environments of Central Asia, the food and clothing reflected much of the nature of the land. While the Sufis of Hadramaut's culture of frugality with doses of coffee and quat suited their arid and barren surroundings. There is a tendency for Sufis to repeat the traditions of what they had inherited from the past and pass it on to the new generation. These established, ongoing habits become sanctified and are repeated by newcomers to the circle. People refer to the past because it bestows a higher authority on the practices and there is a security in perpetuating habits, even if they can become detrimental to spiritual progress. If you are not able to read the present, how can you understand the past?

Until recently, the non-Muslim world knew little about Islam and Sufism. Traditionally, translations of the Quran into other languages had been frowned upon by conservative and traditional scholars and doctors of Islam and discouraged by them. The Quran was not translated until 1153 CE, when a Latin edition appeared. Then, in 1649, an English version (from French) was produced by Alexander Ross. This was followed in 1734 by a translation by George Sales, and others. Even if some of these translations were not deliberately biased, they were difficult to follow and understand.

It was not until 1930 that Mohammad Marmaduke Pickthall published his scholarly and sympathetic translation in Hyderabad.

In 1934, Abdullah Yusuf Ali brought out a translation containing many footnotes and explanations. Arthur J Arberry produced his translation in 1955, followed in 1956 by N J Dawood. From thereon, numerous publishing houses, university presses and Muslim states came out with their own versions. By the end of the 20th century, there were an estimated 400 translations in different languages and well over 100 in English. This demand is largely due to the thirst of the public to benefit from the Quran as well as academic and other interests throughout the world.

A vast body of academic work, including chronicles, biographies, treatises, translations on Islam and Sufism, has arisen out of the interest in religion and spirituality over the recent past. The internet and other media makes this easily accessible to all, rather than being the preserve of the few. This has had a huge impact on the understanding of Sufi *tariqas*, masters and their teachings.

The clear discipline and teachings of the great Sufi masters, such as Ibn 'Ata' Allah al-Iskandari, Abdullah Ansari, Ibn al-'Arabi and Mulla Sadra, can help any serious spiritual seeker. Original Islam can now be practiced and lived by most people without fear of retribution from unjust and rigid authorities, who impose uniformity of thought in their fear of losing control over people's minds and hearts. The rise of social networking and the internet has made access to this rich heritage easy, though one has to sift through the sites judiciously for authentic and transformative teachings.

During the past few decades, research projects on the lives and teachings of numerous Sufi shaykhs and spiritual masters have become popular. These studies have come out of European or American universities with a few from the East. Metaphysical poetry and spiritual songs have also been rediscovered and made public by literary and spiritually oriented individuals and organizations. It is not an accident that Rumi has for many years been so frequently quoted and read in the West and is one of the bestselling poets in the States, probably in large part due to the interpretive translations of Coleman Barks and others.

These are all signs that our scientific and material development is reaching a point that needs the revitalization of the heart and awakening to the inner light of the soul. Normal human consciousness is beginning to be regarded as one of many strands of accessible consciousness, starting from the local and conditioned state to full and boundless light of the cosmic consciousness: Allah.

The golden thread amongst all of these works is the constant reference to an Essence or Reality that transcends all that is discerned by human senses and the mind. The idea of God being the preserve of a specific religion or people is being superseded by the durable idea of universal Oneness or supreme consciousness. Muslims, especially the Sufis, have constantly referred to the return to the truth that there is only one unique Essence (Allah, God) in creation and that everything else is simply an overflow of grace and manifestation of that primal light. Whatever there is in existence contains a trace of its origin. Whatever is born will also die. This encourages the mind to reflect on what is eternally present and constant while also experiencing change and the dualities in creation.

Whenever I asked an enlightened teacher what my duties in life ought to be, I received the same answer: as long as your focus is upon reducing your personal concern or "separate identity", you are on the right track of liberating yourself from your "lower" self. The Prophet Musa (Moses) was ordered to take off his sandals (symbolizing protection and separation) before the Burning Bush. When personal identity or the illusion of independence is lost to a higher consciousness, then every moment and every place is sacred. For those who have the will and interest to transcend the limitations of body and mind, the opportunities exist today, as they have always done. Sacredness is what holds the universe and consciousness of life.

Humans are driven to realize the highest level of consciousness. Sufism is a natural human expression of the quest for knowledge of what connects and unifies the universe in all its diversity; the links of the seen and the unseen – the thread of truth.

The decline of Islamic civilization is partly due to the lack of the transformation of Muslims and their awakening to the truth of human nature – the divine soul within. Such an awakening would result in radical change in conduct and attitude in life, which would affect the entire people and produce a wholesome way of life. It is never too late for individuals and society to regain this glorious promise that is the most worthy cause of life. Individual and collective confusion, chaos and warfare will only end when self and soul are reconciled and balanced within the individual. To live as a soul is to be a passing guest on earth, leaving little trace or damage in your wake.

The relationship between the Muslim world and the West has, as we know, undergone much change and upheaval over the centuries since the advent of Islam, and continues to do so. During the first 400 years after the Prophet Muhammad's message, there was no significant Western power that could have challenged, let alone opposed, the Muslims in their spread and expansion across vast areas of the world. Islam expanded through conquest but also as a result of its promise to bring about social justice on earth by preaching a powerful message of a divine order overruling temporal power.

The Crusades, instigated by the wealthy and influential Roman Catholic Church in order to divert the troublesome nobles of northern Europe, led to a tragic waste of life and wealth and left considerable bitterness and animosity in their wake. With colonial expansion, especially in the economic, military and technological sectors, Muslim power was thoroughly and systematically dismantled. This met with little resistance from the dissipated and spiritually bereft Muslim leadership. By the early 20th century, the Western world regarded Muslims as minor clients of little significance, except when it came to the trade routes to and from India: the lucrative oil and gas reserves were yet to be exploited.

Muslims had travelled to and lived in Europe as early as the 18th century. During the latter part of the 19th century, there were quite a few visitors from the Middle East and North Africa to France, Britain and other European countries. Middle Eastern reformers, such as Jamal al-din Afghani (1839–97) and Muhammad Abduh (1849–1905), travelled in Europe. They were all impressed by Western material success and wrote on the challenge of achieving necessary modernization in the Muslim world without forsaking its Islamic heritage.

As the colonialists retreated, a wave of nationalism swept through Muslim lands, sparked primarily by the desire on the part of the colonies to reclaim political autonomy and economic independence. Although the changes being wrought were largely political, there is no doubt that the Muslim populations in these new nation-states were looking to an Islamic ideal for social justice, irrespective of schools of thought or degrees of adherence to the practices of the faith. However, political freedom from colonial masters did not bring about the kind of stability and social justice that the people had hoped for. Instead, there was more frustration and turmoil for ordinary citizens in the years to come. Having installed their lackeys and strongmen in power, the former Western masters turned a blind eye to the groundswell of deep dissatisfaction that simmered on the streets of the Middle East, the Subcontinent and North Africa.

The Khomeini era and the Iranian Revolution saw the beginning of an entirely new phase for the Muslim world in 1979. The fractious relationship with the West brought about changes. Despite the negative attention Islam and Muslims were eliciting in the Western media and the hawkish direction that Western foreign policy was taking, it led to a popular and academic upsurge in interest and scholarship in the spiritual teachings of Islam, its culture and its history in the West. Muslims, too, started to learn about their own rich and vibrant heritage.

The shocking impact of the events of 11 September 2001 fuelled further anti-Islamic sentiment in the West. Each violation of security by newly emboldened militant Muslims, especially in London, Paris and Madrid, made life miserable for Muslim and non-Muslim ethnic minorities alike in the US, Europe and further afield.

There is no doubt that this difficult period of open hostilities will lead, like it has done before, to a time of greater tolerance, accommodation and sharing helped considerably by the global links formed by social networking and the rapid dissemination of information. Prophetic Islam is slowly being rediscovered by both Muslims and non-Muslims. This new consciousness will increase the popularity of authentic Islam and Sufi spiritual teachings. We are indeed very fortunate today to have available unprecedented amounts of scholarship and research material that reveals the essential unity in the message conveyed by the Abrahamic religions and the transformative teachings of the Quran and the Prophetic Path.

From the mid-20th century onwards, there emerged a genuine desire amongst scholars, academics and the general public for an understanding of teachings from Hinduism, Buddhism, Islam and other Eastern spiritual teachings. Ease of travel and freedom to express and investigate provided the perfect backdrop to explore traditions of all sorts for the spiritual seekers from Europe, the USA and elsewhere. Quite a few seekers embraced Islam and particularly the Way of the Sufis.

Every loss in life I consider the throwing off of an old garment
in order to put on a new one;
And the new garment has always been better than the old.[211]
Hazrat Inayat Khan

Hazrat Inayat Khan (1882–1926), a Chishti master from India, attracted many Westerners to Islam during his years in Europe and America; initially through his music, later through Sufi teachings and the establishment of the World Sufi Movement. His work was carried on by his son, Pir Vilayat Inayat Khan (1916–2004), who taught in the tradition of Universal Sufism and was active in the interfaith movement.

Pir Zia Inayat Khan (b. 1971), Pir Vilayat's son, as head of the Sufi Order International, has taken on his father's mantle.

Gurdjieff (c1866/77–1949), a flamboyant Russian teacher, awoke considerable European interest in Sufism during the early part of the 20th century. This grew with more European converts to Islam and availability of Sufi tales from authors such as Idries Shah (1924–96). It also encouraged a trend of people isolating Sufism from the practice of Islam. No doubt Sufism throughout the centuries adapted some practices from the mystics of other faiths, but representing as it has always done the inner dimension of Islam, with centuries-old traditions of masters steeped in the *deen*, there can be no separation. You don't have to call yourself a Sufi to follow a mystic path, but if you want to benefit from Sufism's rich unveilings, the practice of Islam is an integral part of the package. Boundaries and restrictions are the foundations of openings in higher consciousness.

Gurdjieff popularized the quest for a hidden hierarchy of spiritual masters. He refers in his writings to the survival of the Sarmoung Brotherhood, a spiritual elite coming from all major religions. He claimed this school was founded in Babylon around 2500 BC and taught a method of spiritual transformation that transcends all religious differences. Gurdjieff, Idries Shah and other gurus of the late 19th and 20th centuries found the concept of the hidden spiritual elite convenient in separating Sufism from Islam and adopting some Sufi practices without the necessity of Prophetic Islam.

Seventeen years after Gurdjieff's death in 1949, Idries Shah contacted John Bennett's group, who were carrying on Gurdjieff's work and presented himself as a promoter of the Sarmoung masters. Later he was to claim his work was inspired by the Khwajagan, whom he described as the earliest of mystical chains of transmission in Sufism. He further claimed that only the Naqshabandis have the authority to initiate disciples into all other *tariqas*. The Khwajagan, who spread from Khurasan to Central Asia, were an important early group of spiritual masters who incorporated some of the Malamati teachings in their approach.

Human beings are always looking for the strange and exotic. Gurdjieff's success was partly due to his fantastic tales of hidden masters and travel to remote areas, such as Tibet and Afghanistan, to make contact with these hidden luminaries. This idea must have been difficult for his pupils to follow as it asserts that the higher level of being was far away, rather than within them.

Once there were more Muslims living in the West, the number of Sufi teachers visiting and sometimes establishing centres increased. The Rifa'is, who had been well established in Eastern Europe, kept many *zawiyas* going there in spite of Communist oppression. The Turkish migrants to Germany and other minorities from the Middle East and Subcontinent in European countries made a considerable contribution to the spread of Sufism. The Mevlevi order from Turkey became particularly popular because of the music, singing and whirling *dervishes*. Shaykh Nazim al-Haqqani (1922–2014), a Naqshabandi shaykh, had from his Cyprus base a considerable following in northern Europe, USA and other parts of the world. Dr Javad Nurbaksh (1926–2008), a psychiatrist of Iranian origin and a shaykh of the Nimatullahi Sufi order, moved first to the USA following the Iranian Revolution, and afterwards settled in England.

Various other masters, specifically Shaykh Abdalqadir as-Sufi (b. 1930), Shaykh Asaf Durakovic (b. 1940) and Llewellyn Vaughan-Lee (b. 1953), all of whom are mentioned previously, have brought about an increased interest during past decades.

There were also some so-called Sufis who ignored the basic tenets of Islam and were driven by a desire for power and influence. The pupils of some of these charismatic figures often end up disappointed and disillusioned. In these cases, the group ends up eventually being disbanded. There is often some competition, as happens in human nature, between the different Sufi orders and often a lack of co-operation or friendly connection between teachers. There is invariably the tendency of pupils to exaggerate the power of their master in comparison with others and regard their path as more superior and authentic.

As the number of educated Muslims is increasing in the West, as well as the number of new converts, much of the classical Sufi teachings are becoming popular even in the traditional mosques and religious institutions.

North America was frequently visited by Sufi teachers and visitors from the mid-20th century. Their centres and meeting halls had become popular by the time of the Iranian Revolution. The Naqshabandis, Rifa'is, North African and Subcontinent *tariqas* all had a presence. Several of these were involved in charitable activities both in America and internationally. Some of the teachers I have spoken to have expressed the opinion that America, due to its religious freedom, has a greater receptivity to Sufi teachings.

In the global village of today's world, many educated and professionally flexible people find their needs split between worldly and social activities and the desire to know truth and experience higher spiritual openings. Europeans flocking to the wilderness of India and other exotic destinations is an expression of spiritual thirst and hope to experience the Reality that ever resides within the heart. They look for a guru and then take the teachings back home. Human beings are, in truth, spiritual seekers.

With spiritual maturity and growth, the fortunate seeker will discover that the ultimate authority that he is looking for is already within him or her. God calls to Himself by Himself via the soul within the human breast, which is the personal instigator of all of our motives and drives. The soulmate that you are looking for in the outer world is a noisy distraction from the harmonious calling that is emitted from your own soul. We mix our worldly need for friendship, companions or solace with the spiritual drive to be at one with the spirit within. It is impossible to find an outer soulmate capable of combining all your needs – physical, mental and spiritual.

In the past, religion had played a key role in bonding people together and allowing rulers to enforce a measure of stability with laws and regulations that have had varying degrees of ethics and morality. Religion has also often been used to give legitimacy to human greed, love of conquest and dominance. Despots and autocrats have taken whatever ideas were helpful to reinforce their own dynasties and dogma.

The present-day crisis of global terrorism is forcing us to question why this has been supported in some part by educated people, specifically young Muslims, who have benefitted as migrants to European countries from the living conditions of their adopted lands. Since the end of the formal political and colonial occupation of the Middle East, Subcontinent and Africa, there has been much agitation and fermentation brewing in these countries. The emergence of numerous extreme movements is understandable due to the stagnation of life and lack of durable fulfilment.

CHALLENGE TO ALL

The grim atrocities so extreme,
Beyond language or expression,
The inhuman side of humanity declaring the failure of unity
At lower and higher levels.
We may say that life's purpose is celebrating Oneness,
Yet we are all caught in destructive otherness.
But no deviation ever lasts,
For Allah will attain His purpose,
To know the Ever Present Oneness.

Shaykh Fadhlalla Haeri

Over the past century, the Muslims increasingly realized the extent of the material and technological advancement of the West and wanted the same.

They asked themselves: if Islam was the correct path, why were Muslim nations in such misery? Their confusion, insecurity and challenges of daily living were exacerbated when European hegemony was followed by the advent of despotic autocratic rule, disguised as democratic or Islamic. The people were treated as subjects, rather than citizens, in the new emerging nation states. The hundreds of millions of Muslims who have love and pride in their religion suffered humiliation at many levels in their day-to-day lives. Fear and hatred of their leaders brought about expedient secretiveness. Economic development was accompanied by corruption and the disparity between the haves and have-nots was so wide that injustices and inequalities were glaring at everyone. The response was a range of radical ideas, which went from embracing Communism before the collapse of the Soviet Union to countless versions of Islamic revivals and reforms. In addition, revolutionary fervour was fanned by nationalistic ideals and aspirations.

Under these circumstances, it is not surprising that people would look for an immediate reversal, whether this takes the form of praying for the Mahdi, political agitation or extreme violence. There have been considerable personal and communal confusions causing conflicting forces in people's minds; a real tragedy for Muslims and the whole world.

Some years ago, while I was on holiday at a Red Sea resort, I was assigned a young Egyptian as a room-service attendant. Khalid was a graduate from an agricultural college, but could not find other work, except in the tourist industry, which he regarded with disdain, suspicion and even hatred. He was forced to serve fussy Westerners their alcohol and resented this forced breach of his Islamic principles. Every morning he would come to my room to read Quran for me. He had a melodious voice and recited well. Khalid invited me to accompany him to *Jummah* (Friday) prayers at a new mosque in the nearby town. The imam gave the standard government-approved *khutbah* (sermon) and asked for prayers for the president. When my young friend told me that his father was the imam and I was invited for lunch, I was less than enthusiastic. During lunch, the father told me that he was sent the *khutbah* every week and his job was dependent on using the official version. However, he would now give me his real sermon. He then proceeded to rain curses on the president and the government!

Over the past few decades, numerous new adjectives emerged to describe these new tendencies and forces – Islamist, fundamentalist, salafist, quietist and others. The Muslim Brotherhood was an early attempt to reform government by applying strict Islamic laws. There emerged innumerable factions from this cauldron, all with different tactics and strategies to improve the dire situation in their countries. Draconian laws emerged in some countries using differing versions of interpretations of *shari'a* injunctions. It is not surprising that extreme movements promising instant solutions and reversals of misfortunes have flourished in such hotbeds of unimaginable extremism and inhuman tendencies. This is now a global problem and the suffering such movements have brought about would have been unimaginable a few decades ago. Millions of Muslims have been displaced, lost their homes or have become refugees over the past few years due to the implosions and explosions that are taking place in their lands.

Historically, the Arabs have suffered from the illusion and image of being the fountainhead of Islam. In reality, within a short period after the Quranic revelation, the universal spiritual foundation of Prophetic Islam had fractured into religious and ethnic divisions, spearheaded by an evident Arabism. Despotic rulers emerged through the centuries who sang the aspirations of the populace while creating a deeper tyranny based on military might, secret services and supportive business/trading people. Religion was morphed to become a flag-waving mockery of its original revelation, while the Sufis and a few others tried to preserve the original Prophetic Path. Today the multiple hypocrisies and distortions are clear for anyone that takes the time and trouble to witness the modified versions of Mu'awiya's Islam. The Arab Spring showed how deeply rotten the leadership in many Arab countries is, how they have betrayed their people and the cynical culpability of several Western powers in supporting such corrupt governments.

In the 1950s, Iraq had emerged as an example of co-existence between numerous minorities of different ethnicity and religion. With a few revolutions and the rise to power of Saddam Hussein and his Baath Party, a promising educated generation was corralled to applaud Saddam's caliphate, without it actually being called that. Mubarak's rule in Egypt was a pharaonic-style caliphate. Gaddafi in Libya presented another version of absurd totalitarian governorship.

NEWSMAKERS

Who had done it?
Why?
What authority?
Mockery of legitimacy!
Labelled democracy,
theocracy or some other ocracy.
Actors and promoters
compete to be seen,
as modern caliphs.
Once known
the show game ends.
What can shadows do!
The light is ever there
For those who can see.

Shaykh Fadhlalla Haeri

Human nature is both earthly and heavenly; if these two sides are not addressed and nurtured then the imbalance will either produce secular robots and functionaries or fundamentalism and extremism. Islam is a path of bringing justice and balance to people's daily lives, while encouraging the rise of consciousness through intellect as well as spiritual practices that awaken one to the divine nature of the soul. Outer extremism reflects an inner drive to go beyond earthly limitations and an irrational way of life. We can only be content if we balance our humanity and divinity; the terrestrial with the celestial. The essential message of the Quran is that there is one cosmic force that permeates whatever is known and unknown in the universe. This life on earth is only a preparation for experiencing perpetual life, which is present in the moment but will only be known by everyone after the removal of our survival needs and the illusion that we are the body and the mind, i.e. death. There is no rest or peace for any individual unless there has been an awakening to the truth and magnificence of the sacred soul within the heart. This discovery removes the veil of otherness. Inner personal referencing will have a spiritual GPS, balancing outer experiences with the inner source of life and consciousness.

The spectre of terrorism is due to a past that produced desperation and destitution. There is a different map to living than one that is purely economically driven. Dr Ali Allawi, in his perceptive *Crisis of Islamic Civilization*, points out that any revival of real Islam must be based on the restoration of the sacred. Once the sacred was no longer the source of life, all that was left was an outer shell – the rules and regulations of religion. Rigid fundamentalism refuses any flexibility in interpretation. Innate in human nature is the desire to fix things, hence the absoluteness of the *shari'a* element. Makka represents the soul of Islam, Madina its body. If Madina does not live by the light of Makka, it ends up fascist and despotic. The result is the current wave of fundamentalism.

Ali ibn Ahmad al-Bushanji (d. 348 AH/959–60 CE) is credited with the oft-quoted: "Sufism was originally a reality without a name and had become a name without a reality." I grew up in an environment where the tenets of Sufism were lived without the usual labels of *tariqas*. My grandfather, who was a well-respected religious establishment scholar, shunned his brother who was a Sufi master. In their old age they cheerfully reconciled by discovering that their aim in life was the same – enlightenment and humanity.

The Sufi attempts to interact with the world rationally, while acknowledging the highest potential of humanity and its source of divinity. The link between the visible, material realm and the unseen is now becoming universally accepted as the ultimate goal of humanity. I foresee a wonderful future ahead of us, despite our history of much warfare and injustice, as well as the confusions and atrocities happening in the present day. It may take a few more generations for a class of universal awakened beings to emerge and be an example of a wholesome and balanced way of life. When this happens, people will live with courtesy as responsible guests on earth. They will live as Sufis even if they do not use the name.

Human existence and experience is in two zones: one relates to personal consciousness, biological growth and identity with individuality. The other zone is to do with universal consciousness, which traverses the finite and the infinite, and is within time and beyond time. In the first zone, human growth and evolvement is traceable and has a clear connectedness, until it reaches the edge of supreme consciousness. It is at that border that the issue of *fana'* and *baqa'* has classically been referred to. In our present-day culture these terms can be misleading. At the tipping point, when conditioned consciousness dissolves into its original higher consciousness, it could be said that the death or *fana'* of the first consciousness has taken place. This death is the gateway to *baqa'* or ongoingness. Conditioned consciousness is limited and dependent on higher consciousness, and when it ends the experience of higher consciousness begins and continues. The goal of the real teacher is to live and share a state in which higher consciousness is constantly referred to at all times.

Truth, Reality or Divine Light are all words meaning higher consciousness, pure consciousness or God consciousness – at different levels. This is the source of plurality, duality, otherness and separate consciousness. There is no clear separation within the realm of pure consciousness but there are levels of intensity and potency. Our mental habits may lead us to take our earthly dictionary to a land where that language is no longer valid. The Promised Land, *Jannah* or the heavenly abode, supreme consciousness is clearly timeless or boundless.

Enlightened human consciousness contains numerous levels and stages of awareness and experiences; overlapping images and values can occur at the same time with different levels of intensity. When someone enters into the zone of pure awareness the initial impact can be disturbing, rather like waking up from sleep. The sleeper leaves behind a state called sleep consciousness and enters into wake consciousness; an expanded metaphor for the arc of awakening is that of a newborn taking in outer experiences as it grows to adulthood. Its awakening is incremental but continues until death, the gateway to the liberation of the soul from being entangled with body and mind. In the case of the awakened being, with time and repeated experience the basic normal consciousness becomes inseparably connected with higher consciousness. All events and experiences will, with time and practice, reveal their meaning and essence.

Calling a person awakened implies that they have had the experience of having touched on that zone of higher consciousness, which is accompanied by the shock of fully realizing the transience of so-called normal consciousness. Whatever is in existence is now illumined by the unifying light. Whenever a reflective being stops mind, thought and all other awarenesses, they will touch upon transcendence, which ultimately moves toward a constant state of enlightenment and the plateau of awakening becomes a welcome state. It is there where the end and the beginning are inseparable, time and timelessness are the same. The final stage of enlightenment implies the full spectrum of consciousness – all physical realities are seen as indicators and pointers emanating from and moving toward the origin. Shadows are spotlighted by the constancy of pure consciousness. At the physical level, a big explosion leaves its mark where it has taken place. At the consciousness level, also, when the lower conditioned states have been superseded by the lights of supreme consciousness, energetic changes and traces can be detected. Spiritual transcendence leaves its subtle imprint, which can be accessed by those whose hearts are open to spiritual lights. This explains one of the reasons for the popularity of sacred spaces and shrines.

Many people have some breakthrough in terms of insights or epiphanies. What I term as an awakened person is when the light of the soul always accompanies the shadows of duality. Serious seekers often discuss which teacher is more enlightened. They will understand better if they review the extent of the worldly engagement and whether he or she is affected by their outer activities. There may be two beings that have awoken to the truth but one of them is fully engaged in teaching and showing the path of transcendence to others. I would give a higher status to that being because they are accessing the entire spectrum of consciousness where humanity and divinity are together.

It is also important to remember that, however enlightened a person may be, they will still display behavioural patterns inherited from their past. A shaykh whose early years were spent in service and action will still show some of these traits. Another may be more intellectually oriented. Some have a gentle outer demeanour, while others are more dominating and assertive. Reflecting on years of travels to meet people of light and how they have benefitted me in the quest of reality, I find that all who interested me were pointing in the same direction: toward the unified field of Oneness, whatever the differences in flavours, cultural variations or the extent of their involvement in the surrounding community.

With enlightenment, the awakened person realizes the importance of life experiences and the need for people and their leaders to wake up to the real purpose of life – to witness perfection at different levels of perception and consciousness. An ordinary wise person develops compassion and tolerance, but the enlightened being understands the state of the evolving human beings without disappointment. A well-meaning politician can run the risk of ending up as a fascist, who imposes social engineering. The enlightened being, on the other hand, simply overflows with the truth of utter oneness, which emanates from the heart. The enlightened being and the good leader both wish goodness for everyone, but the leader may act hastily or ineffectively without real reference to the essence of the situation. The enlightened man or woman can only do what is perfect at any precise moment in time, uniting the outer and inner dimensions of life.

DON'T MISS IT

Don't miss an opening
To what?
Life
Don't miss it
Don't talk or reflect
Don't think or meditate
Just don't miss it
Your life
Quest of tomorrow
Knowledge and Love
Fulfilled moment

Don't miss it
Fear disguised as hope
Don't miss it
Life
Now
Forever.

Shaykh Fadhlalla Haeri

The accomplished master will help the seeker to focus on his goal and the devotee to give up attachment to everything. It is important to see the teachings of the prophets and spiritual masters in their full context. Ibn al-'Arabi writes about the virtues of generosity, asceticism and night vigils, but equally emphasizes the importance of giving up identification and the image of being generous. Role-playing, irrespective of how good the role may be, is a spiritual hinderance.

One other important piece of advice to sincere seekers is not to dwell too deeply on descriptions of the path to enlightenment in old Sufi literature early on along their spiritual journey. Once you have a better understanding of these maps of reality, you can learn the various aspects of your experiences. Sufi treatises can be helpful in confirming to you that others have traversed the same terrain and a few describe well the new state of awakening. Embrace the path with trust until you experience intimate interaction with Reality. The mind registers whether something is familiar or not. When you are in a new land you must personally imbibe all its atmosphere and energy, otherwise you may be regurgitating someone else's views or feelings. No two people are the same as humans. Everyone is the same in spirit.

I benefitted from Ibn al-'Arabi when I had experienced the states and stations he described. *The Meaning of Man* by Sidi Ali al-Jamal is a good example of a book that can confuse novices because it addresses people at different levels of spiritual evolvement. I have worked with Shaykh Hosam Raouf on an abridged version to render it more accessible. You talk to a youngster in a different way to a mature seeker. Specialist treatises like this need to be used by qualified teachers, rather than for general consumption. This is the original reason why the brahmans and rabbis claimed an exclusive right over the dissemination of their scriptures: to avoid the danger of confusion and misinterpretation, whether that be purposefully or due to a lack of truly living them.

Before reaching spiritual maturity, Sufi literature can encourage fantasy or act as a placebo with uncertain outcomes. It is best, for this reason, to avoid specific spiritual terms and discussion of spiritual hierarchies. In the material realm, more is sought; in the spiritual realm, the reverse is true. Many spiritual seekers see the path as a process of getting something. The soul within has it all, but needs a pure heart to allow the light to shine through.

PERFECT DESTINY

At first humble,
then comes bliss of loss,
face, base and grace.
Nothing left,
divine madness, earthly disgrace
heavenly light.
Perfect origin –
primal light before matter,
liberation from illusion, confusion and identity,
Illumined by cosmic power of unity,
now and forever.

Shaykh Fadhlalla Haeri

For thousands of years, religion and human leadership were the key bonding factor between people. Religions brought about a certain measure of stability and justice in different societies. The emotional cohesion was horizontal depending on what the others thought of you and what your position and status was. We are heading toward a new zone in our emotional or spiritual connectiveness. It is moving from a horizontal linking to a vertical one. More and more individuals are learning to transcend their mind and connect personal limited consciousness to that of the infinite cosmic reality. When there are many people with direct access to their inner infinitude or soul, a new wave of horizontal evolution will come about.

Formal religions may die out or morph into new hybrids. The word "Sufi" and the idea of brotherhoods or *tariqas* may become the object of study and literature, but the inherent quest in humans to realize a durable purpose and meaning for life will persist. The Sufis always reflected the human state of their day; like a river, the extent of purity, pollution or temperature varied. Yet, with the internet and the ease of communication in today's world, the forces that brought about Sufi movements and other spiritual streams are unlikely to continue in the same way. The one-on-one contact between master and pupil gives the possibility of more rapid progress on the path than Skype and emails can achieve, but the contemporary situation also allows for the seeker to take more personal responsibility. In the past, awakened beings mostly emerged from within Sufi groups; in the future, illumined individuals may connect without the background of a group. For hundreds of years people wished to find an authority and follow it. Nowadays the drive is based on following different authorities to experience the vastness of your own soul. If Sufism is defined as the ever-continuous quest of humanity to live according to its source of Divinity, then as humanity changes in its texture and colour, so will the flavour of Sufism.

UNIQUE JOURNEYS – AT ONE WITH DESTINY

Not as you think
Thoughts are barriers
Not as it seems
All existence from it
Dependent on it
Not another
The Real contains all
differentiations
Veiling the Real.

The source of all
Existences express it
The present moment reveals all
Past, present and future
The link of the seen and the unseen.

Shaykh Fadhlalla Haeri

It is an age for increased personal responsibility, rather than dependency and blame of others. The traditional concept of putting yourself completely into the hands of the master – *fana' fi-shaykh* (annihilation through the shaykh) – can easily become cultish and create an expectancy that can backfire with negative implications for teacher and pupil. The teacher can only act as a mirror for the sincere seeker and sometimes as a wise friend or counsellor.

There will always be the need for guidance and mirrors, but the best master may say to his devoted pupil, "Don't listen to anyone except me, until the time will come when I say, 'Now don't even listen to me, because you can hear your soul.' Then, only follow that voice."

> *I saw my Lord with my heart's sight and declared it is certainly You, oh You and it is You, who is everywhere and all space knows it is only You and it is You, who encompasses everything with Your knowledge and therefore whatever I see it is You and through my annihilation my death vanishes and by that annihilation I find it is only You.*
>
> *Attributed to Imam Ali*

BIBLIOGRAPHY

These are some of the works consulted in the writing of this book. It is by no means a comprehensive bibliography on all the subjects raised.

All Quranic verses that appear in English have been taken from the translation by M H Shakir, published by Tahrike Tarsile Quran Inc., New York, 1982.

Abd al-Qadir, al-Jilani, Shaykh, *Sublime Gems: Selected Teachings of Abd al-Qadir al-Jilani*, Zahra Publications, South Africa, 2005.

Abun-Nasr, Jamil M, *A History of the Maghrib in the Islamic Period*, Cambridge University Press, UK, 1990.

Abdur Rahman Syed Sabahuddin, *Amir Khusrau as a Genius*, Idarah-I Adabiyat-I, Delhi, 1982.

Addas, Claude, *The Voyage of No Return*, The Islamic Text Society, UK, 2000.

Attar, Farid ud-Din, *The Conference of the Birds*, translated by Afkham Darbandi and Dick Davis, Penguin Books, UK 1986.

Attar, Farid ud-Din, *Tadhkaratu'l-Auliya (Memoirs of Saints)*, selected and abridged by Dr Bankey Behari, Shaykh Muhammad Ashraf, Pakistan, 1995.

Brown, John P, *The Dervishes or Oriental Spiritualism*, Frank Cass & Co. Ltd., by arrangement with Oxford University Press, UK, 1968.

Birge, John Kingsley, *The Bektashi Order of Dervishes*, Luzac Oriental, UK, 1994.

Bilgrami, Muna Haeri, *Iran through Our Eyes*, Zahra Publications, South Africa, 2009

Bibliography

Bonney, Richard, *Jihad: From Quran to bin Laden*, Palgrave Macmillan, UK, 2004.

Bulliet, Richard W, *The Patricians of Nishapur*, ACLS Humanities ebook, USA, 1972.

Bulleh Shah The Love-Intoxicated Iconoclast, translated by J R Puri and T R Shangari, Radha Soami Satsang Beas, India, 1995.

Chinmayananda, Swami, *Collection of Quotes*, Central Chinmaya Mission Trust, India, 2000.

Chinmayananda, Swami, *The Journey of a Master*, Central Chinmaya Mission Trust, India, 1994.

Chittick, William C, *Sufism: A Beginner's Guide*, Oneworld Publications, India, 2009.

Chodkiewicz, Michel, *Seal of the Saints: Prophethood and Sainthood in the Doctrine of Ibn Arabi*, translated by Liadain Sherrard, Islamic Texts Society, UK, 1993.

Chodkiewicz, Michel, *The Spiritual Writings of Amir Abd al-Kader*, SUNY Series in Western Esoteric Traditions, USA, 1995.

Clancy-Smith, Julia A, *Rebel and Saint: Muslim Notables, Populist Protest, Colonial Encounters (Algeria and Tunisia, 1800–1904)*, University of California Press, USA, 1994.

Cooke, Miriam & Lawrence, Bruce R (eds), *Muslim Networks from Hajj to Hip Hop*, University of North Carolina Press, 2005.

Darqawi, Shaykh Mawlay al-'Arabi, *The Darqawi Way: Letters of Shaykh Mawlay al-'Arabi ad-Darqawi*, Diwan Press, UK, 1979.

The Diwans of the Darqawa, translated by Aisha Abd ar-Rahman at-

Tarjumana, Diwan Press, UK, 1980.Dunn, Philip, Dunn Mascetti, Manuela and Nicholson, R A, *The Illustrated Rumi*, Harper Collins, USA, 2000.

Douglas-Klotz, Neil, *The Sufi Book of Life: 99 Pathways of the Heart for the Modern Dervish*, Penguin Compass, USA, 2005.

El Eflaki, Shemsu-d-Din Ahmed, *Legends of the Sufis (selections from Menaquibul Arifin)*, translated by James W Redhouse, The Theosophical Publishing House Ltd., UK, 1976.

Ernst, Carl W, *Teachings of Sufism*, Shambala South Asia Editions, India, 1999.

Ezekiel, I A, *Sarmad (Jewish Saint of India)*, Radha Soami Satsang Beas, India, 1974.

Frembgen, Jurgen Wasim, *At the Shrine of the Red Sufi*, translation by Jane Ripken, Oxford University Press, Pakistan, 2011.

Garbett, Sir Colin, *The Ringing Radiance*, Radha Soami Satsang Beas, India, 1968.

Haeri, Shaykh Fadhlalla (compiled by), *Prophetic Traditions in Islam: On the Authority of the Family of the Prophet*, translation by Asadullah adh-Dhaakir Yate, The Muhammadi Trust in association with Zahra Publications, UK, 1999.

Haeri, Shaykh Fadhlalla, *The Elements of Sufism*, Elements Books Ltd., UK, 1990.

Haeri, Shaykh Fadhlalla, *Ripples of Light*, Zahra Publications, South Africa, 1998.

Haeri, Shaykh Fadhlalla (compiled by), *Path to Light: The Haydari Handbook*, Zahra Publications, South Africa.

Bibliography

Haeri, Shaykh Fadhlalla, *Son of Karbala: The Spiritual Journey of an Iraqi Muslim*, O Books, UK, 2006.

Haeri, Shaykh Fadhlalla (compiled by), *Sayings of the Prophet Muhammad*, Zahra Publications, South Africa, 2010.

Haeri, Shaykh Fadhlalla, *The Four Journeys*, Zahra Publications, South Africa 2014.

Haeri, Muneera, *The Chishtis: A Living Light*, Oxford University Press, Karachi, 2000.

Habib, Muhammad, *Politics & Society During the Early Medieval Period*, Delhi, 1974.

Hasrat, Bikrama Jit, *Dara Shikuh: Life and Works*, Munshiram Manoharlal Publishers Pvt. Ltd., India, 1982.

Helminski, Camille Adams (compiled by), *Women of Sufism: A Hidden Treasure, Writings and Stories of Mystic Poets, Scholars and Saints*, Shambala, USA, 2003.

Honerkamp, Kenneth, "Abu Abd Al-Rahman Al-Sulami (d. 412 AH/1201 CE) on Sama, Ecstasy and Dance", *Journal of the History of Sufism*, 4 (2003): 1–13.

Honerkamp, Kenneth, *A Sufi Itinerary of Tenth Century Nishapur*, based on a treatise by Abu Abd al-Rahman al-Sulami, *Journal of Islamic Studies*, 17/1 (January 2006): 43–67.

Ibn 'Ajiba, Shaykh Ahmad, *The Immense Ocean (Al-Bahr al-Madid)*, translated and annotated by Mohamed Fouad Aresmouk and Michael Abdurrahman Fitzgerald, Fons Vitae, USA, 2009.

Ibn 'Ajiba, Shaykh Ahmad, *Al-Fahrasa: Autobiography of Ibn 'Ajiba*, translation by Jean-Louis Michon, Fons Vitae, USA, 1999.

Ibn 'Ata' Allah al-Iskandari, *The Hikam*, translation and commentary by Shaykh Fadhlalla Haeri, Zahra Publications, Karachi, 2004.

Ibn Mashish, Mawlai Abd as-Salam, *As-Salat al-Mashishiyyah*, translation and commentary by Abu Faydan Faridi, Nalayn Publications, Karachi, 2014.

Iqbal, Muhammad, *Shikwa and Jawab-i-Shikwa*, translation by Khushwant Singh, Oxford University Press, India, 1999.

Jamal, Sidi Ali, *Advice to the Seeker on the Path or Asceticism*, extracts entitled *Sabeel al Irfan wal Furqan* (*The Path of Knowledge and Discernment*), translation by Shaykh Fadhlalla Haeri and Shaykh Hosam Raouf, 2002 (unpublished).

Kalabadhi, Abu Bakr, *The Doctrine of the Sufis* (*Kitab al-Ta'rruf li-madhhab ahl al-tasawwuf*), translation by A J Arberry, Ashraf Press, Pakistan, 1966.

Karamustafa, Ahmet T, *Sufism: The Formative Period*, The American University in Cairo Press, Egypt, 2007.

Karrar, Ali Salih, *The Sufi Brotherhoods in the Sudan*, Northwestern University Press, by arrangement with Hurst and Company, London, Hong Kong, 1992.

Khan, Hazrat Inayat, *The Sufi Message of Hazrat Inayat Khan*, Gaydan, Vadan, Nirtan, Barrie and Rockcliff, UK, for International Headquarters of Sufi Movement, 1960.

Khayyam, Omar, *Rubaiyat of Omar Khayyam*, translation by Edward FitzGerald, Adam & Black, UK, 1909.

Khusrau, Amir, *In the Bazaar of Love: The Selected Poetry of Amir Khusrau*, translation by Paul Losensky and Sunil Sharma, Penguin Books, India, 2011.

Bibliography

Krynicki, Annie Krieger, *Captive Princess: Zebunissa, Daughter of Emperor Aurangzeb*, Oxford University Press, Pakistan, 2005.

Lapidus, Ira M, *A History of Islamic Societies*, Cambridge University Press, UK, 2002.

Lawrence, Bruce B, *The Early Chishti Approach to Sama'*, JAAR Thematic Studies L/1.

Lewis, Samuel L, *Sufi Vision and Initiation: Meetings with Remarkable Beings*, edited by Neil Douglas-Klotz, Sufi Ruhaniat International, San Francisco, CA, 1986, 2013.

Lings, Martin, *A Sufi Saint of the Twentieth Century: Shaikh Ahmad al-'Alawi*, Premier Publishing Company, India, 1993.

Martin, B G, *Muslim Brotherhoods in 19th-Century Africa*, Cambridge University Press, USA, 1978.

Magali, Morsy, *North Africa 1800–1900: A survey from the Nile Valley to the Atlantic*, Longman, USA, 1984.

Malamud, Margaret, "Sufi Organisations and Structures of Authority in Medieval Nishapur", *International Journal of Middle East Studies*, 26/3 (August 1994), Cambridge University Press.

Muzaffer Ozak al-Jerrahi al-Halveti, Sheikh, *The Unveiling of Love*, translation by Muhtar Holland, Inner Traditions International, USA, 1981.

Nasr, Seyyed Hossein, *The Garden of Truth: The Vision and Promise of Sufism, Islam's Mystical Tradition*, Harper Collins, USA, 2007.

Nasr, Seyyed Hossein, with Ramin Jahanbegloo, *In Search of the Sacred: A Conversation with Seyyed Hossein Nasr on His Life and Thought*, Praeger, 2010.

Niffari, Muhammad Ibn 'Abdi'l-Jabbar, *The Mawaqif and Mukhatabat*, translation and commentary by A J Arberry, Cambridge University Press, UK, 1935.

Nizami, Khaliq Ahmad, *The Life and Times of Shaikh Farid-Ud-Din Ganj-i-Shakar*, Universal Books, Pakistan, 1955.

Nizami, Khaliq Ahmad, *Some Aspects of Religion and Politics in India During the Thirteenth Century*, Idarah-I Adabiyat-I Delli, India, 1974.

O'Fahey, R S, *Enigmatic Saint: Ahmad Ibn Idris and the Idrisi Tradition*, Hurst and Company, UK, 1990.

Patchen, Nancy, *The Journey of a Master: Swami Chinmayananda*, Central Chinmaya Mission Trust, India, 1994.

Qureshi, Samina, *Sacred Spaces: A Journey with the Sufis of the Indus*, Mapin Publishing, Singapore.

Rabb, Muhammad Abdur, *Al-Junayd's Doctrine of Tawhid: An Analysis of his Understanding of Islamic Monotheism*, Institute of Islamic Studies, McGill University, Canada, 1967 (unpublished MA thesis).

Rabb, Muhammad Abdur, *Persian Mysticism: Abu Yazid al-Bistami*, The Academy for Pakistani Affairs, Pakistan, 1971.

Ridgeon, Lloyd (ed), *The Cambridge Companion to Sufism*, Cambridge University Press, UK, 2015.

Rizvi, Saiyid Athar Abbas, *A History of Sufism in India: Volume One*, Munshiram Manoharlal Publishers Pvt. Ltd., India, 1978.

Rizvi, Saiyid Athar Abbas, *A History of Sufism in India: Volume Two*, Munshiram Manoharlal Publishers Pvt. Ltd., India, 1983.Rumi, Jalal ad-Din, *The Sun of Tabriz*, translation by Sir Colin Garbett, Johnston and Neville, Cape Town, 1969.

Bibliography

Sanai, Hakim, *The Walled Garden of Truth*, translated and abridged by D L Pendelbury, Octagon Press, UK, 1974.

Schimmel, Annemarie, *My Soul is a Woman*, translation by Susan H Hay, The Continuum International Publishing Group Inc., USA, 1997.

Sells, Michael A, *Early Islamic Mysticism*, Suhail Academy, Pakistan, 2004.

Shah Abdul Lati Bhitai, *The Risalo*, selections translated by Elsa Kazi, Muhammad Ashraf, Pakistan, 1965.

Shaikh Sadiyya, *Sufi Narratives of Intimacy: Ibn Arabi, Gender and Sexuality*, University of North Carolina Press, USA, 2012.

Shams-i-Tabriz, *Me and Rumi: The Autobiography of Shams-i-Tabriz*, translated, introduced and annotated by William C Chittick, Fons Vitae, USA, 2004.

Sijzi, Amir Hasan, *Morals for the Heart (Fawa'id al-Fu'ad)*, translated and annotated by Bruce B Lawrence, Paulist Press, USA, 1992.

Shah-Kazemi, Reza (ed), *Algeria: Revolution Revisited, Islamic World Report*, UK, 1997.

Shakoor, Muhyiddin, *The Writing on the Water*, Element Books, UK, 1987.

Sugich, Michael, *Signs on the Horizon: Meetings with Men of Knowledge and Illumination*, 2013 (self-published).

Sulami, Abdu Abd ar-Rahman, *Early Sufi Women*, translation by Rkia E Cornell, Fons Vitae, USA, 1999.

Sultan Bahu, *Death Before Dying: The Sufi Poems of Sultan Bahu*, translated and introduced by Jamal J Elias, University of California Press, USA, 1998.

Sviri, Sara, *The Taste of Hidden Things*, The Golden Sufi Center, USA, 1997.

Sviri Sara, "Hakim Tirmidhi and the Malamati Movement in Early Sufism", from Lewisohn, L (ed), *The Heritage of Sufism: Volume One*, Oneworld Publications, UK, 1999.

Sultanova, Razia, *From Shamanism to Sufism: Women, Islam and Culture in Central Asia*, I B Tauris, UK, 2011.

Toussulis, Yannis, *Sufism and the Way of Blame: Hidden Sources of a Sacred Psychology*, Quest Books, USA, 2010.

Tweedie, Irina, *The Chasm of Fire*, Element Books, UK, 1979.

Trimingham, J Spencer, *The Sufi Orders in Islam*, Oxford University Press, USA, 1998.

Vaughan-Lee, Llewellyn, *Spiritual Power: How It Works*, The Golden Sufi Center, USA, 2005.

Zauqi, Syed Muhammad, *Vision for Seekers of the Truth*, Ferozsons (Pvt) Ltd., Pakistan, 2005.

GLOSSARY

We have tried to keep the transliteration of Arabic words as simple as possible, avoiding most diacritics, especially for the hamza (glottal stop), but retaining the ' for the 'ayn. We have dropped the 'h' which often appears at the end of words ending in the Arabic letter 'ta' marbuta'; also for simplicity's sake, where there are long vowels in the Arabic, we have only indicated them in a few words, like *deen*. Preference has been given to conventional spellings where names are concerned.

abd	slave
adab	courtesy, appropriate conduct
adhan	call to prayer
Ahl al-Bayt	Household of the Prophet
akhira	ultimate realm; the hereafter
Al-'Eid al-Adha	Hajj Eid
Allah Raad	God willed it
Allahu Akbar	God is greater
'alim	one trained in the religious sciences, pl. *'ulama*
Ana'l-Haqq	I am the Truth
ashraf	of noble descent, from "*shareef*"
Assalamu Alaykum	Peace be upon you
awliya	friends of God, sing. *wali*
ayah	verse from Quran, sign or mark, pl. *ayat*
Ayat al-Kursi	Throne Verse in the Quran, 2:225
'Ayn al-Ruman	"Source of Pomegranates"
baqa'	on-going in God, mystic state once *fana'* has taken place

Glossary

baraka	blessing, grace
Bari Imam	Leader of the Earth
Bayt ad-Deen	House of Religion
bay'a	spiritual allegiance
Bismillah	in the name of Allah
burda	mantle
burnous	cloak
chilla	lit. "forty", from the Persian *chehel* indicating a period of 40 days; ritual retreat for the purpose of spiritual awakening.
Chiragh-i-Delhi	"Lamp of Delhi"
dacoit	robber
Dar al-Bayda	Casablanca
Dar al-Ehsan	"Abode of Selfless Action"
dargah	shrine, implying a sanctuary
Data Ganj Baksh	"Distributor of Unlimited Treasure"
deen	religion, life-transaction between Allah and man
dervish	follower of Sufism
dhikr	invocation, remembrance of Allah
dhimmi	non-Muslim citizen of a Muslim state
diwan	collection of odes
djellaba	traditional Moroccan robe with hood
dunya	this world
fana'	annihilation of self
faqir	poor one, someone in need of God, i.e. on the Sufi path, pl. *fuqara*

fatwa	legal opinion issued by a canon lawyer
fiqh	Islamic law
firman	edict
fu'ad	innermost of the heart
fuqara	pupils of spiritual master, pl. of *faqir*
futuh	unsolicited gift
futuwwa	spiritual chivalry
gazavat	sanctified war
Gharib Nawaz	Helper of the Poor
ghazal	rhymed couplet
ghusul	ritual ablution
hadith	tradition, saying (usually of the Prophet Muhammad but sometimes narrated by the holy imams relating his deeds and utterances)
Hadith Qudsi	Divine saying, via the tongue of the Prophet
hadra	lit. Presence, invocation done at Sufi gatherings
hafiz	one who has memorized all the Quran
Hajj	pilgrimage to Makka in the last month of the Islamic calendar year
Hajji	pilgrim
hal	state
haqiqa	Truth, inner reality, true nature of creation
haqq	Truth, inner reality, one of the Attributes of Allah
harraq	He who sets others on flames
hijab	veil
hijra	migration

Glossary

himma	spiritual yearning
'ibadat	worship
idhn	permission
ijtihad	an exercise of reason to establish the ruling of the *shari'a* on a given point, by a mujtahid, a person qualified for the enquiry
'irfan	gnosis, enlightenment
isharat	sign
ishraq	momentary illumination
jahiliyya	ignorance
Jannah	paradise
Jannat al-Baqi	the cemetery in Madina where many of the Prophet's family were buried, near his own grave, markers of which have been utterly razed to the ground by the regime in Saudi Arabia
jihad	lit. intense striving, often used in context of "holy" war as well as spiritual striving
jinn	creatures made out of fire, who exist in a parallel universe to man, who is made out of clay
Jummah	Friday
Kaaba	Arabian ancient sacred place of worship, situated within the sacred enclosure of Makka
Kaki	Man of Bread
khadim	servant of the shrine
khalifa	deputy appointed by shaykh

Khidr	the Green Man, ever green, ever-living guide, associated with the Prophet Elijah of the Old Testament and in the Quran as the teacher of the Prophet Musa
khirqa	lit. rag, patched cloak of Sufi
killidar	keeper of the key
khalwa	spiritual retreat, seclusion
khanqah	Sufi centre
khutba	sermon, address, generally taken to mean discourse at Friday prayers
khwaja	title of respect, often used to denote spiritual authority
kohl	traditional eye make-up; antimony
kramats	burial places of saints
La ilaha illallah	there is no god but God
lal	red
langarkhana	kitchen feeding poor, attached to a shrine
madhhab	school of law
madrasa	school for religious studies
majdhub	ecstatic
majlis	assembly, pl. *majalis*
makhfi	the hidden one
maqam	station
masnavi	rhymed couplet
mawaqif	when all stops or at the stop
mawlid	birthday

mawsim	lit. season; annual gathering commemorating a *wali*'s death or union with God (in the Indian tradition called *'urs* or wedding).
memsahebs	wives of colonial officers
mu'adhdhin	one who calls to prayer (muezzin in English parlance)
mujaddid	reformer
mujtahid	practitioner of *ijtihad*
mumin	believer
muqaddam	senior Sufi, appointed deputy of a spiritual master
murid	seeker, pupil in Sufism
nafs	ego, lower self
nikah	marriage
nur	light
qadi	judge
qalandar	wandering *dervish*
qasidah	ode
qawwal(s)	singer(s) of devotional song(s)
qawwali(s)	devotional song(s)
qibla	direction Muslims face, when praying, toward the Kaaba in Makka
qutb	axial saint
rafiullah	elevated by Allah
ratib	litany
ribat	Sufi lodge
sadaqa	charity, payment to the poor

sajda	prostration
Salafi or Salafist	literalist reform movement within Sunni Islam, support implementation of *shari'a* law, try to follow the behaviour of the Prophet Muhammad and his close companions, reject innovations. They are divided into those who avoid politics, those who enter the political arena but do not advocate *jihad* and the jihadists.
sama'	spiritual recital, audition party
sajjada nasheen	he who sits on the prayer mat, i.e. representative.
salat	ritual prayer
Samandari Baba	"Man of the Sea"
saradib	cellar
Seyyed	lit. "mister", as honorific title denotes males accepted as descendants of the Prophet Muhammad through his grandsons, Hasan and Hussein
shahada	declaration of embracing Islam
shahbaz	noblest species of falcon
shalwar qameez	Baggy pants and long tunic, traditional garb of parts of the Indo-Pak Subcontinent.
shareef	noble descent, from "*ashraf*"
shari'a	Islamic law or code of conduct, outward path
shaykh al-ta'lim	shaykh of instruction
shaykh al-terbiya	shaykh of upbringing
shirk	associating other-than-Allah with Allah, idolatry, polytheism
silsila	chain, spiritual lineage

Glossary

suffa	sofa, bench. Ahl al-Suffa: people of the bench (ascetic devotees)
suf	wool
Sultan ul-Mashaikh	Sultan of the Shaykhs
Sultan al-'Ashiqin	Sultan of the Lovers
sunna	customary practice, line of conduct used in reference to Allah or the Prophet Muhammad
Sultan-i-Hind	Ruler of India
Surat Fatiha	"The Opening"; first chapter of the Quran
tafsir	interpretation of Quran
tajalli	divine inner manifestation witnessed by the inner eye of a seeker, theophany
tajrid	lit. stripping off, transcend form toward meaning, from the visible to the Essence, to see the One behind the two
tariqa	order, way, mystical school of guidance for those following Sufi path
Tariqat al-Khawajagan	the Path of the Masters
Tariqat al-Sahabat	Path of the Prophet's Companions
tasawwuf	Sufism
tasbih	prayer beads
tawhid	Divine unity, belief in Allah's Oneness
tayyammum	ritual ablution using sand, dust or stone instead of water where the latter is unavailable
tekke	Sufi lodge or centre
'ulama	those trained in the religious sciences; pl. of *'alim*

'urs	wedding; specifically the celebration of a *wali*'s death, a "marriage" of reunification with origin
ustadh	teacher
Wahhabi	puritanical offshoot of Sunni Islam, opposed to Sufism, originating in the 18th century CE
wali	friend of God
waqf	religious endowment
wird	litany
wudu	ritual ablution
zakat	mandatory charitable contribution or tax
zawiya	lit. corner, Sufi sanctuary
zuhr	midday

ENDNOTES

Introduction

1. This invocation is implied every time the Prophet Muhammad's name is mentioned.

2. *The Hikam: The Wisdom of Ibn 'Ata' Allah*, translation and commentary by Shaykh Fadhlalla Haeri; Zahra Publications, Pakistan, 2004, p.284.

3. *Shikwa and Jawab-i-Shikwa*, Muhammad Iqbal, translation by Khushwant Singh; OUP, India, 1999, p.77.

4. *The Sufi Message of Hazrat Inayat Khan*, Hazrat Inayat Khan; Barrie and Rockcliff, UK, 1960, p.57.

Chapter 1

5. *The Hikam: The Wisdom of Ibn 'Ata' Allah*, op. cit., p.41.

6. *The Four Journeys*, Shaykh Fadhlalla Haeri, Zahra Publications, South Africa, 2014, p.142.

7. *Prophetic Traditions in Islam*, compiled by Shaykh Fadhlalla Haeri, The Muhammadi Trust in association with Zahra Publications, UK, 1999, p.134.

8. *Selections from the Risalo of Shah Abdul Latif Bhitai*, translation by Elsa Kazi, Sindhi Adabi Board, Pakistan, 1965, p.234.

9. *The Journey of a Master: Swami Chinmayananda*, Nancy Patchen, Central Chinmaya Mission Trust, India, 1994, p.188.

10. Ibid., p.240.

Chapter 2

11. *The Hikam: The Wisdom of Ibn 'Ata' Allah,* op. cit., p.136.

12. *From Shamanism to Sufism: Women, Islam and Culture in Central Asia*, Razia Sultanova, I B Tauris, UK, 2011, p.39.

13. *The Hikam: The Wisdom of Ibn 'Ata' Allah,* op. cit., p.13.

14. *The Sufi Orders in Islam*, J Spencer Trimingham, translation by R A Nicholson, OUP, USA, 1998, p.167.

15. *Morals for the Heart (Fawa'id al-Fu'ad)*, Amir Hasan Sijzi, translation by Bruce B Lawrence, Paulist Press, USA, 1992, p.104.

16. Adapted from *Morals for the Heart (Fawa'id al-Fu'ad)*, op. cit., p.322.

17. *The Voyage of No Return*, Claude Addas, The Islamic Text Society, 2000, p.73.

18. *Al-Junayd's Doctrine of Tawhid: An Analysis of his Understanding of Islamic Monotheism*, Muhammad Abdur Rabb, Institute of Islamic Studies, McGill University, Canada, 1967 (unpublished MA thesis), p.113.

19. *The Sufi Book of Life: 99 Pathways of the Heart for the Modern Dervish*, Neil Douglas-Klotz, Penguin Compass, USA, 2005, p.181.

20. *Sufism: A Beginner's Guide*, William C Chittick, Oneworld, India, 2009, p.21.

21. *Me and Rumi: The Autobiography of Shams-i-Tabriz*, translation by William C Chittick, Fons Vitae, USA, 2004, p.88.

22. *Ithaf as-Sada* (commentary on *Ihya 'Ulum ad-Din* by Abu-Hamid al-Ghazali), M Al-Murtada az-Zabidi.

Endnotes

Chapter 3

23. *Prophetic Traditions in Islam*, op. cit., p.138.

24. *The Writing on the Water*, Muhyiddin Shakoor, Element Books, UK, 1987, p.216.

25. *Husein: Epic of Shaykh Asaf Durakovic*, World Life Institute Publishing House, USA, 2012.

26. *The Sufi Orders in Islam*, op. cit., p.37–8.

27. Ibid., p.38–9.

28. *The Unveiling of Love*, Shaykh Muzaffer Ozak al-Jerrahi, translation by Muhtar Holland, Inner Traditions International, USA, 1981, p.170–71.

29. Ibid., p.59.

30. *The Walled Garden of Truth*, Hakim Sanai, translated and abridged by D L Pendlebury, Octagon Press, UK, 1974, p.10.

Chapter 4

31. *Kashf al-Mahjub* (*Uncovering the Veiled*), Ali al-Hujweri, translation by R A Nicholson, Islamic Book Foundation, Lahore, 1976.

32. *Some Aspects of Religion and Politics in India During the Thirteenth Century*, K A Nizami, Delhi, 1974, p.242. Source: *Siyaru'l-Awliya*, Amir Khurd, Saiyyid Muhammad bin Mubarak, Delhi, 1302/1885.

33. *The Life and Times of Shaikh Farid-Ud-Din Ganj-i-Shakar*, K A Nizami, Universal Books, Pakistan, 1955, p.103. Source: Ibid.

34. *Some Aspects of Religion and Politics in India During the Thirteenth Century*, op. cit.

35. Adapted from *The Life and Times of Shaikh Farid-Ud-Din Ganj-i-Shakar*, op. cit.

36. *Morals for the Heart (Fawa'id al-Fu'ad)*, op. cit., p.166.

37. The biographical information about Shah Shahidullah Faridi was extracted from notes on his life prepared for the author by Muhammad Harun Riedinger, who had been Shah Shahidullah's murid.

38. *Morals for the Heart (Fawa'id al-Fu'ad)*, op. cit.

39. *The Sufi Message of Hazrat Inayat Khan*, op. cit., p.201.

40. *Prophetic Traditions in Islam*, op. cit., p.14.

41. *Me and Rumi*, op. cit., p.226.

42. *Sublime Gems: Selected Teachings of Abd al-Qadir al-Jilani*, Zahra Publications, South Africa, 2005, p.1.

43. *The Sufi Orders in Islam*, op. cit., p.42.

44. *Sublime Gems*, op. cit., p.94.

45. *Advice to the Seeker on the Path of Asceticism*, Sidi Ali al-Jamal, unpublished translation by Shaykh Fadhlalla Haeri and Shaykh Hosam Raouf, p.102.

Chapter 5

46. *Prophetic Traditions in Islam*, op. cit., p.178.

47. *The Tarjuman al-Ashwaq*, Ibn al-'Arabi, translation by R A Nicholson, UK, 1911.

48. *Futuhat Makkiyya IV*, Ibn al-'Arabi, p.591, Source: The Vision of God according to *Ibn al-'Arabi*, translation by Michel Chodkiewicz.

49. *Death Before Dying: The Sufi Poems of Sultan Bahu*, translation by Jamal J Elias, University of California Press, USA, 1998, p.31.

50. Ibid., p.39.

51. Ibid., p.33.

52. Ibid., p.48.

53. Ibid., p.113.

54. Ibid., p.115.

55. Ibid., p.135.

56. *At the Shrine of the Red Sufi*, Jurgen Wasim Frembgen, translation by Jane Ripken, OUP, Pakistan, 2011, p.48.

57. *The Risalo*, Shah Abdul Lati Bhitai, translation by Elsa Kazi, Muhammad Ashraf, Pakistan, 1965, p.132.

58. Ibid., p.236.

59. Ibid., p.232.

60. Ibid., p.237.

61. *Bulleh Shah: The Love-Intoxicated Iconoclast*, translation by J R Puri and T R Shangari, Radha Soami Satsang Beas, India, 1995, p.264.

62. Ibid., p.130.

63. Ibid., p.131.

64. *The Hand of Poetry: Five Mystic Poets of Persia*, translation by Coleman Barks.

65. *Mathnawi III 1833–1834*, Jalal ad-Din Rumi, translation by Camille and Kabir Helminski, from *The Rumi Collection: An Anthology of Translations of Mevlana Jalaluddin Rumi*, edited by Kabir Helminski, Shambala Publications, 2005.

66. *The Hikam: The Wisdom of Ibn 'Ata' Allah*, op. cit., p.36.

67. *The Sufi Message of Hazrat Inayat Khan*, op. cit., p.213.

68. *The Hikam: The Wisdom of Ibn 'Ata' Allah*, op. cit., p.30.

Chapter 6

69. *The Four Journeys*, op. cit., p.191.

70. Ibid., p.136.

71. *Morals for the Heart (Fawa'id al-Fu'ad)*, op. cit., p.99–100.

72. *Vision for Seekers of Truth*, Syed Muhammad Zauqi, Ferozsons (Pvt) Ltd., Pakistan, 2005, p.340.

73. *The Life and Times of Shaikh Farid Ud-Din Ganj-i-Shakar*, op. cit.

74. *State and Culture in Medieval India*, K A Nizami, Delhi, 1985, p.193.

75. *A History of Sufism in India: Volume One*, S A A Rizvi, Munshiram Manoharlal Publishers Pvt. Ltd., India, 1978, p.174. Source: *Akhbaru'l-Akhyar*, Shaykh Abdul'l-Haqq Muhaddis Dihlawi, Delhi, 1914.

76. Ibid., p.166. Source: *Anwaru'l-'Uyun*, Shaykh Abdul'l-Quddus Gangohi, Delhi, 1895.

77. *The Early Chishti Approach to Sama'*, Bruce B Lawrence, JAAR Thematic Studies L/1.

78. *In the Bazaar of Love: The Selected Poetry of Amir Khusrau*, translation by Paul Losensky and Sunil Sharma, Penguin Books, India, 2011, p.xxx.

79. Adapted from *Safinat-u'l-Awliya*, Dara Shikoh.

80. *Amir Khusrau as a Genius*, Syed Sahabuddin Abdur Rahman, Idarah-I Adabiyat-l, India, 1982, p.10. Source: *Safinat-u'l Awliya*, Dara Shikoh.

81. Ibid., p.11.

82. *In the Bazaar of Love: The Selected Poetry of Amir Khusrau*, op. cit., p.xxxvi.

83. Ibid., p.xxxi.

84. *A History of Sufism in India: Volume Two*, S A A Rizvi, Munshiram Manoharlal Publishers Pvt. Ltd., India, 1983, p.278.

85. *Politics and Society During the Early Medieval Period*, Mohammad Habib, India, 1974, p.380. Source: *Khair ul-Majlis*, compiled by Maulana Hamid Qalandar, K A Nizami, Muslim University, Aligarh.

86. Ibid., p.363.

87. *Notes from a Distant Flute*, Sufi Literature in Pre-Mughal India, Bruce B Lawrence, Iran, 1978, p.29. Source: *Khair-u'l Majalis*, op. cit.

88. English introduction to *Khair ul-Majlis: Conversations with Shaykh Nasir ad-Din Chiragh-i-Delhi*, op. cit.

89. *Politics and Society During the Early Medieval Period*, op. cit., p.374. Source: *Siyaru'l Awliya*, Amir Khurd, Saiyyid Muhammad bin Mubarak, Delhi, 1302–1885.

90. *Dara Shikuh: Life and Works*, Bikram Jit Hasrat, Munshiram Manoharlal Publishers Pvt. Ltd., India, 1982, p.138.

91. *Sarmad (Jewish Saint of India)*, I A Ezekiel, Radha Soami Satsang Beas, India, 1974, p.19.

92. *The Hikam: The Wisdom of Ibn 'Ata' Allah*, op. cit., p.40.

Chapter 7

93. *Al Mathal Al A'la (The Likeness of the One Without Semblance)*: *A Commentary on As-Salat al Mashishiyyah*, Abu Faydan Faridi, Na'layn Publications, Pakistan, 2014, p.4–5.

94. Ibid., p.15–19.

95. *Dalail al-Khayrat (Proof of the Blessing)*, Muhammad al-Jazuli, translation of Moroccan version by Aisha Bewley.

96. *Untold Marrakesh: The Seven Saints*, Mohammed Khan. www.sacredfootsteps.org/2015/05/16/untold-marrakesh-the-seven-saints/.

97. *Dalail al-Khayrat*, op. cit.

98. www.salawat.net/burdaintroduction.

99. *The Sufi Orders in Islam*, op. cit., p.27.

100. *The Hikam: The Wisdom of Ibn 'Ata' Allah*, op. cit., p.116.

101. *A Biography of Abu l-Hasan al-Shadhili Dating from the Fourteenth Century*, Kenneth Honerkamp, p.5.

102. Ibid., p.8.

103. Ibid.

104. *The Hikam: The Wisdom of Ibn 'Ata' Allah*, op. cit., p.215.

105. *Al-Farasa: The Autobiography of Ibn 'Ajiba*, English translation by Jean-Louis Michon, Fons Vitae Press, USA, 1999. Source: *The Immense Ocean (Al-Bahr al-Madid)*, Ahmad ibn 'Ajiba, translation by Mohamed Fouad Aresmouk and Michael Abdurrahman Fitzgerald, Fons Vitae, USA, 2009, p.xviii.

106. *The Darqawa Way: The Letters of Shaykh Darqawa*, translation by Aisha Abd ar-Rahman at-Tarjumana, Diwan Press, UK, 1979, p.320.

107. Ibid., p.133.

108. *The Immense Ocean (Al-Bahr al-Madid)*, op. cit., p.1.

109. *Al Risala al-Qushayriyya*, Abu Qasim al-Qushayri, (eds) Abd al-Halim Mahmud and Mahmud ibn al-Sharif, Dar al-Kutub al-Haditha, Egypt, 1974; *The Teachings of Sufism*, Carl W Ernst, Shambala, India, 1999, p.152.

110. *The Hikam: The Wisdom of Ibn 'Ata' Allah*, op. cit., p.28.

111. *A Sufi Saint of the Twentieth Century: Shaikh Ahmad Al-'Alawi, His Spiritual Heritage and Legacy*, Martin Lings, Premier Publishing Company, India, 1993, p.52.

112. Ibid., p.108.

113. Ibid., p.108–9.

114. *Algeria Revolution Revisited*, (ed) Reza Shah-Kazemi, Islamic World Report, London, 1997, p.20.

115. *A Sufi Saint of the Twentieth Century*, op. cit.

116. *The Diwans of the Darqawa: The Fayturiyya of Shaykh Muhammad al-Fayturi Hamudah*, translation by Aisha Abd ar-Rahman at-Tarjumana, Diwan Press, UK, 1980, p.360.

117. Ibid., p.362.

118. *The Hikam: The Wisdom of Ibn 'Ata' Allah*, op. cit., p.288.

119. Ibid., p.263.

120. *The Poem of the Sufi Way: Umar Ibn al-Farid*, translation by Th. Emil Homerin in *Umar al-Farid: Sufi Verse, Saintly Life*, Paulist Press, USA, 2001.

Chapter 8

121. *The Faith and Practice of al-Ghazali*, translation by W Montgomery Watt, Allen & Unwin, UK, 1967.

122. *Muslim Brotherhoods in 19th-Century Africa*, B G Martin, Cambridge University Press, USA, 1978, p.20. Source: *Majmu thalatha kutub (Litattafai uku a habe)*, Usman dan Fodio, Zaria, 1961, p.1.

123. Ibid., p.34. Source: *Hidayat at-Tullah*, Usman dan Fodio, Zaria, p.1–2.

124. Ibid., p.35. Source: *Infaq al-Maysur*, Muhammad Bello, Cairo, 1383/1964, p.94–5.

125. *The Hikam: The Wisdom of Ibn 'Ata' Allah*, op. cit., p.242.

126. *Abdelkader: Le Chevalier de la Foi*, Mohamed Cherif Sahli, Entreprise Algerienne de Press, 1967, p.131–2.

127. *The Spiritual Writings of Amir 'Abd al-Kader*, Michel Chodkiewicz, translation by a team under the direction of James Chrestensen and Tom Manning, State University of New York Press, USA, 1995, p.2. Source: *L'Emir 'Abd el-Kader, Du Fanatisme Musulman au Patriotisme Français*, Paul Azan, Paris, 1925.

128. Ibid. Source: M Habart in introduction to French translation of *The Life of 'Abdal-Kadir*, Charles Henry Churchill, 2nd edition, Algiers, 1974.

129. *The Life of Abdel Kader*, Charles Henry Churchill, Chapman and Hall, UK, 1867, p.323.

130. Ibid., p.321–2.

131. *The Spiritual Writings of Amir 'Abd al-Kader*, op. cit., Mawqif 197, p.50.

132. *Prophetic Traditions in Islam*, op. cit., p.89.

133. *North Africa 1800–1900*, Magali Morsy, Longman, USA, 1984, p.252.

134. *Prisoners of the Mahdi*, Byron Farwell, Longmans, UK, 1967, p.334.

135. *Sayings of the Prophet Muhammad: Selected Traditions*, compiled by Shaykh Fadhlalla, Zahra Publications, South Africa, 2010, p.24, 30.

Chapter 9

136. *Nafahat al-uns*, Nur ad-Din Jami. Source: *Mystical Dimensions of Islam*, Annemarie Schimmel, Chapel Hill, NC, 1975, p.435.

137. *Early Sufi Women (Dhikr an-niswa al-muta'abbidat as-sufiyyat)*, Abu Abd ar-Rahman as-Sulami, translation by Rkia E Cornell, Fons Vitae, USA, 1999, p.232.

138. Ibid., p.80.

139. *The Sufi Book of Life*, op. cit., p.231.

140. *My Soul is a Woman: The Feminine in Islam*, Annemarie Schimmel, translation by Susan H Ray, Continuum, USA, 1997, p.38.

141. Extracted from *Early Sufi Women*, op. cit.

142. Ibid., p.244.

143. Ibid., p.144.

144. Ibid., p.168.

145. Ibid., p.168, n.127.

146. Ibid., p.70.

147. *The Secrets of God's Mystical Oneness (Asrar al-Towhid)*, Mohammad Ebn-e Monavaar, Mazda Publishers, USA, 1992, p.412.

148. *Sufi Narratives of Intimacy: Ibn 'Arabi, Gender and Sexuality*, Sa'diyya Shaikh, UNC Press, USA, p.84. Source: *Al-Futuhat al-makkiyya*, 3:89, Ibn al-'Arabi.

149. Ibid., p.101. Source: *Sufis of Andalusia*, Ibn al-'Arabi, p.143–5.

150. Ibid., p.102. Source: *Diwan Ibn al-'Arabi*, Ibn al-'Arabi, p.54.

151. *The Teachings of Sufism*, op. cit., p.198.

152. The Diwan of Princess Zebunissa XXXX. Source: *Captive Princess: Zebunissa Daughter of Emperor Aurangzeb*, Annie Krieger Krynicki, OUP, Pakistan, 2005.

153. The Diwan of Princess Zebunissa XXXII. Source: Ibid.

154. The Diwan of Princess Zebunissa V. Source: Ibid.

155. The Diwan of Princess Zebunissa XVI. Source: Ibid.

156. *The Unveiling of Love*, op. cit., p.99–100.

157. *The Path of Truth*, Nana Asma'u, vv 94–6. Source: *One Woman's Jihad: Nana Asma'u, Scholar and Scribe*, Indiana University Press, USA, 2000.

158. *Sufi Women*, Nana Asma'u, vv 59–60. Source: Ibid.

159. *From Shamanism to Sufism*, op. cit., p.154–5.

160. *Morals for the Heart (Fawa'id al-Fu'ad)*, op. cit., p.103.

161. *The Unveiling of Love*, op. cit., p.194–5.

162. *The Four Journeys*, op. cit., p.147.

Chapter 10

163. *Sayings of the Prophet Muhammad: Selected Traditions*, op. cit., p.43.

164. Ibid., p.66.

165. From *Khatum: The Prayers of Hazrat Inayat Khan*.

166. *Illuminating the Shadow: Life, Love and Laughter of a 20th-Century Sufi*, (ed) Neil Douglas-Klotz, Sufi Ruhaniat International, USA, 2016. p.108–9.

167. From 'Good Night', Hakim Sanai, http://www.gtalkir/#post1709513.

168. *The Window Within the Soul: Mathnawi III 2401–2405*, Jalal ad-Din Rumi, op. cit.

169. *The Sun of Tabriz: The Diwan of Jalal ad-Din Rumi*, translation by Sir Colin Garbett, Johnston and Neville, South Africa, 1969, p.19–21.

170. Ibid., p.65–6.

171. *The Illustrated Rumi*, translation by Philip Dunn, Manuela Dunn Mascetti and R A Nicholson, Harper Collins, USA, 2000, p.16.

172. *The Unveiling of Love*, op. cit., p.196.

173. *The Illustrated Rumi*, op. cit.,p.141.

174. "Bektashi Wit and Humour", www.bektashiorder.com/nodequeue11?page=7.

175. *The Bektashi Order of Dervishes*, John Kingsley Birge, Luzac Oriental, UK, 1994, p.16.

176. https://en.m.wikipedia.org/wiki/bektashi_order.

177. *A History of Sufism in India: Volume One*, op. cit., p.316–17.

178. *Sayings of the Prophet Muhammad: Selected Traditions*, op. cit., p.18.

179. *The Masters of Wisdom*, J G Bennett, Touchstone Books, UK, 1977.

180. *The Chasm of Fire*, Irina Tweedie, Element Books, UK, 1979, p.71.

181. Ibid., p.202.

182. *Spiritual Power: How It Works*, Llewellyn Vaughan-Lee, The Golden Sufi Center, USA, 2005, p.41.

183. Ibid., p.122.

184. *The Hikam: The Wisdom of Ibn 'Ata' Allah*, op. cit., p.85.

185. Ibid., p.192.

Chapter 11

186. http://www.allgreatquotes.com/hafizquotes.shtml, translation by Daniel Ladinsky.

187. *Taste of Hidden Things*, Sara Sviri, The Golden Sufi Center, USA, 1997, p.124.

188. *Sufism and the Way of Blame*, Yannis Toussulis, Theosophical Publishing House, USA, 2010, p.67.

189. Ibid., p.192.

190. *Early Islamic Mysticism*, Michael A Sells, Suhail Academy, Pakistan, 2004, p.123–4.

191. *Morals for the Heart (Fawa'id al-Fu'ad)*, op. cit., p.287.

192. *The Sufi Book of Life*, op. cit., p.84.

193. *The Rubaiyat of Omar Khayyam*, translation by Edward FitzGerald, Adam and Charles Black, UK, 1909, p.134.

194. Ibid., p.130.

195. Ibid., p.107.

196. *The Walled Garden of Truth*, op. cit., p.10.

197. Ibid., p.50.

198. *The Conference of the Birds*, Farid ud-Din Attar, translation by Dick Davis and Afkham Darbandi, Penguin, UK, 1984.

199. Ibid., p.229.

200. Ibid., p.40.

201. www.goodreads.com/author/quotes/279656

202. Ibid.

203. *Sufism: A Beginner's Guide*, op. cit., p.94.

204. *The Mystics of Islam*, R A Nicholson, Routledge and Kegan Paul, UK, 1963.

205. *Prophetic Traditions In Islam*, op. cit.

206. Ibid., p.80.

207. Ibid., p.188.

208. Ibid., p.58.

209. *The Four Journeys*, op. cit., p.196.

210. *The Garden of Truth*, Seyyed Hossein Nasr, Harper Collins, USA, 2007, p.209.

Chapter 12

211. *The Sufi Message of Hazrat Inayat Khan*, op. cit., p.68.